# Verbal
# Workbook for
# SAT*I

## Ninth Edition

MITCHEL WEINER
Former Member, Department of English
James Madison High School, Brooklyn, New York

SHARON WEINER GREEN
Former Instructor in English
Merritt College, Oakland, California

**BARRON'S**

*SAT is a registered trademark of the College Entrance Examination Board,
which does not endorse this book.

# ACKNOWLEDGMENTS

SAT directions selected from The Official Guide to the SAT I: Taking the SAT I Reasoning Test, (1995) College Entrance Examination Board and Educational Testing Service. Reprinted by permission of the College Board and Educational Testing Service, the copyright owners.

Permission to reprint SAT I directions does not constitute review or endorsement by the College Board or Educational Testing Service as a whole or of any other questions or testing information it may contain.

The authors gratefully acknowledge the following copyright holders for permission to reprint material used in reading passages:

Page 4: From *A Handbook to Literature, 6/E* by Holman. © 1992. Reprinted by permission of Prentice-Hall, Inc.

Page 21: From "The Spider and the Wasp" by Alexander Petrunkevitch in *Scientific American*, August 1952.

Page 28: From "Symbolic Language of Dreams" by Erich Fromm in *Language: An Enquiry into Its Meaning and Function* by Ruth Nanda Anshen, ed. Copyright 1957. HarperCollins Publishers, Inc.

Page 31: From *Small Town America* by Richard Lingerman. Copyright © 1980 with permission of Putnam Publishing Group.

Page 32: From *A Pocket History of the United States* by Alan Nevins and Henry Steele Commager. Copyright 1991. Alfred A. Knopf, New York.

Page 127: From *The Most Beautiful House in the World* by Witold Rybczynski. Copyright 1989. With permission of Viking Penguin.

Page 130: From *La Vida* by Oscar Lewis. Copyright 1965. Random House, New York.

Page 130: From "What is Poverty?" by Jo Goodwin Parker. Originally published in *America's Other Children: Public Schools Outside Suburbia* by George Henderson, ed. Copyright 1971. University of Oklahoma Press.

Page 133: From "Living in Two Cultures" by Jeanne Wakatsuki Houston in *Outlooks and Insights*. Copyright 1983. St. Martin's Press.

Page 134: From "Introduction" by Antonio Castro Leal to *Twenty Centuries of Mexican Art*. Copyright 1940 by the Museum of Modern Art.

Page 136: From *The Press and the Presidency* by John Tebbel and Sarah Miles Watts. Copyright 1985. Oxford University Press, New York.

Page 139: From "The Desert Smells Like Rain: A Naturalist in Papago Indian Country" by Gary Nabhan. With permission of North Point Press; div. of Farrar, Straus & Giroux, Inc.

Page 141: From *Indian Country* by Peter Matthiessen. Copyright 1984. Used by permission of Viking Penguin.

Page 142: From "Social Characteristics and Socialization of Wild Chimpanzees" by Yukimaru Sugiyama in *Primate Socialization* by Frank E. Poirer, ed. Copyright 1972. Random House, New York.

Page 144: From *War, Peace and International Politics* by David W. Zeigler, Copyright 1977. Reprinted by permission of Addison-Wesley Educational Publishers, Inc.

Page 147: From *Picasso on Art: A Selection of Views* by Dore Ashton. Copyright 1972. The Viking Press, New York.

Page 147: From *Picasso: The Early Years* by Jiri Padrta. Undated. Tudor Publishing Co., New York.

Page 151: From "The Dynamic Abyss" by Charles D. Hollister, Arthur R. M. Nowell, and Peter A. Jumars in *Scientific American*, March 1984.

Page 152: From *Organizing the World's Money* by Benjamin J. Cohen. Copyright 1977. Basic Books, a div. of HarperCollins Publishers, Inc.

Page 155: From *F. Scott Fitzgerald* by Kenneth Eble. Copyright 1963. Twayne Publishers, an imprint of Simon & Schuster Macmillan.

Page 155: From "F. Scott Fitzgerald" by Edmund Wilson in *Shores of Light*. © 1985 with permission from Farrar, Straus & Giroux, Inc.

Page 212: From *Picasso: Fifty Years of His Art* by Alfred H. Barr. Copyright 1946 by the Museum of Modern Art.

Page 223: From *The Magic Years* by Selma H. Fraiberg. Copyright 1959. By permission of Scribner, a division of Simon & Schuster.

Page 223: From *Essentials of Psychology and Life* by Philip G. Zimbardo. Reprinted with permission of Addison-Wesley Educational Publishers, Inc. Copyright 1980. Scott, Foresman and Co., Glenview, Illinois.

Page 238: From "The Canopy of the Tropical Rain Forest" by Donald R. Perry in *Scientific American*, November 1984.

Page 246: From *The Joy of Music* by Leonard Bernstein. Copyright 1959. Used by permission of Doubleday, a div. of BDD Publishing Group.

Page 249: From *The Politics of Prejudice* by Roger Daniels. Copyright 1962. University of California Press, Berkeley.

Page 249: From "American Antisemitism Historically Reconsidered" by John Higham, in *Jews in the Mind of America* by Herbert Stember, et al, eds. Copyright 1966. American Jewish Committee, Basic Books, New York. Reprinted in *Antisemitism in the United States* by Leonard Dinnerstein, ed. Copyright 1971. Holt, Rinehart, and Winston, Inc., New York.

Page 264: From *The Way to Rainy Mountain* by N. Scott Momaday. Copyright 1969. University of New Mexico Press.

Page 265: From *Mortal Lessons: Notes on the Art of Surgery* by Richard Selzer. Copyright © 1974, 1975, 1976 by Richard Selzer. Reprinted by permission of Georges Borchardt, Inc. for the author.

Page 272: From "The Man Who Hitched the Reindeer To Santa Claus's Sleigh" by X. J. Kennedy in *The New York Times Book Review*, December 5, 1993. © 1993 The New York Times Co.

Page 275: From *Montana 1948* by Larry Watson. Copyright © 1993 by Larry Watson. (Milkweed Editions, 1993)

**Library of Congress Cataloging-in-Publication Data**

Weiner, Mitchel, 1907–
  Verbal workbook for SAT I / Mitchel Weiner, Sharon Weiner Green. — 9th ed.
    p.   cm.
  ISBN 0-8120-9640-1
  1. English language—Examinations—Study guides.
2. Universities and colleges—United States—Entrance examinations—Study guides.   3. Scholastic Assessment Test—Study guides.
I. Green, Sharon.   II. Title.
LB1631.5.W45   1997
428'.0076—dc20                                    96-36295
                                                  CIP

Library of Congress Catalog Card No. 96-36295

International Standard Book No. 0-8120-9640-1

Printed in The United States of America

19 18 17 16 15 14 13 12 11 10

# CONTENTS

## PART VII TESTS FOR PRACTICE

## PART VIII SUGGESTED STUDY PROGRAM

# PREFACE

Welcome to the world of SAT I, where *air* and *lumber* can be verbs, and *apathy* and *phenomena* are common everyday words. Welcome to the ninth edition of Barron's *Verbal Workbook*. If you are preparing for the verbal reasoning sections of SAT I, this is the book you need.

Over the past two and a half years, our research staff has been analyzing the SAT I, studying each new test that has been released. The result of our investigations is in your hands.

This ninth edition represents a major expansion in America's leading book focusing on the verbal portions of the SAT. Containing the best of the time-tested features of earlier editions, today's ninth edition provides much, much more.

It features four complete verbal reasoning tests, each three sections long. Here are four crucial "dress rehearsals" for the day you walk into the examination room.

It briefs you on the vocabulary-in-context and critical reading questions, giving you key tips on how to tackle these important verbal question types.

It takes you through the double reading passages, showing you how to work your way through a pair of reading passages without wasting effort or time.

It offers you a year-long study program so that you don't have to settle for last minute cram sessions. Pace yourself as you work your way through the wealth of practice exercises designed for you.

It gives you the *newly revised and expanded* SAT I High-Frequency Word List, incorporating vocabulary from actual SAT I tests through 1996. These words are *vital*—computer analysis shows that they occur test after test on actual SATs. Master them and you'll be well on your way to building a college-level vocabulary.

With dozens of clear, helpful pointers and hundreds of brand-new questions modeled closely on verbal questions appearing on today's SAT, Barron's *Verbal Workbook* gives you a down-to-earth introduction to the sometimes intimidating world of the SAT. Don't let SAT I get you down. With the Barron's team behind you, go for your personal best: take time today to build your verbal skills for SAT I.

This ninth edition of Barron's *Verbal Workbook* is a sign of Barron's ongoing commitment to make this publication America's outstanding guide to the verbal reasoning sections of the SAT. It has benefited from the dedicated labors of the editorial staff of Barron's, in particular Liza Burby and Jackie Dwyer, from the research and writing skills of Lexy Green, and from the critical insights of Judy Makover, our longtime colleague and friend. We are greatly indebted to them.

# PART I

# INTRODUCING SAT I: VERBAL REASONING

# NATURE OF THE TEST

SAT I is a standardized test designed to help predict how well you are likely to do in your academic work as a college freshman. By looking at your school grades and your SAT I scores, college admissions officers get a sense of you as a potential student—a person they'd like to have in their school.

SAT I tries to measure your ability to reason using facts that are part of your general knowledge or facts that are included in your test booklet.

You're not required to recall great chunks of history or literature or science. You're not even required to recall most math formulas—they're printed right in the test booklet.

Assessment tests are essentially multiple-choice tests. Your score depends upon how many correct answers you get within a definite period of time. Speed is important. So is accuracy. You have to pace yourself so that you don't sacrifice speed to gain accuracy (or sacrifice accuracy to gain speed).

# OVERVIEW AND CONTENT

This is the basic format of SAT I. The total time allowed is $3\frac{1}{2}$ hours. There are six sections on the test. You are given 30 minutes apiece to complete five of them. They are:

    30-question verbal section
    35-question verbal section
    25-question math section
    35-question math section
    (experimental section—verbal or math)

The sixth section is divided into two 15-minute mini-sections. They are:

    13-question verbal section
    10-question math section

These sections should always appear on SAT I, but the order in which they appear is likely to vary from test to test.

Not counting the experimental section, the three verbal sections ordinarily contain a total of 19 sentence completions, 19 analogies, and 40 critical reading questions. *More than half* of the verbal questions on SAT I directly test your reading.

The three verbal sections have different formats. However, the organization within each section does not vary greatly; this is how they should look:

30-Question Verbal Section
1–9 sentence completion questions
10–15 analogy questions
16–30 critical reading questions

35-Question Verbal Section
1–10 sentence completion questions
11–23 analogy questions
24–35 critical reading questions

13-Question Verbal Section
1–13 critical reading questions on paired
    passages

Pay particular attention to how these sections are organized. The first two sections contain groups of sentence completion questions followed by groups of analogy questions. These groups of questions are arranged in order of difficulty: they start out with easy "warm-up" questions and get more and more difficult as they go along. (The critical reading questions are arranged to follow the passage's organization; questions about material found early in the passage come before questions about material occurring later.)

Here are the sorts of verbal questions you can expect:

## SENTENCE COMPLETION QUESTIONS

Sentence completion questions ask you to fill in the blanks. Your job is to find the word or phrase that best completes the sentence's meaning.

> Directions: Choose the word or set of words that, when inserted in the sentence, best fits the meaning of the sentence as a whole.

Brown, this biography suggests, was an ____ employer, giving generous bonuses one day, ordering pay cuts the next.

(A) indifferent
(B) objective
(C) unpredictable
(D) ineffectual
(E) unobtrusive

If you insert the different answer choices in the sentence, (C) *by definition* makes the most sense. Someone who gives bonuses one day and orders pay cuts the next clearly is *unpredictable*—no one can tell what he's going to do next.

To learn how to handle sentence completion questions, turn to Part III.

## ANALOGY QUESTIONS

An analogy is a likeness. Your job is to figure out the relationship between a pair of words and then find the pair of words whose relationship is *most* like the one linking the original pair.

> Directions: Select the lettered pair that best expresses a relationship similar to that expressed in the original pair.

WOLF : PACK ::
(A) horse : saddle
(B) goose : flock
(C) fox : lair
(D) dog : sled
(E) lion : cub

The correct answer is (B). A wolf is a member of a pack (a group of wolves). A goose is a member of a flock.

You'll get a thorough briefing on analogy questions in Part IV.

## CRITICAL READING QUESTIONS

Typically, a 30-question verbal section has two reading passages; a 35-question verbal section has only one. Each of these passages is followed by six to twelve critical reading questions. They ask about the passage's main idea or specific details, the author's attitude to the subject, the author's logic and techniques, the implications of the discussion, or the meaning of specific words.

> Directions: The passage below is followed by questions based on its content. Answer the questions on the basis of what is stated or implied in the passage and in any introductory material that may be provided.

[The following passage is considerably shorter than those in the SAT I.]

Certain qualities common to the sonnet should be noted. Its definite restrictions make it a challenge to the artistry of the poet and
Line call for all the technical skill at the poet's
(5) command. The more or less set rhyme patterns occurring regularly within the short space of fourteen lines afford a pleasant effect on the ear of the reader, and can create truly musical effects. The rigidity of the form precludes a

*(10)* too great economy or too great prodigality of words. Emphasis is placed on exactness and perfection of expression. The brevity of the form favors concentrated expression of ideas or passion.

1.  The author's primary purpose is to

    (A) contrast different types of sonnets
    (B) criticize the limitations of the sonnet
    (C) describe the characteristics of the sonnet
    (D) explain why the sonnet lost popularity as a literary form
    (E) encourage readers to compose formal sonnets

2.  The word "afford" in line 7 means

    (A) initiate
    (B) exaggerate
    (C) are able to pay for
    (D) change into
    (E) provide

3.  The author's attitude toward the sonnet form can best be described as one of

    (A) amused toleration
    (B) grudging admiration
    (C) strong disapprobation
    (D) effusive enthusiasm
    (E) scholarly appreciation

The first question asks you to find the author's main idea. In the opening sentence, the author says certain qualities of the sonnet should be noted or observed. He then goes on to tell you which of these qualities deserve your attention, characterizing them in some detail. Thus, he *describes certain of the sonnet's qualities or characteristics.* The correct answer is (C). You can eliminate the other answers with ease. The author is upbeat about the sonnet: he doesn't say that the sonnet has limitations or that it has become less popular. Similarly, he doesn't discuss different types of sonnets. And while he talks about the challenge of composing formal sonnets, he never invites his readers to try writing them.

The second question asks you to figure out a word's meaning from its context. The rhyme patterns have a pleasant effect on the ear of the listener; indeed they *provide* or afford this effect. The correct answer is (E).

The third question asks you to figure out how the author feels about his subject. All the author's comments about the sonnet form are positive, but he doesn't go so far as to gush (he's not *effusive).* The only answer that reflects this attitude is (E), *scholarly appreciation.*

See Part V for tactics that will help you handle the entire range of critical reading questions.

# BEFORE THE TEST

What you do on your actual test day clearly matters a lot. However, what you do *before the test*, as you organize yourself and learn how to handle tests of this nature, may in the long run matter even more to you.

## SIX MONTHS BEFORE

### Expand Your Verbal Horizons

If you haven't started studying for the test by this time, you'd better get started now. There's no point killing yourself with last-minute cramming sessions and overnight flash card marathons. Now's the time to pick up some good habits that will expand your verbal horizons and increase your verbal skills.

Make a habit of reading a good, high-quality newspaper every day. Try *The Christian Science Monitor*, *The New York Times*, or *The Washington Post*, not something written in short sound bites like *U.S.A. Today*. These newspapers, written for **discriminating** readers, **exemplify** what is best in journalism today. Note how their editorials **address** the day's issues **dispassionately**, **delineating** schemes to **rectify** society's ills.

Note also the number of boldface words in the previous two sentences. We have highlighted them because they are key SAT words: you can find them all on our SAT I High-Frequency Word List (Part VI). Were any of them unfamiliar to you? Then turn to the high-frequency list. You can jumpstart your SAT I preparations if you follow the directions given there for building your vocabulary. You can also design a study plan to cover both building your vocabulary and mastering the major verbal question types if you simply model your plan on our Suggested Study Program (Part VIII). You have the time—get to it!

## TWO MONTHS BEFORE

### Register

First, get the paperwork out of the way. Unless you like paying late registration fees, be sure to pick up a test registration form at your high school guidance office and send it in to the College Board at least 6–7 weeks before the date on which you want to take the test. Plan ahead: if you want to take the test in October, you have to mail your form in early September, when you are bound to be busy getting off to a good start with your new classes at school.

To get a registration form, or to order a copy of *The New Sat I: Reasoning Test,* a guide to the test including a sample SAT I, call or write the College Board:

College Board SAT I
P.O. Box 6200
Princeton, NJ 08541-6200

(609) 771–7588
(8:30 A.M.–9:30 P.M. weekdays)

### Rehearse

The best way to practice for a race is to run the course in advance. Likewise, the best way to practice for a test is to take a simulated test, going over all the different question types in advance.

First, memorize the directions for each type of question. These are only slightly different from the exact words you'll find on SAT I. The test time you would normally spend reading directions can be better spent answering questions.

Then take your practice test. In this workbook, you have four verbal reasoning model tests—one self-assessment test in the next chapter, plus three more at the end of the book. To get the most out of these tests, try taking them under test conditions—no breaks in mid-section, no talking, no help from friends.

You'll find this kind of run-through will help build your test-taking stamina and strengthen you for those three and one half vital hours after you walk through that test center door.

## Learn to Pace Yourself

In taking SAT I, your job is to answer as many questions as you can, rapidly, economically, *correctly*, without getting hung up on any one question and wasting time you could have used to answer two or three additional ones.

As you go through this book, if you find you do get bogged down on an individual question, think things through. First, ask yourself whether it's a question you might be able to answer if you had a bit more time or whether it's one you have *no* idea how to tackle. If you think it's one you'll be able to answer if you give it a second try, mark it with a check or an arrow, and plan to come straight back to it after you've worked through the easy questions in the section. If you think it's a lost cause, mark it with an X and come back to it only after you've answered all the other questions in the section and double-checked your answers. With practice, you should be able to distinguish a "second chancer" from a lost cause. In any case, if you're taking too long, your best bet is to move on.

## Learn When (and When Not) to Guess

Students always worry about whether they should or shouldn't guess on standardized tests. Because wrong answers do count fractionally against you on SAT I, you may think that you should never guess if you aren't sure of the right answer to a question. But even if you guessed wrong four times for every time you guessed right, you would still come out even. A wrong answer costs you only $1/4$ of a point ($1/3$ on the quantitative comparison questions). *On the multiple-choice questions,* the best advice for top students is to guess if you can eliminate one or two of the answer choices. You have a better chance of hitting the right answer when you make this sort of "educated" guess.

As you go through this book, try this experiment to find out what kind of guesser you are. Take part of any test that you have not taken before. You don't have to take an entire test section, but you should take at least 25 questions. First, answer only those questions you are sure about. Then, with a different color pen, answer those remaining questions for which you can make educated guesses.

Finally, with yet another color pen, guess blindly on all the other questions.

Score each of the three tests separately. Compare your scores from the three different approaches to the test. For many people, the second score (the one with the educated guesses) will be the best one. But you may be different. Maybe you are such a poor guesser that you should never guess at all. That's okay. Or maybe you are such a good guesser that you should try every question. That's okay, too. The important thing is to know yourself.

## Learn to Concentrate

Another important technique for you to work on is building your powers of concentration. As you go through the practice exercises and model tests, notice when you start to lose your focus. Does your mind drift off in the middle of long reading passages? Do you catch yourself staring off into space, or watching the seconds ticking away on the clock? The sooner you spot these momentary lapses of concentration, the sooner you'll be back working toward your goal.

By the way, there's nothing wrong with losing focus for a moment. Everybody does it. When you notice you're drifting, smile. You're normal. Breathe in slowly and let the air ease out. Then take a fresh look at that paragraph or question you were working on. You've had your mini-break. Now you're ready to pick up a few points.

## Learn There's No Need to Panic

Despite all rumors to the contrary, *your whole college career is not riding on the results of this one test.* SAT I is only one of the elements that colleges take into account when they are deciding about admissions. Admissions officers like the test because the scores give them a quick way to compare applicants from different high schools without worrying whether a B+ from the District High School is the equivalent of a B+ from the Elite Preparatory School. But colleges never rely on SAT I scores alone. Admissions officers are perfectly well aware that there are brilliant students who fall apart on major tests, that students who are not feeling well can do much worse than normal on a test, and that all sorts of things can affect your SAT I score on any given day. What's more, every college accepts students with a *wide* range of SAT I scores.

You do not need to answer every question on SAT I correctly to be accepted by the college of your choice. In fact, if you answer only 50 to 60 percent of the questions correctly, you'll get a better than average score, and that, plus a decent GPA, will get you into most colleges. Consider the following chart:

| | Verbal Score | Correct Answers Needed (out of 78) |
|---|---|---|
| (Average) | 500–510 | 35 or 36 |
| | 570 | 47 or 48 |
| (About the top 5 percent) | 650 | 61 or 62 |

As you can see, *there's no need to panic about taking SAT I.* However, not everybody taking SAT I realizes this simple truth.

It's hard to stay calm when those around you are tense, and you're bound to run into some pretty tense people when you take SAT I. (Not everyone works through this book, unfortunately.) So you may experience a slight case of "exam nerves" just before the big day. Don't worry about it.

1. Being keyed up for an examination isn't always bad; you may outdo yourself because you are so worked up.
2. Total panic is unlikely to set in; by the time you face the exam, you'll know too much.

Keep that in mind and those tensions should just fade away.

## THE NIGHT BEFORE

### Rest

The best thing you can do for yourself before any test is to get a good night's sleep. If you find you're so keyed up that you don't think you'll be able to sleep, try listening to relaxing music, or exercising and then taking a warm bath. If you're lying in bed wakefully, try concentrating on your breathing: breathe in for 4 to 6 counts, hold your breath for another 4 to 6 counts, exhale for 4 to 6 counts. Concentrating on breathing or on visualizing an image of a person or place often helps people block out distractions and enables them to relax.

### Organize Your Gear

The night before the test, set out everything you're going to need the next day. You will need your admission ticket, a photo ID (a driver's license or a non-driver picture ID, a passport, or a school ID), four or five sharp No. 2 pencils (with erasers), plus a map or directions showing how to get to the test center. Set out an accurate watch as well, plus a calculator with charged batteries to use on the math.

Lay out comfortable clothes for the next day, including a sweater in case the room is cold. Consider bringing along a snack, a treat you can munch on during the break.

### Plan Your Route

Allow plenty of time for getting to the test site. If you haven't been there before, locate the test center on a map and figure out the best route. If you're using public transportation, check your bus or subway schedule, and be sure you've got a token or ticket or the correct change. If you're driving, check that there's gas in the car. Your job is taking the test. You don't need the extra tension that comes from worrying about whether you will get to the test on time, or the extra distraction that comes from kicking yourself for losing test time by being late.

# DURING THE TEST

## Use Time Wisely

In the course of working through the model tests and practice exercises in this book, you should have developed your own personal testing rhythm. You know approximately how many questions you need to get right to meet your academic goals.

Don't get bogged down on any one question. By the time you get to SAT I, you should have a fair idea of how much time to spend on each question. (About 30 to 40 seconds for a sentence completion or analogy question, 75 seconds for a critical reading question if you average in your passage reading time.) If a question is taking too long, leave it and move on to the next question. Keep moving on to maximize your score.

### Note Down Questions You Skip

Before you move on, put a mark in your test booklet next to the question you're skipping. You're probably going to want to find that question easily later on.

What sort of mark? First, ask yourself whether it's a question you might be able to answer if you had a bit more time or whether it's one you have *no* idea how to tackle. If you think it's one you'll be able to answer if you give it a second try, mark it with a check or an arrow and plan to come straight back to it after you've worked through the easy questions in the section. If you think it's a lost cause, mark it with an X and come back to it only after you've answered all the other questions in the section and double-checked your answers. Either way, mark that test booklet and move on.

Whenever you skip a question, check frequently to make sure you are answering later questions in the right spots. No machine is going to notice that you made a mistake early in the test, answered question 9 in the space for question 8, and all your following answers are in the wrong place. Line up your answer sheet with your test booklet. That way you'll have an easier time checking that you're getting your answers in the right spots.

Never just skip for skipping's sake. Always try to answer each question before you decide to move on. Keep up that "can do" spirit—the more confident you are that you can answer these questions, the more likely you are to give each question your best shot.

### Answer Easy Questions First

*First* answer all the easy questions; *then* tackle the hard ones if you have time. You know that the questions in each segment of the test get harder as you go along (except for the reading comprehension questions). But there's no rule that says you have to answer the questions in order. You're allowed to skip. So, if the last three analogy questions are driving you crazy, move on to the reading passages right away. Take advantage of the easy questions to boost your score.

### Tackle Shorter Questions Before Longer Ones

If you're running out of time on a verbal section and you're smack in the middle of a critical reading passage, look for the shortest questions on that passage and try answering them. Aim for questions with answer choices that are only two or three words long. You don't need much time to answer a vocabulary-in-context question or a straightforward question about the author's attitude or tone, and one or two extra correct answers can boost your score an additional 10 to 20 points.

### Eliminate Wrong Answers as You Go

Eliminate as many wrong answers as you can. Sometimes you'll be able to eliminate all the choices until you have just one answer left. Even if you wind up with two choices that look good, deciding between two choices is easier than deciding among five. What's more, the reasoning that helped you decide which answer choices to eliminate may also give you new insights into the question and help you figure out which of the remaining answer choices is correct.

Draw a line through any answer you decide to eliminate. That way if you decide to move on to another question and come back to this one later, you won't forget which answer choices you thought were wrong. (However, when you cross out an answer choice, do so *lightly*. Don't obliterate it totally. You may want to look it over again later if you decide your first impulse to eliminate it was wrong.)

Even if you can't settle on a correct answer and decide to guess, every answer you eliminate as definitely wrong improves your chances of guessing right.

## CENTER ON THE TEST

Focus on the question in front of you. At this moment, it's all that matters. Answer it and fill in your answer choice, *being careful you're filling in the right space*. Then move on to the next question, and the next. Find your steady, even testing rhythm and keep it going. Notice if your mind starts to wander, or your eyes.

### Block Out Distractions

When Steffi Graf plays tennis at Wimbledon, she has her mind on one thing: the game. Not the movements of the crowd in the stands, not the occasional plane flying overhead, not the applause of the spectators, not even the handsome guy in the third row. She blocks them out.

SAT I is your game. To play it well, block out the distractions. Don't start looking around at the other students taking the test. You don't get any points for watching other people answer questions. You only get points for answering questions yourself. Keep your eye on the test booklet and your mind on the game.

### When Things Get Tight, Stay Loose

Sooner or later, as you go through the test, you're going to hit a tough spot. You may run into a paragraph that seems totally unintelligible, or a couple of hard questions that throw you, so that you stop thinking about the question you're working on and sit there panicking instead.

If you come to a group of questions that stump you, relax. There are bound to be a few brainbenders on a test of this nature. *Remember, you don't have to answer every question correctly to do just fine on the test.*

There will be a break about halfway through the test. Use this period to clear your thoughts. Take a few deep breaths. Stretch. Close your eyes and imagine yourself floating. In addition to being under mental pressure, you're under physical pressure from sitting so long in a hard seat with a No. 2 pencil clutched in your hand. Anything you can do to loosen up and get the kinks out will ease your body and help the oxygen get to your brain.

### Keep a Positive Outlook

The best thing you can do for yourself during the test is to keep a positive frame of mind. Too many people walk into tests and interviews defeated before they start. Instead of feeling good about what they have going for them, they worry about what can go wrong instead. They let negative thoughts distract them and drag them down.

You are a motivated, hard-working student. That's why you've chosen to work through this book. You're exactly the sort of person the colleges are looking for. For you, SAT I isn't an unknown terror. It's something you can handle, something for which you are prepared. It's okay for you not to answer every question. It's okay for you to get some questions wrong. You'll do better figuring out the answers to the questions you tackle if you know you're doing okay. Have confidence in yourself.

### Note What's Going Right

Whenever you cross out an answer you *know* is incorrect, whenever you skip a question so that you can come back to it later, notice that you're doing the right thing. Whenever you catch yourself drifting off and quickly get back to work, whenever you stretch to get out the kinks, recognize how much you're in control. In applying these tactics you've mastered, you're showing you know how to do the job and do it right.

### Pat Yourself on the Back

As you go through the test, each time you get a correct answer, pat yourself on the back. "Yes! Ten more points!" Enjoy your successes, and keep an eye out for more successes, more correct answer choices ahead. Feel good about the progress you're making and the rewarding college years to come.

# PART II

# SELF-ASSESSMENT

# INTRODUCTION

Call this chapter "Seventy-Five Minutes to a Better Score on SAT I." Just $1^1/4$ hours from now you will have a much better idea of how well prepared you are to face the verbal portions of SAT I.

This chapter contains three verbal reasoning test sections modeled on the ones you will face when you take SAT I. You are allowed 30 minutes each for Sections 1 and 2, 15 minutes for Section 3. Make every minute count. Take each test section under exam conditions, or as close to exam conditions as you can get—no talking, no consulting dictionaries, no taking a soda break. Limit yourself to the time allowed; that way you'll develop a sense of how to pace yourself on SAT I.

As soon as you've completed all three sections, see how many questions you've answered correctly. (The correct answers are given on page 35.) Then read the answer explanations and go back over any questions you got wrong. Note unfamiliar words you came across so that you can look them up in your dictionary. Check to see whether any particular question types are giving you special trouble. Do this follow-up thoroughly to get the most out of the time you've spent.

# ANSWER SHEET FOR SELF-ASSESSMENT TEST

## Section 1

1. Ⓐ Ⓑ Ⓒ Ⓓ Ⓔ
2. Ⓐ Ⓑ Ⓒ Ⓓ Ⓔ
3. Ⓐ Ⓑ Ⓒ Ⓓ Ⓔ
4. Ⓐ Ⓑ Ⓒ Ⓓ Ⓔ
5. Ⓐ Ⓑ Ⓒ Ⓓ Ⓔ
6. Ⓐ Ⓑ Ⓒ Ⓓ Ⓔ
7. Ⓐ Ⓑ Ⓒ Ⓓ Ⓔ
8. Ⓐ Ⓑ Ⓒ Ⓓ Ⓔ
9. Ⓐ Ⓑ Ⓒ Ⓓ Ⓔ
10. Ⓐ Ⓑ Ⓒ Ⓓ Ⓔ
11. Ⓐ Ⓑ Ⓒ Ⓓ Ⓔ
12. Ⓐ Ⓑ Ⓒ Ⓓ Ⓔ
13. Ⓐ Ⓑ Ⓒ Ⓓ Ⓔ
14. Ⓐ Ⓑ Ⓒ Ⓓ Ⓔ
15. Ⓐ Ⓑ Ⓒ Ⓓ Ⓔ
16. Ⓐ Ⓑ Ⓒ Ⓓ Ⓔ
17. Ⓐ Ⓑ Ⓒ Ⓓ Ⓔ
18. Ⓐ Ⓑ Ⓒ Ⓓ Ⓔ
19. Ⓐ Ⓑ Ⓒ Ⓓ Ⓔ
20. Ⓐ Ⓑ Ⓒ Ⓓ Ⓔ
21. Ⓐ Ⓑ Ⓒ Ⓓ Ⓔ
22. Ⓐ Ⓑ Ⓒ Ⓓ Ⓔ
23. Ⓐ Ⓑ Ⓒ Ⓓ Ⓔ
24. Ⓐ Ⓑ Ⓒ Ⓓ Ⓔ
25. Ⓐ Ⓑ Ⓒ Ⓓ Ⓔ
26. Ⓐ Ⓑ Ⓒ Ⓓ Ⓔ
27. Ⓐ Ⓑ Ⓒ Ⓓ Ⓔ
28. Ⓐ Ⓑ Ⓒ Ⓓ Ⓔ
29. Ⓐ Ⓑ Ⓒ Ⓓ Ⓔ
30. Ⓐ Ⓑ Ⓒ Ⓓ Ⓔ

## Section 2

1. Ⓐ Ⓑ Ⓒ Ⓓ Ⓔ
2. Ⓐ Ⓑ Ⓒ Ⓓ Ⓔ
3. Ⓐ Ⓑ Ⓒ Ⓓ Ⓔ
4. Ⓐ Ⓑ Ⓒ Ⓓ Ⓔ
5. Ⓐ Ⓑ Ⓒ Ⓓ Ⓔ
6. Ⓐ Ⓑ Ⓒ Ⓓ Ⓔ
7. Ⓐ Ⓑ Ⓒ Ⓓ Ⓔ
8. Ⓐ Ⓑ Ⓒ Ⓓ Ⓔ
9. Ⓐ Ⓑ Ⓒ Ⓓ Ⓔ
10. Ⓐ Ⓑ Ⓒ Ⓓ Ⓔ
11. Ⓐ Ⓑ Ⓒ Ⓓ Ⓔ
12. Ⓐ Ⓑ Ⓒ Ⓓ Ⓔ
13. Ⓐ Ⓑ Ⓒ Ⓓ Ⓔ
14. Ⓐ Ⓑ Ⓒ Ⓓ Ⓔ
15. Ⓐ Ⓑ Ⓒ Ⓓ Ⓔ
16. Ⓐ Ⓑ Ⓒ Ⓓ Ⓔ
17. Ⓐ Ⓑ Ⓒ Ⓓ Ⓔ
18. Ⓐ Ⓑ Ⓒ Ⓓ Ⓔ
19. Ⓐ Ⓑ Ⓒ Ⓓ Ⓔ
20. Ⓐ Ⓑ Ⓒ Ⓓ Ⓔ
21. Ⓐ Ⓑ Ⓒ Ⓓ Ⓔ
22. Ⓐ Ⓑ Ⓒ Ⓓ Ⓔ
23. Ⓐ Ⓑ Ⓒ Ⓓ Ⓔ
24. Ⓐ Ⓑ Ⓒ Ⓓ Ⓔ
25. Ⓐ Ⓑ Ⓒ Ⓓ Ⓔ
26. Ⓐ Ⓑ Ⓒ Ⓓ Ⓔ
27. Ⓐ Ⓑ Ⓒ Ⓓ Ⓔ
28. Ⓐ Ⓑ Ⓒ Ⓓ Ⓔ
29. Ⓐ Ⓑ Ⓒ Ⓓ Ⓔ
30. Ⓐ Ⓑ Ⓒ Ⓓ Ⓔ
31. Ⓐ Ⓑ Ⓒ Ⓓ Ⓔ
32. Ⓐ Ⓑ Ⓒ Ⓓ Ⓔ
33. Ⓐ Ⓑ Ⓒ Ⓓ Ⓔ
34. Ⓐ Ⓑ Ⓒ Ⓓ Ⓔ
35. Ⓐ Ⓑ Ⓒ Ⓓ Ⓔ

## Section 3

1. Ⓐ Ⓑ Ⓒ Ⓓ Ⓔ
2. Ⓐ Ⓑ Ⓒ Ⓓ Ⓔ
3. Ⓐ Ⓑ Ⓒ Ⓓ Ⓔ
4. Ⓐ Ⓑ Ⓒ Ⓓ Ⓔ
5. Ⓐ Ⓑ Ⓒ Ⓓ Ⓔ
6. Ⓐ Ⓑ Ⓒ Ⓓ Ⓔ
7. Ⓐ Ⓑ Ⓒ Ⓓ Ⓔ
8. Ⓐ Ⓑ Ⓒ Ⓓ Ⓔ
9. Ⓐ Ⓑ Ⓒ Ⓓ Ⓔ
10. Ⓐ Ⓑ Ⓒ Ⓓ Ⓔ
11. Ⓐ Ⓑ Ⓒ Ⓓ Ⓔ
12. Ⓐ Ⓑ Ⓒ Ⓓ Ⓔ
13. Ⓐ Ⓑ Ⓒ Ⓓ Ⓔ

# SELF-ASSESSMENT TEST
## Section 1

TIME—30 MINUTES
30 QUESTIONS

For each of the following questions, select the best answer from the choices provided and fill in the appropriate circle on the answer sheet.

Directions: Each sentence below has one or two blanks, each blank indicating that something has been omitted. Beneath the sentence are five words or sets of words labeled A through E. Choose the word or set of words that, when inserted in the sentence, best fits the meaning of the sentence as a whole.

Example:

Medieval kingdoms did not become constitutional republics overnight; on the contrary, the change was _____ .

(A) unpopular
(B) unexpected
(C) advantageous
(D) sufficient
(E) gradual

Ⓐ Ⓑ Ⓒ Ⓓ ●

1. Though their lack of external ears might suggest otherwise, mole rats are able to use _____ to communicate.

(A) gestures
(B) touch
(C) smells
(D) sounds
(E) symbols

2. A map purporting to show that the Vikings _____ North America long before the arrival of Columbus, branded as a fraud in 1974, could turn out to be _____ after all, according to California scientists.

(A) visited...questionable
(B) charted...genuine
(C) assessed...fragmentary
(D) retraced...superficial
(E) advocated...extant

3. The word *tephra*, from the Greek word meaning ash, has come into use among geologists to describe the assortment of fragments, ranging from blocks of material to dust, that is _____ into the air during a volcanic eruption.

(A) amassed
(B) ejected
(C) repressed
(D) wafted
(E) absorbed

4. Hummingbirds use spider silk to strengthen nest walls to better _____ the weight and pressure of wriggling hatchlings.

(A) withstand
(B) discern
(C) expose
(D) transmute
(E) induce

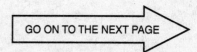
GO ON TO THE NEXT PAGE

1   1   1   1   1   1   1   1   1   1   1

5.  The strike was settled when the outside ____
    brought the reluctant representatives of labor
    and management together to hear their ____
    views.

    (A) auditors…banal
    (B) media…irreconcilable
    (C) arbitrators…conflicting
    (D) opportunists…tentative
    (E) agitators…bellicose

6.  Warner's emotional power and her magic as an
    author stem from her choice of details that
    ____ emotions rather than simply describing
    them.

    (A) deny
    (B) diminish
    (C) evoke
    (D) disdain
    (E) nullify

7.  Although the poet Stevie Smith had a child-
    hood that was far from ____, she always
    envied children, believing they alone had the
    ideal life.

    (A) idyllic
    (B) envious
    (C) indifferent
    (D) dubious
    (E) neutral

8.  Scientists are hard-line ____; only after
    failing to ____ a controversial theory do
    they accept the evidence.

    (A) militarists...exploit
    (B) optimists...believe
    (C) martinets...punish
    (D) innovators...refute
    (E) cynics...debunk

9.  A prudent, thrifty, New Englander, DeWitt was
    naturally ____ of investing money in junk
    bonds, which he looked on as ____ ventures.

    (A) enamored...worthless
    (B) terrified...sound
    (C) chary...risky
    (D) tired...profitable
    (E) cognizant...provincial

GO ON TO THE NEXT PAGE

1    1    1    1    1    1    1    1    1    1    1    1

<u>Directions:</u> Each question below consists of a related pair of words or phrases, followed by five pairs of words or phrases labeled A through E. Select the pair that <u>best</u> expresses a relationship similar to that expressed in the original pair.

Example:

CRUMB : BREAD ::

(A) ounce : unit
(B) splinter : wood
(C) water : bucket
(D) twine : rope
(E) cream : butter

10. PLAY : ACT ::
    (A) statue : base
    (B) room : window
    (C) building : story
    (D) book : title
    (E) ballet : score

11. ABRIDGE : NOVEL ::
    (A) excavate : tunnel
    (B) polish : rhyme
    (C) span : gap
    (D) produce : play
    (E) cut : speech

12. CALCULATED : SPONTANEITY ::
    (A) verbose : glibness
    (B) rehearsed : performance
    (C) familiar : novelty
    (D) premeditated : justification
    (E) vivid : color

13. FLAUNT : DISPLAY ::
    (A) transform : modify
    (B) brag : declare
    (C) demonstrate : prove
    (D) rehearse : perform
    (E) cancel : initiate

14. CONFLUENCE : RIVERS ::
    (A) deluge : showers
    (B) junction : highways
    (C) deforestation : trees
    (D) detour : traffic
    (E) construction : buildings

15. QUERY : INTERROGATIVE ::
    (A) quibble : objectionable
    (B) allusion : literary
    (C) statement : factual
    (D) metaphor : figurative
    (E) comment : argumentative

GO ON TO THE NEXT PAGE

1   1   1   1   1   1   1   1   1   1   1   1

---

> Directions: Each passage below is followed by questions based on its content. Answer the questions on the basis of what is stated or implied in that passage and in any introductory material that may be provided.

---

**Questions 16–21 are based on the following passage.**

*In the following excerpt from Jane Austen's* Pride and Prejudice, *the members of the Bennet family react to news of the marriage of Lydia, the youngest Bennet daughter, to Mr. Wickham. Elizabeth, oldest of the Bennet daughters and the novel's heroine, is in love with Mr. Darcy and worries how this unexpected marriage may affect her relationship with him.*

A long dispute followed this declaration; but Mr. Bennet was firm: it soon led to another; and Mrs. Bennet found, with amazement
Line and horror, that her husband would not
(5) advance a guinea[1] to buy clothes for his daughter. He protested that she should receive from him no mark of affection whatever, on the occasion of her marriage. Mrs. Bennet could hardly comprehend it. That his anger
(10) could be carried to such a point of inconceivable resentment, as to refuse his daughter a privilege, without which her marriage would scarcely seem valid, exceeded all that she could believe possible. She was more alive to
(15) the disgrace, which the want of new clothes must reflect on her daughter's nuptials, than to any sense of shame at her eloping and living with Wickham, a fortnight before they took place.
(20) Elizabeth was now most heartily sorry that she had, from the distress of the moment, been led to make Mr. Darcy acquainted with their fears for her sister; for since her marriage would so shortly give the proper termination
(25) to the elopement, they might hope to conceal its unfavorable beginning, from all those who were not immediately on the spot.
She had no fear of its spreading farther, through his means. There were few people on
(30) whose secrecy she would have more confidently depended; but at the same time, there was no one, whose knowledge of a sister's frailty would have mortified her so much. Not, however, from any fear of disadvantage from
(35) it, individually to herself; for at any rate, there seemed a gulf impassable between them. Had Lydia's marriage been concluded on the most honorable terms, it was not to be supposed that Mr. Darcy would connect himself with a
(40) family, where to every other objection would now be added, an alliance and relationship of the nearest kind with the man whom he so justly scorned.
From such a connection she could not
(45) wonder that he should shrink. The wish of procuring her regard, which she had assured herself of his feeling in Derbyshire, could not in rational expectation survive such a blow as this. She was humbled, she was grieved; she
(50) repented, though she hardly knew of what. She became jealous of his esteem, when she could no longer hope to be benefitted by it. She wanted to hear of him, when there seemed the least chance of gaining intelligence. She
(55) was convinced that she could have been happy with him, when it was no longer likely they should meet.

---
[1] A British coin.

GO ON TO THE NEXT PAGE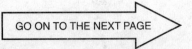

**1   1   1   1   1   1   1   1   1   1   1   1**

16. All of the following statements about Mrs. Bennet may be inferred from the passage EXCEPT

(A) She finds a lack of proper attire more shameful than a lack of proper conduct.
(B) She is ready to welcome home her newly married daughter.
(C) She is sensitive to the nature of her husband's scruples about the elopement.
(D) She is unable to grasp the degree of emotion her daughter's conduct has aroused.
(E) She is primarily concerned with external appearances.

17. The "privilege" that Mr. Bennet refuses to grant his daughter (line 12) is the privilege of

(A) marrying Mr. Wickham
(B) buying a new wardrobe
(C) running away from home
(D) seeing her mother and sisters
(E) having a valid wedding ceremony

18. According to the passage, Elizabeth Bennet presently

(A) has ceased to crave Darcy's affection
(B) regrets having told Darcy of her sister's elopement
(C) no longer desires to conceal Lydia's escapade
(D) fears Darcy will spread the word about the sudden elopement
(E) cares more for public opinion than for her family's welfare

19. The expression "a sister's frailty" (lines 32–33) refers to Elizabeth's sister's

(A) delicate health since birth
(B) embarrassing lack of proper wedding garments
(C) reluctant marriage to a man whom she disdained
(D) fear of being considered an old maid
(E) moral weakness in running away with a man

20. According to lines 38–43, Mr. Darcy feels contempt for

(A) Lydia's hasty marriage
(B) secrets that are entrusted to him
(C) Elizabeth's confession to him
(D) Lydia's new husband
(E) Mr. Bennet's harshness

21. The passage can best be described as

(A) a description of the origins of a foolish and intemperate marriage
(B) an account of one woman's reflections on the effects of her sister's runaway marriage
(C) an analysis of the reasons underlying the separation of a young woman from her lover
(D) a description of a conflict between a young woman and her temperamental parents
(E) a discussion of the nature of sacred and profane love

**Questions 22–30 are based on the following passage.**

*The following passage is taken from a classic study of tarantulas published in* Scientific American *in 1952.*

A fertilized female tarantula lays from 200 to 400 eggs at a time; thus it is possible for a single tarantula to produce several thousand
*Line* young. She takes no care of them beyond
(5) weaving a cocoon of silk to enclose the eggs. After they hatch, the young walk away, find convenient places in which to dig their burrows and spend the rest of their lives in solitude. Tarantulas feed mostly on insects and
(10) millipedes. Once their appetite is appeased, they digest the food for several days before eating again. Their sight is poor, being limited

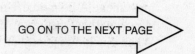
GO ON TO THE NEXT PAGE

to sensing a change in the intensity of light
and to the perception of moving objects. They
(15) apparently have little or no sense of hearing,
for a hungry tarantula will pay no attention to
a loudly chirping cricket placed in its cage
unless the insect happens to touch one of its
legs.

(20)     But all spiders, and especially hairy ones,
have an extremely delicate sense of touch.
Laboratory experiments prove that tarantulas
can distinguish three types of touch: pressure
against the body wall, stroking of the body
(25) hair, and riffling of certain very fine hairs on
the legs called trichobothria. Pressure against
the body, by a finger or the end of a pencil,
causes the tarantula to move off slowly for a
short distance. The touch excites no defensive
(30) response unless the approach is from above,
where the spider can see the motion, in which
case it rises on its hind legs, lifts its front legs,
opens its fangs and holds this threatening posture as long as the object continues to move.
(35) When the motion stops, the spider drops back
to the ground, remains quiet for a few seconds, and then moves slowly away.

     The entire body of a tarantula, especially
its legs, is thickly clothed with hair. Some of it
(40) is short and woolly, some long and stiff.
Touching this body hair produces one of two
distinct reactions. When the spider is hungry,
it responds with an immediate and swift
attack. At the touch of a cricket's antennae the
(45) tarantula seizes the insect so swiftly that a
motion picture taken at the rate of 64 frames
per second shows only the result and not the
process of capture. But when the spider is not
hungry, the stimulation of its hairs merely
(50) causes it to shake the touched limb. An insect
can walk under its hairy belly unharmed.

     The trichobothria, very fine hairs growing
from disklike membranes on the legs, were
once thought to be the spider's hearing organs,
(55) but we now know that they have nothing to do
with sound. They are sensitive only to air
movement. A light breeze makes them vibrate
slowly without disturbing the common hair.
When one blows gently on the trichobothria,

(60) the tarantula reacts with a quick jerk of its four
front legs. If the front and hind legs are stimulated at the same time, the spider makes a sudden jump. This reaction is quite independent
of the state of its appetite.

(65)     These three tactile responses—to pressure
on the body wall, to moving of the common
hair, and to flexing of the trichobothria—are
so different from one another that there is no
possibility of confusing them. They serve the
(70) tarantula adequately for most of its needs and
enable it to avoid most annoyances and dangers. But they fail the tarantula completely
when it meets its deadly enemy, the digger
wasp Pepsis.

22. According to the author, which of the following attributes is (are) characteristic of female
tarantulas?

   I. Maternal instincts
  II. Visual acuity
 III. Fertility

   (A) I only
   (B) II only
   (C) III only
   (D) I and III only
   (E) II and III only

23. Lines 6–9 primarily suggest that the female
tarantula

   (A) becomes apprehensive at sudden noises
   (B) is better able to discern pressure than
       stroking
   (C) must consume insects or millipedes daily
   (D) constructs a cocoon for her young
   (E) is reclusive by nature

GO ON TO THE NEXT PAGE

**1    1    1    1    1    1    1    1    1    1    1**

24. The word "excites" in line 29 most nearly
    means

    (A) irritates
    (B) delights
    (C) stimulates
    (D) exhilarates
    (E) infuriates

25. The author's attitude toward tarantulas would
    best be described as

    (A) fearful
    (B) sentimental
    (C) approving
    (D) objective
    (E) incredulous

26. The main purpose of the passage is to

    (A) report on controversial new discoveries
        about spider behavior
    (B) summarize what is known about the physi-
        cal and social responses of tarantulas
    (C) challenge the findings of recent laboratory
        experiments involving tarantulas
    (D) explain the lack of social organization in
        the spider family
    (E) discuss the physical adaptations which
        make tarantulas unique

27. The description of what happens when one
    films a tarantula's reaction to the touch of a
    cricket (lines 44–48) chiefly is intended to
    convey a sense of the tarantula's

    (A) omnivorous appetite
    (B) photogenic appearance
    (C) graceful movement
    (D) quickness in attacking
    (E) lack of stimulation

28. The word "independent" in line 63 most nearly
    means

    (A) individualistic
    (B) self-governing
    (C) affluent
    (D) regardless
    (E) detached

29. In the passage, the author does all of the fol-
    lowing EXCEPT

    (A) deny a possibility
    (B) describe a reaction
    (C) correct a misapprehension
    (D) define a term
    (E) pose a question

30. In the paragraphs immediately following this
    passage, the author most likely will

    (A) explain why scientists previously confused
        the tarantula's three tactile responses
    (B) demonstrate how the tarantula's three tac-
        tile responses enable it to meet its needs
    (C) point out the weaknesses of the digger
        wasp that enable the tarantula to subdue it
    (D) report on plans for experiments to explore
        the digger wasp's tactile sense
    (E) describe how the digger wasp goes about
        attacking tarantulas

# STOP

**IF YOU FINISH BEFORE TIME IS CALLED, YOU MAY CHECK YOUR WORK ON THIS
SECTION ONLY. DO NOT WORK ON ANY OTHER SECTION IN THE TEST.**

**2   2   2   2   2   2   2   2   2   2   2**

## Section 2

TIME—30 MINUTES
35 QUESTIONS
For each of the following questions, select the best answer from among the choices provided and fill in the appropriate circle on the answer sheet.

---

Directions: Each sentence below has one or two blanks, each blank indicating that something has been omitted. Beneath the sentence are five words or sets of words labeled A through E. Choose the word or set of words that, when inserted in the sentence, best fits the meaning of the sentence as a whole.

Example:

Medieval kingdoms did not become constitutional republics overnight; on the contrary, the change was _____.

(A) unpopular
(B) unexpected
(C) advantageous
(D) sufficient
(E) gradual

Ⓐ  Ⓑ  Ⓒ  Ⓓ  ●

---

1. While there were some tasks the candidate could _____, others she had to attend to herself.

    (A) perform
    (B) endorse
    (C) delegate
    (D) misconstrue
    (E) rehearse

2. Considering that caterpillars and spiders belong to distinctly different classes of arthropods and evolved silk quite independently, the silks they produce have a remarkably _____ composition.

    (A) delicate
    (B) diaphanous
    (C) mutable
    (D) similar
    (E) durable

3. Formed by Puerto Rican tenants who refused to move from Boston's South End when it was scheduled to be razed, the community development group has not only _____ hundreds of apartments but has also built New England's first center _____ to Hispanic culture.

    (A) relegated…pertinent
    (B) demolished…convenient
    (C) renovated…dedicated
    (D) remodeled…indifferent
    (E) eliminated…restricted

4. Concrete actually is _____, like a sponge—it can absorb up to 10 percent of its weight in water.

    (A) delicate
    (B) elastic
    (C) porous
    (D) ubiquitous
    (E) washable

GO ON TO THE NEXT PAGE ⇒

2  2  2  2  2  2  2  2  2  2  2

5. Some of Kandinsky's artistic innovations are now so much a part of our visual world that they appear on everything from wallpaper to women's scarves without causing the slightest _____.

   (A) profit
   (B) remorse
   (C) boredom
   (D) effort
   (E) stir

6. Short stories, in Hemingway's phrase, have plots that show only "the tip of the iceberg"; such stories _____ a _____ shape below but do not describe that shape in detail.

   (A) cover up...distinctive
   (B) hint at...bulkier
   (C) depart from...nebulous
   (D) thaw out...colder
   (E) revolve around...grimmer

7. The title *Rage of a Privileged Class* seems _____, for such a privileged group would seem on the surface to have no _____ sustained anger with anyone.

   (A) incongruous...time for
   (B) paradoxical...reason for
   (C) ambiguous...familiarity with
   (D) ironic...indifference to
   (E) witty...capacity for

8. Lyell's and Darwin's ideas, which saw nature as the result of cumulative, _____ change, triumphed over the older, catastrophist theories, which _____ that mountains and species were created by a few sudden and dramatic events.

   (A) gradual...supposed
   (B) drastic...anticipated
   (C) regular...denied
   (D) frequent...disproved
   (E) abrupt...intimated

9. In Christopher's _____ family, _____ begun over dinner frequently carried over for days.

   (A) contentious...arguments
   (B) abstemious...accusations
   (C) garrulous...doubts
   (D) assiduous...conversations
   (E) irreverent...rituals

10. The founder of the Children's Defense Fund, Marian Wright Edelman, strongly _____ the lack of financial and moral support for children in America today.

    (A) advocates
    (B) condones
    (C) feigns
    (D) abets
    (E) decries

GO ON TO THE NEXT PAGE

2 2 2 2 2 2 2 2 2 2 2 2

<u>Directions:</u> Each question below consists of a related pair of words or phrases, followed by five pairs of words or phrases labeled A through E. Select the pair that <u>best</u> expresses a relationship similar to that expressed in the original pair.

Example:

CRUMB : BREAD ::

(A) ounce : unit
(B) splinter : wood
(C) water : bucket
(D) twine : rope
(E) cream : butter

Ⓐ ● Ⓒ Ⓓ Ⓔ

11. JAR : RECEPTACLE ::

(A) book : story
(B) cottage : building
(C) rifle : ammunition
(D) trunk : lid
(E) barrel : wood

12. WRIGGLE : EEL ::

(A) bite : snake
(B) leap : frog
(C) gobble : turkey
(D) roost : hen
(E) muzzle : dog

13. BREEZE : GALE ::

(A) course : voyage
(B) hurricane : destruction
(C) affection : passion
(D) stream : current
(E) fame : recognition

14. DEPOT : TRAIN ::

(A) cockpit : plane
(B) pier : ship
(C) ticket : performance
(D) brakes : automobile
(E) sidecar : motorcycle

15. GUSHER : OIL ::

(A) bucket : water
(B) sewer : rain
(C) piston : grease
(D) tanker : gasoline
(E) geyser : steam

16. CLUE : DETECTIVE ::

(A) cloud : astronomer
(B) prescription : doctor
(C) confession : criminal
(D) symptom : diagnostician
(E) prediction : prophet

17. SILKWORM : SILK ::

(A) termite : wood
(B) mollusk : pearl
(C) snakebite : snake
(D) necklace : diamond
(E) fly : cobweb

18. POLLSTER : OPINION ::

(A) debater : speech
(B) hitchhiker : ride
(C) witness : testimony
(D) trespasser : property
(E) peddler : merchandise

GO ON TO THE NEXT PAGE ⇒

2   2   2   2   2   2   2   2   2   2   2

19. TANNERY : LEATHER ::

  (A) mine : coal
  (B) bolt : fabric
  (C) inventory : merchandise
  (D) foundation : cement
  (E) mill : flour

20. ACCLIMATE : CLIMATE ::

  (A) habituate : familiarity
  (B) initiate : action
  (C) orient : situation
  (D) economize : money
  (E) articulate : speech

21. BLEAK : HOPE ::

  (A) harsh : voice
  (B) weak : joy
  (C) modest : faith
  (D) drab : color
  (E) insipid : food

22. FORBEAR : PATIENCE ::

  (A) snarl : amicability
  (B) endure : suffering
  (C) attack : hostility
  (D) perjure : treachery
  (E) denounce : resignation

23. IMPOSING : IMPRESS ::

  (A) winsome : attract
  (B) majestic : oppress
  (C) devastating : surrender
  (D) disquieting : encourage
  (E) relaxing : inspire

GO ON TO THE NEXT PAGE

2  2  2  2  2  2  2  2  2  2  2

Directions: The passage below is followed by questions based on its content. Answer the questions on the basis of what is stated or implied in the passage and in any introductory material that may be provided.

**Questions 24–35 are based on the following passage.**

*In this excerpt from an essay on the symbolic language of dreams, the writer Erich Fromm explores the nature of symbols.*

One of the current definitions of a symbol is that it is "something that stands for something else." We can differentiate between three
Line kinds of symbols: the *conventional*, the *acci-*
(5) *dental*, and the *universal* symbol.

The *conventional* symbol is the best known of the three, since we employ it in everyday language. If we see the word "table" or hear the sound "table," the letters *t-a-b-l-e* stand for
(10) something else. They stand for the thing "table" that we see, touch, and use. What is the connection between the *word* "table" and the *thing* "table"? Is there any inherent relationship between them? Obviously not. The
(15) *thing* table has nothing to do with the *sound* table, and the only reason the word symbolizes the thing is the convention of calling this particular thing by a name. We learn this connection as children by the repeated experience
(20) of hearing the word in reference to the thing until a lasting association is formed so that we don't have to think to find the right word.

There are some words, however, in which the association is not only conventional. When
(25) we say "phooey," for instance, we make with our lips a movement of dispelling the air quickly. It is an expression of disgust in which our mouths participate. By this quick expulsion of air we imitate and thus express our
(30) intention to expel something, to get it out of our system. In this case, as in some others, the symbol has an inherent connection with the feeling it symbolizes. But even if we assume that originally many or even all words had

(35) their origins in some such inherent connection between symbol and the symbolized, most words no longer have this meaning for us when we learn a language.

Words are not the only illustration for con-
(40) ventional symbols, although they are the most frequent and best known ones. Pictures also can be conventional symbols. A flag, for instance, may stand for a specific country, and yet there is no intrinsic connection between
(45) the specific colors and the country for which they stand. They have been accepted as denoting that particular country, and we translate the visual impression of the flag into the concept of that country, again on conventional
(50) grounds.

The opposite to the conventional symbol is the *accidental* symbol, although they have one thing in common: there is no intrinsic relationship between the symbol and that which it
(55) symbolizes. Let us assume that someone has had a saddening experience in a certain city; when he hears the name of that city, he will easily connect the name with a mood of sadness, just as he would connect it with a mood
(60) of joy had his experience been a happy one. Quite obviously, there is nothing in the nature of the city that is either sad or joyful. It is the individual experience connected with the city that makes it a symbol of a mood.

(65) The same reaction could occur in connection with a house, a street, a certain dress, certain scenery, or anything once connected with a specific mood. We might find ourselves dreaming that we are in a certain city. We ask
(70) ourselves why we happened to think of that city in our sleep and may discover that we had

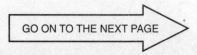

GO ON TO THE NEXT PAGE

2    2    2    2    2    2    2    2    2    2    2

fallen asleep in a mood similar to the one symbolized by the city. The picture in the dream
represents this mood, the city "stands for" the
(75) mood once experienced in it. The connection
between the symbol and the experience symbolized is entirely accidental.

The *universal* symbol is one in which there
is an intrinsic relationship between the symbol
(80) and that which it represents. Take, for instance,
the symbol of fire. We are fascinated by certain qualities of fire in a fireplace. First of all,
by its aliveness. It changes continuously, it
moves all the time, and yet there is constancy
(85) in it. It remains the same without being the
same. It gives the impression of power, of
energy, of grace and lightness. It is as if it
were dancing, and had an inexhaustible source
of energy. When we use fire as a symbol, we
(90) describe the *inner experience* characterized by
the same elements which we notice in the sensory experience of fire—the mood of energy,
lightness, movement, grace, gaiety, sometimes
one, sometimes another of these elements
(95) being predominant in the feeling.

The universal symbol is the only one in
which the relationship between the symbol
and that which is symbolized is not coincidental, but intrinsic. It is rooted in the experience
(100) of the affinity between an emotion or thought,
on the one hand, and a sensory experience, on
the other. It can be called universal because it
is shared by all men, in contrast not only to the
accidental symbol, which is by its very nature
(105) entirely personal, but also to the conventional
symbol, which is restricted to a group of people sharing the same convention. The universal
symbol is rooted in the properties of our body,
our senses, and our mind, which are common
(110) to all men and, therefore, not restricted to individuals or to specific groups. Indeed, *the language of the universal symbol is the one common tongue developed by the human race, a
language which it forgot before it succeeded in
(115) developing a universal conventional language.*

24. The passage is primarily concerned with
   (A) refuting an argument
   (B) illustrating an axiom
   (C) describing a process
   (D) proving a thesis
   (E) refining a definition

25. The term "stand for" in line 9 means
   (A) tolerate
   (B) represent
   (C) withstand
   (D) endorse
   (E) rise

26. According to lines 8–32, "table" and "phooey"
   differ in that
   (A) only one is a conventional symbol
   (B) "table" is a better known symbol than
       "phooey"
   (C) "phooey" has an intrinsic natural link with
       its meaning
   (D) children learn "phooey" more readily than
       they learn "table"
   (E) only one is used exclusively by children

27. It can be inferred from the passage that another
   example of a word with both inherent and con-
   ventional associations to its meaning is
   (A) hiss
   (B) hike
   (C) hold
   (D) candle
   (E) telephone

28. The author contends that conventional symbols
   (A) are less meaningful than accidental ones
   (B) necessarily have an innate connection with
       an emotion
   (C) can be pictorial as well as linguistic
   (D) are less familiar than universal symbols
   (E) appeal chiefly to conventionally minded
       people

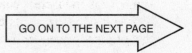
GO ON TO THE NEXT PAGE

2 2 2 2 2 2 2 2 2 2 2

29. Which of the following would the author be most likely to categorize as a conventional symbol?

(A) a country road
(B) a patchwork quilt
(C) a bonfire
(D) the city of London
(E) the Statue of Liberty

30. According to the author's argument, a relationship between the city of Paris and the mood of joy can best be described as

(A) innate
(B) dreamlike
(C) elemental
(D) coincidental
(E) immutable

31. A major factor distinguishing a universal symbol from conventional and accidental symbols is

(A) its origins in sensory experience
(B) its dependence on a specific occasion
(C) the intensity of the mood experienced
(D) its unmemorable nature
(E) its appeal to the individual

32. By saying "Take . . . the symbol of fire" (lines 80–81), the author is asking the reader to

(A) grasp it as an element
(B) consider it as an example
(C) accept it as a possibility
(D) prefer it as a category
(E) assume it as a standard

33. Which of the following would the author most likely categorize as a universal symbol?

(A) the word f-i-r-e
(B) the word p-h-o-o-e-y
(C) a red dress
(D) an American flag
(E) water in a stream

34. The word "properties" in line 108 means

(A) possessions
(B) attributes
(C) investments
(D) titles
(E) grounds

35. The author contends in lines 111–115 that the language of the universal symbol

(A) antedates the development of everyday conventional language
(B) restricts itself to those capable of comprehending symbolism
(C) should be adopted as the common tongue for the human race
(D) grew out of mankind's efforts to create a universal conventional language
(E) developed accidentally from the human desire to communicate

## STOP

**IF YOU FINISH BEFORE TIME IS CALLED, YOU MAY CHECK YOUR WORK ON THIS SECTION ONLY. DO NOT WORK ON ANY OTHER SECTION IN THE TEST.**

3  3  3  3  3  3  3  3  3  3  3

## Section 3

TIME—15 MINUTES
13 QUESTIONS

For each of the following questions, choose the best answer and fill in the appropriate circle on the answer sheet.

Directions: The two passages below are followed by questions based on their content and on the relationship between the two passages. Answer the questions on the basis of what is stated or implied in the passages and in any introductory material that may be provided.

### Questions 1–13 are based on the following passages.

*The following passages describe the settling of the American West during the nineteenth century. The first was written by a social historian and scholar. The second comes from a widely used textbook in American history.*

#### Passage 1

The populating of nearly one billion acres of empty land west of the Mississippi occurred in a series of peristaltic waves, beginning in
Line the 1840s and continuing for the rest of the
(5) century. First to arrive was the advance guard, the trailblazers—explorers, trappers, and mountain men, hide and tallow traders, free-lance adventurers, the military. Then the set-tlers in their wagon trains lumbering over the
(10) Oregon Trail to the lush meadows of the Oregon Territory and the inland valleys of California. Next, the gold-seekers, bowling across the plains and deserts pell-mell in 1848, working up and down the California mountain
(15) ranges, then backtracking to the gold and sil-ver country in the Rockies and the Southwest. And finally, a last great wave, first by wagons, then by railroads, to mop up the leapfrogged Great Plains. By 1890 the great movement
(20) west was over, ending in a final hurrahing stampede of boomers into Oklahoma Territory, a rush of humanity that created entire towns in an afternoon.

The vast, empty land demanded new tools,
(25) new social organizations, new men and women. And it produced a new canon of

myths and heroes—the stuff of countless dime novels, Wild West shows, movies, and televi-sion series for later generations. The heroes
(30) are familiar enough—the cowboys, the law-men, the gamblers, the gold-hearted dance-hall girls, the bad men too, for heroes need evil to conquer. The western town played a part, too, mainly as backdrop and chorus,
(35) before which the central figures enacted their *agon* (struggle; contest). The fictional western town was as rigidly formalized as the set for a Japanese No play—the false-front stores on a dusty street lined with hitching rails, the
(40) saloons with bar, gambling tables, and stage for the dancers, the general store, the jail, and the church. The people of the chorus had a stereotypical form—women in crinolines and the men in frock coats and string ties, their
(45) striped pants tucked into boots. Their lives were projected as dim, ordinary, law-abiding shadows, against which were contrasted the bold-hued dramas of the principals. These were the "decent folk," whom the heroic law-
(50) men died for; they were the meek who would inherit the set after the leading actors left and the last wild cowboy was interred in Boot Hill. Colorless, sober, conservative, salt-of-the-earth, they represented the future—and a dull one it
(55) was. Occasionally, as in the film *High Noon*, their passive virtues were transmogrified into hypocrisy and timidity, mocking the lonely courage of the marshal they had hired to risk

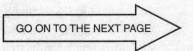
GO ON TO THE NEXT PAGE

3   3   3   3   3   3   3   3   3   3   3

his life for them. The implication was: Are
(60) these dull, cautious folk really the worthy
heirs of the noble cowboys? In Steven Crane's
short story *The Bride Comes to Yellow Sky*, the
last cowboy is a drunken anachronism, wearing his nobility in tatters, yet not to be
(65) scorned.

**Passage 2**

It was the miners who established the first
outposts of the Far West. The discovery of
gold in California had transformed that com-
monwealth from a pastoral outpost of New
(70) Spain to a thriving American state and had
opened up new and varied economic activities—farming, shipping, railroading, and manufacturing. That experience was to be repeated
again and again in the history of the mining
(75) kingdom; in the rush to Pike's Peak country in
1859, to Alder Gulch and Last Chance in
Montana and the banks of the Sweetwater in
Wyoming in the middle sixties, to the Black
Hills of the Dakota country in the seventies.
(80) Everywhere the miners opened up the country,
established political communities, and laid the
foundations for more permanent settlements.
As the gold and silver played out or fell into
the hands of eastern corporations and mining
(85) fever abated, the settlers would perceive the
farming and stock-raising possibilities around
them or find work on the railroads that were
pushing in from the East and West. Some
communities remained almost exclusively
(90) mining, but the real wealth of Montana and
Colorado, Wyoming and Idaho, as of
California, was in their grass and their soil.
Even in mineral wealth the value of the precious metals which had first lured adventurers
(95) was shortly exceeded by that of the copper
and coal and oil which were so abundant. . . .
Even while the miners were grubbing in
the hills of Nevada and Montana, a new and
more important chapter was being written in
(100) the history of the West. This was the rise of
the cattle kingdom. The physical basis of the
kingdom was the grasslands of the West,
stretching unbroken from the Rio Grande to

the northern frontier, from Kansas and
(105) Nebraska into the Rocky Mountain valleys.
Here millions of buffaloes had roamed at will,
but within two decades the buffalo was to
become almost extinct and its place taken by
even more millions of Texas longhorns and
(110) Wyoming and Montana steers. . . .
The cattle kingdom, like the mining, had
its romantic side, and the remembrance of this
has persisted in the American consciousness
after the cattle kingdom itself has vanished.
(115) The lonely life on the plain, the roundup, the
hieroglyphic brands, the long drive, the stampede, the war with cattle rustlers, the splendid
horsemanship, the picturesque costume
designed for usefulness, not effect—the wild
(120) life of the cow towns like Abilene and
Cheyenne, all have found their way into
American folklore and song. Children array
themselves now in imitation cowboy suits,
moving-picture ranchmen shoot down rustlers
(125) with unerring aim, and the whole country
sings what was reputed to be President
Franklin Roosevelt's favorite song:
Home, home on the range,
Where the deer and the antelope play
(130) Where seldom is heard, a discouraging word,
And the skies are not cloudy all day.

1. According to Passage 1, the settling of the
West took place
(A) during a steady migration that lasted sixty
years
(B) intermittently as people went farther and
farther west
(C) in two waves, the first during the 1840s,
the last in the 1890s
(D) in no discernible order
(E) sometimes slowly and sometimes rapidly
during a fifty-year period

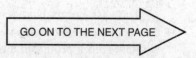
GO ON TO THE NEXT PAGE

2. Passage 1 implies that the settlers went to the West largely for

    (A) economic advancement
    (B) adventure
    (C) a desire for more space
    (D) free land
    (E) more individual liberty

3. The comparison between western towns and the set of a Japanese No play (line 38) is intended to make the point that

    (A) in the Old West, people mattered more than towns
    (B) every town in the Old West looked alike
    (C) the towns looked good on the surface but not underneath
    (D) in books and films, western towns are all the same
    (E) towns were all show and no substance

4. The author of Passage 1 believes that after the westward migration, the settlers were portrayed as people who

    (A) settled into routine lives
    (B) yearned for a return to the romantic days of the past
    (C) turned into hypocrites
    (D) failed to do what was expected of them
    (E) recreated their past in books, movies, and TV shows

5. The allusion to the cowboy in *The Bride Comes to Yellow Sky* (lines 62–65) is meant to show that

    (A) the people rejected the heroes of the Old West
    (B) many of the myths of the Old West were false
    (C) the legendary heroes of the Old West became obsolete
    (D) drunkenness and reckless behavior tarnished the image of the heroic cowboys of the Old West
    (E) all glamorous and romantic eras eventually die out

6. The center of the so-called "mining kingdom" (lines 67–82), as described in Passage 2,

    (A) was located in California
    (B) stretched from the Mississippi River to the Western mountains
    (C) shifted from place to place
    (D) began in the Far West and then jumped to the East
    (E) drifted west throughout the second half of the 19th century

7. According to Passage 2, when the gold and silver ran out, the miners switched to

    (A) working on the land
    (B) searching for oil and other fuels
    (C) cattle rustling
    (D) their previous occupations
    (E) digging for other minerals

8. The author of Passage 2 believes that the defining event in the history of the West was

    (A) the founding of new cities and towns
    (B) the discovery of precious metals
    (C) the growth of the cattle industry
    (D) the development of the mining kingdom
    (E) the coming of the railroad

9. Passage 2 implies that the buffalo became almost extinct in the Great Plains because

    (A) they roamed westward
    (B) their land was fenced off for agriculture
    (C) the land could no longer support huge buffalo herds
    (D) they were killed to make room for cattle-grazing
    (E) they were driven north to Canada and south to Mexico

GO ON TO THE NEXT PAGE

**3 3 3 3 3 3 3 3 3 3 3**

10. According to Passage 2, the cowboy of the Old West is remembered today for all of the following EXCEPT his

(A) distinctive clothing
(B) ability to ride horses
(C) law-abiding nature
(D) skill with a gun
(E) rugged individualism

11. Both passages suggest that settlers were attracted to California because of its

(A) gold
(B) mountains
(C) seacoast
(D) scenic splendor
(E) fertile valleys

12. The authors of both Passage 1 and Passage 2 seem to have a common interest in

(A) defining the American dream
(B) political history
(C) mining
(D) American folklore and legend
(E) the social class structure in America

13. Compared to the account of the westward movement in Passage 1, Passage 2 pays more attention to the role of

(A) pioneer families
(B) miners
(C) politicians
(D) entrepreneurs
(E) outlaws

## STOP

**IF YOU FINISH BEFORE TIME IS CALLED, YOU MAY CHECK YOUR WORK ON THIS SECTION ONLY. DO NOT WORK ON ANY OTHER SECTION IN THE TEST.**

# ANSWER KEY

## Section 1

| | | | | | | | | | |
|---|---|---|---|---|---|---|---|---|---|
| 1. D | 4. A | 7. A | 10. C | 13. B | 16. C | 19. E | 22. C | 25. D | 28. D |
| 2. B | 5. C | 8. E | 11. E | 14. B | 17. B | 20. D | 23. E | 26. B | 29. E |
| 3. B | 6. C | 9. C | 12. C | 15. D | 18. B | 21. B | 24. C | 27. D | 30. E |

## Section 2

| | | | | | | | | | |
|---|---|---|---|---|---|---|---|---|---|
| 1. C | 5. E | 9. A | 13. C | 17. B | 21. D | 24. E | 27. A | 30. D | 33. E |
| 2. D | 6. B | 10. E | 14. B | 18. B | 22. C | 25. B | 28. C | 31. A | 34. B |
| 3. C | 7. B | 11. B | 15. E | 19. E | 23. A | 26. C | 29. E | 32. B | 35. A |
| 4. C | 8. A | 12. B | 16. D | 20. C | | | | | |

## Section 3

| | | | | | | |
|---|---|---|---|---|---|---|
| 1. E | 3. D | 5. C | 7. A | 9. D | 11. A | 13. B |
| 2. A | 4. A | 6. C | 8. C | 10. C | 12. D | |

## ANALYSIS OF TEST RESULTS

I.   Check your answers against the answer key.
II.  Fill in the following chart.

| | | | | Total |
|---|---|---|---|---|
| **Sentence Completions** <br> Number Correct | Section 1 (Questions 1–9) <br> 2 7 | Section 2 (Questions 1–10) <br> 10 | | 17 |
| **Analogies** <br> Number Correct | Section 1 (Questions 10–15) <br> 3 | Section 2 (Questions 11–23) <br> 11 | | 14 |
| **Critical Reading** <br> Number Correct | Section 1 (Questions 16–30) <br> 9 11 | Section 2 (Questions 24–35) <br> 5 | Section 3 (Questions 1–13) <br> 9 | 25 |

III. Interpret your results.     9 4/8 5/22

| | | |
|---|---|---|
| Sentence Completions | Number Correct | 17 |
| Analogies | Number Correct | 14 |
| Critical Reasoning | Number Correct | 25 |
| | Subtotal | 56 |

*Guessing Penalty:* Subtract 1/4 point for each incorrect answer.     5
(Do not take off points for questions you left blank.)

TOTAL SCORE     51

| | Sentence Completion/Analogy Score | Reading Score | Total |
|---|---|---|---|
| Excellent | 18–19 Correct | 37–40 | 73–78 |
| Very Good | 14–17 Correct | 27–36 | 55–72 |
| Good | 11–13 Correct | 19–26 | 41–54 |
| Fair | 9–10 Correct | 15–18 | 33–40 |
| Poor | 6–8  Correct | 10–14 | 20–32 |
| Very Poor | 0–5  Correct | 0–9 | 0–19 |

You can get a rough idea of which areas you most need to work on by comparing your sentence completion, analogy, and critical reading scores.

The College Board uses a guessing formula to compensate for the effect of wild guesses on people's scores. The formula is

Raw Score = _____ – (_____ divided by 4)
                no. correct    no. incorrect

In calculating your Raw Score, do not count any questions you left blank as incorrect.

A Raw Score of 73 to 78 is excellent.
A Raw Score of 55 to 72 is very good.
A Raw Score of 41 to 54 is above average.
A Raw Score of 25 to 40 is average to below average.

If your Raw Score differs from your total number of correct answers by more than 3 points, you should be very cautious about guessing on this test. Guess intelligently. Guess only when you can eliminate one or more of the five answer choices to the question.

## IV. List any unfamiliar words you came across. Then look the words up in a dictionary and write down their definitions.

| Word | Definition |
|---|---|
| Anachronym | repres. of something as existing or occuring out of the period. |
| | |
| | |
| | |

## V. Read the answer explanations and think about your performance.

Go over the questions you omitted as well as the ones you got wrong. Did you mark down any answers in the wrong spot? Did you run out of time and have to leave out questions you could have answered correctly? Did you misread any questions, overlooking key words like "except" and "best"? Were you too cautious about guessing, omitting questions that you had a chance of getting right if you had just guessed? If necessary, reread the relevant sections in Part I. Then get to work on mastering the different question types.

# ANSWER EXPLANATIONS

## SECTION 1

1. **D**  Our experience suggests to us that a creature without visible ears would be unable to hear *sounds*.

2. **B**  Although the map that *charted* (mapped) Viking explorations has been considered a fake, new evidence may prove it to be authentic or *genuine*.

3. **B**  In a volcanic eruption, ash and other matter is *ejected* or forced out of the volcano.

4. **A**  If the silk makes the nest walls stronger, they will be more able to *withstand* or resist the weight and pressure of the small birds.

5. **C**  *Arbitrators* (people chosen to decide disputes) labor to reconcile people with *conflicting* views.

6. **C**  The writer gains emotional force by choosing details that *evoke* or call up emotions.

7. **A**  Despite Stevie Smith's belief in an ideal childhood, her childhood was not *idyllic* or charmingly simple.

8. **E**  A *cynic* is someone who distrusts human nature and motives. Such a person would suspect the motives of anyone advancing a controversial theory and would only accept evidence in favor of that theory after having tried hard to *debunk* that evidence (expose it as a sham or false).

9. **C**  Someone prudent or cautious would look on junk bonds as *risky*, uncertain investments. Such a person would be *chary of* (cautiously hesitant about) investing in such poor risks.

10. **C**  An *act* is a major division of a *play*. A *story* is a major division of a *building*.

11. **E**  One *abridges* (condenses) a *novel* to shorten it. One *cuts* a *speech* to shorten it.

12. **C**  Something *calculated* or contrived lacks *spontaneity* (naturalness). Something *familiar* lacks *novelty* (newness).

13. **B**  To *flaunt* something is to *display* it in a showy or boastful manner. To *brag* about something is to *declare* it in a showy or boastful manner.

14. **B**  The *confluence* of two *rivers* is the place where they come together or meet. The *junction* of two *highways* is the place where they come together or meet.

15. **D**  A *query* or question is by definition *interrogative*. A *metaphor* or figure of speech is by definition *figurative* (metaphorical; expressing a comparison).

16. **C**  Far from being *sensitive to the nature of her husband's scruples* or ethical considerations about what he can and cannot do for his rash daughter, Mrs. Bennet can hardly comprehend them.

17. **B**  The privilege Mr. Bennet refuses his daughter is a *new wardrobe*. In the opening sentence, we learn that Mr. Bennet would not come up with any money ("would not advance a guinea") to buy his daughter new clothes. To Mrs. Bennet, the purchase of new clothes on the occasion of a wedding was a privilege automatically granted the bride.

18. **B**  The opening sentence of the second paragraph indicates Elizabeth's *regret*: she "was most heartily sorry."

19. **E**  Frailty here is the *moral weakness* of giving way to temptation and running off to "live in sin" with a man.

20. **D**  The concluding sentence of the third paragraph indicates that Darcy scorned or felt contempt for the man Lydia married.

21. **B**  Three of the four paragraphs trace Elizabeth's *reflections* or thoughts in detail.

22. **C**  Neither maternal instincts nor visual keenness is characteristic of female tarantulas. Only *fertility* (the quality of being prolific) is.

23. **E**   Since it is stated that young tarantulas go off to spend their lives in solitude, it follows that female tarantulas are *reclusive* or solitary by nature.
24. **C**   To excite a defensive response is to *stimulate* that kind of reaction.
25. **D**   The author's presentation of factual information about tarantulas is scientifically *objective* (impartial).
26. **B**   Rather than covering new ground or challenging current theories, the passage *sums up general knowledge.*
27. **D**   The key words here are "seizes the insect so swiftly." The spider's attack is quicker than even the movie camera's eye.
28. **D**   Under these conditions, the spider will jump whether or not it is hungry. Thus its reaction occurs quite *regardless* of the state of its appetite.
29. **E**   Use the process of elimination to answer this question. In lines 65–69 the author *denies the possibility* that the viewer could confuse the spider's three tactile responses. You can eliminate (A).

   In the second, third, and fourth paragraphs the author *describes* the spider's three tactile responses or *reactions*. You can eliminate (B).

   In lines 52–56 the author *corrects the misapprehension* that the trichobothria might be hearing organs. You can eliminate (C).

   In lines 52–53, the author *defines* trichobothria as very fine hairs growing from disklike membranes on the spider's legs. You can eliminate (D).

   Only (E) is left. At no time does the author *pose* or ask *a question.* By elimination, (E) is the correct answer.
30. **E**   The concluding sentence of the passage states that the tarantula's tactile responses do not help it when it meets (that is, is attacked by) its deadly enemy, the digger wasp. It follows that subsequent paragraphs will discuss *digger wasp attacks* in more detail.

# Section 2

1. **C**   If you *delegate* or assign a task to someone else, you do not have to attend to it yourself.
2. **D**   If you realize how very different caterpillars and spiders are, you will find it remarkable that they produce silks that are *similar.*
3. **C**   The group has both *renovated* (fixed up) housing that was scheduled to be torn down or razed and has built a center devoted or *dedicated* to Hispanic culture.
4. **C**   Like a sponge, concrete can soak up water because it is *porous* or permeable to fluids.
5. **E**   We are now so used to Kandinsky's innovative designs that they can turn up anywhere without causing any widespread notice or *stir.*
6. **B**   Just as the tip of the iceberg suggests or *hints at* the greater mass of the iceberg under the water, to Hemingway short stories *hint at* a *bulkier,* heavier tale underlying the small part of the story the reader gets to see.
7. **B**   To have so many advantages that one would have no *reason for* anger and yet to be angry all the same is clearly *paradoxical* (puzzling; contradictory).
8. **A**   The catastrophist theory hypothesized or *supposed* that species were created by means of sudden dramatic events or catastrophes. Darwin and Lyell, however, theorized that species were created through cumulative, *gradual* change.
9. **A**   A *contentious* (quarrelsome, disputatious) family by definition is given to *arguments.*
10. **E**   As a supporter of children's rights, Edelman would be likely to *decry* or condemn such a lack of support for young people.
11. **B**   A *jar* is a kind of *receptacle* or container. A *cottage* (small, humble house) is a kind of *building.*
12. **B**   In its characteristic movement, an *eel wriggles.* In its characteristic movement, a *frog leaps.*

13. **C**  A *breeze* (light wind) is less intense than a *gale* (windstorm). *Affection* (liking) is less intense than *passion*.

14. **B**  A *train* loads and unloads passengers and cargo at a *depot*. A *ship* loads and unloads passengers and cargo at a *pier*.

15. **E**  A *gusher* is a copious natural outpouring of *oil*, as from an oil well. A *geyser* is a copious natural outpouring of *steam* and heated water.

16. **D**  A *detective* scrutinizes *clues* to solve a mystery. A *diagnostician* scrutinizes *symptoms* to identify a disease.

17. **B**  A *silkworm* is able to produce *silk*. A *mollusk* (shellfish, such as an oyster) is able to produce *pearls*.

18. **B**  A *pollster* (poll taker) asks people for their *opinions*. A *hitchhiker* asks people for *rides*.

19. **E**  In a *tannery*, hides are processed into *leather*. In a *mill*, grain is processed into *flour*.

20. **C**  To *acclimate* oneself is to become accustomed to the *climate*. To *orient* oneself is to become accustomed to one's *situation* or locality.

21. **D**  Something *bleak* (bare; grim; hopeless) lacks *hope*. Something *drab* (dingy; dull; colorless) lacks *color*.

22. **C**  To *forbear* (control oneself when provoked) is to show *patience*. To *attack* is to show *hostility*.

23. **A**  Something *imposing* (striking; impressive) by definition *impresses*. Something *winsome* (engaging; attractive) by definition *attracts*.

24. **E**  The author begins by giving a definition of the term *symbol* and proceeds to analyze three separate types of symbols. Thus, he is *refining* or further defining his somewhat rudimentary original definition.

25. **B**  For groups of letters or words to stand for an object, they must in some way *represent* that object to the people who accept them as a conventional symbol for it.

26. **C**  In describing the associations of the word "phooey," the author states that "the symbol has an inherent connection with the feeling it symbolizes." In other words, there is an *intrinsic natural link* between the symbol and its meaning.

27. **A**  When we say "hiss," we expel air in a sibilant manner, making a sharp "s" sound as we thrust our tongue toward the tooth ridge and dispel the air quickly. Thus we express our disapproval of something, our desire to push it away from us.

28. **C**  The author gives the example of the flag as a conventional symbol that is *pictorial* rather than linguistic.

29. **E**  To the author, the image of the *Statue of Liberty* would be a conventional symbol, one agreed upon by a group of people to stand for the abstract idea of freedom.

30. **D**  If by some accident you were to have a memorably joyful time in Paris, the city of Paris might come to have some symbolic value for you, bringing a mood of joy to your mind. However, the relationship between the city and the mood is not an inherent, built-in one; it is purely *coincidental*.

31. **A**  The author describes how one's inner experience of a universal symbol is rooted in or grows out of one's *sensory experience*.

32. **B**  The author offers fire as an *example* of a universal symbol and asks us to consider it.

33. **E**  Like fire, *water* is a universal symbol that we experience through our senses, feeling its fluidity, its movement, its power. The words *fire* and *phooey* are conventional symbols, as is the flag. The red dress, if it has any symbolic value at all, is an accidental symbol at best.

34. **B**  The *properties* of our body mentioned here are our body's *attributes* or characteristics. To answer vocabulary-in-context questions, substitute each of the answer choices in the sentence in place of the word in quotes.

35. **A**  The closing sentence states that the human race forgot the language of universal symbols before it developed conventional language. Thus, the language of the universal symbol *antedates* or comes before the development of our everyday conventional tongues.

## SECTION 3

1. **E**   As described in the first paragraph of Passage 1, the settling of the West occurred in "peristaltic waves." In other words, it did not occur at a steady rate. Rather, it took place *sometimes slowly and sometimes rapidly during a fifty-year period* from the 1840s to the 1890s. Nor did the settlers go farther and farther west. California was settled before the Rockies and the Great Plains.

2. **A**   Those who went west were, among others, trappers and traders, gold- and oil-seekers, all hoping for *economic advancement* by cashing in on the rich resources of the area.

3. **D**   The "fictional western town was as rigidly formalized" (lines 36–37) as the set in a Japanese No play. It follows, therefore, *that in books and films, western towns are all the same*. In reality, of course, towns vary considerably.

4. **A**   The passage describes a stereotype of townspeople frequently used in books, movies, and plays set in the period. The people seem always to be portrayed as "decent folk" (line 49) who had *settled into routine lives*.

5. **C**   The cowboy in Crane's story is called a "drunken anachronism" (line 64), a label implying that he is a sad relic of a bygone era. In other words, he's a *hero of the Old West who has become obsolete*.

6. **C**   The original center of the mining kingdom was California. Then, it shifted to Colorado (Pike's Peak), to Montana, Wyoming, and the Black Hills of South Dakota. As new sources of precious metals were discovered throughout the nineteenth century, the center *shifted from place to place*.

7. **A**   Many ex-miners turned to farming and to raising cattle, occupations that required them to *work on the land*.

8. **C**   Passage 2 says that although mining had been a major influence in shaping the history of the American West, *the growth of the cattle industry* wrote an even "more important chapter" (line 99).

9. **D**   The passage indicates that prior to becoming "almost extinct" (line 108), millions of buffalo had "roamed at will" (line 107) throughout the Great Plains. Because ranchers needed the land to graze their "Texas longhorns and Wyoming and Montana steers," the buffalo *were killed to make room for cattle*.

10. **C**   The qualities of the cowboy mentioned by the passage are his "picturesque costume," his "splendid horsemanship," his "unerring aim" (with a gun), and his "lonely life on the plain." Only the cowboy's *law-abiding nature* is not mentioned in the passage.

11. **A**   Passage 1 tells of *gold*-seekers "working up and down the California mountain ranges" (lines 14–15). Passage 2 says that "the discovery of *gold* in California" (lines 67–68) triggered a rush of settlers to the area.

12. **D**   Both authors also discuss the impact of the westward movement on American culture, *folklore and legend*. In particular, the cowboy epitomizes the romanticism of the westward movement.

13. **B**   In Passage 1 the *miner* is mentioned as one of several figures who participated in the settling of the West. On the other hand, almost half of Passage 2 is devoted to a discussion of the *miner*.

# PART III

# SENTENCE COMPLETION QUESTIONS

Overview

Tips

Sentence Completion Exercises

Answers to Sentence
  Completion Exercises

Answer Explanations

# OVERVIEW

Sentence completion questions are the first verbal questions you encounter as you take SAT I. These questions test your ability to use your vocabulary and to recognize how the different parts of a sentence fit together to make sense.

The sentence completion questions ask you to choose the best way to complete a sentence from which one or two words have been omitted. You must be able to recognize the logic, style, and tone of the sentence, so that you will be able to choose the answer that makes sense in this context. You must also be able to recognize the different ways in which words are normally defined. At some time or another, you have probably had a vocabulary assignment in which you were asked to define a word and use it in a sentence. In these questions, you have to *fit* words into sentences. Once you understand the implications of the sentence, you should be able to choose the answer that will make the sentence clear, logical, and consistent in style and tone.

The subject matter of these sentences comes from a wide variety of fields—music, art, science, literature, history. However, this is not a test of your general knowledge. Though at times your knowledge of a particular fact may guide you in choosing the correct answer, you should be able to handle any of the sentences using your understanding of the English language.

# TIPS ON HANDLING SENTENCE COMPLETION QUESTIONS

**TIP 1**

## BEFORE YOU LOOK AT THE ANSWER CHOICES, THINK OF A WORD THAT MAKES SENSE

Your first step in answering a sentence completion question is, *without looking at the answer choices,* to try to come up with a word that fits in the blank. The word you think of may not be the exact word that appears in the answer choices, but it will probably be similar in meaning to the right answer. That way when you turn to the answer choices you'll have an idea of what you're looking for.

Try going through the sentence substituting the word *blank* for each missing word. Doing this will give you a feel for what the sentence means.

Example:

Unlike her gabby brother Bruce, Bea seldom __*blanks*__.

Just from looking at the sentence, you know the answer must be a synonym for *chatters* or *talks*.

At this point, look at the answer choices. If the word you thought of is one of your five choices, select it as your answer. If the word you thought of is *not* one of your five choices, look for a synonym of that word.

See how the process works in dealing with a more complex sentence.

The psychologist set up the experiment to test the rat's ____; he wished to see how well the rat adjusted to the changing conditions it had to face.

Even before you look at the answer choices, you can figure out what the answer *should* be.

Look at the sentence. A psychologist is trying to test some particular quality or characteristic of a rat. What quality? How do you get the answer?

Note how the part of the sentence following the semi-colon (the second clause, in technical terms) is being used to define or clarify what the psychologist is trying to test. He is trying to see how well the rat *adjusts*. What words does this suggest to you? *Flexibility*, possibly, or *adaptability*. Either of these words could complete the sentence's thought.

Here are the five answer choices given.

(A) reflexes
(B) communicability
(C) stamina
(D) sociability
(E) adaptability

The answer clearly is *adaptability*, (E).

Be sure to check out all five answer choices before you make your final choice. Don't leap at the first word that seems to fit. You are looking for the word that *best* fits the meaning of the sentence as a whole. In order to be sure you have not been hasty in making your decision, substitute each of the answer choices for the missing word. That way you can satisfy yourself that you have come up with the answer that best fits.

---

**TIP 2**

## SPOT CLUES IN THE SENTENCE: SIGNAL WORDS

Writers use transitions to link their ideas logically. These transitions or signal words are clues that can help you figure out what the sentence actually means.

## Support Signals

Look for words that indicate that the omitted portion of the sentence continues a thought developed elsewhere in the sentence. Examples are *and*, *moreover*, *in addition*, and *furthermore*. In such cases, a synonym or near-synonym should provide the correct answer.

Here is an example of a sentence completion question in which a support signal provides a helpful clue.

He was habitually so docile and ____ that his friends could not understand his sudden outburst against his employers.

(A) submissive
(B) incorrigible

(C) contemptuous
(D) erratic
(E) hasty

The signal word *and* is your clue that the writer is trying to reinforce the notion of docility introduced in the sentence. Not only is this person docile, he is also ___*blank*___. Look through the answer choices for a synonym or near-synonym of *docile* or obedient. You find one immediately: (A), *submissive*. Check through the other answer choices. Nothing else makes sense. The correct answer is (A).

## Contrast Signals

Look for words or phrases that indicate a contrast between one idea and another. Examples are *but*, *although*, *nevertheless*, *despite*, *however*, *even though*, and *on the other hand*. In such cases, an antonym or near-antonym for another word in the sentence should provide the correct answer.

Here is an example of a sentence completion question in which a contrast signal pinpoints the correct answer for you.

We expected her to be jubilant over her victory, but she was ____ instead.

(A) triumphant
(B) adult
(C) morose
(D) loquacious
(E) culpable

The signal word *but* suggests that the winner's expected reaction contrasts with her actual one. Instead of being "jubilant" (extremely joyful), she is sad. Look through the answer choices to find a word that is the *opposite* of jubilant. The correct answer is (C), *morose* or gloomy.

## Cause and Effect Signals

Look for words or phrases that indicate that one thing causes another—words like *because*, *since*, *therefore*, *consequently*, *accordingly*, *hence*, or *thus*.

Here is an example of a sentence completion question in which a cause and effect signal should prove helpful to you.

Because his delivery was ____, the effect of his speech on the voters was nonexistent.

(A) plausible

(B) moving
(C) audible
(D) halting
(E) respectable

What sort of delivery would cause a speech to have no effect? A *plausible* (superficially pleasing and persuasive) delivery would probably have some effect on the voters. A *moving* or eloquent delivery certainly would. An *audible* delivery, one the audience could hear, would be more likely to have an effect than an inaudible one would. A *respectable*, appropriate delivery probably would have some impact as well. Only a *halting* or stumbling delivery would mar the voters' appreciation of the speech and cause it to have little or no effect on them. Thus, the correct answer is (D).

## TIP 3
# NOTICE NEGATIVES

Watch out for negative words and words with negative prefixes. *No, not, none*; *non-, un-, in-*. These negative words and word parts are killers, especially in combination.

The damage to the car was insignificant.
("Don't worry about it—it's just a scratch.")
The damage to the car was not insignificant.
("Oh, no, Bart! We totaled Mom's car!")

In particular, watch out for *not*: it's easy to overlook, but it's a key word, as the following sentence clearly illustrates.

Madison was not ____ person and thus made few public addresses; but those he made were memorable, filled with noble phrases.

(A) a reticent
(B) a stately
(C) an inspiring
(D) an introspective
(E) a communicative

What would happen if you overlooked *not* in this question? Probably you'd wind up choosing (A): Madison was a *reticent* (quiet; reserved) man. *For this reason* he made few public addresses.

Unfortunately, you'd have gotten things backward. The sentence isn't telling you what Madison was like. It's telling you what he was *not* like. And he was not a *communicative* person; he didn't

express himself freely. However, when he did get around to expressing himself, he had some good things to say.

## TIP 4
# TAKE ONE BLANK AT A TIME

Dealing with double-blank sentences can be tricky. Testing the first word of each answer pair helps you narrow things down.

Here's how to do it. Read through the entire sentence. Then insert the first word of each answer pair in the sentence's first blank. Ask yourself whether this particular word makes sense in this blank. If the initial word of an answer pair makes no sense in the sentence, you can eliminate the entire answer pair.

Next, check out the second word of each of the answer pairs that you haven't ruled out. Be careful. Remember, just as each word of the correct answer pair must make sense in its individual context, both words must make sense when used together.

Try this question to practice working with double-blank sentences.

The opossum is ____ the venom of snakes in the rattlesnake subfamily and thus views the reptiles not as ____ enemies but as a food source.

(A) vulnerable to...natural
(B) indicative of...mortal
(C) impervious to...lethal
(D) injurious to...deadly
(E) defenseless against...potential

Your first job is to eliminate any answer choices you can on the basis of their first word. Opossums might be *vulnerable* to snake poison. Keep (A). Opossums are unlikely to be *indicative* or suggestive of snake poison. Cross out (B). Opossums could be *impervious* to (unaffected by; immune to) snake poison. Keep (C). Opossums couldn't be *injurious* or harmful to snake poison. Cross out (D). Opossums could be *defenseless against* snake poison. Keep (E).

Now examine the second half of the sentence. Opossums look on rattlesnakes as a food source. They can eat rattlers for a reason. Why? Is it because they are *vulnerable to* or *defenseless against* the poison? No. It's because they're *imper-*

*vious* to the poison (that is, unharmed by it). That's the reason they can treat the rattlesnake as a potential source of food and not as a *lethal* or deadly enemy. The correct answer is (C).

Note the cause-and-effect signal *thus*. The nature of the opossum's response to the venom explains *why* it can look on a dangerous snake as a possible prey.

# SENTENCE COMPLETION EXERCISES

To develop your ability to handle sentence completion questions, work your way through the following three series of exercises. Warning: These series of exercises are graded in difficulty. The further you go, the harder it gets, just like on a video game. Go all the way. Even if you do less well on Level C than you did on Level A, look on every error as an opportunity to learn. Study all the sentences that you found difficult. Review all the vocabulary words that you didn't know. Remember, these are all college-level sentences, set up to test your knowledge of college-level words.

After completing each exercise, see how many questions you answered correctly. (The correct answers are given on page 72.) Then *read those answer explanations* for questions you answered incorrectly, questions you omitted, and questions you answered correctly but found difficult.

## LEVEL A ✓

Most high school students feel comfortable answering sentence completion questions on this level of difficulty. Consider the four practice exercises that follow to be a warm-up for the harder questions to come.

---

<u>Directions:</u> Each sentence below has one or two blanks, each blank indicating that something has been omitted. Beneath the sentence are five words or sets of words labeled A through E. Choose the word or set of words that, when inserted in the sentence, <u>best</u> fits the meaning of the sentence as a whole.

Example:

Medieval kingdoms did not become constitutional republics overnight; on the contrary, the change was _____ .

(A) unpopular
(B) unexpected
(C) advantageous
(D) sufficient
(E) gradual

Ⓐ Ⓑ Ⓒ Ⓓ ●

---

# Exercise 1

1. The Cabinet member's resignation was not a total ____: rumors of his imminent departure had been making the rounds in Washington for a week.

   (A) withdrawal
   (B) success
   (C) shock
   (D) eclipse
   (E) pretense

2. A major outbreak of food poisoning in 1993 underlined the serious ____ in the then-current system of food inspection.

   (A) expectations
   (B) innovations
   (C) objectivity
   (D) deficiencies
   (E) uniformity

3. It is possible to analyze a literary work to death, ____ what should be a living experience as if it were a laboratory specimen.

   (A) questioning
   (B) dissecting
   (C) amending
   (D) nurturing
   (E) reviving

4. Anthropologists traditionally argue that the male-female division of labor in hunter-gatherer societies arose because it ____ the nuclear family's joint interests and thereby represented a sound, ____ strategy.

   (A) impaired...collaborative
   (B) respected...divisive
   (C) ignored...disinterested
   (D) restricted...provisional
   (E) promoted...cooperative

5. Because of its strength and adhesiveness, ____ qualities in nest building, many species of birds incorporate silk into their nests.

   (A) questionable
   (B) intangible
   (C) invaluable
   (D) hypothetical
   (E) irrelevant

6. In the constant battle for newsstand supremacy, with newsstands groaning from the weight of specialty publications, the biggest challenge facing any new magazine is ____ itself from the crowd, making its mission ____.

   (A) transforming...plausible
   (B) separating...impossible
   (C) distinguishing...clear
   (D) acquiring...public
   (E) distancing...futile

7. Her memoirs are quite unlike those of her predecessors, for she is bold and aggressive where they are ____ and comfortable.

   (A) audacious
   (B) vivid
   (C) bland
   (D) brazen
   (E) contentious

8. The report was relentlessly ____ to the scientist, interpreting one complex event after another to his ____.

   (A) magnanimous...dismay
   (B) disparaging...initiative
   (C) innocuous...indifference
   (D) hostile...discredit
   (E) obsequious...detriment

9. People who don't outgrow their colleges often don't grow in other ways; there remained in Forster's life and imagination a ____ of the undergraduate, clever but ____.

   (A) dislike...talented
   (B) touch...judicious
   (C) streak...immature
   (D) fear...dormant
   (E) trace...sincere

10. She ____ recognition and fame, yet she felt a deep suspicion and ___ for the world in which recognition and fame are granted, the world of money and opinion and power.

    (A) mistrusted...antagonism
    (B) worked for...respect
    (C) endured...veneration
    (D) shunned...enmity
    (E) yearned for...contempt

11. Unfortunately, excessive care in choosing one's words often results in a loss of ____.

    (A) precision
    (B) atmosphere
    (C) selectivity
    (D) spontaneity
    (E) credibility

12. Just as the earliest stone tools left by humans may seem nothing more than rock fragments to a layperson, so a lot of fossils require a trained eye to ____ them.

    (A) excavate
    (B) appreciate
    (C) disseminate
    (D) antedate
    (E) educate

13. According to a noted art critic, one would have to be completely immune to the sensuous pleasures of painting to be ____ Lucien Freud's mesmerizing art.

    (A) drawn to
    (B) overcome by
    (C) enamored of
    (D) unaffected by
    (E) consistent about

14. Most people who are color-blind actually can distinguish several colors; some, however, have a truly ____ view of a world all in shades of gray.

    (A) monochromatic
    (B) opalescent
    (C) translucent
    (D) astigmatic
    (E) roseate

15. For years no one could make this particular therapy work in animals larger than rodents, but now two research groups have demonstrated its ____ in dogs.

    (A) efficacy
    (B) defects
    (C) variability
    (D) origin
    (E) virulence

16. Thanks to the emerging technology of active noise control, automakers may soon be able to ____ noise inside a car and create the long-promised "quiet ride."

    (A) dampen
    (B) energize
    (C) undertake
    (D) concentrate
    (E) augment

17. Despite her father's ____ that "a woman's place is in the home" and a ____ reception from her professors and fellow graduate students, Marian Cleeves went on to become the first woman to receive a doctorate in anatomy from the University of California at Berkeley.

    (A) warning...gratifying
    (B) reprimand...lavish
    (C) encouragement...respectful
    (D) admonition...cool
    (E) maxim...hospitable

18. John Keats, Dylan Thomas, Arthur Rimbaud—all these were poets who *had* to be poets, whom no one or nothing short of death could have ____ their courses.

    (A) confirmed in
    (B) derailed from
    (C) lauded for
    (D) interested in
    (E) convinced of

19. For someone suffering from stress, a holiday can act as a tonic, ____ rancor, transforming indecision, and renewing the spirit.

    (A) enhancing
    (B) exaggerating
    (C) manifesting
    (D) dispelling
    (E) compounding

20. The philosopher Auguste Comte ____ the term *altruism* to ____ unselfish regard for the welfare of others.

    (A) avoided...rationalize
    (B) coined...denote
    (C) applied...lessen
    (D) explained...refute
    (E) understood...terminate

# Exercise 2

1. Given the ability of modern technology to
_____ the environment, it is clear that if we are
not careful, the human race may soon be as
extinct as the dinosaur.

   (A) enhance
   (B) destroy
   (C) analyze
   (D) repair
   (E) nurture

2. As founder and president of the Children's
Defense Fund, Marian Wright Edelman has
ensured that, even though the young cannot
vote or make campaign contributions, they are
nevertheless not _____ in Washington.

   (A) represented
   (B) distrusted
   (C) ignored
   (D) committed
   (E) welcome

3. Using novel concepts and techniques previously unknown in commercial advertising, the
_____ advertising campaign broke new ground
in the field of marketing.

   (A) questionable
   (B) interminable
   (C) imitative
   (D) inadequate
   (E) innovative

4. The attorney's vibrant voice and _____ sense of
timing were as useful to him as his prodigious
preparation, attention to detail, and _____ of the law.

   (A) deficient...conception
   (B) excellent...ignorance
   (C) shaky...command
   (D) outstanding...mastery
   (E) impeccable...deprecation

5. Thomas Jefferson called *The Federalist* papers
"the best commentaries on the principles of
government ever written," and two centuries
later they still _____ as the most _____ statements of American political philosophy.

   (A) stand...derivative
   (B) rate...abstruse
   (C) rank...impressive
   (D) fascinate...ambiguous
   (E) compete...underrated

6. Some spiderwebs are sheets or tangles of
threads that delay the _____ of prey, allowing
the spider, _____ by vibrations that travel
through the threads, time to make its way over
to the entangled victim.

   (A) escape...alerted
   (B) consumption...frightened
   (C) capture...thwarted
   (D) pursuit...soothed
   (E) sighting...irritated

7. Janet Malcolm depicts the biographer as a
nosy, intrusive figure, _____ his subject's
private papers.

   (A) annotating
   (B) restoring
   (C) invading
   (D) acknowledging
   (E) compiling

8. Because fruit juice fills babies' small stomachs
and ruins their appetite for foods that contain
nutrients they _____, consuming large quantities
can actually prove _____ to babies less than 24
months old.

   (A) prefer...beneficial
   (B) choose...counterproductive
   (C) require...helpful
   (D) need...detrimental
   (E) ingest...advantageous

9. Telling gripping tales about a central character
engaged in a mighty struggle with events,
modern biographies satisfy the American
appetite for _____ narratives.

   (A) lyrical
   (B) colloquial
   (C) digressive
   (D) undemanding
   (E) epic

10. A leading philosopher of our time, Ludwig
Wittgenstein, laid down a _____ to which good
historians _____: "Of that of which nothing is
known nothing can be said."

   (A) burden...protest
   (B) law...amend
   (C) rule...adhere
   (D) maxim...succumb
   (E) weapon...surrender

11. Muskoxen survived in isolated arctic habitats, but in the nineteenth century, they declined rapidly even there, their numbers _____ by the armed enthusiasm of explorers, whalers, fur traders, and Eskimo.

    (A) swelled
    (B) augmented
    (C) devastated
    (D) underestimated
    (E) calculated

12. In a nation where the economic reversals of the past few years have taken a psychological as well as a financial toll on many regions, what most _____ the South may be the degree of _____ throughout the region.

    (A) distinguishes...optimism
    (B) grieves...prosperity
    (C) typifies...disenfranchisement
    (D) distresses...reflection
    (E) appeases...idealism

13. He loved his friends, but he held people in general in _____ and maintained that human virtues were unworthy to be compared with a dog's devotion.

    (A) reverence
    (B) abeyance
    (C) contempt
    (D) affection
    (E) honor

14. Stunned by Professor Marian Diamond's work showing how the rat brain structure can increase by 5 to 7 percent, one _____ neuroanatomist stated flatly, "Young lady, that brain cannot _____!"

    (A) astounded...function
    (B) aghast...deteriorate
    (C) dumbfounded...think
    (D) skeptical...grow
    (E) finicky...die

15. For all his protestations of _____, Judge Learned Hand had been deeply _____ at being passed over for the United States Supreme Court, where Oliver Wendell Holmes, Jr., Benjamin Cardozo, and countless others said he belonged.

    (A) innocence...embarrassed
    (B) disbelief...enervated
    (C) indifference...disappointed
    (D) despondency...frustrated
    (E) affection...commiserated

16. Halls and audiences for *lieder* recitals tend to be smaller than for opera and thus more _____ the intimacy and sense of close involvement, which is the recital's particular charm.

    (A) inauspicious for
    (B) destructive of
    (C) conducive to
    (D) compromised by
    (E) indifferent to

17. In this survey of Revolutionary America, the author finds a remarkable homogeneity of opinion from Massachusetts to Georgia; the differences between the sections are _____, almost always explainable by differences in climate or topography.

    (A) sharp
    (B) nonexistent
    (C) irreconcilable
    (D) superficial
    (E) enormous

18. According to Lionel Trilling, the paradox of liberalism was that in its quest for freedom it must move toward greater organization, stricter legislation, and increasing _____.

    (A) anarchy
    (B) self-realization
    (C) stagnation
    (D) control
    (E) levity

19. Our mood swings about the economy grow more extreme: when things go well, we become _____; when things go poorly, _____ descends.

    (A) restive...anxiety
    (B) euphoric...gloom
    (C) prudent...benevolence
    (D) ascetic...misery
    (E) ambivalence...optimism

20. Abandoning the moral principles of his youth, the aging emperor Tiberius led a _____, wanton life.

    (A) celibate
    (B) rudimentary
    (C) debauched
    (D) circumspect
    (E) peripatetic

# Exercise 3

1. Although a few of her contemporaries ____ her book, most either ignored it or mocked it.

   (A) dismissed
   (B) disregarded
   (C) deprecated
   (D) misconstrued
   (E) appreciated

2. All critics have agreed that the opera's score is ____, but, curiously, no two critics have agreed which passages to praise and which to damn.

   (A) intolerable
   (B) melodious
   (C) unsurpassed
   (D) conventional
   (E) uneven

3. A man incapable of ____ action, he never had an opinion about something that he had not worked up beforehand, fashioning it with lengthy care.

   (A) premeditated
   (B) coherent
   (C) spontaneous
   (D) calculated
   (E) self-conscious

4. Even as the local climate changed from humid to arid and back—a change that caused other animals to become extinct—our almost-human ancestors ____ by learning how to use the new flora.

   (A) anticipated
   (B) survived
   (C) diverged
   (D) deteriorated
   (E) migrated

5. Marketing specialists have begun ____ what had once been a ____ audience into innumerable segments based on age, sex, income, and a host of pop sociological categories.

   (A) carving up...mass
   (B) bringing together...fragmented
   (C) tearing apart...sophisticated
   (D) unifying...distinct
   (E) transforming...responsive

6. Like a balloon that is ____, aneurysms (swellings in the walls of arteries) sometimes enlarge so much that they ____.

   (A) expanding...contract
   (B) punctured...dilate
   (C) elastic...stratify
   (D) weightless...stretch
   (E) overinflated...burst

7. Critics ____ the ____ in developing the new weather satellite to unexpected problems in manufacturing and testing its components.

   (A) credit...timeliness
   (B) impute...success
   (C) attribute...delay
   (D) assign...importance
   (E) deny...threat

8. As former Supreme Court Justice Warren Burger was fond of pointing out, many lawyers are not legal hotshots; they often come to court ____ and ____ professional skills.

   (A) ill-prepared...lacking
   (B) hot-tempered...criticizing
   (C) reluctant...demonstrating
   (D) argumentative...manifesting
   (E) conservative...excelling

9. A hypothesis must not only account for what we already know, but it must also be ____ by continued observation.

   (A) refuted
   (B) interrupted
   (C) verified
   (D) discredited
   (E) outmoded

10. *Elizabeth Gaskell: A Habit of Stories* is a considerable ____, superseding Winifred Gerin's learned biography of the English novelist.

    (A) failure
    (B) rationalization
    (C) accomplishment
    (D) recollection
    (E) muddle

11. Boccherini was a good and interesting composer whose reputation has not sufficiently ____ the decline into which it fell after his death.

    (A) contributed to
    (B) benefited from
    (C) recovered from
    (D) conflicted with
    (E) derived from

12. Having billed himself as "Mr. Clean," Hosokawa could not ____ the ____ of a major financial scandal.

    (A) survive...acclaim
    (B) withstand...notoriety
    (C) identify...exposure
    (D) resist...charms
    (E) censure...temptation

13. A curious ____ of Florence's history is that this great center of Italian ____ should time and again have been home to acts of appalling savagery and inhumanity.

    (A) example...conflict
    (B) paradox...civilization
    (C) result...brutality
    (D) convention...culture
    (E) distinction...quality

14. While some Southern writers see the past as a heavy burden, others see it as a subject for ____ reflection.

    (A) gloomy
    (B) wearisome
    (C) interminable
    (D) nostalgic
    (E) bleak

15. Lamenting that something horrid had recently befallen the craft of biography, biographer Arthur Schlesinger ____ the glut of gossipy new lives on the market.

    (A) deplored
    (B) forgot
    (C) acclaimed
    (D) composed
    (E) abridged

16. Instead of taking exaggerated precautions against touching or tipping or jarring the bottle of wine, the waitress handled it quite ____, being careful only to use a napkin to keep her hands from the cool bottle itself.

    (A) fastidiously
    (B) reverently
    (C) nonchalantly
    (D) tentatively
    (E) ambivalently

17. The eighteenth century was a kind of golden age in deaf history because with the establishment of deaf schools, deaf people emerged from ____ and began to appear in positions of eminence and ____—as writers, engineers, philosophers, and intellectuals.

    (A) retirement...ambiguity
    (B) seclusion...compromise
    (C) obscurity...responsibility
    (D) hiding...ignominy
    (E) solicitude...disrepute

18. Left to endure a penniless old age, the ____ man lived to regret his ____ youth.

    (A) miserly...friendless
    (B) reclusive...affable
    (C) eccentric...fleeting
    (D) egotistical...frugal
    (E) improvident...prodigal

19. When Dorothy and her friends realized that, despite his claims, the Wizard of Oz didn't know how to get them back to Kansas, they were sure they'd been ____ by a ____.

    (A) befriended...philanthropist
    (B) succored...magician
    (C) captured...genius
    (D) duped...charlatan
    (E) delayed...miser

20. Egocentric, at times vindictive when he believed his authority was being questioned, White could also be kind, gracious, and even ____ when the circumstances seemed to require it.

    (A) self-deprecating
    (B) authoritarian
    (C) provocative
    (D) taciturn
    (E) disdainful

# Exercise 4

1. Repeat offenders who continue to drive under the influence of alcohol face having their drivers' licenses permanently ____.

   (A) issued
   (B) recorded
   (C) authorized
   (D) revoked
   (E) disregarded

2. Excited and unafraid, the ____ child examined the stranger with bright-eyed curiosity.

   (A) apathetic
   (B) drowsy
   (C) timorous
   (D) inquisitive
   (E) hesitant

3. Though masterminded by the Metropolitan Museum's Guy Bauman, this survey of Flemish paintings in America was clearly a ____ operation, aided by scholars throughout North America.

   (A) marginal
   (B) derivative
   (C) worthwhile
   (D) circuitous
   (E) collective

4. I am seeking an ____ solution to this dispute, one that will be fair and acceptable to both sides.

   (A) equivocal
   (B) infamous
   (C) equitable
   (D) idiosyncratic
   (E) overrated

5. A New World lizard, the basilisk, occasionally does something that seems to ____ physics: it runs across the surface of water for distances of up to thirty feet.

   (A) defy
   (B) quantify
   (C) assess
   (D) exemplify
   (E) corroborate

6. The most consistent qualities of Forster's novels are the human isolation and passivity in them; his principal characters stand slightly apart and ____, but rarely ____.

   (A) sneer...collapse
   (B) interact...adapt
   (C) mourn...recollect
   (D) observe...act
   (E) domineer...participate

7. Far from being distracted or immobilized by his inner conflicts, Keynes was ____ by them into becoming one of the most productive, effective and buoyant personalities of the twentieth century.

   (A) neutralized
   (B) energized
   (C) incapacitated
   (D) enervated
   (E) inhibited

8. A born teller of tales, Olsen used her impressive ____ skills to advantage in her story "I Stand Here Ironing."

   (A) domestic
   (B) metaphysical
   (C) narrative
   (D) diagnostic
   (E) argumentative

9. Waving broadly at the still-applauding crowd, the speaker was highly ____ by the ____ response to her talk.

   (A) exasperated...vehement
   (B) gratified...enthusiastic
   (C) bewildered...profound
   (D) intimidated...sincere
   (E) delighted....skeptical

10. As a scientific document, the book should stand for several years until further ____ again make revision ____.

   (A) developments...impossible
   (B) obstacles...optional
   (C) attempts...undesirable
   (D) failures...detrimental
   (E) advances...necessary

11. The jazz musician cannot play well if he is completely ____, as if lying half asleep in a Jacuzzi.

   (A) untruthful
   (B) autonomous
   (C) sincere
   (D) relaxed
   (E) talented

12. Why do some plant stems develop a protective bark that enables them to survive the winter, while others ____ at the first frost?

   (A) blossom
   (B) adapt
   (C) shrivel
   (D) mature
   (E) wake

13. Salvador Dali's tendency to fabricate events makes it difficult for the biographer to tell the story of his life with any degree of ____.

   (A) vividness
   (B) accuracy
   (C) solemnity
   (D) spontaneity
   (E) artistry

14. If Amelia Earhart's acceptance was by no means ____, her fame was unusually widespread and her popularity long-lived.

   (A) universal
   (B) ambiguous
   (C) expedient
   (D) partial
   (E) genuine

15. Throughout his career he demonstrated strong belief in individual faith but powerful ____ about the organized church.

   (A) modesty
   (B) skepticism
   (C) devotion
   (D) discernment
   (E) ambition

16. For a young person, Winston seems remarkably ____; you'd expect someone his age to show a little more life.

   (A) sophomoric
   (B) vigorous
   (C) stodgy
   (D) tidy
   (E) sensitive

17. Complaints about the inanity of popular leisure activities, long a staple of American intellectual life, are routinely ____ these days as nostalgic elitism.

   (A) lauded
   (B) reinforced
   (C) celebrated
   (D) offered
   (E) dismissed

18. It would be beneficial if someone so radical could be brought to believe that old customs need not necessarily be ____ and that change may possibly be ____.

   (A) defensible...premature
   (B) outdated...required
   (C) evil...salutary
   (D) invaluable...temporary
   (E) worthless...inadvisable

19. T.S. Eliot, famous for his ____, nevertheless accepted posterity's interest in his life, ____ that his correspondence with his lady friends eventually would be read.

   (A) reticence...assuming
   (B) modesty...prohibiting
   (C) boastfulness...remembering
   (D) vanity...intimating
   (E) curiosity...regretting

20. Waiting impatiently in line to see Santa Claus, even the best-behaved children grow ____ and start to fidget.

   (A) restive
   (B) noisome
   (C) sonorous
   (D) pungent
   (E) ambivalent

# LEVEL B ✓

Most high school students have some difficulty answering sentence completion questions on this level. Consider the four practice exercises that follow to be a good sample of the mid-range sentence completion questions you will face on SAT I.

---

<u>Directions:</u> Each sentence below has one or two blanks, each blank indicating that something has been omitted. Beneath the sentence are five words or sets of words labeled A through E. Choose the word or set of words that, when inserted in the sentence, <u>best</u> fits the meaning of the sentence as a whole.

Example:

Medieval kingdoms did not become constitutional republics overnight; on the contrary, the change was ____ .

(A) unpopular
(B) unexpected
(C) advantageous
(D) sufficient
(E) gradual

Ⓐ Ⓑ Ⓒ Ⓓ ●

---

## Exercise 1

1. In the 1920s Hollywood became a magnet for men and women on the cutting edge—____ artists genuinely excited by the possibilities of the up-and-coming film medium.

   (A) irritable
   (B) innovative
   (C) untalented
   (D) outdated
   (E) inferior

2. According to poet John Berryman, there were so many ways to ____ a poem that it was quite amazing good ones ever got written.

   (A) dedicate
   (B) begin
   (C) ruin
   (D) recite
   (E) categorize

3. One by one, she ____ almost all of her supporters until, at the end, only a handful of her closest allies really wanted her to stay in office.

   (A) promoted
   (B) alienated
   (C) represented
   (D) exaggerated
   (E) liberated

4. The aorta is like a tree trunk from which other major arteries ____.

   (A) escape
   (B) subtract
   (C) clamber down
   (D) branch off
   (E) strip away

5. By putting the entire Woolf archive on microfilm, the project directors hope to make the contents of the manuscripts more ____ to scholars.

   (A) accessible
   (B) objective
   (C) appealing
   (D) implicit
   (E) relevant

6. Land is no less ____ just because it has not yet been ____.

   (A) eroded...subdivided
   (B) exhausted...cultivated
   (C) imaginary...discovered
   (D) fallow...settled
   (E) real...charted

7. Peter has a bad habit of making ____ remarks that cause us to forget the gist of what he is saying.

    (A) awkward
    (B) pertinent
    (C) digressive
    (D) telling
    (E) tentative

8. Though set in a mythical South American country, Isabel Allende's novel is _____ the tragic history of Chile.

    (A) irrelevant to
    (B) rooted in
    (C) inconsistent with
    (D) exceeded by
    (E) indifferent to

9. The marketers' ____ in donating the new basketball backboards to the school system are not solely ____; they plan to sell advertising space on the backboards, turning them into miniature billboards.

    (A) losses...obvious
    (B) expectations...peculiar
    (C) aims...mercenary
    (D) reasons...sensitive
    (E) motivations...philanthropic

10. Justice Harry Blackmun's retirement, while unlikely to bring about a drastic change at the Supreme Court, will remove a distinctly ____ voice from the Court's often featureless mix.

    (A) bland
    (B) personal
    (C) moderate
    (D) neutral
    (E) derivative

11. Having just published his fourth novel in an almost 40-year career, Gaddis describes himself, with some ____, as a writer who has never been in a ____ to get into print.

    (A) expectation...mood
    (B) impatience...technique
    (C) understatement...rush
    (D) indecision...position
    (E) exaggeration...school

12. Actors fade out of view with depressing frequency; the theater is a ____ profession at best.

    (A) romantic
    (B) demanding
    (C) chancy
    (D) disinterested
    (E) degenerate

13. Though Phil had expected to feel overawed when he met Joe Montana, he found the world-famous quarterback friendly and ____.

    (A) querulous
    (B) acerbic
    (C) domineering
    (D) unintimidating
    (E) taciturn

14. Flying in the face of ____, the writer George Sand shocked her contemporaries by taking lovers and by wearing men's clothes.

    (A) immodesty
    (B) reconciliation
    (C) emancipation
    (D) convention
    (E) modernism

15. In the poem *Annabel Lee*, the speaker reveals that he is not ____ to the death of his beloved; on the contrary, he is ____.

    (A) indifferent...apathetic
    (B) reconciled...acquiescent
    (C) resigned...inconsolable
    (D) accustomed...inured
    (E) relevant...responsive

16. The artists of the Chinese avant-garde have used Western styles ____ and meaningfully to accomplish artistic ends of their own.

    (A) obsequiously
    (B) shamefully
    (C) cannily
    (D) fortuitously
    (E) problematically

17. He continually describes what superhuman labor it has cost him to compose his poems and ____ that, in comparison with his own work, the poetry of other poets is ____.

    (A) insists...meritorious
    (B) insinuates...profound
    (C) asserts...laborious
    (D) intimates...superficial
    (E) maintains...meticulous

18. The biographer may not have ____ the depths of her subject's self-contradictory character, but she has traced its intriguingly complex ____.

(A) plumbed...tedium
(B) sounded...surface
(C) thwarted...background
(D) reached...insipidity
(E) disregarded...psyche

19. Because of the trauma they have experienced, survivors of a major catastrophe are likely to exhibit ____ of behavior and may require the aid of competent therapists.

(A) concessions
(B) diminutions
(C) aberrations
(D) restrictions
(E) altercations

20. The reader has the happy impression of watching an extraordinarily inventive and intellectually ____ novelist working at the ____ of her powers.

(A) dishonest...apex
(B) creative...eclipse
(C) fecund...height
(D) effete...limits
(E) amenable...diminution

## Exercise 2

1. Illness can be ____ as how disease *feels*, the experience of being sick: at once a physical or natural condition and a social and cultural one.

(A) cured
(B) survived
(C) acclaimed
(D) defined
(E) deprecated

2. One of Detroit's great success stories tells of Lee Iacocca's revitalization of the moribund Chrysler Corporation, turning it into a ____ competitor.

(A) vigorous
(B) tentative
(C) marginal
(D) negligent
(E) superficial

3. A journalist rather than a scholar, Mr. Cose seems nevertheless to be ____ most of the serious studies relevant to his topic.

(A) overawed by
(B) ignorant of
(C) associated with
(D) wearied by
(E) familiar with

4. Now better known for its racetrack, Saratoga Springs first gained attention for the ____ qualities of its famous "healing waters."

(A) diagnostic
(B) commercial
(C) therapeutic
(D) overlooked
(E) experimental

5. The benefits of telecommuting—working at home by means of various electronic communication devices rather than ____ commuting to an office—have been so clearly and consistently ____ that telework is on the rise in virtually every country with a functioning telephone system.

(A) personally...forgotten
(B) instantly...underrated
(C) physically...demonstrated
(D) painfully...denounced
(E) intermittently...discredited

6. Polls indicate that many prospective voters in the next presidential election are ____ about the outcome; they do not seem to care who wins.

(A) enthusiastic
(B) inadequate
(C) antagonistic
(D) apathetic
(E) suspicious

7. If you need car parts that the dealers no longer stock, try ____ for odd bits and pieces at the auto wreckers' yards.

(A) waiting
(B) bantering
(C) scavenging
(D) riveting
(E) insuring

8. Grateful as we are for these splendid books, they remain isolated examples of excellence in a literature of ____.

   (A) competition
   (B) distinction
   (C) grandeur
   (D) mediocrity
   (E) affirmation

9. Despite the ____ discussions of recent months, observers say that the administration and the developer have made progress in their negotiations and are close to ____ on a purchase price.

   (A) amicable...haggling
   (B) acrimonious...defaulting
   (C) heated...agreeing
   (D) fruitful...settling
   (E) constructive...compromising

10. People expected Winston Churchill to take his painting lightly, but Churchill, no ____, regarded his artistic efforts most seriously indeed.

    (A) virtuoso
    (B) zealot
    (C) dilettante
    (D) altruist
    (E) renegade

11. Aimed at curbing European attempts to seize territory in the Americas, the Monroe Doctrine was a warning to ____ foreign powers.

    (A) magnanimous
    (B) credulous
    (C) reticent
    (D) predatory
    (E) allied

12. It is a spotty sort of book, with many pages that, if not exactly ____, are less than ____.

    (A) bland...tedious
    (B) pretentious...conventional
    (C) dull...exciting
    (D) eventful...newsworthy
    (E) murky...obscure

13. Unlike her sister, the Widow Douglass, who ____ Huck's minor offenses, Miss Watson did nothing but scold the boy.

    (A) believed
    (B) rebuked

    (C) condoned
    (D) evaded
    (E) corroborated

14. In discussing Rothko's art, Breslin is ____ in keeping to the facts and resisting the ____ of fanciful interpretation.

    (A) scrupulous...temptation
    (B) meticulous...integrity
    (C) ungainly...reward
    (D) uninterested...echo
    (E) inept...bias

15. Burdened by debt, Lydgate abandons his dreams of reforming medicine to take a conventional but ____ practice in London.

    (A) lucrative
    (B) ordinary
    (C) innovative
    (D) intangible
    (E) exotic

16. The observers hope to find out how important ____ foraging is to these endangered shorebirds in order to ____ the importance of restricting nighttime human use of beaches to specific places or times.

    (A) nocturnal...ascertain
    (B) aerial...convey
    (C) underwater...rectify
    (D) sporadic...mitigate
    (E) desultory...mandate

17. When I listened to her cogent arguments, all my ____ were ____ and I was forced to agree with her point of view.

    (A) senses...stimulated
    (B) opinions...confirmed
    (C) preconceptions...substantiated
    (D) questions...interpolated
    (E) doubts...dispelled

18. The ____, by definition, possesses wisdom; the virtuoso, by definition, possesses ____.

    (A) scholar...morality
    (B) sage...expertise
    (C) zealot...sincerity
    (D) visionary...idealism
    (E) pedant...proficiency

19. Samuel Johnson gave more than ____ cooperation to his biographer, James Boswell; he made himself available to Boswell night after night, furnished Boswell with correspondence, even read his biographer's notes.

(A) innocuous
(B) collusive
(C) tacit
(D) edifying
(E) diplomatic

20. Where lesser scholars would have been ____ by the vast collection of unpublished letters, rough drafts, and journals left by Henry James, Leon Edel was emboldened by its discovery and began to plan an ambitious series of studies on the life and works of the novelist.

(A) intrigued
(B) encouraged
(C) incensed
(D) taxed
(E) daunted

## Exercise 3

1. In their determination to discover ways to ____ human life, doctors fail to take into account that longer lives are not always happier ones.

(A) ease
(B) prolong
(C) eradicate
(D) recuperate
(E) dissect

2. The most crucial issue for wildlife in this arid land is unimpeded ____ water.

(A) passage through
(B) freedom from
(C) access to
(D) saturation in
(E) overflow of

3. Always trying to look on the bright side of every situation, she is a born ____.

(A) opportunist
(B) antagonist
(C) optimist
(D) maverick
(E) zealot

4. Despite their reputations as soothing love songs sung by mothers to lull fretful infants to sleep, many lullabies are of a dark, even ____ nature.

(A) soporific
(B) manipulative
(C) threatening
(D) auspicious
(E) innocuous

5. The mayor and school superintendent let their dispute over budget cuts ____ to ugly and destructive proportions.

(A) escalate
(B) automate
(C) stagnate
(D) condense
(E) dwindle

6. Wherever Lao Li travels, he makes slides of contemporary works of art; his archives ____ every meaningful artistic effort in modern China.

(A) deride
(B) ignore
(C) perpetrate
(D) document
(E) abridge

7. Contrary to her customary ____ behavior, Susan began leaving parties early to seek the solitude of her room.

(A) reclusive
(B) circumspect
(C) decorous
(D) gregarious
(E) altruistic

8. Science is always ____, expecting that modifications of its present theories will sooner or later be found necessary.

(A) conclusive
(B) irrefutable
(C) original
(D) tentative
(E) inflexible

9. One of the great killers until barely 50 years ago, tuberculosis ("consumption" as it was then named) seemed a scourge or ____ rather than the long-term ____ illness it was.

   (A) plague...chronic
   (B) detriment...ominous
   (C) antiseptic...prevalent
   (D) vestige...contemporary
   (E) epidemic...salutary

10. Gaddis is a formidably talented writer whose work has been, unhappily, more likely to intimidate or ____ his readers than to lure them into his fictional world.

    (A) entice
    (B) strengthen
    (C) invigorate
    (D) transform
    (E) repel

11. Compared with the ostentatious glamour of opera, classical song (increasingly called *lieder* everywhere) is a more ____ tradition.

    (A) articulate
    (B) unrepresentative
    (C) subdued
    (D) broad-minded
    (E) worldly

12. This well-documented book is ____ researched, fluently written, and unfailingly intelligent in tracing the ____ course of its subject's tormented career.

    (A) indifferently...triumphant
    (B) inadequately...unfortunate
    (C) painstakingly...tragic
    (D) carefully...auspicious
    (E) thoroughly...promising

13. Lexy's joy at finding the perfect Christmas gift for John was ____, for she still had to find presents for the cousins and Uncle Bob.

    (A) transient
    (B) antithetical
    (C) exuberant
    (D) exhaustive
    (E) incontrovertible

14. Life is a ____ of the sacred and the profane, of good and evil; to try to ____ them is futile.

    (A) rejection...embrace
    (B) commingling...separate
    (C) misalliance...endure
    (D) defamation...reform
    (E) confusion...promulgate

15. Under the rule of the foreign invaders, the land seemed asleep, save for a small group of rebels who sought to kindle the ____ nationalism of the people.

    (A) valid
    (B) blatant
    (C) dormant
    (D) pretentious
    (E) contemplated

16. Many of the early Hollywood moguls sought to ____ themselves and enhance their celluloid empires by snaring ____ writers and intellectuals as screenwriters.

    (A) advance...presumptuous
    (B) aggrandize...prestigious
    (C) intimidate...unsuspecting
    (D) glorify...superannuated
    (E) sabotage...distinguished

17. The Turner Network's new production is an absorbing *Heart of Darkness*, watchful, surreptitious, almost ____ as it waits to ____ our emotions.

    (A) lighthearted...cater to
    (B) melancholy...cheer up
    (C) mercenary...pay for
    (D) predatory...pounce on
    (E) furtive...figure out

18. Helen valued people who behaved as if they respected themselves; nothing irritated her more than an excessively ____ waiter or a fawning salesclerk.

    (A) austere
    (B) domineering
    (C) grave
    (D) obsequious
    (E) contentious

19. Whereas most scholars have tended to regard Monteverdi's opera *L'Orfeo* as the beginning of a tradition, Mr. Pickett sensibly considers it the ____ of one.

    (A) origin
    (B) example
    (C) presence
    (D) culmination
    (E) birthright

20. Though ostensibly teaching posture, Feher brings into play techniques of ballet, yoga, and vocal projection to come up with lessons that can best be described as ____.

    (A) problematic
    (B) eclectic
    (C) homogeneous
    (D) unpretentious
    (E) doctrinaire

## Exercise 4

1. During the troubles of 1750, the ____ of Scotland was terrible; many Scots could afford nothing to eat but oatmeal porridge.

    (A) anarchy
    (B) reputation
    (C) punishment
    (D) apathy
    (E) poverty

2. The biographer of Tennyson is confronted with the problem, rarely solved, of how to make a basically ____ life interesting.

    (A) dramatic
    (B) bewildering
    (C) intriguing
    (D) controversial
    (E) uneventful

3. If, like the mole rat, you could run backward as easily as forward but had weak eyes that could see only dim shadows of light and dark, you too might want touch-sensitive whiskers to help ____ you through the tunnels of your underground home.

    (A) carry
    (B) illuminate
    (C) excavate
    (D) distract
    (E) guide

4. Getting into street brawls is no minor matter for professional boxers, who are required by law to restrict their ____ impulses to the ring.

    (A) humorous
    (B) aggressive
    (C) obligatory
    (D) amateurish
    (E) legitimate

5. For all of his turn-of-the-century trappings, the novel's hero is basically a ____ voice; his values and cultural ____ are of the 1990s more than the 1890s.

    (A) derivative...antecedents
    (B) modern...antiquity
    (C) contemporary...background
    (D) familiar...descendants
    (E) hollow...premises

6. She wondered whether triangles, which had only three sides, ____ as polygons, which she thought of as many-sided.

    (A) theorized
    (B) estimated
    (C) qualified
    (D) subsisted
    (E) multiplied

7. Kepler's observations of the supernova would have been more ____ and valuable had they been made with a telescope; unfortunately, Kepler's supernova lighted the night skies five full years before Galileo made the first ____ telescopic scan of the heavens.

    (A) remote...skeptical
    (B) solemn...unseemly
    (C) infamous...extraneous
    (D) detailed...documented
    (E) fortuitous...recorded

8. As a product of the Soviet literary establishment, the author was brave enough to ____ the hand that fed him, but not heroic enough to bite it.

    (A) give up
    (B) nibble at
    (C) cringe from
    (D) worship
    (E) devour

9. It is a relief to see people who can be interested in the arts without being "arty"—collectors who collect for their own ____ rather than for ____.

   (A) enjoyment...satisfaction
   (B) interest...pleasure
   (C) reputation...amusement
   (D) delight...show
   (E) education...fulfillment

10. The periodic nature of her complaints began to concern us: alarmed by these ____ attacks, we decided to consult a doctor in spite of her opposition.

    (A) trivial
    (B) recurrent
    (C) superficial
    (D) spontaneous
    (E) tentative

11. Though critic John Simon seldom has a good word to say about most contemporary plays, his review of *All in the Timing* was a total ____.

    (A) mistake
    (B) dismissal
    (C) fraud
    (D) rave
    (E) farce

12. Traditional Chinese painters trained by copying their teachers; ____ was reserved for old age, when you might make changes so ____ that they were almost invisible.

    (A) imitation...ubiquitous
    (B) emulation...dramatic
    (C) novelty...marked
    (D) originality...slight
    (E) honor...petty

13. Satisfied that her name had been ____, she dropped her libel suit after the newspaper finally published a ____ of its original defamatory statement.

    (A) praised...summary
    (B) maligned...glossary
    (C) vindicated... repetition
    (D) enhanced...reaffirmation
    (E) cleared...retraction

14. Like Machiavelli before him, Henry Kissinger has a keen appreciation for the hard-headed, even ____, use of power, to the point of admiring some traits in leaders who were otherwise ____.

    (A) cynical...benevolent
    (B) gentle...insignificant
    (C) ruthless...detestable
    (D) resentful...charismatic
    (E) forceful...exemplary

15. Some thought Dali was a brilliant painter; others ____ him as a conceited poseur.

    (A) respected
    (B) venerated
    (C) dismissed
    (D) vindicated
    (E) exasperated

16. The late James Beard was ____ with his time and knowledge—a ____ trait in the narrow world of food writing, a milieu notorious for its pettiness and infighting.

    (A) unselfish...common
    (B) unconcerned...standard
    (C) stingy...remarkable
    (D) occupied...negative
    (E) generous...rare

17. *New Yorker* short stories often include ____ allusions to ____ people and events: the implication is, if you are in the in-crowd, you'll get the reference; if you come from Cleveland, you won't.

    (A) esoteric...obscure
    (B) redundant...celebrated
    (C) tedious...notorious
    (D) provincial...major
    (E) passing...common

18. Her growing bitterness was ____ by her professional rivalry with her sister, whose fortunes rose while her own ____.

    (A) represented...ascended
    (B) mitigated...dwindled
    (C) exemplified...soared
    (D) nurtured...multiplied
    (E) exacerbated...declined

19. Such was Brandon's _____ that he was at times described as being honest as the day was long.

    (A) vigilance
    (B) munificence
    (C) probity
    (D) gravity
    (E) eminence

20. While the movie *Spellbound* is a testimonial to the powers of psychoanalysis to overcome the evils of unreason, its portrait of the analytic profession is not entirely _____.

    (A) malignant
    (B) obscure
    (C) adulatory
    (D) vehement
    (E) derivative

## LEVEL C

Most high school students have trouble answering many sentence completion questions on this level of difficulty. Consider the four practice exercises that follow to be a chance for you to acquaint yourself with the toughest sorts of sentence completion questions that occur on SAT I.

---

Directions: Each sentence below has one or two blanks, each blank indicating that something has been omitted. Beneath the sentence are five words or sets of words labeled A through E. Choose the word or set of words that, when inserted in the sentence, best fits the meaning of the sentence as a whole.

Example:

Medieval kingdoms did not become constitutional republics overnight; on the contrary, the change was _____ .

(A) unpopular
(B) unexpected
(C) advantageous
(D) sufficient
(E) gradual

Ⓐ Ⓑ Ⓒ Ⓓ ●

---

## Exercise 1

1. The moon was hidden and the night had grown very dark; she had to _____ to see.

    (A) blink
    (B) strain
    (C) mask
    (D) remember
    (E) reflect

2. The Battle of Lexington was not, as most of us have been taught, a _____ rising of individual farmers, but was instead a tightly organized, well-planned event.

    (A) premeditated
    (B) cautionary
    (C) spontaneous
    (D) coordinated
    (E) theoretical

3. The book will arouse antagonism, disagreement, and animosity among theologians because it will _____ many _____ rituals and beliefs.

    (A) undermine...iconoclastic
    (B) tolerate...accepted
    (C) disturb...established
    (D) disregard...forgotten
    (E) observe...pious

4. What made Ann such a fine counselor was her
____, her ability to put herself in her client's place
and feel his emotions as if they were her own.

   (A) integrity
   (B) empathy
   (C) tenacity
   (D) impartiality
   (E) aloofness

5. The text brims with details, but there are no
overarching theses to ____ them.

   (A) specify
   (B) exaggerate
   (C) confound
   (D) unify
   (E) modify

6. The true historian finds the facts about
Marlowe and Shakespeare far more interesting
than people's unfounded ____.

   (A) complaints
   (B) evidence
   (C) conjectures
   (D) qualms
   (E) certainty

7. Even Cormac McCarthy, Don DeLillo, and
William Gaddis—eminent novelists who are
notoriously ____ when it comes to ____—have
surrendered to the exigencies of modern publishing and agreed to be the subjects of magazine articles.

   (A) prolific...writing
   (B) egotistical...fame
   (C) overrated...style
   (D) irate...delays
   (E) shy...publicity

8. Tom prided himself on knowing the latest
news, the secrets of the rich and the poor; it
____ him that there was something he did not
know about his friend.

   (A) delighted
   (B) flattered
   (C) reminded
   (D) galled
   (E) reassured

9. Uncertain which suitor she ought to marry, the
princess ____, saying now one, now the other.

   (A) improvised
   (B) vacillated
   (C) threatened
   (D) compromised
   (E) divulged

10. Factory trawlers, large fishing vessels that drag
heavy nets over the seafloor, "vacuum" the
North Pacific seas, trapping fish ____.

   (A) unintentionally
   (B) indiscriminately
   (C) paradoxically
   (D) collaboratively
   (E) temporarily

11. According to the Senator, it was not ____ for a
politician in search of votes to ____ a mother
on the beauty of her plain child; it was merely
sound political common sense.

   (A) kindness...ridicule
   (B) folly...intimidate
   (C) hypocrisy...compliment
   (D) sensitivity...evaluate
   (E) wisdom...reprimand

12. Duke Ellington's jazz symphonies were
attacked by classical critics who felt that the
entire attempt to fuse jazz as a form with classical music should be ____.

   (A) promoted
   (B) documented
   (C) discouraged
   (D) acclaimed
   (E) repeated

13. During the last four decades of Tennyson's
long life, his creative powers never ____, some
of his most remarkable work coming after the
age of 70.

   (A) recovered
   (B) manifested
   (C) flagged
   (D) blossomed
   (E) broadened

14. The villagers fortified the town hall, hoping this improvised ____ could ____ them from the guerrilla raids.

    (A) stronghold...alienate
    (B) refuge...distinguish
    (C) bastion...protect
    (D) venture...intimidate
    (E) disguise...safeguard

15. Lovejoy, the hero of Jonathan Gash's mystery novels, is an antique dealer who gives the reader advice on how to tell ____ antiques from the real thing.

    (A) priceless
    (B) spurious
    (C) classical
    (D) authentic
    (E) antiquated

16. The omniscient narrator stands above the story he is telling, ____ his knowledge of what will occur.

    (A) disheartened by
    (B) unlimited in
    (C) ostracized for
    (D) vindicated by
    (E) uncertain of

17. Today employers no longer fire or discharge employees; instead, according to the latest ____, they simply "effect a separation."

    (A) digression
    (B) overstatement
    (C) euphemism
    (D) paradox
    (E) proverb

18. The TV news magazine sits precisely at the ____ of information and entertainment, for while it is not a silly sitcom, it is not a documentary either.

    (A) foundation
    (B) juncture
    (C) cessation
    (D) institution
    (E) eclipse

19. Even though nonbreeding female mole rats are ____, when the queen mole rat dies, several females suddenly ____ their sexual and reproductive powers and battle one another to replace her.

    (A) prolific...accept
    (B) sterile...regain
    (C) barren...relinquish
    (D) fecund...recover
    (E) fragile...lose

20. ____ by life's ____, the last emperor of China worked as a lowly gardener in the palace over which he had once ruled.

    (A) Fortified...generosity
    (B) Deluded...coincidences
    (C) Humbled...vicissitudes
    (D) Venerated...survivors
    (E) Recognized...impostors

## Exercise 2

1. Numerous studies have found that people who choose to represent themselves in court on the whole exercise pretty good judgment—they seem to have a ____ sense of when they need a lawyer and when they don't.

    (A) faulty
    (B) capricious
    (C) reliable
    (D) transient
    (E) drastic

2. Skulls are the Rosetta stones of anthropology, because they bear unique features that let scientists ____ whether two fossil samples come from the same type of creature.

    (A) determine
    (B) prophesy
    (C) disregard
    (D) initiate
    (E) recollect

3. Even when being ____ in method, people can come up with incorrect answers by basing their arguments on false premises.

    (A) original
    (B) logical
    (C) slipshod
    (D) realistic
    (E) careless

4. Was he so thin-skinned, then, to ____ any small ____ at his expense?

   (A) support...purchase
   (B) repeat...compliment
   (C) comprehend...mystery
   (D) resent...jest
   (E) disregard...insult

5. We look with pride at our new bridges and dams, for they are works of art as well as of ____.

   (A) leisure
   (B) aesthetics
   (C) drudgery
   (D) utility
   (E) anachronism

6. When clay dries out, it loses its plasticity and becomes less ____.

   (A) synthetic
   (B) expensive
   (C) malleable
   (D) tangible
   (E) brittle

7. For many years an unheralded researcher, Barbara McClintock gained international ____ when she won the Nobel Prize in Physiology and Medicine.

   (A) condemnation
   (B) notoriety
   (C) renown
   (D) affluence
   (E) camaraderie

8. In judging the degree of his guilt, the question remains whether he acted out of purely ____ motives or whether he acted with thoughts of his own ____ in mind.

   (A) benevolent...fame
   (B) disinterested...advantage
   (C) selfish...benefit
   (D) mercenary...profit
   (E) malicious...cleverness

9. Rosa was such a last-minute worker that she could never start writing a paper till the deadline was ____.

   (A) known
   (B) problematic

   (C) imminent
   (D) superseded
   (E) recent

10. Even while enraptured by the glorious sound produced by Miss Norman, critics ____ a certain absurdity in setting an ____ recital in the cavernous Royal Festival Hall.

    (A) decried...unmelodious
    (B) implied...impractical
    (C) overlooked...explicit
    (D) acknowledged...intimate
    (E) fostered...oppressive

11. Trying to prove Hill a liar, Senator Specter repeatedly questioned her ____.

    (A) intelligence
    (B) veracity
    (C) optimism
    (D) autonomy
    (E) brevity

12. It was only the first day of summer vacation, but his nerves were already ____ by the constant clamor of the children.

    (A) eliminated
    (B) alleviated
    (C) replete
    (D) vacillated
    (E) frayed

13. Donald Trump's latest casino in Atlantic City is the most ____ gambling palace in the East, easily outglittering its competitors.

    (A) professional
    (B) speculative
    (C) ostentatious
    (D) lucrative
    (E) restrained

14. Mrs. Thatcher had a better eye for the weaknesses and ____ of her contemporaries than for their virtues.

    (A) responsibilities
    (B) foibles
    (C) merits
    (D) talents
    (E) attractions

15. American culture now stigmatizes, and sometimes even heavily ____, behavior that was
once taken for granted: overt racism, cigarette
smoking, the use of sexual stereotypes.

    (A) advocates
    (B) penalizes
    (C) ignores
    (D) indoctrinates
    (E) advertises

16. Because we have completed our analysis of the
major components of the proposed project, we
are free to devote the remainder of this session
to a study of the project's ____ details.

    (A) lurid
    (B) scrupulous
    (C) unquestionable
    (D) incidental
    (E) involuntary

17. When we encounter a tentative thought of our
own in someone else's writings, any ____ we
may have had of its validity is ____, and what
we were hesitant to believe is confirmed as
truth.

    (A) assurance...unfounded
    (B) intimation...imprudent
    (C) doubt...dispelled
    (D) proof...unjustified
    (E) suspicion...reinforced

18. Determined to hire employees on the basis of
their merits rather than on the basis of their
family connections, Johnson refused to ____
nepotism and other forms of favoritism in the
engagement of new workers.

    (A) obscure
    (B) proscribe
    (C) countenance
    (D) misrepresent
    (E) discern

19. Just as sloth is the mark of the idler, ____ is
the mark of the ____.

    (A) grief...miser
    (B) obsequiousness...toady
    (C) wanderlust...trespasser
    (D) suspicion...tyrant
    (E) brevity...wit

20. Unlike Sartre, who was born into a cultivated
environment, receiving culture in his feeding
bottle, so to speak, the child Camus had to
fight to ____ a culture that was not ____.

    (A) acquire...innate
    (B) encourage...barbarous
    (C) develop...frivolous
    (D) restrain...inferior
    (E) justify...conventional

## Exercise 3

1. Because the damage to his car had been ____,
Michael decided he wouldn't bother to report
the matter to his insurance company.

    (A) intermittent
    (B) gratuitous
    (C) negligible
    (D) spontaneous
    (E) significant

2. Mr. Levi is ____ learned; he has read everything bearing on his subject and on poetry in
general (in several languages), and he has
forgotten little if anything.

    (A) moderately
    (B) spottily
    (C) inadvertently
    (D) formidably
    (E) inadequately

3. Because vast organizations are an inevitable
element in modern life, it is ____ to aim at
their abolition.

    (A) necessary
    (B) important
    (C) customary
    (D) realistic
    (E) futile

4. Hoping for a rave review of his new show, the
playwright was ____ when the critics ____ it
unanimously.

    (A) gloomy...condoned
    (B) incredulous...appraised
    (C) vexed...selected
    (D) miserable...panned
    (E) impressed...divulged

5. Because it had not been blasted into a stable orbit, the satellite moved _____ through space.

   (A) innocuously
   (B) gradually
   (C) erratically
   (D) effortlessly
   (E) routinely

6. When railroads first began to supplant rivers and canals as highways of commerce, they were regarded as blessings and their promoters were looked upon as _____.

   (A) hucksters
   (B) upstarts
   (C) atheists
   (D) benefactors
   (E) diehards

7. Though she tried to be happy living with Clara in the city, Heidi _____ for the mountains and for her gruff but loving grandfather.

   (A) pined
   (B) searched
   (C) cheered
   (D) labored
   (E) trembled

8. The discovery by George Poinar and Roberta Hess that amber could preserve intact tissue from million-year-old insects _____ the possibility, since proved correct, that it also could preserve intact DNA.

   (A) eliminated
   (B) distorted
   (C) raised
   (D) precluded
   (E) predestined

9. The new dance troupe's gravest problem, one that mars the current production, is a desire for correctness and technical accuracy that _____ both energy and musical response.

   (A) enhances
   (B) stifles
   (C) transforms
   (D) reflects
   (E) supplies

10. New judges often fear that the influence of their own backgrounds will _____ their verdicts, no matter how sincere they are in wanting to be _____.

    (A) contradict...revered
    (B) corroborate...silent
    (C) condition...impartial
    (D) disclose...secretive
    (E) falsify...humane

11. Because he had abandoned his post and joined forces with the Indians, his fellow officers considered the hero of *Dances with Wolves* a _____.

    (A) martinet
    (B) braggart
    (C) renegade
    (D) skinflint
    (E) laggard

12. To take a _____ attitude, looking down on others as one's inferiors, often is to _____ any chance of favorable relations with them.

    (A) promising...negate
    (B) patronizing...eliminate
    (C) modest...reduce
    (D) pertinent...violate
    (E) benign...deny

13. Contemporary critics often _____ the poet Longfellow as a simple sentimentalist who relied too much on poetic meters only suitable for light verse.

    (A) heed
    (B) endorse
    (C) dismiss
    (D) embellish
    (E) acclaim

14. On some occasions Monteverdi specifies the instruments he wishes to make up his orchestra, but more often he is _____ or silent on the issue.

    (A) enigmatic
    (B) precise
    (C) eloquent
    (D) resolute
    (E) vehement

15. Just as an ____ dish lacks flavor, an inane remark lacks ____.

(A) intriguing...spice
(B) insipid...sense
(C) inedible...listeners
(D) occasional...implications
(E) offensive...taste

16. Deeply ____ by the insult to his dignity, he maintained that no true gentleman would accept such an ____ calmly.

(A) mortified...opportunity
(B) incensed...affront
(C) puzzled...honor
(D) shamed...iconoclasm
(E) gratified...admonition

17. Isozaki's love for detail is apparent everywhere in the new museum, but fortunately the details are ____ to the building's larger formal composition, which is ____ by the busyness of much recent architecture.

(A) important...harmed
(B) irrelevant...fragmented
(C) subordinated...unencumbered
(D) appropriate...echoed
(E) incidental...nullified

18. Although most worthwhile criticism concentrates on the positive, one should not ____ praise everything.

(A) argumentatively
(B) constructively
(C) derogatorily
(D) analytically
(E) indiscriminately

19. Strindberg's plays are marked by his extreme ____; he felt modern woman needed to ____ man and by subordinating him invalidate his masculinity.

(A) acrimony...comfort
(B) misogyny...dominate
(C) hypocrisy...reinvigorate
(D) philosophy...abstract
(E) altruism...civilize

20. Learned though she was, her ____ never degenerated into ____.

(A) erudition...pedantry
(B) knowledge...ignorance
(C) scholarship...research
(D) speculation...thought
(E) education...inquiry

## Exercise 4

1. Biologists categorize many of the world's environments as deserts: regions where the ____ availability of some key factor, such as water, sunlight, or an essential nutrient, places sharp constraints on the existence of living things.

(A) ready
(B) gradual
(C) limited
(D) nearby
(E) unprecedented

2. The sea was so rough that the safest thing to do was to seize the railing of the ship and hang on; walking was too ____ a pastime.

(A) leisurely
(B) pleasant
(C) tempting
(D) precarious
(E) prosaic

3. Though the ad writers had come up with a highly creative campaign to publicize the company's newest product, the head office rejected it for a more ____, down-to-earth approach.

(A) innovative
(B) drastic
(C) prosaic
(D) noteworthy
(E) philosophic

4. The Americans and the British seem to have a dog-in-the-manger attitude toward the island of Malta, no longer needing it themselves but nevertheless wishing to ____ it to others.

(A) interpret
(B) offer
(C) deny
(D) praise
(E) reveal

5. Why bother with facts? Facts that are significant we probably already know, and facts that
are new seem essentially _____.

   (A) momentous
   (B) antiquated
   (C) improbable
   (D) undemonstrable
   (E) trivial

6. When you learn archaeology solely from lectures, you get only _____ sense of the concepts
presented, but when you hold a five-thousand-
year-old artifact in your hands, you have a
chance to involve your senses, not just your
intellect.

   (A) an invalid
   (B) an anachronistic
   (C) an abstract
   (D) a specious
   (E) a tangential

7. Paradoxically, while it is relatively easy to
prove a fraudulent work of art is a fraud, it is
often virtually impossible to prove that an
authentic one is _____.

   (A) unpretentious
   (B) objective
   (C) impartial
   (D) dubious
   (E) genuine

8. The humorist Mark Twain had a great _____ for
history and historians, observing that each year
the antiquarians shed new darkness on the past.

   (A) reverence
   (B) affinity
   (C) tolerance
   (D) contempt
   (E) empathy

9. Since novelty of presentation is apt to add to a
performer's popularity, the most successful
troubadours were those who were also the most
_____ in their delivery.

   (A) spontaneous
   (B) lyrical
   (C) academic
   (D) practiced
   (E) repetitious

10. Unfortunately, in developing countries rapid
economic growth often _____ the overexploitation of natural resources and _____ distribution
of wealth.

   (A) halts...indiscriminate
   (B) holds off...inadequate
   (C) leads to...inequitable
   (D) continues...evenhanded
   (E) goes beyond...ungrateful

11. Untempered by any _____, she spread an ever
more militant message to her followers.

   (A) conviction
   (B) enthusiasm
   (C) radicalism
   (D) hardship
   (E) moderation

12. The idea that people are basically economic
creatures, intent only upon their own material
advantage, induces disbelief in the _____ of any
_____ motive.

   (A) purpose...natural
   (B) desirability...ulterior
   (C) stupidity...altruistic
   (D) seemliness...egoistic
   (E) integrity...unselfish

13. Leavening his decisions with humorous, down-
to-earth anecdotes, Judge Wapner was not at all
the _____ legal scholar.

   (A) considerate
   (B) pedantic
   (C) indecisive
   (D) competent
   (E) pragmatic

14. The Apache are a _____ society, where husbands
typically move into wives' dwellings and women
take the leadership role in family affairs.

   (A) sedentary
   (B) defunct
   (C) fragmented
   (D) matrilineal
   (E) xenophobic

15. _____ James Baldwin, who wrote of black Americans as being in a perpetual state of rage, Mr. Cose remarks that few human beings could _____ the psychic toll of uninterrupted anger.

    (A) Corroborating...endure
    (B) Refuting...enhance
    (C) Dismissing...refine
    (D) Challenging...survive
    (E) Upholding...weather

16. Rather than allowing these dramatic exchanges between her characters to develop fully, Ms. Norman unfortunately tends to _____ the discussions involving the two women.

    (A) exacerbate
    (B) protract
    (C) truncate
    (D) augment
    (E) elaborate

17. "The show must go on" is the oldest _____ of show business; every true performer lives by that creed.

    (A) euphemism
    (B) allegory
    (C) precursor
    (D) tenet
    (E) corroboration

18. Wincing at the _____ of the interviewer's wording, the scholar was as _____ to words and phrases as a sectarian is to creeds.

    (A) brusqueness...indifferent
    (B) vagueness...sensitive
    (C) repetitiveness...dogmatic
    (D) clarity...addicted
    (E) fluency...responsive

19. From the critic's perspective, M.F.K. Fisher was a writer who _____ classification, for her food writing read like love stories, her fiction like memoirs.

    (A) remembered
    (B) relished
    (C) skirted
    (D) complied with
    (E) matured with

20. Because the apelike members of *Australopithecus afarensis* were capable both of walking and of swinging through trees, the anthropologist described them as a mosaic, bipedal from the waist down and _____ from the waist up.

    (A) ethereal
    (B) arboreal
    (C) dysfunctional
    (D) articulated
    (E) pedestrian

# ANSWERS TO SENTENCE COMPLETION EXERCISES

## LEVEL A

### Sentence Completion Exercise 1

| | | | | | | | | | |
|---|---|---|---|---|---|---|---|---|---|
| 1. **C** | 3. **B** | 5. **C** | 7. **C** | 9. **C** | 11. **D** | 13. **D** | 15. **A** | 17. **D** | 19. **D** |
| 2. **D** | 4. **E** | 6. **C** | 8. **D** | 10. **E** | 12. **B** | 14. **A** | 16. **A** | 18. **B** | 20. **B** |

### Sentence Completion Exercise 2

| | | | | | | | | | |
|---|---|---|---|---|---|---|---|---|---|
| 1. **B** | 3. **E** | 5. **C** | 7. **C** | 9. **E** | 11. **C** | 13. **C** | 15. **C** | 17. **D** | 19. **B** |
| 2. **C** | 4. **D** | 6. **A** | 8. **D** | 10. **C** | 12. **A** | 14. **D** | 16. **C** | 18. **D** | 20. **C** |

### Sentence Completion Exercise 3

| | | | | | | | | | |
|---|---|---|---|---|---|---|---|---|---|
| 1. **E** | 3. **C** | 5. **A** | 7. **C** | 9. **C** | 11. **C** | 13. **B** | 15. **A** | 17. **C** | 19. **D** |
| 2. **E** | 4. **B** | 6. **E** | 8. **A** | 10. **C** | 12. **B** | 14. **D** | 16. **C** | 18. **E** | 20. **A** |

### Sentence Completion Exercise 4

| | | | | | | | | | |
|---|---|---|---|---|---|---|---|---|---|
| 1. **D** | 3. **E** | 5. **A** | 7. **B** | 9. **B** | 11. **D** | 13. **B** | 15. **B** | 17. **E** | 19. **A** |
| 2. **D** | 4. **C** | 6. **D** | 8. **C** | 10. **E** | 12. **C** | 14. **A** | 16. **C** | 18. **E** | 20. **A** |

## LEVEL B

### Sentence Completion Exercise 1

| | | | | | | | | | |
|---|---|---|---|---|---|---|---|---|---|
| 1. **B** | 3. **B** | 5. **A** | 7. **C** | 9. **E** | 11. **C** | 13. **D** | 15. **C** | 17. **D** | 19. **C** |
| 2. **C** | 4. **D** | 6. **E** | 8. **B** | 10. **B** | 12. **C** | 14. **D** | 16. **C** | 18. **B** | 20. **C** |

### Sentence Completion Exercise 2

| | | | | | | | | | |
|---|---|---|---|---|---|---|---|---|---|
| 1. **D** | 3. **E** | 5. **C** | 7. **C** | 9. **C** | 11. **D** | 13. **C** | 15. **A** | 17. **E** | 19. **C** |
| 2. **A** | 4. **C** | 6. **D** | 8. **D** | 10. **C** | 12. **C** | 14. **A** | 16. **A** | 18. **B** | 20. **E** |

### Sentence Completion Exercise 3

| | | | | | | | | | |
|---|---|---|---|---|---|---|---|---|---|
| 1. **B** | 3. **C** | 5. **A** | 7. **D** | 9. **A** | 11. **C** | 13. **A** | 15. **C** | 17. **D** | 19. **D** |
| 2. **C** | 4. **C** | 6. **D** | 8. **D** | 10. **E** | 12. **C** | 14. **B** | 16. **B** | 18. **D** | 20. **B** |

### Sentence Completion Exercise 4

| | | | | | | | | | |
|---|---|---|---|---|---|---|---|---|---|
| 1. **E** | 3. **E** | 5. **C** | 7. **D** | 9. **D** | 11. **D** | 13. **E** | 15. **C** | 17. **A** | 19. **C** |
| 2. **E** | 4. **B** | 6. **C** | 8. **B** | 10. **B** | 12. **D** | 14. **C** | 16. **E** | 18. **E** | 20. **C** |

## LEVEL C

**Sentence Completion Exercise 1**

| | | | | | | | | | |
|---|---|---|---|---|---|---|---|---|---|
| 1. **B** | 3. **C** | 5. **D** | 7. **E** | 9. **B** | 11. **C** | 13. **C** | 15. **B** | 17. **C** | 19. **B** |
| 2. **C** | 4. **B** | 6. **C** | 8. **D** | 10. **B** | 12. **C** | 14. **C** | 16. **B** | 18. **B** | 20. **C** |

**Sentence Completion Exercise 2**

| | | | | | | | | | |
|---|---|---|---|---|---|---|---|---|---|
| 1. **C** | 3. **B** | 5. **D** | 7. **C** | 9. **C** | 11. **B** | 13. **C** | 15. **B** | 17. **C** | 19. **B** |
| 2. **A** | 4. **D** | 6. **C** | 8. **B** | 10. **D** | 12. **E** | 14. **B** | 16. **D** | 18. **C** | 20. **A** |

**Sentence Completion Exercise 3**

| | | | | | | | | | |
|---|---|---|---|---|---|---|---|---|---|
| 1. **C** | 3. **E** | 5. **C** | 7. **A** | 9. **B** | 11. **C** | 13. **C** | 15. **B** | 17. **C** | 19. **B** |
| 2. **D** | 4. **D** | 6. **D** | 8. **C** | 10. **C** | 12. **B** | 14. **A** | 16. **B** | 18. **E** | 20. **A** |

**Sentence Completion Exercise 4**

| | | | | | | | | | |
|---|---|---|---|---|---|---|---|---|---|
| 1. **C** | 3. **C** | 5. **E** | 7. **E** | 9. **A** | 11. **E** | 13. **B** | 15. **D** | 17. **D** | 19. **C** |
| 2. **D** | 4. **C** | 6. **C** | 8. **D** | 10. **C** | 12. **E** | 14. **D** | 16. **C** | 18. **B** | 20. **B** |

# ANSWER EXPLANATIONS

## LEVEL A

### Sentence Completion Exercise 1

1. **C** If Washington political circles had been aware for a week that the Cabinet member was on the way out, his resignation did not come as a *shock* or surprise to them.

2. **D** An epidemic of food poisoning would indicate flaws or *deficiencies* in the system of inspecting food (a system set up to prevent food poisoning and other public health problems).

3. **B** The key phrase "as if it were a laboratory specimen" signals you that this sort of excessive literary analysis is analogous to the *dissecting* or cutting apart of animals and plants one does in a biology lab.

4. **E** Customs generally arise because they serve a function. In this case, the division of labor by gender probably came about because it *promoted* or furthered the interests of the family and in this way was a sensible *cooperative* strategy.

5. **C** If birds use silk in building their nests *because* it is strong and sticky, it follows that strength and adhesiveness are highly desirable, *invaluable* qualities in nest building.

6. **C** The new magazine's challenge is to make itself stand out from its competitors. Thus, it seeks to *distinguish* or differentiate itself from the crowd by making its mission *clear*.

7. **C** The earlier writers' reminiscences differ from this writer's memoirs in being *bland* and unexciting.

8. **D** A report that constantly interpreted things to reflect badly on or *discredit* someone would clearly be unfriendly or *hostile* to that person.

9. **C** By not growing up fully, Forster remained in some ways *immature*.

10. **E** Although she felt *contempt* (scorn) for the world of money and opinion and power, she nevertheless desired or *yearned for* the fame that only that world could give.

11. **D** If you are excessively careful about what you say, you are not likely to be *spontaneous* or free in your choice of words.

12. **B** A layperson or nonexpert by definition lacks the training to *appreciate* or recognize the importance of fossils and ancient artifacts.

13. **D** It would be extremely hard to be *unaffected* or unmoved by truly mesmerizing, enchanting art.

14. **A** If you can see only shades of gray, your view is by definition *monochromatic* (made up of one color or hue).

15. **A** If the therapy has been shown to work in dogs (animals larger than rodents), then its *efficacy* or effectiveness in larger animals has been proven.

16. **A** To *dampen* or muffle the noise in a car should make a trip in the car quieter.

17. **D** Neither her father's *admonition* (warning or counsel) nor her classmates' *cool* (unsociable; distant) reception stopped Cleeves from following her chosen path.

18. **B** To *derail* someone from his course is to throw him off track.

19. **D** To *dispel* rancor is to get rid of the brooding and ill will that can afflict a person suffering from stress.

20. **B** Comte *coined* (invented; created) a term to *denote* (stand for; mean) the concept of unselfishness.

### Sentence Completion Exercise 2

1. **B** If we manage to *destroy* the environment, we will be well on the way to extinction as a species.

2. **C** *Even though* children cannot influence affairs in the usual ways, thanks to Edelman's work they are nevertheless not *ignored*.

3. **E**   A campaign that breaks new ground is by definition *innovative*.

4. **D**   Both an *outstanding* sense of timing and a *mastery* of the law would be helpful to an attorney.

5. **C**   The papers *rank* as (have the status or position of) the most *impressive* statements of American political philosophy.

6. **A**   The entangling threads that slow down the victim's *escape* vibrate from the victim's struggles. These vibrations *alert* (warn; inform) the spider that it has trapped something in its web.

7. **C**   In poking through the subject's private papers, the biographer *invades* the subject's privacy.

8. **D**   If the babies drink so much fruit juice that they do not get the varied nourishment they *need*, then drinking large amounts of juice could be *detrimental* (harmful) to them.

9. **E**   *Epics* or accounts of heroic exploits by definition narrate the mighty struggles of a central character or protagonist.

10. **C**   Wittgenstein's comment is a *rule* for historians, which good historians should stick to or *adhere*. It says, "If you don't know anything about a subject, you can't say anything about it." In other words, write about what you know.

11. **C**   The muskoxen declined or grew fewer in number because the herds were *devastated* (destroyed; ravaged) by hunters.

12. **A**   What marks the South as different (*distinguishes* it) is that as a region it is *optimistic* at a time when much of the rest of the country is pessimistic.

13. **C**   Someone who looks on human virtues as less worthy than canine virtues clearly views people in general with *contempt* (scorn).

14. **D**   The dumbfounded neuroanatomist disbelieved Diamond's work. *Skeptical* of the results of her experiments, he maintained that a rat's brain could not increase or *grow*.

15. **C**   Though he maintained that he did not care ("protested his *indifference*"), Judge Hand was *disappointed* that he had not been nominated to the Supreme Court.

16. **C**   A small hall would tend to promote a sense of closeness appropriate to recitals. In other words, such a hall would be particularly *conducive to* the intimacy that is the recital's special charm.

17. **D**   If the colonies appeared remarkably homogeneous or uniform in opinion, then clearly only *superficial*, very minor differences differentiated them.

18. **D**   One would expect that a liberal political movement advocating freedom would favor less authority, not more. However, Trilling asserts that, paradoxically, contrary to expectations, liberalism must move in the direction of increasing *control*.

19. **B**   The contrast here is between the extremes of *euphoria* (elation) and *gloom* (melancholy; depression).

20. **C**   By definition, to lead a lewd and wanton life is to be *debauched* (corrupted by sensuality).

## Sentence Completion Exercise 3

1. **E**   Though most people disregarded or made fun of her book, some *appreciated* it (admired it, grasped its worth).

2. **E**   If the critics all say the opera's score has both praiseworthy and wretched sections, then they agree that the score varies in quality. In other words, it is *uneven*.

3. **C**   Someone who plans everything out in advance is not *spontaneous*.

4. **B**   Our almost-human ancestors did not become extinct. Instead, they *survived*.

5. **A**   The marketing experts have divided or *carved up* the *mass* (whole) audience into segments.

6. **E**   If you *overinflate* a balloon, it *bursts*.

7. **C**   Unexpected problems generally lead to *delays*.

8. **A**   A hotshot is someone conspicuously talented and successful. These lawyers are *not* legal hotshots. They are *ill-prepared* and they *lack* professional skills.

9. **C**   Scientists continue to test hypotheses against experience, *verifying* them or establishing their accuracy by keeping on making observations.

10. **C**   To supersede or replace a learned, scholarly biography, this new life of Gaskell must be a very good book. In other words, it must be a considerable *accomplishment* or achievement for the author.

11. **C**   After Boccherini's death, the composer's reputation fell into a decline or weakened. It has not yet *recovered* or improved enough to satisfy the writer of this sentence.

12. **B**   *Because* he had emphasized his scandal-free, virtuous reputation, Hosokawa could not *withstand* or successfully resist the ill fame (*notoriety*) of being connected with a scandal.

13. **B**   It is *paradoxical* (incongruous; puzzlingly contradictory) that a *civilized* center should have been the site of horribly uncivilized, inhumane acts.

14. **D**   The writers who are not negative about the past look on it positively, even *nostalgically* (sentimentally, with a sense of wistful longing).

15. **A**   If Schlesinger laments or mourns the state of biography, then he is unhappy about the gossipy new biographies currently on sale. Thus, he *deplores* (disapproves of) them.

16. **C**   The waitress handled the bottle *nonchalantly* or casually, without undue excitement.

17. **C**   To begin to appear in prominent, *responsible* positions is to emerge from *obscurity* or anonymity into the public view.

18. **E**   Someone who has *improvidently* squandered his money without thinking about the future would regret his *prodigal*, wasteful ways.

19. **D**   A *charlatan* falsely pretends to know more than he actually does. When Dorothy finds out that the Wizard does not know how to get her home, she thinks he has *duped* or made a fool of her.

20. **A**   Despite his self-centeredness, White could be kind to others and even belittle or be modest about himself (be *self-deprecating*).

## Sentence Completion Exercise 4

1. **D**   To *revoke* a license is to cancel it, to make it void.

2. **D**   A curious child is by definition *inquisitive*.

3. **E**   Since many scholars helped to put together the survey, it was a *collective* (combined; cooperative) effort, not an individual one.

4. **C**   A fair solution is by definition *equitable* or just.

5. **A**   It is physically impossible for most living creatures to walk on water. Thus, by running across the surface of water, the basilisk seems to *defy* or challenge the laws of physics.

6. **D**   Passive, inactive people tend to *observe* rather than to *act*.

7. **B**   Keynes was not immobilized. Instead, he was *energized* or invigorated.

8. **C**   The telling of tales is by definition *narrative*.

9. **B**   An *enthusiastic*, spirited response would be likely to please or *gratify* a speaker.

10. **E**   *Advances* or new developments in science would make it *necessary* to revise the book.

11. **D**   Someone lying half asleep in a hot tub is clearly *relaxed*.

12. **C**   Plants that do not survive *shrivel* (wither) and die.

13. **B**   To fabricate events is to make them up, to invent them. Dali's tendency to make things up makes it hard for people to get an *accurate* idea of his life.

14. **A**   Many people accepted and liked Earhart ("her fame was unusually widespread and her popularity long-lived"). However, not everyone did: her acceptance was not *universal*.

15. **B**   His belief in individual faith contrasts with his doubts (*skepticism*) about the organized church.

16. **C**   Someone old for his years, slow and conservative, could well be called *stodgy*.

17. **E**   By calling these complaints "nostalgic elitism" (sentimental snobbery), one *dismisses* or rejects them as a subject for serious consideration.

18. **E**   Radicals tend to believe that old customs are nonsense and that change is always a good idea. This author thinks it would be good for radicals to rethink their beliefs. They need to realize that old customs are not always *worthless* and that change can sometimes be a bad idea (be *inadvisable*).

19. **A**   Though Eliot was personally *reticent* (reserved; uncommunicative about himself), he was realistic enough to *assume* that his private papers someday would be read.

20. **A**   To be *restive* by definition is to exhibit or be marked by impatience.

# LEVEL B

## Sentence Completion Exercise 1

1. **B**  People on the cutting edge—at the forefront of a new movement—are likely to be *innovative*.
2. **C**  If it is so amazing that good poems ever get written, there must be many ways to *ruin* poems.
3. **B**  If only a few of her allies stood by her, she must have *alienated* or estranged all the others.
4. **D**  Just as the limbs of a tree *branch off* from the trunk, the major arteries branch off from the aorta.
5. **A**  The goal of the project is to make Woolf's work more *accessible* or available to scholars.
6. **E**  The map is not the territory. Land exists (is *real*) even if it has not yet been mapped (*charted*).
7. **C**  *Digressive* remarks that wander from the topic may make you forget the gist or main point of what's being said.
8. **B**  Allende's book is based on or *rooted in* actual Chilean history.
9. **E**  If they plan on selling ad space, their *motivations* in making the donation are at least partially financial and not solely charitable or *philanthropic*.
10. **B**  Blackmun's voice stood out from the featureless mix of the other Justices' voices: it was an individual, *personal* voice.
11. **C**  It is somewhat of an *understatement* for Gaddis to describe himself as never having been in a *rush* to get into print. At a rate of one book every ten years, he's been markedly slow to publish.
12. **C**  *Chancy* means uncertain in prospects; risky. Acting as a career certainly is that.
13. **D**  Montana was *unintimidating*: he did not frighten or overawe those who met him.
14. **D**  In Sand's time, for a woman to take lovers or wear men's clothes was a shocking departure from *convention* (usual social custom).
15. **C**  The speaker is not *resigned* or reconciled to her death. Instead, he is *inconsolable* (heartbroken; unable to be comforted or consoled).
16. **C**  The Chinese artists have been clever. They have made *canny* (shrewd) use of Western styles.
17. **D**  Given the extreme amount of work he has put into his poems, it is understandable that he finds the poems of others *superficial* or lacking substance.
18. **B**  To *sound* the depths is to ascertain just how deep something is. This biographer has not reached the depths, but she has examined the *surface*.
19. **C**  Traumas or major shocks can lead to *aberrations* or abnormalities of behavior in survivors.
20. **C**  Someone intellectually *fecund* (fertile; prolific) is bursting with ideas. Clearly, this productive novelist is at the *height* of her powers.

## Sentence Completion Exercise 2

1. **D**  The sentence serves to *define* the term *illness*.
2. **A**  By revitalizing Chrysler, Iacocca made it a *vigorous*, energetic company.
3. **E**  One expects a scholar to know the serious works on his subject. Though Cose is not a scholar, he nevertheless is *familiar with* the appropriate serious works.
4. **C**  Healing waters are by definition *therapeutic* (curative).
5. **C**  Because the benefits of telecommuting have been shown or *demonstrated*, more people are choosing to work at home.
6. **D**  By definition, someone *apathetic* does not care.
7. **C**  To *scavenge* is to hunt through discarded items to find useful bits.
8. **D**  Most of the books are not excellent, but are *mediocre* instead.
9. **C**  Angry, *heated* discussions suggest no settlement is near. However, the two sides actually are close to *agreeing*.
10. **C**  Churchill was not a *dilettante* or dabbler; he was a serious artist.
11. **D**  Foreign powers that look on territory in the Americas as prey to be seized are by definition *predatory*.

12. **C**    A spotty book is uneven in quality. This particular book suffers from sections that are relatively uninteresting, less than *exciting* though not precisely *dull*.

13. **C**    Widow Douglass did not always scold Huck. Instead, she *condoned* (voluntarily overlooked; forgave) his minor misdeeds.

14. **A**    To interpret art fancifully, inventing things, is a *temptation* to the critic. This critic resists the temptation; he is *scrupulous* (carefully painstaking) in sticking to the facts.

15. **A**    Because he owes money, Lydgate must take a *lucrative*, well-paying position.

16. **A**    Before they can *ascertain* or figure out how important it is to limit the human use of the beaches at night, the observers must determine just how much the shorebirds depend on their *nocturnal* (nighttime) feeding.

17. **E**    For the listener to come to agree with the speaker, any *doubts* he might have had must have been *dispelled* (made to vanish).

18. **B**    By definition, a *sage* is a wise person. Likewise, a virtuoso is a skilled person, one who has *expertise*.

19. **C**    *Tacit* cooperation is implied but not expressed actively. Johnson's cooperation with Boswell went far beyond this.

20. **E**    Lesser scholars would have been intimidated or *daunted* by the amount of material to be explored.

## Sentence Completion Exercise 3

1. **B**    The key phrase here is "longer lives." The doctors are trying to lengthen or *prolong* human life.

2. **C**    In an arid, extremely dry land, one needs *access to* water.

3. **C**    Someone consistently hopeful is by definition an *optimist*.

4. **C**    *Even* intensifies what is being said. Lullabies not only have a dark side, they even have a *threatening*, menacing quality.

5. **A**    For a dispute to become ugly and destructive, the level of disagreement must *escalate* (intensify; increase).

6. **D**    Lao Li's archives *document* or record contemporary Chinese art.

7. **D**    Someone who leaves parties in order to go off alone clearly can no longer be described as *gregarious* (sociable).

8. **D**    If science is always ready to change or modify its theories, it clearly is *tentative* (provisional) rather than absolute in making its statements.

9. **A**    Because we today are able to cure tuberculosis, we think of it as simply another long-term *chronic* illness. In the past, however, people regarded it as a pestilence or *plague*.

10. **E**    Rather than lure or attract readers, Gaddis's work *repels* or drives them away instead.

11. **C**    Instead of being showily glamorous like opera, classical song is more restrained or *subdued*.

12. **C**    The writer is uniformly positive about the book being reviewed, calling it *painstakingly* or carefully researched. The life the book describes, however, is not positive: the subject's tormented career was *tragic*.

13. **A**    Lexy's pleasure did not last long; it was *transient* or fleeting.

14. **B**    It would be futile or pointless to try to *separate* elements that have been thoroughly *commingled* or mixed.

15. **C**    By describing the land as asleep, the writer means that the nation had yet to rouse itself to confront the foreign invaders. Clearly the people's sense of nationalism was *dormant* or sleeping.

16. **B**    In order to enhance or improve their empires, the moguls (cinema magnates) needed the services of *prestigious*, eminent writers whose prestige would rub off on them. In this way the moguls would *aggrandize* themselves, making themselves appear greater through their association with great intellectuals.

17. **D**    The production is described metaphorically as if it were a jungle creature, alert, stealthy, almost *predatory* (ready to seize its victim) as it waits to *pounce*.

18. **D**    *Obsequious* means servile or fawningly attentive.

19. **D**  *Whereas* signals a contrast. *L'Orfeo* is not the beginning of a tradition. Instead, it is the *culmination* or highest achievement of one.

20. **B**  In combining so many different approaches, Feher's lessons are clearly *eclectic* (composed of elements drawn from different sources).

## Sentence Completion Exercise 4

1. **E**  If you could afford only such meager nourishment, clearly you would be very poor—in other words, suffering from *poverty*.

2. **E**  An *uneventful* life, one in which nothing much important or notable happened, would be difficult to make seem interesting.

3. **E**  Unable to rely on its poor vision to help it move in the darkness, the mole rat depends on the sensitivity of its whiskers to what they touch to give it a feel for its surroundings. Thus, the whiskers help *guide* the mole rat.

4. **B**  *Aggressive*, belligerent impulses push people to get into street brawls. However, professional boxers are allowed to fight only in professional competitions—that is, in the ring.

5. **C**  The phrase "for all" as used here means "in spite of." It signals a contrast. The novel's hero does not really belong in the 1890s. He is a *contemporary* voice and has a contemporary, 1990s cultural *background*.

6. **C**  She wondered whether triangles *qualified* (demonstrated the required characteristics) to be called polygons.

7. **D**  Telescopic observations are more *detailed* (complete) than ones made with the naked eye. However, the first *documented* or recorded use of the telescope came after Kepler saw the supernova.

8. **B**  The author was not brave enough to attack the people who had the power to prevent his books from being published; he did not bite the hand that fed him. However, he was brave enough to make an occasional negative remark about these people; thus, he *nibbled at* the hand that fed him.

9. **D**  People who are "arty" are showily or pretentiously artistic: they collect art in order to show off their belongings. True art lovers, however, collect for their own pleasure or *delight*, not for *show*.

10. **B**  *Recurrent* (periodically reappearing) attacks or bouts of illness could well alarm someone's friends and family.

11. **D**  "Though" signals a contrast. In this case, Simon does have good things to say about a contemporary play. He *raves* about it, praising it extravagantly.

12. **D**  In their old age, Chinese painters no longer copied their teachers. Instead, they were *original*. However, they did not make major changes; they made *slight*, barely visible ones.

13. **E**  If you had your reputation damaged by a libelous statement, you would want your name *cleared* or freed of blame. Thus, you would welcome a *retraction* (disavowal; withdrawal) of the libel.

14. **C**  Kissinger appreciates the hard-headed, realistic use of power. He even appreciates power when it is used *ruthlessly*, without compassion or remorse. For this reason, he is able to admire the ability to use power effectively even when he sees it in people who are otherwise *detestable* (odious).

15. **C**  Poseurs by definition pretend to be something they are not. Some people thought Dali was a great artist. Others *dismissed* (slighted; made little of) him as a painter who pretended to be great.

16. **E**  If the world of food writing is known for its pettiness (small-mindedness) and infighting (internal quarrels), then *generosity* would be *rarely* found there.

17. **A**  *Esoteric* allusions are by definition references that are understood only by a small, restricted group. References to *obscure*, little-known people and events clearly would not be understood by people in general.

18. **E**  To see her sister's fortunes rise while her own *declined* or fell would be likely to *exacerbate* or intensify the subject's bitterness.

19. **C**  *Probity* is by definition honesty or integrity.

20. **C**  In calling *Spellbound* a testimonial to (expression of the benefits received from) the powers of psychoanalysis to do good, the writer maintains that the movie presents a favorable picture of psychoanalysis. However, it is not an excessively admiring, *adulatory* picture.

## LEVEL C

### Sentence Completion Exercise 1

1. **B**   In the dark, one's eyes have to work hard or *strain* to be able to see.
2. **C**   The uprising was organized and planned. Thus, it was not *spontaneous* or unpremeditated.
3. **C**   Theologians (specialists in the study of religious faith and practices) would be upset by a book that *disturbed established* rituals and beliefs.
4. **B**   *Empathy* by definition is sensitivity to the feelings and thoughts of others.
5. **D**   *Theses* is the plural form of *thesis*, which here means theory or contention. The details are disconnected; no overarching or encompassing theories bring them together or *unify* them.
6. **C**   Preferring facts, the historian is uninterested in speculations or *conjectures*.
7. **E**   By agreeing to be the subjects of magazine articles, these famously *shy* novelists have given in to their publishers' insistence on *publicity*.
8. **D**   Caring so much about being in the know, Tom was vexed or *galled* by his ignorance.
9. **B**   To waver between choices is by definition to *vacillate*.
10. **B**   With their huge nets, the trawlers scoop up everything in their path. Thus, they trap fish *indiscriminately*, hauling them in without distinguishing among them.
11. **C**   The statement is cynical. In *complimenting* the child of a potential voter, the politician is not so much being *hypocritical*, feigning to see beauty where it doesn't exist, as he or she is being practical (showing good political sense).
12. **C**   The symphony is a classical music form. In writing jazz symphonies, Ellington was combining or fusing jazz with a classical form. He was attacked for this by critics who wished to *discourage* such fusions.
13. **C**   If Tennyson managed to produce particularly impressive work in his last years, clearly his creative powers had not declined or *flagged*.
14. **C**   A *bastion* (stronghold; fortified area) by definition is a place set up to *protect* people from attack.
15. **B**   Lovejoy advises the reader how to avoid being fooled by *spurious*, fake antiques.
16. **B**   Someone omniscient (all-knowing) would by definition be *unlimited* in knowledge.
17. **C**   A *euphemism* is a mild expression used in place of a blunt, unpleasant one.
18. **B**   By definition, a *juncture* is a point of convergence, here the point where televised information and entertainment are joined together in a new format.
19. **B**   For a nonbreeding female to be able to replace a queen, taking over her breeding functions, the female must *regain* her reproductive abilities. In other words, the nonbreeding female suddenly reverses her *sterility* (barrenness; inability to reproduce).
20. **C**   Life's *vicissitudes* are the changes of fortune one experiences in the course of a lifetime. Going from ruling an empire to laboring in a garden, China's last emperor clearly would have been *humbled* or lowered in condition by these changes.

### Sentence Completion Exercise 2

1. **C**   The writer is relatively positive about people's decisions in choosing to represent themselves in court. He or she concludes that people have a *reliable* or dependable sense of when lawyers are and are not necessary.
2. **A**   Anthropologists attempt to *determine* (discover; learn) the origins of the fossils they find.
3. **B**   A faulty premise or underlying assumption can undermine the most *logically* reasoned argument.
4. **D**   To be thin-skinned by definition is to be quick to *resent* any insult or joking remark (*jest*) that might reflect on one's dignity.
5. **D**   Bridges and dams are built to serve useful functions: they are works of *utility*. However, this writer asserts that the new bridges and dams are works of art as well.
6. **C**   By definition, something that loses its plasticity (capacity for being molded or shaped) is less *malleable* (capable of being shaped).

7. **C** McClintock went from being unheralded (not celebrated or famous) to being *renowned* (celebrated; acclaimed).

8. **B** A *disinterested* (unselfishly motivated) act would not be motivated by selfish thoughts of one's own *advantage*.

9. **C** *Imminent* means near at hand, hanging threateningly over one's head. A procrastinator or last-minute worker often delays till the deadline is nearly upon her.

10. **D** The key word here is "cavernous." The critics *acknowledged* or admitted that it was silly to hold an *intimate* (close, personal) performance in a huge, impersonal hall.

11. **B** *Veracity* means truthfulness. By calling someone a liar, you attack their truthfulness.

12. **E** Nerves would be *frayed* or strained by constant clamor (noise).

13. **C** Something that outglitters its rivals is more showy or *ostentatious* than they are.

14. **B** *Foibles* by definition are minor flaws or weaknesses. The support signal *and* suggests that the missing word must be a synonym or near-synonym for "weaknesses."

15. **B** To stigmatize behavior is to characterize or mark it as disgraceful or wicked. To *penalize* behavior is to go even further and punish it.

16. **D** Now that they have dealt with the major items, they can move on to the minor, *incidental* ones.

17. **C** If you now believe what you had been reluctant to believe, your *doubts* or uncertainties have been *dispelled* (dissipated; driven away).

18. **C** Johnson would not *countenance* (tolerate; approve) such unfair hiring practices.

19. **B** A *toady* (sycophant; flatterer in search of getting favors) is characterized by *obsequiousness* (servile attentiveness).

20. **A** Camus had to fight to *acquire* or gain the culture that was not his by birth (in other words, was not *innate* or inborn).

## Sentence Completion Exercise 3

1. **C** One wouldn't bother to make an insurance claim for *negligible* (small; inconsequential) damage.

2. **D** To have retained so much information is to be *formidably*, awe inspiringly learned.

3. **E** It is *futile* or useless to try to abolish something whose existence is inevitable (unavoidable).

4. **D** To have his work *panned* or harshly criticized would be likely to make a playwright *miserable*.

5. **C** The satellite is off course and is moving *erratically* (irregularly or inconsistently) through space.

6. **D** A *benefactor* by definition is someone who confers benefits or blessings on others.

7. **A** *Though* signals a contrast. In spite of her attempts to be happy, Heidi was unhappy because she *pined* (fruitlessly longed) to be back home.

8. **C** The couple's discovery *raised* or suggested a possibility that further investigation showed to be correct.

9. **B** An overemphasis on correctness that *stifled* or repressed the performers' liveliness would mar or spoil a production.

10. **C** Your background can *condition* or determine your thinking, subtly prejudicing you so that you cannot be truly *impartial* or fair.

11. **C** A *renegade* by definition deserts one allegiance in favor of another.

12. **B** A *patronizing* or condescending attitude may offend others and *eliminate* or rule out the possibility of good relations.

13. **C** To *dismiss* Longfellow in this way is to reject him as unworthy of serious critical consideration.

14. **A** By not specifically stating his wishes, Monteverdi leaves them a mystery. Thus, he is *enigmatic* (mysterious).

15. **B** By definition, *insipid* means lacking flavor. By definition, inane means lacking *sense*.

16. **B** An *affront* (deliberate offense or insult) would clearly *incense* or anger someone.

17. **C** Because the details were *subordinated* or made less important than the building's total design, the building was *unencumbered* (unimpeded; unhampered) by a sense of busyness.

18. **E** To praise things *indiscriminately*, making no distinctions between treasures and trash, is to fail to exercise proper critical selectivity.

19. **B**   To believe, as Strindberg did, that women need to *dominate* or control men, emasculating them, is to be a *misogynist*, a hater of women.

20. **A**   *Erudition* means great learning or scholarship. *Pedantry*, however, is a great show of learning, an excessive attention to petty details that lacks the true scholarly spirit.

## Sentence Completion Exercise 4

1. **C**   A *limited* availability of necessities would put constraints or restrictions on the creatures needing them.

2. **D**   Under such rough conditions, it would be too risky or *precarious* to walk without holding on.

3. **C**   *Though* signals a contrast. Rather than being creative, the eventual publicity campaign was *prosaic* or unimaginative.

4. **C**   To *deny* or refuse to others something you yourself do not need or want is to behave like the proverbial dog-in-the-manger, who did not want to eat the hay in the manger but refused to let the hungry cattle get at it.

5. **E**   If there is no point in bothering with these new facts, they must be insignificant or *trivial*.

6. **C**   Something understood only theoretically or intellectually is known only in the *abstract*.

7. **E**   It is incongruous that it is easier to prove something a fake than it is to prove it *genuine* or real.

8. **D**   When we say historians shed new light on or illuminate the past, we express respect for historians. When Twain observed that the antiquarians (students of ancient things) shed new darkness on the past, he expressed *contempt* or scorn for historians.

9. **A**   *Spontaneous* performances, performances arising from the impulse of the moment, would tend to be fresh or *novel*.

10. **C**   The key word here is "unfortunately." To have rapid economic growth *lead to* the overexploitation or excessive, unjust use of resources and the unfair, *inequitable* sharing of wealth is truly unfortunate.

11. **E**   If she became increasingly militant (aggressively active), then she was not tempered (mellowed) by a spirit of *moderation* or restraint.

12. **E**   If you think that people are motivated only by selfish thoughts of their own advantage, you would be unlikely to believe in the *integrity* or trustworthiness of any *unselfish* motive.

13. **B**   Wapner was not a *pedantic* scholar, fussing about minute points of law.

14. **D**   By definition, a *matrilineal* society, one in which inheritance is determined through the female line, is one in which women have a significant role.

15. **D**   In remarking that few humans could *survive* living in a state of uninterrupted anger, Cose *challenges* or disputes Baldwin's statement about anger as a constant in black American life.

16. **C**   Instead of allowing the exchanges to develop fully, the playwright cuts short or *truncates* them.

17. **D**   By definition, a *tenet* is a belief generally held to be true. Here it is used as a synonym for guiding principle or *creed*.

18. **B**   A sectarian (person who adheres to the beliefs of a particular religious faction) will not tolerate heretical statements, being *sensitive* to creeds. Similarly, this scholar will not tolerate *vague* wording, being *sensitive* to words.

19. **C**   Fisher's work evades or *skirts* classification because it does not fall neatly into set categories.

20. **B**   *Arboreal* means inhabiting or frequenting trees.

# PART IV

# ANALOGY QUESTIONS

# OVERVIEW

To most people, the analogy questions are the ones that stand out when they think about SAT I and the new PSAT. Analogies may well be the most unfamiliar kind of question on the test, but they aren't impossible, and at least some of them will be fairly easy. If you're unfamiliar with this type of question, a sure way for you to boost your SAT I verbal score is for you to get acquainted with the form and content of some typical analogies.

Analogy questions ask you to look at relationships between words. You are given two words, linked by a colon. Think of how the dictionary defines these words. Ask yourself why these words belong together. What connects them? In what context have you seen them together? How are they generally used? Then look for a pair of words among the answer choices that are related in the same way.

Your correct answer choice has got to have the same characteristics as the original pair. The words must have a clear relationship. They must be related *by definition*. Be careful—remember that many words are defined in multiple ways. If you stay alert to the range of possibilities, you'll come up with correct answers, time after time.

# TIPS ON HANDLING ANALOGY QUESTIONS

## TIP 1 SET UP A TEST SENTENCE THAT LINKS THE CAPITALIZED WORDS

Your first step in answering an analogy question is to make a test sentence that defines the two capitalized words and shows how they relate. You must think what each word means and then link them together. It's not that hard to do.

Here's an example for you to try.

CHAPTER : BOOK ::

(A) title : story
(B) paper : page
(C) sentence : essay
(D) tune : melody
(E) act : play

In a short, clear sentence, state the relationship between the two words in capital letters. Then use that sentence to test the words in the answer choices.

A CHAPTER is a major piece of a BOOK.
A *blank* is a major piece of a *blank* .

Now substitute the words in each of the answer choices for the words in capital letters. You should wind up with one pair of words that makes good sense.

(A) A TITLE is a major piece of a STORY.
(B) A PAPER is a major piece of a PAGE.
(C) A SENTENCE is a major piece of an ESSAY.
(D) A TUNE is a major piece of a MELODY.
(E) An ACT is a major piece of a PLAY.

The correct answer is (E). An ACT is a major piece of a PLAY. Or, reversing the word order to make your sentence clearer, just as a BOOK is divided into CHAPTERS, a PLAY is divided into ACTS.

Note that (C), while tempting, is incorrect. A sentence is defined as a grammatically self-contained group of words. While an essay is composed of sentences, a sentence is not *by definition* a major piece of an essay.

## FINE-TUNE YOUR TEST SENTENCE

Sometimes when you set up a test sentence it just doesn't work. More than one answer choice may fit your test sentence, leaving you looking for a way to narrow things down. *No* answer choice may fit your test sentence, leaving you unsure what to try next. In such cases, you need to fine-tune your test sentence, adjusting it till everything works.

When you fine-tune your test sentence, try different approaches. Look for other meanings of the individual words, other ways the words can relate. If more than one answer choice seems to fit, try making your sentence more specific. If *no* answer choice fits, try making your sentence more general.

Here's an example:

MITTEN : HAND ::

(A) belt : leather
(B) ring : finger
(C) muffler : neck
(D) bracelet : clasp
(E) sandal : foot

You set up a test sentence:

You wear a MITTEN on your HAND.
You wear a _ blank _ on your _ blank _ .

Then you see that *several* answer choices could fit your test sentence. You wear a ring on your finger. You wear a muffler on your neck. You wear a sandal on your foot. Your test sentence is too general. It doesn't work.

Ask yourself *why* you wear a mitten on your hand. The answer is,

You wear a MITTEN to keep your HAND warm.

Similarly, you wear a *muffler* to keep your *neck* warm. The correct answer is (C).

## KNOW COMMON ANALOGY PATTERNS

Analogies tend to fall into certain basic patterns. You'll have an easier time coming up with good test sentences for analogy questions if you familiarize yourself with the most common analogy types.

One word of caution. Do not go overboard and try to memorize these analogy types. Just try to get a feel for them, so that you'll be able to recognize how each pair of words is linked.

## Common Analogy Patterns

### Definition

REFUGE : SHELTER
A *refuge* (place of asylum) by definition *shelters.*

### Defining Characteristic

TIGER : CARNIVOROUS
A *tiger* is by definition *carnivorous* or meat eating.

### Class and Member

RODENT : SQUIRREL
A *squirrel* is a member of the *rodent* family.

### Group and Member

WOLF : PACK
A *wolf* is a member of a *pack.*

### Antonyms

WAX : WANE
*Wax,* to grow larger, and *wane,* to dwindle, are opposites.

### Antonym Variants

WILLFUL : OBEDIENCE
*Willful* means lacking in *obedience.*

### Synonyms

NARRATE : TELL
*Narrate* and *tell* are synonyms; they have the same meaning.

### Synonym Variants

VERBOSE : WORDINESS
Someone *verbose* is wordy; he or she exhibits *wordiness.*

### Degree of Intensity

FLURRY : BLIZZARD
A *flurry* or shower of snow is less extreme than a *blizzard.*

### Part to Whole

FINGER : HAND
The *finger* is part of the *hand.*

## Function

BALLAST : STABILITY
*Ballast* provides *stability*.

## Manner

STRUT : WALK
To *strut* is to *walk* in a proud manner.

## Action and Its Significance

WINCE : PAIN
A *wince* is a sign that one feels *pain*.

## Worker and Article Created

POET : SONNET
A *poet* creates a *sonnet*.

## Worker and Tool

PAINTER : BRUSH
A *painter* uses a *brush* to paint.

## Worker and Action

ACROBAT : CARTWHEEL
An *acrobat* performs a *cartwheel*.

## Worker and Workplace

MINER : QUARRY
A *miner* works in a *quarry* or pit.

## Tool and Its Action

CROWBAR : PRY
A *crowbar* is a tool used to *pry* things apart.

## Cause and Effect

VIRUS : INFLUENZA
A *virus* causes *influenza*.

## Sex

DOE : STAG
A *doe* is a female deer; a *stag,* a male deer.

## Age

COLT : STALLION
A *colt* is a young *stallion*.

## Time Sequence

CORONATION : REIGN
The *coronation* precedes the *reign*.

## Spatial Location

CREST : WAVE
The *crest* is the highest point of the *wave*.

## Symbol and Quality It Represents

DOVE : PEACE
A *dove* is the symbol of *peace*.

## TIP 4    WORDS HAVE MANY MEANINGS: STAY ALERT

Watch out for those words that have more than one meaning. *Lie*, for example, can mean *recline*. It can also mean *fib*. Similarly, the noun *minute* means sixty seconds. As an adjective, *minute* (my-NYOOT) can mean very, very small.

Be on the lookout for familiar-looking words defined in unfamiliar ways. Try this example:

PAN : CAMERA ::

(A) ban : book
(B) tune : radio
(C) charge : battery
(D) filter : lens
(E) rotate : periscope

Before you can answer this question, you have to know the definition of *pan*. You're not dealing with a frying pan or a gold miner's pan or a dishpan; *pan* here is a verb, not a noun. You can tell because the first word of each answer choice is also a verb. The verb ending *-ate* at the end of *rotate* gives that away.

The verb *pan*, however, has several meanings:

The miner panned for gold. (The miner washed gravel to separate out the gold.)

The chef panned the carrots. (The chef cooked the carrots in a pan with a small amount of fat or water.)

The critic panned the comedy. (The critic severely criticized the comedy.)

None of these is the meaning you want.

Think how *pan* relates to *camera*. When someone *pans* a *camera*, what happens? The cameraperson rotates the camera on its axis so that he or she can film a panoramic scene (or a moving person or object). Similarly, a submarine crew member *rotates* or revolves a *periscope* on its axis so that he or she can make a panoramic observation. The correct answer is (E).

# ANALOGY EXERCISES

To develop your ability to handle analogy questions, work your way through the following three series of exercises. Warning: These series of exercises are graded in difficulty. The further you go, the harder it gets, just like on a video game. Go all the way. Even if you do less well on Level C than you did on Level A, look on every error as an opportunity to learn. Study all the analogies that you found difficult. Review all the vocabulary words that you didn't know. Remember, these are all typical SAT I analogy types made up of typical SAT I words.

After completing each exercise, see how many questions you answered correctly. (The correct answers are given on page 108.) Then *read those answer explanations*. Pay particular attention to the way the analogies are expressed in clear, concise sentences. Your job is to learn to express these relationships in sentences just as concise and clear.

## ✓LEVEL A

Most high school students feel comfortable answering analogy questions on this level of difficulty. Consider the four practice exercises that follow to be a warm-up for the harder questions to come.

---

Directions: Each question below consists of a related pair of words or phrases, followed by five pairs of words or phrases labeled A through E. Select the pair that best expresses a relationship similar to that expressed in the original pair.

Example:

CRUMB : BREAD ::

(A) ounce : unit
(B) splinter : wood
(C) water : bucket
(D) twine : rope
(E) cream : butter

(A) ● (C) (D) (E)

---

## Exercise 1

1. GRAPEFRUIT : CITRUS ::

   (A) lemon : rind
   (B) tulip : bulb
   (C) mansion : cottage
   (D) product : label
   (E) cat : feline

2. GOLF : CLUB ::

   (A) baseball : team
   (B) hockey : stick
   (C) football : field
   (D) debate : trophy
   (E) swimming : flippers

3. COLANDER : DRAIN ::

   (A) refrigerator : chill
   (B) outlet : plug
   (C) television : watch
   (D) composure : lose
   (E) evidence : collect

4. CERTIFICATE : MARRIAGE ::

   (A) license : permission
   (B) legacy : death
   (C) frame : photograph
   (D) deed : purchase
   (E) advertisement : product

5. HUSK : CORN ::

   (A) pick : grapes
   (B) peel : orange
   (C) plant : wheat
   (D) boil : rice
   (E) slice : pineapple

6. ORGANDY : FABRIC ::

   (A) margin : paper
   (B) branch : tree
   (C) bonnet : hat
   (D) bolt : cloth
   (E) laundry : garment

7. HANG : PICTURE ::

   (A) suspend : service
   (B) admire : view
   (C) limit : observation
   (D) post : notice
   (E) straighten : tie

8. JUROR : PANEL ::

   (A) suitor : rivals
   (B) actor : audience
   (C) player : team
   (D) sculptor : statue
   (E) jewel : setting

9. RETREAT : POSITION ::

   (A) retire : resignation
   (B) vacate : opening
   (C) overhaul : equipment
   (D) withdraw : agreement
   (E) explore : territory

10. SPINE : CACTUS ::

    (A) backbone : vertebra
    (B) petal : rose
    (C) quill : porcupine
    (D) swamp : alligator
    (E) root : evergreen

11. PHARMACIST : DRUGS ::

    (A) dentist : drills
    (B) electrician : wires
    (C) consumer : merchandise
    (D) detective : clues
    (E) optician : lenses

12. PODIUM : SPEECH ::

    (A) bench : judge
    (B) newspaper : editorial
    (C) tedium : lecture
    (D) preface : book
    (E) pulpit : sermon

13. OUTLAST : ENDURANCE ::

    (A) outshout : anger
    (B) outgrow : clothing
    (C) outstrip : turbulence
    (D) outsmart : cleverness
    (E) outweigh : judgment

14. ETERNAL : END ::

    (A) astronomical : star
    (B) purposeful : goal
    (C) conclusive : argument
    (D) amorphous : form
    (E) peripheral : border

15. STILTED : SPEECH ::

    (A) peckish : appetite
    (B) wooden : movement
    (C) standard : dialect
    (D) colloquial : jargon
    (E) slanted : bias

16. COMPANION-WAY : LADDER ::

    (A) porthole : window
    (B) banister : staircase
    (C) highway : barrier
    (D) building : fire escape
    (E) friendship : elopement

17. CENSUS : POPULATION ::

(A) limit : expansion
(B) assessment : tax
(C) catalog : collection
(D) authority : government
(E) review : performance

18. ENLARGE : SCOPE ::

(A) clarify : viewpoint
(B) measure : extent
(C) protract : duration
(D) overburden : capacity
(E) reflect : vision

19. INDEMNIFY : REIMBURSEMENT ::

(A) intimidate : resistance
(B) refuse : shipment
(C) vaccinate : immunization
(D) contradict : corroboration
(E) condemn : building

20. UNGAINLY : GRACE ::

(A) unsightly : vision
(B) unruly : discipline
(C) unseemly : attitude
(D) unlikely : symmetry
(E) untimely : death

# Exercise 2

1. SLICE : BREAD ::

(A) yolk : egg
(B) strip : bacon
(C) muffin : wheat
(D) glass : goblet
(E) orange : fruit

2. TOWEL : RACK ::

(A) napkin : stack
(B) coat : hook
(C) stove : burner
(D) rung : ladder
(E) curtain : window

3. PIT : PEACH ::

(A) slice : watermelon
(B) rind : orange
(C) stone : cherry
(D) vine : grape
(E) stem : apple

4. TUTOR : STUDENT ::

(A) captain : team
(B) prosecutor : juror
(C) guide : tourist
(D) actor : audience
(E) dentist : hygienist

5. HANG : WALLPAPER ::

(A) strip : paint
(B) lay : carpet
(C) air : mattress
(D) clean : chimney
(E) cut : paste

6. CARTOONIST : COMIC STRIP ::

(A) editor : text
(B) actor : stage
(C) artist : palette
(D) ventriloquist : dummy
(E) composer : tune

7. CROCK : CONTAINER ::

(A) lid : jar
(B) mop : bucket
(C) jeep : vehicle
(D) marble : sculpture
(E) seed : plant

8. TWINE : ROPE ::

(A) bolt : cloth
(B) ladder : wood
(C) belt : apron
(D) twig : bough
(E) bead : string

9. REFEREE : OFFICIATE ::

(A) subject : govern
(B) opposition : eliminate
(C) chairperson : preside
(D) secretary : dictate
(E) umpire : compete

10. DAREDEVIL : RASH ::

(A) dullard : bookish
(B) infant : cranky
(C) braggart : modest
(D) trickster : deceitful
(E) laughingstock : witty

11. FLUTE : FLAUTIST ::

(A) symphony : conductor
(B) harp : harpsichord
(C) kettledrum : tympanist
(D) lute : madrigalist
(E) taps : bugler

12. INVENTORY : MERCHANDISE ::

(A) patent : device
(B) revenue : wealth
(C) pharmacy : prescription
(D) promontory : height
(E) roster : players

13. DECK : ORNAMENTS ::

(A) equip : paraphernalia
(B) furnish : references
(C) safeguard : valuables
(D) salvage : remains
(E) pack : belongings

14. REAM : PAPER ::

(A) medley : song
(B) pitcher : milk
(C) cord : wood
(D) pane : glass
(E) ear : corn

15. LAUGH : GUFFAW ::

(A) sing : hum
(B) cry : whimper
(C) smile : amuse
(D) applaud : heckle
(E) speak : bellow

16. LITTER : KITTENS ::

(A) sty : pigs
(B) brood : chickens
(C) kennel : dogs
(D) herd : cattle
(E) fertilizer : plants

17. GLIMPSE : BRIEF ::

(A) courtship : swift
(B) observation : furtive
(C) guess : accurate
(D) hope : genuine
(E) stare : fixed

18. FRACTURE : BONE ::

(A) cast : leg
(B) graft : wood
(C) orbit : planet
(D) lava : volcano
(E) schism : church

19. EPISODIC : CONTINUITY ::

(A) lengthy : durability
(B) cinematic : authority
(C) ambiguous : clarity
(D) theatrical : performance
(E) spectacular : flamboyance

20. CHURLISH : BREEDING ::

(A) mulish : stubbornness
(B) foolish : consistency
(C) boorish : sensitivity
(D) oafish : affluence
(E) loutish : servility

## Exercise 3

1. MUSICIAN : SYMPHONY ::

(A) conductor : orchestra
(B) comedian : nightclub
(C) anchor : newsroom
(D) actor : play
(E) brigand : band

2. SAGE : HERB ::

(A) leaf : tree
(B) bud : flower
(C) poodle : dog
(D) salt : meal
(E) rose : bouquet

3. SKIT : PLAY ::

(A) quiz : examination
(B) injury : scar
(C) detour : journey
(D) ambush : retreat
(E) accompanist : recital

4. GRAIN : SAND ::

(A) texture : wood
(B) wave : water
(C) flake : snow
(D) drop : bucket
(E) grit : oil

5. THANKFUL : INGRATITUDE ::

   (A) despotic : tyranny
   (B) fashionable : snobbery
   (C) hopeful : despair
   (D) melancholy : gloom
   (E) pessimistic : rejection

6. QUAKE : FEAR ::

   (A) shiver : omen
   (B) tremble : earth
   (C) shake : indifference
   (D) wriggle : dread
   (E) shudder : horror

7. SWARM : BEES ::

   (A) sheaf : wheat
   (B) sliver : crumbs
   (C) sting : wasps
   (D) school : fish
   (E) strip : bacon

8. TORNADO : WIND ::

   (A) whirlpool : current
   (B) current : electricity
   (C) dune : sand
   (D) fan : breeze
   (E) levee : river

9. CONSTRUCT : EDIFICE ::

   (A) raze : building
   (B) fabricate : lie
   (C) invent : patent
   (D) exaggerate : effect
   (E) correct : flaw

10. DEMONSTRABLE : SHOWN ::

    (A) malleable : shaped
    (B) insufferable : discouraged
    (C) hypothetical : refuted
    (D) exhausted : replenished
    (E) communicable : quarantined

11. MOUNT : ASSAULT ::

    (A) scale : ladder
    (B) launch : campaign
    (C) increase : donation
    (D) conclude : speech
    (E) cease : hostilities

12. ANTHOLOGY : WRITINGS ::

    (A) thesaurus : questions
    (B) bibliography : indexes
    (C) sampler : delicacies
    (D) chronology : topics
    (E) poem : stanzas

13. HAMPER : LAUNDRY ::

    (A) cabinet : wood
    (B) dryer : clothespins
    (C) cooler : picnic
    (D) pail : mop
    (E) coffer : valuables

14. KNIT : NEEDLE ::

    (A) embroider : hoop
    (B) stitch : thread
    (C) macrame : belt
    (D) crochet : hook
    (E) weave : yarn

15. ETCH : GLASS ::

    (A) smash : pottery
    (B) hem : fabric
    (C) stretch : rubber
    (D) tattoo : skin
    (E) fold : paper

16. FURY : EMOTION ::

    (A) vice : instinct
    (B) hunger : drive
    (C) digression : path
    (D) color : spectrum
    (E) grief : memory

17. SYMPATHETIC : COMPASSION ::

    (A) honorable : infamy
    (B) miserable : hate
    (C) confident : fear
    (D) aghast : horror
    (E) brazen : indifference

18. PALM : VICTORY ::

    (A) date : sugar
    (B) harvest : faith
    (C) forearm : strength
    (D) cornucopia : abundance
    (E) palliation : defeat

19. MOPE : UNHAPPINESS ::

(A) smirk : nervousness
(B) sulk : petulance
(C) ogle : friendliness
(D) cope : confidence
(E) josh : seriousness

20. CHARLATAN : KNOWLEDGE ::

(A) hypocrite : virtue
(B) masquerade : disguise
(C) pseudonym : identity
(D) swindler : fraud
(E) dupe : deceit

## Exercise 4

1. PARK : CAR ::

(A) submerge : submarine
(B) launch : satellite
(C) dock : ship
(D) saddle : horse
(E) pedal : bicycle

2. HEAD : CAULIFLOWER ::

(A) seed : wheat
(B) petal : rose
(C) eye : potato
(D) ear : corn
(E) stem : tomato

3. WAGON : CARAVAN ::

(A) track : train
(B) lifeboat : steamship
(C) photograph : album
(D) float : parade
(E) route : procession

4. THOROUGHBRED : HORSE ::

(A) prolific : rabbit
(B) independent : cat
(C) timid : deer
(D) sterile : mule
(E) pedigreed : dog

5. TWEEZERS : PLUCK ::

(A) guitar : strum
(B) goose : peck
(C) lipstick : smear
(D) wheelbarrow : convey
(E) doorbell : connect

6. CLATTER : POTS ::

(A) shatter : windowpane
(B) rustle : leaves
(C) wrinkle : clothes
(D) stack : dishes
(E) collect : coins

7. MUZZLE : BITE ::

(A) saddle : ride
(B) gag : speak
(C) collar : choke
(D) whip : obey
(E) tether : stay

8. DOWNY : SOFTNESS ::

(A) bulky : lightness
(B) wispy : quietness
(C) sickly : sweetness
(D) risky : trickiness
(E) silky : smoothness

9. ON-RAMP : HIGHWAY ::

(A) aisle : airplane
(B) gangway : ship
(C) curb : road
(D) toll : tunnel
(E) crash : speedway

10. DECIBEL : VOLUME ::

(A) foot : length
(B) earthquake : magnitude
(C) silence : noise
(D) chimes : harmony
(E) scale : weight

11. TRAILER : SCREEN ::

(A) poster : billboard
(B) sidecar : motorcycle
(C) automobile : windshield
(D) vine : trellis
(E) clipping : film

12. PETITION : ASK ::

(A) narrate : tell
(B) refuse : request
(C) whisper : state
(D) intimidate : hint
(E) classify : risk

13. CEASE-FIRE : FIGHTING ::

    (A) alimony : divorce
    (B) skirmish : battle
    (C) recess : proceedings
    (D) applause : catcalls
    (E) ashes : blaze

14. STAND : WITNESS ::

    (A) brief : lawyer
    (B) evidence : juror
    (C) ruling : judge
    (D) dock : prisoner
    (E) alibi : criminal

15. SENSITIVE : DISTRESS ::

    (A) submissive : master
    (B) repulsive : disgust
    (C) gullible : upset
    (D) arrogant : impress
    (E) sympathetic : condemn

16. PLOW : FURROW ::

    (A) scatter : seed
    (B) paint : wall
    (C) bore : hole
    (D) haul : barrow
    (E) cultivate : soil

17. PIQUE : RAGE ::

    (A) thrift : parsimony
    (B) warmth : cordiality
    (C) intemperance : moderation
    (D) rash : irritation
    (E) lethargy : indifference

18. DILEMMA : PERPLEXITY ::

    (A) comedy : amusement
    (B) alternative : argument
    (C) secrecy : trepidation
    (D) tact : indiscretion
    (E) folly : deliberation

19. DISCURSIVE : FOCUS ::

    (A) argumentative : thesis
    (B) meandering : journey
    (C) expository : clarity
    (D) verbose : brevity
    (E) narrative : detail

20. PROCESSION : FORMAL ::

    (A) march : rapid
    (B) hike : brief
    (C) saunter : leisurely
    (D) migration : annual
    (E) stroll : rural

## Level B

Most high school students have some difficulty answering analogy questions on this level. Consider the four practice exercises that follow to be a good sample of the mid-range analogy questions you will face on SAT I.

---

Directions: Each question below consists of a related pair of words or phrases, followed by five pairs of words or phrases labeled A through E. Select the pair that best expresses a relationship similar to that expressed in the original pair.

Example:

CRUMB : BREAD ::

(A) ounce : unit
(B) splinter : wood
(C) water : bucket
(D) twine : rope
(E) cream : butter

# Exercise 1

1. BLEACHERS : GYMNASIUM ::

    (A) detergents : laundromat
    (B) scoreboard : ballpark
    (C) pews : church
    (D) aisles : theater
    (E) laps : track

2. PERFORMANCE : REHEARSAL ::

    (A) improvisation : memorization
    (B) itinerary : journey
    (C) cinema : stage
    (D) parade : drill
    (E) work : vacation

3. BLADES : ICE SKATES ::

    (A) laces : boots
    (B) runners : sled
    (C) bumpers : automobile
    (D) stripes : sneakers
    (E) boots : skis

4. MUSSEL : SHELLFISH ::

    (A) bushel : wheat
    (B) statue : marble
    (C) flock : sheep
    (D) snake : reptile
    (E) cub : bear

5. BED : GARDEN ::

    (A) hammock : campsite
    (B) exhibit : gallery
    (C) plot : cemetery
    (D) patio : lawn
    (E) foundation : house

6. MIGRAINE : HEAD ::

    (A) vertebra : neck
    (B) cast : leg
    (C) diaphragm : lungs
    (D) heartburn : stomach
    (E) wart : finger

7. CONDENSE : COMPACT ::

    (A) evaporate : moist
    (B) describe : concise
    (C) distend : soft
    (D) refine : pure
    (E) contract : ill

8. CATCHY : TUNE ::

    (A) memorable : slogan
    (B) intermittent : rain
    (C) staccato : rhythm
    (D) successful : film
    (E) matchless : performance

9. HUBBUB : NOISY ::

    (A) tumult : dangerous
    (B) killjoy : talkative
    (C) blackball : objectionable
    (D) free-for-all : wild
    (E) razzle-dazzle : sudden

10. FLAX : LINEN ::

    (A) sand : glass
    (B) palm : tree
    (C) window : curtain
    (D) spool : thread
    (E) wax : linoleum

11. PASTEURIZE : FOOD ::

    (A) sterilize : heat
    (B) recirculate : water
    (C) fumigate : area
    (D) illuminate : light
    (E) vaccinate : immunity

12. FIB : LIE ::

    (A) kneel : recline
    (B) quibble : complain
    (C) regret : admonish
    (D) evade : pursue
    (E) convince : mislead

13. COPIOUS : SCARCE ::

    (A) expeditious : slow
    (B) intermittent : occasional
    (C) ambitious : earnest
    (D) durable : massive
    (E) extinct : rare

14. SPRUCE UP : CLOTHING ::

    (A) discard : leftovers
    (B) store : belongings
    (C) publish : books
    (D) purchase : furniture
    (E) tidy : room

15. ABSCOND : DEPART ::

    (A) eavesdrop : listen
    (B) abstain : indulge
    (C) blunder : rectify
    (D) flee : escape
    (E) invest : speculate

16. HEINOUS : INIQUITY ::

    (A) conspicuous : invisibility
    (B) egregious : excellence
    (C) ingenuous : innocence
    (D) notable : benevolence
    (E) notorious : levity

17. BEES : APIARY ::

    (A) silkworms : silk
    (B) caterpillar : moth
    (C) geese : gaggle
    (D) snakes : herpetology
    (E) rabbits : hutch

18. DECOROUS : PROPRIETY ::

    (A) ornate : simplicity
    (B) fashionable : attire
    (C) insignificant : timidity
    (D) masterful : munificence
    (E) reserved : reticence

19. IMPLACABLE : APPEASE ::

    (A) inexplicable : explain
    (B) imperceptible : bother
    (C) intolerable : fear
    (D) interminable : begin
    (E) immobile : alarm

20. EVANESCENT : PERMANENCE ::

    (A) glittering : radiance
    (B) fleeting : timorousness
    (C) wealthy : affluence
    (D) desultory : methodicalness
    (E) gleaming : iridescence

## Exercise 2

1. SNOW : MELTS ::

    (A) rain : falls
    (B) glass : shatters
    (C) dew : evaporates
    (D) moisture : spreads
    (E) ice : gleams

2. BLANKET : WARMTH ::

    (A) drink : thirst
    (B) cottage : house
    (C) furnace : thermostat
    (D) lamp : illumination
    (E) bed : slumber

3. ORTHODONTIST : TEETH ::

    (A) scalp : hair
    (B) cranium : head
    (C) pediatrician : health
    (D) dermatologist : skin
    (E) surgeon : scalpel

4. BLINDFOLD : VISION ::

    (A) cane : motion
    (B) bandage : wound
    (C) gag : speech
    (D) megaphone : hearing
    (E) fog : highway

5. GRAIN : MARBLE ::

    (A) splinter : wood
    (B) surface : earth
    (C) texture : fabric
    (D) cardboard : paper
    (E) mine : ore

6. BOOK : FLIGHT ::

    (A) list : departure
    (B) plan : escape
    (C) reserve : table
    (D) determine : priority
    (E) publish : schedule

7. MUDDLE : UNTIDY ::

    (A) appearance : disheveled
    (B) huddle : unfriendly
    (C) riddle : insoluble
    (D) snarl : tangled
    (E) cottage : filthy

8. STOCK : AQUARIUM ::

    (A) drain : tank
    (B) furnish : apartment
    (C) inspect : hospital
    (D) purchase : birdcage
    (E) scour : kennel

9. SAW : TEETH ::

(A) map : chart
(B) fork : tines
(C) camera : film
(D) floss : dentures
(E) garden : shrubbery

10. ANARCHIC : ORDER ::

(A) aimless : purpose
(B) meticulous : detail
(C) warped : distortion
(D) authoritative : command
(E) indifferent : regularity

11. SEEDY : APPEARANCE ::

(A) run-down : health
(B) fruitful : harvest
(C) threadbare : poverty
(D) wistful : glance
(E) seemly : behavior

12. PATRICIAN : ARISTOCRACY ::

(A) professor : faculty
(B) peasant : feudalism
(C) father : parenthood
(D) commoner : sense
(E) fascist : democracy

13. ABYSS : GULLY ::

(A) rice : grain
(B) mountain : trail
(C) drizzle : fog
(D) tidal wave : ripple
(E) thunderstorm : cloud

14. INSURMOUNTABLE : DISADVANTAGE ::

(A) impermeable : water
(B) indomitable : defeat
(C) interminable : tedium
(D) inevitable : drawback
(E) insuperable : barrier

15. CLAP : THUNDER ::

(A) applause : performance
(B) clatter : noise
(C) river : waterfall
(D) report : explosion
(E) tap : windstorm

16. HOARY : YOUTHFULNESS ::

(A) somnolent : alertness
(B) evanescent : transience
(C) tractable : submissiveness
(D) energetic : vigor
(E) innovative : currency

17. PENITENT : CONTRITE ::

(A) pragmatist : prompt
(B) hedonist : apologetic
(C) skeptic : arrogant
(D) stoic : remorseful
(E) zealot : fanatical

18. QUIP : WITTY ::

(A) outburst : tentative
(B) proverb : original
(C) quibble : petty
(D) epithet : appropriate
(E) quarrel : irreconcilable

19. STAMPS : PHILATELIST ::

(A) museum : curator
(B) words : grammarian
(C) coins : numismatist
(D) donations : altruist
(E) gold : miser

20. EXTRACT : QUAGMIRE ::

(A) condense : fog
(B) purify : essence
(C) fertilize : acreage
(D) release : incarceration
(E) uproot : sycamore

## Exercise 3

1. HEAP : SNOW ::

(A) icicle : ice
(B) dam : water
(C) drizzle : rain
(D) stack : hay
(E) bed : flowers

2. ANT : COLONY ::

(A) goose : flock
(B) bee : industry
(C) farmer : field
(D) government : assembly
(E) pygmy : giant

3. COTTAGE : MANSION ::

    (A) jet : helicopter
    (B) necklace : diamond
    (C) compact : limousine
    (D) library : museum
    (E) wing : building

4. MUTTON : SHEEP ::

    (A) kennel : dog
    (B) udder : cow
    (C) gander : goose
    (D) veal : calf
    (E) colt : horse

5. SCRIBE : WRITE ::

    (A) glutton : eat
    (B) minstrel : sing
    (C) seer : worry
    (D) mason : strike
    (E) admiral : obey

6. ECSTATIC : JOYFUL ::

    (A) seemly : proper
    (B) exuberant : melancholy
    (C) despairing : discouraged
    (D) marked : significant
    (E) emotional : spiritual

7. BEE : BEEHIVE ::

    (A) fly : flyspeck
    (B) moth : cocoon
    (C) termite : nest
    (D) sheep : fleece
    (E) horse : saddle

8. UPROOT : TREE ::

    (A) upset : equilibrium
    (B) outstrip : rival
    (C) dissect : specimen
    (D) extract : tooth
    (E) extricate : snare

9. SATISFY : CRAVING ::

    (A) quench : thirst
    (B) appreciate : desire
    (C) acknowledge : benefactor
    (D) demur : objection
    (E) convince : opinion

10. RECRUITER : ENLISTMENT ::

    (A) student : enrollment
    (B) salesperson : purchase
    (C) physician : certification
    (D) banker : embezzlement
    (E) witness : testimony

11. JERK : SUDDEN ::

    (A) shove : forcible
    (B) footwork : smooth
    (C) error : hasty
    (D) stumble : foolish
    (E) nudge : inquisitive

12. STERN : LENIENCY ::

    (A) angry : annoyance
    (B) willing : ambition
    (C) impertinent : reluctance
    (D) harsh : authority
    (E) grave : frivolity

13. MUSEUM : GALLERY ::

    (A) aquarium : fish
    (B) hospital : ward
    (C) library : book
    (D) boutique : merchandise
    (E) station : train

14. EXTRICATE : ENTANGLEMENT ::

    (A) release : confinement
    (B) unfold : relationship
    (C) engross : involvement
    (D) extrapolate : argument
    (E) assume : subterfuge

15. ROLL : WALLPAPER ::

    (A) bolt : cloth
    (B) brush : paint
    (C) floor : carpet
    (D) archway : door
    (E) string : parcel

16. PANHANDLER : MONEY ::

    (A) volunteer : expertise
    (B) investor : profit
    (C) cobbler : shoe
    (D) pollster : opinion
    (E) heretic : faith

17. ENSLAVE : LIBERTY ::

(A) disenfranchise : vote
(B) entitle : autonomy
(C) segregate : race
(D) deny : equality
(E) emancipate : independence

18. FLYSPECK : MINUTE ::

(A) splotch : irregular
(B) runway : long
(C) mothball : clean
(D) anthill : crowded
(E) crease : smooth

19. MALCONTENT : GRUMBLE ::

(A) spendthrift : squander
(B) desperado : snarl
(C) pessimist : compromise
(D) mutineer : endure
(E) deadbeat : pay

20. HIDEBOUND : FLEXIBILITY ::

(A) concrete : tangibility
(B) mercurial : stability
(C) concealed : determination
(D) destined : opportunity
(E) resolute : indifference

## Exercise 4

1. SHEET : PAPER ::

(A) lumber : wood
(B) pane : glass
(C) page : book
(D) lightbulb : lamp
(E) hem : fabric

2. STEERING WHEEL : AUTOMOBILE ::

(A) propeller : plane
(B) chassis : truck
(C) rudder : ship
(D) tire pump : bicycle
(E) road sign : highway

3. BAKE : SOUFFLE ::

(A) parch : moisture
(B) simmer : kettle
(C) boil : porridge
(D) pan : performance
(E) grill : suspect

4. GRAPES : WINE ::

(A) flock : sheep
(B) corn : stalk
(C) farm : church
(D) tree : paper
(E) oil : drum

5. MEGAPHONE : SPEAK ::

(A) dictaphone : write
(B) lever : pry
(C) pillow : sleep
(D) telephone : answer
(E) metronome : tick

6. DEFLATE : AIR ::

(A) erode : soil
(B) deplete : dearth
(C) dehydrate : water
(D) muffle : engine
(E) crush : rock

7. SOAPBOX : ORATOR ::

(A) coffin : mourner
(B) pulpit : preacher
(C) gavel : judge
(D) rehearsal : actor
(E) bucket : janitor

8. CREASES : PAPER ::

(A) shrinkage : surface
(B) planks : wood
(C) ripples : laughter
(D) furrows : brow
(E) throngs : people

9. APPRAISER : BUILDING ::

(A) artist : masterpiece
(B) critic : book
(C) miser : gold
(D) tailor : suit
(E) judge : courtroom

10. SPAT : QUARREL ::

(A) battle : hostility
(B) rudeness : injury
(C) grounds : enmity
(D) quibble : objection
(E) faction : rivalry

11. FOOTING : SECURE ::

   (A) vision : impaired
   (B) grasp : firm
   (C) sympathy : hopeful
   (D) path : meandering
   (E) energy : exuberant

12. JITTERY : FIDGET ::

   (A) foolish : weep
   (B) touchy : snap
   (C) drowsy : lull
   (D) mulish : roam
   (E) cranky : excite

13. DOOR : BUILDING ::

   (A) hatch : plane
   (B) porthole : boat
   (C) lumber : construction
   (D) dashboard : car
   (E) trunk : tree

14. WILLFUL : OBEDIENCE ::

   (A) careful : caution
   (B) joyous : ecstasy
   (C) tuneful : harmony
   (D) fretful : patience
   (E) outspoken : candor

15. COMPACT : POWDER ::

   (A) dustpan : dirt
   (B) pipeline : oil
   (C) lightbulb : electricity
   (D) stack : lumber
   (E) flask : liquor

16. MOOR : SHIP ::

   (A) tether : horse
   (B) hover : helicopter
   (C) sterilize : surgery
   (D) renovate : building
   (E) refuel : airplane

17. BRUSQUE : ABRUPTNESS ::

   (A) arrogant : haste
   (B) momentous : swiftness
   (C) servile : obsequiousness
   (D) benevolent : ingratitude
   (E) bankrupt : generosity

18. BAND : NOMAD ::

   (A) orchestra : conductor
   (B) colony : artist
   (C) handcuff : prisoner
   (D) ward : patient
   (E) tepee : warrior

19. BARNACLE : HULL ::

   (A) tick : skin
   (B) sail : mast
   (C) cottage : house
   (D) hangar : plane
   (E) tomato : stem

20. INADVERTENT : ERROR ::

   (A) inauspicious : omen
   (B) inherent : defect
   (C) unintended : slight
   (D) irreparable : damage
   (E) unfortunate : mistake

## LEVEL C 

Most high school students have trouble answering many analogy questions on this level of difficulty. Consider the four practice exercises that follow to be a chance for you to acquaint yourself with the toughest sorts of analogy questions that occur on SAT I.

<u>Directions:</u> Each question below consists of a related pair of words or phrases, followed by five pairs of words or phrases labeled A through E. Select the pair that <u>best</u> expresses a relationship similar to that expressed in the original pair.

Example:

CRUMB : BREAD ::

(A) ounce : unit
(B) splinter : wood
(C) water : bucket
(D) twine : rope
(E) cream : butter

Ⓐ ● Ⓒ Ⓓ Ⓔ

## Exercise 1

1. CLUSTER : GRAPES ::

    (A) jam : cherries
    (B) crate : oranges
    (C) vineyard : wine
    (D) bunch : bananas
    (E) oak : acorns

2. ALGAE : POND ::

    (A) ink : stamp pad
    (B) wax : linoleum
    (C) moss : tree trunk
    (D) moisture : sponge
    (E) fertilizer : garden

3. HYMN : SONG ::

    (A) prayer : silence
    (B) sermon : address
    (C) lullaby : slumber
    (D) procession : cadence
    (E) pulpit : church

4. EAGLE : SWOOP ::

    (A) salmon : spawn
    (B) beaver : gnaw
    (C) sheep : shear
    (D) panther : spring
    (E) raven : croak

5. SHAMBLES : ORDERLY ::

    (A) meadow : rolling
    (B) pathway : direct
    (C) rubble : fragmentary
    (D) pigsty : clean
    (E) shed : ramshackle

6. CLINCH : DEAL ::

    (A) inaugurate : campaign
    (B) reduce : price
    (C) settle : argument
    (D) suggest : trade
    (E) debate : issue

7. TAP : SAP ::

(A) pinch : skin
(B) draw : blood
(C) chop : tree
(D) pour : milk
(E) purify : air

8. HILT : DAGGER ::

(A) heft : axe
(B) handle : trowel
(C) sheath : sword
(D) blade : knife
(E) eye : needle

9. DIN : LOUD ::

(A) ambush : silent
(B) skirmish : fierce
(C) flood : sudden
(D) mob : unruly
(E) detour : lengthy

10. QUERULOUS : GRUMBLE ::

(A) precarious : risk
(B) malevolent : curse
(C) mutable : endure
(D) garrulous : talk
(E) pensive : disregard

11. BRISTLE : ANGER ::

(A) shave : tidiness
(B) pose : arrogance
(C) sneer : petulance
(D) cavil : acquiescence
(E) cower : fear

12. QUARRY : LIMESTONE ::

(A) journey : goal
(B) well : oil
(C) girder : steel
(D) ream : paper
(E) flask : liquor

13. SKETCH : REVUE ::

(A) tracing : outline
(B) audition : role
(C) essay : anthology
(D) caricature : portrait
(E) performance : stage

14. ALLAY : FEAR ::

(A) slake : thirst
(B) allege : attack
(C) appall : horror
(D) inspire : dread
(E) alarm : threat

15. CIRCUMSPECT : CONSEQUENCES ::

(A) wary : dangers
(B) prudent : squeamishness
(C) cautious : plans
(D) roundabout : aims
(E) circumstantial : evidence

16. CRAVEN : COURAGE ::

(A) impotent : power
(B) venerable : reverence
(C) overwhelming : force
(D) credulous : truth
(E) sagacious : wisdom

17. QUANDARY : SOLUTION ::

(A) cause : effect
(B) impasse : traffic
(C) captive : escape
(D) chemical : compound
(E) maze : exit

18. IMPECUNIOUS : HOVEL ::

(A) mendacious : cell
(B) prosperous : mansion
(C) affluent : tent
(D) indigent : castle
(E) defenseless : fortress

19. SURREPTITIOUS : STEALTH ::

(A) basic : superficiality
(B) profound : facetiousness
(C) obsequious : servility
(D) fugitive : robbery
(E) superfluous : dearth

20. ACROPHOBIA : HEIGHTS ::

(A) hydrophobia : dogs
(B) agoraphobia : crowds
(C) kleptomania : valuables
(D) claustrophobia : shelter
(E) arachnophobia : snakes

## Exercise 2

1. HOOF : CAMEL ::

    (A) tail : squirrel
    (B) paw : dog
    (C) mane : lion
    (D) wing : pigeon
    (E) horn : rhinoceros

2. ROLL : THUNDER ::

    (A) velocity : wind
    (B) cloud : fog
    (C) valley : mountain
    (D) rumble : traffic
    (E) droplet : rain

3. MAGICIAN : CONJURE ::

    (A) acrobat : slip
    (B) prophet : predict
    (C) actor : rehearse
    (D) professor : recite
    (E) thief : confess

4. BOOK : RESERVATION ::

    (A) place : order
    (B) state : qualification
    (C) inscribe : acknowledgment
    (D) educate : institution
    (E) cancel : restriction

5. PLANE : SMOOTH ::

    (A) ship : founder
    (B) motorcycle : swerve
    (C) cube : measure
    (D) road : widen
    (E) saw : cut

6. TRANSLATE : INTERPRETER ::

    (A) prosecute : culprit
    (B) edit : reviewer
    (C) officiate : philosopher
    (D) jeer : laughingstock
    (E) expurgate : censor

7. THIN-SKINNED : INSULT ::

    (A) strong-minded : resist
    (B) hot-blooded : distract
    (C) hard-nosed : offend
    (D) weak-willed : sway
    (E) thick-headed : convince

8. UNLIMITED : ACCESS ::

    (A) unfettered : chains
    (B) interminable : monotony
    (C) unrestricted : entry
    (D) circular : argument
    (E) wide : border

9. EXCAVATE : TUNNEL ::

    (A) collect : fossil
    (B) burrow : hole
    (C) fill : cavity
    (D) pour : foundation
    (E) drill : oil

10. CLUMP : WEEDS ::

    (A) seed : grass
    (B) stem : roots
    (C) stand : trees
    (D) basket : fruit
    (E) clipper : hair

11. PORTFOLIO : PAPERS ::

    (A) blueprint : sketches
    (B) quiver : arrows
    (C) sampler : threads
    (D) roof : rafters
    (E) prototype : copies

12. ABATE : STORM ::

    (A) interrupt : conversation
    (B) devastate : cyclone
    (C) withstand : outburst
    (D) peak : flood
    (E) relax : pressure

13. SYLLABUS : COURSE ::

    (A) title page : text
    (B) entry : dictionary
    (C) space bar : keyboard
    (D) flow chart : procedure
    (E) result : competition

14. BOLT : FOOD ::

    (A) lock : door
    (B) race : automobile
    (C) preserve : rations
    (D) guzzle : beverage
    (E) stockpile : supplies

15. POACHER : GAME ::

    (A) traitor : country
    (B) competitor : contest
    (C) pickpocket : wallet
    (D) commuter : train
    (E) composer : melody

16. PLUMAGE : FEATHERS ::

    (A) foliage : leaves
    (B) coat : furs
    (C) sorcery : charms
    (D) pillow : down
    (E) courage : deeds

17. CISTERN : WATER ::

    (A) furrow : earth
    (B) official : power
    (C) tank : oxygen
    (D) museum : antiquity
    (E) conflagration : fire

18. DISOBEDIENT : COMPLIANCE ::

    (A) lethargic : listlessness
    (B) inconsistent : dependability
    (C) haughty : elaboration
    (D) reverent : innocence
    (E) taciturn : solemnity

19. APPLAUD : APPROBATION ::

    (A) wince : boredom
    (B) jeer : derision
    (C) sneer : apathy
    (D) hiss : apprehension
    (E) cheer : ambivalence

20. CREDULOUS : BELIEVE ::

    (A) elusive : imply
    (B) discreet : warn
    (C) intrepid : fear
    (D) trustworthy : confide
    (E) censorious : criticize

# Exercise 3

1. RECITAL : MUSICIAN ::

    (A) easel : artist
    (B) exhibition : sculptor
    (C) program : announcer
    (D) wares : peddler
    (E) commercial : advertiser

2. PICTURE : FRAME ::

    (A) egg : shell
    (B) window : pane
    (C) diamond : setting
    (D) portrait : canvas
    (E) lamp : shade

3. CLEAR : FOREST ::

    (A) open : door
    (B) plant : bulb
    (C) wash : car
    (D) shave : hair
    (E) free : prisoner

4. BUOY : SHIP ::

    (A) radar : obstruction
    (B) steering wheel : automobile
    (C) paddle : canoe
    (D) bell : channel
    (E) runway light : plane

5. BULLET : RICOCHET ::

    (A) revolver : fire
    (B) sword : wound
    (C) ball : bounce
    (D) rifle : load
    (E) gunpowder : pour

6. PACKRAT : ACCUMULATE ::

    (A) speculator : disburse
    (B) pickpocket : catch
    (C) miser : hoard
    (D) blackguard : steal
    (E) nomad : retreat

7. ALLEVIATE : CURE ::

    (A) hinder : help
    (B) annul : create
    (C) retard : stop
    (D) eliminate : avoid
    (E) squander : hoard

8. TEPID : BOILING ::

    (A) leisurely : plodding
    (B) insufferable : emphatic
    (C) content : dispassionate
    (D) icy : blazing
    (E) swollen : inflated

9. CONGLOMERATE : COMPANY ::

   (A) brokerage : commission
   (B) deed : purchaser
   (C) university : school
   (D) conspiracy : partnership
   (E) truce : army

10. EPICURE : FOOD ::

   (A) chef : pastry
   (B) connoisseur : art
   (C) professional : salary
   (D) gourmet : gluttony
   (E) fanatic : religion

11. DOWEL : POLE ::

   (A) gangway : plank
   (B) redwood : tree
   (C) chandelier : ceiling
   (D) foundation : house
   (E) twig : branch

12. CONDUIT : FLOW ::

   (A) trench : wallow
   (B) chute : slide
   (C) tide : recede
   (D) canal : connect
   (E) sparrow : fly

13. SPEECH : EXTEMPORANEOUS ::

   (A) dance : graceful
   (B) drawing : freehand
   (C) report : controversial
   (D) tune : syncopated
   (E) architecture : modern

14. DAUNTLESS : FEAR ::

   (A) persistent : endurance
   (B) fortuitous : luck
   (C) eager : reluctance
   (D) just : severity
   (E) aware : vigilance

15. CIRCUMSPECT : WARY ::

   (A) meaningful : inane
   (B) respectful : pert
   (C) detrimental : misleading
   (D) reckless : foolhardy
   (E) wicked : abstemious

16. QUACK : EXPERTISE ::

   (A) physician : accreditation
   (B) mentor : guidance
   (C) hypocrite : virtue
   (D) debtor : honesty
   (E) preacher : ministry

17. VIOLATE : AGREEMENT ::

   (A) abrogate : treaty
   (B) ratify : contract
   (C) renovate : building
   (D) erase : error
   (E) adjourn : meeting

18. CRAFTY : SHREWDNESS ::

   (A) sagacious : wisdom
   (B) brazen : cunning
   (C) rare : calculation
   (D) specious : reasoning
   (E) tricky : honesty

19. LEXICOGRAPHER : WORDS ::

   (A) photographer : charts
   (B) gardener : weeds
   (C) philosopher : customs
   (D) archaeologist : fossils
   (E) surveyor : deeds

20. QUIRK : IDIOSYNCRATIC ::

   (A) neurosis : curable
   (B) decision : arbitrary
   (C) skill : spontaneous
   (D) defect : fatal
   (E) whim : fanciful

# Exercise 4

1. SONG : VOCALIST ::

   (A) monologue : speaker
   (B) diatribe : author
   (C) soliloquy : director
   (D) melody : composer
   (E) forecast : prestidigitator

2. SPRINGBOARD : DIVER ::

   (A) club : golfer
   (B) target : archer
   (C) trampoline : gymnast
   (D) helmet : cyclist
   (E) podium : conductor

3. RELAPSE : PATIENT ::
   (A) retaliate : avenger
   (B) return : refugee
   (C) backslide : convert
   (D) expose : criminal
   (E) resign : official

4. SKYLIGHT : ROOF ::
   (A) radiance : shelter
   (B) windshield : garage
   (C) illumination : beam
   (D) porthole : hull
   (E) flap : tent

5. PIECE : JIGSAW PUZZLE ::
   (A) swatch : fabric
   (B) tile : mosaic
   (C) solution : anagram
   (D) fringe : carpet
   (E) frame : picture

6. QUILL : PORCUPINE ::
   (A) mask : raccoon
   (B) sticker : blackberry
   (C) muzzle : dog
   (D) aquarium : goldfish
   (E) flock : goat

7. DEFORESTATION : TREES ::
   (A) debris : rubble
   (B) conservation : energy
   (C) dissemination : seeds
   (D) demolition : buildings
   (E) deception : lies

8. IMAGE : DISTORT ::
   (A) account : slant
   (B) report : disparage
   (C) lens : focus
   (D) audience : confuse
   (E) lie : falsify

9. ONSET : DISEASE ::
   (A) infraction : regulation
   (B) commencement : hostilities
   (C) plague : pestilence
   (D) symptom : diagnosis
   (E) disturbance : panic

10. CHORTLE : GLEE ::
    (A) smirk : smugness
    (B) snarl : fright
    (C) jeer : remorse
    (D) glower : enlightenment
    (E) grin : fury

11. SPIN : YARN ::
    (A) recount : anecdote
    (B) debate : issue
    (C) illuminate : sun
    (D) confess : defendant
    (E) study : text

12. SEASONED : EXPERIENCE ::
    (A) molded : character
    (B) embryonic : maturity
    (C) skilled : proficiency
    (D) gifted : industry
    (E) tempered : steel

13. ROAR : CANNON ::
    (A) wheeze : wind
    (B) flare : skirt
    (C) load : revolver
    (D) buck : horse
    (E) peal : bells

14. ARGUMENTS : DEBATER ::
    (A) triumphs : victor
    (B) blows : pugilist
    (C) warfare : combatant
    (D) failings : sinner
    (E) laws : anarchist

15. PIRATE : BOOTY ::
    (A) informer : source
    (B) waiter : food
    (C) angler : catch
    (D) sailor : yacht
    (E) traitor : loyalty

16. MENDACITY : HONESTY ::
    (A) hypocrisy : wisdom
    (B) duplicity : deceit
    (C) belligerence : inhumanity
    (D) poverty : authenticity
    (E) avarice : generosity

17. DEVOUT : PIETY ::

 (A) restless : energy
 (B) superstitious : zeal
 (C) officious : competence
 (D) compliant : submissiveness
 (E) fallacious : accuracy

18. JUNCTURE : CONNECT ::

 (A) future : occur
 (B) terminus : end
 (C) interruption : retract
 (D) puncture : inflate
 (E) ramification : center

19. PRUDERY : MODESTY ::

 (A) circumspection : caution
 (B) stinginess : thrift
 (C) pride : humility
 (D) tolerance : virtue
 (E) propriety : decorum

20. BLATANT : OBVIOUSNESS ::

 (A) patent : novelty
 (B) noisome : stench
 (C) propitious : harmfulness
 (D) illicit : legality
 (E) averse : harshness

# ANSWERS TO ANALOGY EXERCISES

## LEVEL A

**Analogy Exercise 1**

| | | | | | | | | | |
|---|---|---|---|---|---|---|---|---|---|
| 1. **E** | 3. **A** | 5. **B** | 7. **D** | 9. **D** | 11. **E** | 13. **D** | 15. **B** | 17. **C** | 19. **C** |
| 2. **B** | 4. **D** | 6. **C** | 8. **C** | 10. **C** | 12. **E** | 14. **D** | 16. **A** | 18. **C** | 20. **B** |

**Analogy Exercise 2**

| | | | | | | | | | |
|---|---|---|---|---|---|---|---|---|---|
| 1. **B** | 3. **C** | 5. **B** | 7. **C** | 9. **C** | 11. **C** | 13. **A** | 15. **E** | 17. **E** | 19. **C** |
| 2. **B** | 4. **C** | 6. **E** | 8. **D** | 10. **D** | 12. **E** | 14. **C** | 16. **B** | 18. **E** | 20. **C** |

**Analogy Exercise 3**

| | | | | | | | | | |
|---|---|---|---|---|---|---|---|---|---|
| 1. **D** | 3. **A** | 5. **C** | 7. **D** | 9. **B** | 11. **B** | 13. **E** | 15. **D** | 17. **D** | 19. **B** |
| 2. **C** | 4. **C** | 6. **E** | 8. **A** | 10. **A** | 12. **C** | 14. **D** | 16. **B** | 18. **D** | 20. **A** |

**Analogy Exercise 4**

| | | | | | | | | | |
|---|---|---|---|---|---|---|---|---|---|
| 1. **C** | 3. **D** | 5. **D** | 7. **B** | 9. **B** | 11. **A** | 13. **C** | 15. **A** | 17. **A** | 19. **D** |
| 2. **D** | 4. **E** | 6. **B** | 8. **E** | 10. **A** | 12. **A** | 14. **D** | 16. **C** | 18. **A** | 20. **C** |

## LEVEL B

**Analogy Exercise 1**

| | | | | | | | | | |
|---|---|---|---|---|---|---|---|---|---|
| 1. **C** | 3. **B** | 5. **C** | 7. **D** | 9. **D** | 11. **C** | 13. **A** | 15. **A** | 17. **E** | 19. **A** |
| 2. **D** | 4. **D** | 6. **D** | 8. **A** | 10. **A** | 12. **B** | 14. **E** | 16. **C** | 18. **E** | 20. **D** |

**Analogy Exercise 2**

| | | | | | | | | | |
|---|---|---|---|---|---|---|---|---|---|
| 1. **C** | 3. **D** | 5. **C** | 7. **D** | 9. **B** | 11. **A** | 13. **D** | 15. **D** | 17. **E** | 19. **C** |
| 2. **D** | 4. **C** | 6. **C** | 8. **B** | 10. **A** | 12. **A** | 14. **E** | 16. **A** | 18. **C** | 20. **D** |

**Analogy Exercise 3**

| | | | | | | | | | |
|---|---|---|---|---|---|---|---|---|---|
| 1. **D** | 3. **C** | 5. **B** | 7. **C** | 9. **A** | 11. **A** | 13. **B** | 15. **A** | 17. **A** | 19. **A** |
| 2. **A** | 4. **D** | 6. **C** | 8. **D** | 10. **B** | 12. **E** | 14. **A** | 16. **D** | 18. **A** | 20. **B** |

**Analogy Exercise 4**

| | | | | | | | | | |
|---|---|---|---|---|---|---|---|---|---|
| 1. **B** | 3. **C** | 5. **B** | 7. **B** | 9. **B** | 11. **B** | 13. **A** | 15. **E** | 17. **C** | 19. **A** |
| 2. **C** | 4. **D** | 6. **C** | 8. **D** | 10. **D** | 12. **B** | 14. **D** | 16. **A** | 18. **B** | 20. **C** |

# LEVEL C

**Analogy Exercise 1**

| 1. D | 3. B | 5. D | 7. B | 9. D | 11. E | 13. C | 15. A | 17. E | 19. C |
|------|------|------|------|------|-------|-------|-------|-------|-------|
| 2. C | 4. D | 6. C | 8. B | 10. D | 12. B | 14. A | 16. A | 18. B | 20. B |

**Analogy Exercise 2**

| 1. B | 3. B | 5. E | 7. D | 9. B | 11. B | 13. D | 15. C | 17. C | 19. B |
|------|------|------|------|------|-------|-------|-------|-------|-------|
| 2. D | 4. A | 6. E | 8. C | 10. C | 12. E | 14. D | 16. A | 18. B | 20. E |

**Analogy Exercise 3**

| 1. B | 3. D | 5. C | 7. C | 9. C | 11. E | 13. B | 15. D | 17. A | 19. D |
|------|------|------|------|------|-------|-------|-------|-------|-------|
| 2. C | 4. E | 6. C | 8. A | 10. B | 12. B | 14. C | 16. C | 18. A | 20. E |

**Analogy Exercise 4**

| 1. A | 3. C | 5. B | 7. D | 9. B | 11. A | 13. E | 15. C | 17. D | 19. B |
|------|------|------|------|------|-------|-------|-------|-------|-------|
| 2. C | 4. D | 6. B | 8. A | 10. A | 12. C | 14. B | 16. E | 18. B | 20. B |

# ANSWER EXPLANATIONS

## LEVEL A

**Analogy Exercise 1**

1. **E**    A *grapefruit* is a kind of *citrus*. A *cat* is a kind of *feline*.
2. **B**    In playing *golf*, you strike the ball with a golf *club*. In playing *hockey*, you strike the puck with a hockey *stick*.
3. **A**    You use a *colander* to *drain* foods. You use a *refrigerator* to *chill* foods.
4. **D**    A *certificate* is a written document testifying to a *marriage*. A *deed* is a written document testifying to a *purchase*.
5. **B**    To *husk corn* is to strip away the corn's inedible outer covering. To *peel* an *orange* is to strip away the orange's inedible outer covering.
6. **C**    *Organdy* is a kind of cloth or *fabric*. A *bonnet* is a kind of *hat*.
7. **D**    To *hang* a *picture* is to put it up so that it can be viewed. To *post* a *notice* is also to put it up so that it can be viewed.
8. **C**    A *juror* (person who serves on a jury) is a member of a *panel* (group of jurors). A *player* is a member of a *team*.
9. **D**    To *retreat* from a *position* is to abandon or remove oneself from that position or place. To *withdraw* from an *agreement* is to abandon or remove oneself from that agreement or deal.
10. **C**    A *spine* is a sharp-pointed outgrowth on a *cactus*. A *quill* is a sharp-pointed outgrowth on a *porcupine*.
11. **E**    A *pharmacist* prepares and dispenses *drugs*. An *optician* prepares and dispenses *lenses* for spectacles.
12. **E**    One delivers a *speech* from the *podium* (raised platform). One delivers a *sermon* from the *pulpit* (raised platform in a house of worship).
13. **D**    By definition, to *outlast* someone is to show greater *endurance* (stamina) than that person. Similarly, to *outsmart* someone is to show greater *cleverness* than that person.
14. **D**    By definition, something *eternal* is without an *end*. Likewise, something *amorphous* is without *form* or shape.
15. **B**    *Speech* that is *stilted* is stiff, lacking in spontaneity. *Movement* that is *wooden* is also stiff, lacking in vitality.
16. **A**    A *companion-way* is a kind of *ladder* found on ships. A *porthole* is a kind of *window* found on ships.
17. **C**    A *census* is a list of persons who make up the *population*. A *catalog* is a list of items that make up the *collection*.
18. **C**    By definition, to *enlarge* something is to increase its *scope* or extent. To *protract* (prolong) something is to increase its *duration*.
19. **C**    By definition, to *indemnify* someone is to provide that person with *reimbursement* (repayment). To *vaccinate* someone is to provide that person with *immunization*.
20. **B**    Someone *ungainly* (awkward) by definition lacks *grace*. Someone *unruly* (willful; unmanageable) by definition lacks *discipline*.

## Analogy Exercise 2

1. **B**   A *slice* is a single piece of *bread*. A *strip* is a single piece of *bacon*.
2. **B**   Typically, one hangs a *towel* from a *rack*. Similarly, one hangs a *coat* from a *hook*.
3. **C**   The *pit* of a *peach* is its hard central seed. The *stone* of a *cherry* is its hard central seed.
4. **C**   A *tutor* leads a *student* through his or her studies. A *guide* leads a *tourist* on his or her tour.
5. **B**   To *hang wallpaper* is to place it in proper position, attaching it to the wall. To *lay* a *carpet* is to place it in proper position, attaching it to the floor.
6. **E**   A *cartoonist* is the person who creates a *comic strip*. A *composer* is the person who creates a melody or *tune*.
7. **C**   A *crock* is a kind of *container*. A *jeep* is a kind of *vehicle*.
8. **D**   Just as *twine* is less thick than *rope*, a *twig* (slender shoot) is less thick than a *bough* (branch).
9. **C**   By definition, a *referee officiates* during a game, ensuring that the game runs properly. Similarly, a *chairperson presides* over a meeting, ensuring that the meeting runs properly.
10. **D**   A *daredevil* (daring adventurer) by definition is *rash* (heedless of dangers). Similarly, a *trickster* by definition is *deceitful*.
11. **C**   A *flute* is played by a *flautist*. A *kettledrum* is played by a *tympanist*.
12. **E**   An *inventory* is a list of *merchandise* in stock. A *roster* is a list of *players* on a team.
13. **A**   By definition, one *decks* (arrays or clothes) a place or person with decorations or *ornaments*. Similarly, one *equips* (supplies or furnishes) a place or person with *paraphernalia* (gear).
14. **C**   In large units, *paper* is sold by the *ream*. Similarly, in large units, *wood* is sold by the *cord*.
15. **E**   To *guffaw* is to *laugh* in a loud, boisterous manner. Similarly, to *bellow* or shout is to *speak* in a loud, boisterous manner.
16. **B**   A *litter* of *kittens* is a number of kittens produced in one birth. A *brood* of *chickens* is a number of chickens produced in one hatching.
17. **E**   By definition, a *glimpse* is a *brief*, hasty look. By definition, a *stare* is a *fixed*, hard look.
18. **E**   A *fracture* is a break or splitting of a *bone* into fragments. A *schism* is a break or splitting of a *church* into factions.
19. **C**   By definition, something *episodic* (divided into separate sections) lacks *continuity* (the quality of being uninterrupted). By definition, something *ambiguous* (vague or unclear) lacks *clarity*.
20. **C**   Someone *churlish* (peasantlike; uncouth) shows a lack of *breeding* (good manners). Someone *boorish* (crude; insensitive) shows a lack of *sensitivity*.

## Analogy Exercise 3

1. **D**   A *musician* performs a *symphony*. An *actor* performs a *play*.
2. **C**   *Sage* is a kind of *herb*. A *poodle* is a kind of *dog*.
3. **A**   A *skit* is a short dramatic piece, one less significant than a full-scale *play*. A *quiz* is a short oral or written test, one less significant than a full-scale *examination*.
4. **C**   An individual bit of *sand* is a *grain*. An individual bit of *snow* is a *flake*.
5. **C**   Someone *thankful* (appreciative of the benefits he or she has received) is not characterized by *ingratitude* (ungratefulness). Someone *hopeful* is not characterized by *despair* (hopelessness).
6. **E**   One *quakes* or shivers from *fear*. One *shudders* or shivers from *horror* (dread).
7. **D**   A *swarm* is a group of *bees*. A *school* is a group of *fish*.
8. **A**   A *tornado* is a violent, destructive whirling *wind*. A *whirlpool* is a violent, destructive whirling *current* of water.
9. **B**   To *construct* an *edifice* (building) is to create or make it. To *fabricate* a *lie* is likewise to create or make it.
10. **A**   By definition, something *demonstrable* can be *shown* or demonstrated. By definition, something *malleable* can be *shaped* or molded.
11. **B**   To *mount* an *assault* is to originate and set in motion an attack. To *launch* a *campaign* is to originate and set in motion a series of operations.
12. **C**   An *anthology* is a collection of *writings* for people to read. A *sampler* is a collection of *delicacies* for people to taste.

13. **E**   One keeps *laundry* in a *hamper* (large basket). One keeps *valuables* in a *coffer* (chest or box).
14. **D**   To *knit*, one uses a knitting *needle*. To *crochet*, one uses a crochet *hook*.
15. **D**   To *etch glass* is to mark or produce a design on the glass. Likewise, to *tattoo skin* is to mark or produce a design on the skin.
16. **B**   By definition, *fury* (rage) is an *emotion* or feeling. Likewise, by definition, *hunger* is a *drive* or basic physiological need.
17. **D**   Someone *sympathetic* feels *compassion* or pity. Someone *aghast* (struck with abhorrence or dread) feels *horror*.
18. **D**   The *palm* is the traditional symbol of *victory*. The *cornucopia* (horn of plenty) is the traditional symbol of *abundance* or plentifulness.
19. **B**   By definition, to *mope* (brood) is to exhibit *unhappiness*. Likewise, by definition, to *sulk* is to exhibit *petulance* (peevishness).
20. **A**   A *charlatan* (quack; fraud) puts on a false appearance of *knowledge*. A *hypocrite* puts on a false appearance of *virtue*.

## Analogy Exercise 4

1. **C**   To *park* a *car* is to bring it to a stop at a particular place. To *dock* a *ship* is to bring it to a stop at a particular place.
2. **D**   A *head* of *cauliflower* is the topmost, largely edible portion. An *ear* of *corn* is likewise the topmost, largely edible portion.
3. **D**   A *wagon* forms part of a *caravan* (group of vehicles traveling together in a file). A *float* (vehicle carrying a parade exhibit) forms part of a *parade*.
4. **E**   Both a *thoroughbred horse* and a *pedigreed dog* are certified for their purity of breeding.
5. **D**   The function of *tweezers* is to *pluck* or extract something. The function of a *wheelbarrow* is to *convey* or bear something.
6. **B**   When *pots clatter*, they make a characteristic rattling sound. When *leaves rustle*, they make a characteristic crackly, whispery sound.
7. **B**   A *muzzle* prevents one from *biting*. A *gag* prevents one from *speaking*.
8. **E**   By definition, something *downy* (soft, fluffy) is characterized by *softness*. Likewise, something *silky* is characterized by *smoothness*.
9. **B**   An *on-ramp* (sloping road) gives access to a *highway*. A *gangway* (movable bridge) gives access to a *ship*.
10. **A**   The *decibel* is a measure of *volume*. The *foot* is a measure of *length*.
11. **A**   A *trailer* is a kind of advertisement (preview for movies) that appears on a *screen*. A *poster* is a kind of advertisement that appears on a *billboard*.
12. **A**   To *petition* is to *ask* something formally and in some detail. To *narrate* is to *tell* something formally and in some detail.
13. **C**   A *cease-fire* (truce) is a pause or break in *fighting*. A *recess* is a pause or break in legal or other *proceedings*.
14. **D**   In court, a *witness* appears in the witness *stand*. Likewise, in court, a *prisoner* appears in the *dock*.
15. **A**   Someone *sensitive* is easy to *distress* or upset. Someone *submissive* is easy to *master* or overcome.
16. **C**   To *plow* is to cut open or dig a *furrow* (trench in the earth). To *bore* is to drill or dig a *hole*.
17. **A**   By definition, *pique* (irritation) is less extreme than *rage* (intense anger). By definition, *thrift* (frugality) is less extreme than *parsimony* (stinginess).
18. **A**   A *dilemma* (difficult predicament) is a source of *perplexity* (bewilderment). A *comedy* is a source of *amusement*.
19. **D**   Writing or speech that is *discursive* (rambling; digressive) lacks *focus*. Writing or speech that is *verbose* (wordy) lacks *brevity* (conciseness).
20. **C**   By definition, a *procession* is *formal* in movement. By definition, a *saunter* (stroll) is *leisurely* in movement.

## LEVEL B

### Analogy Exercise 1

1. **C** The seats in a *gymnasium* are the *bleachers*. The seats in a *church* are the *pews*.
2. **D** The practice for a *performance* is called a *rehearsal*. The practice for a *parade* is called a *drill*.
3. **B** *Ice skates* slide over the ice on their *blades*. Likewise, a *sled* slides over the ice or snow on its *runners*.
4. **D** A *mussel* is a kind of *shellfish*. A *snake* is a kind of *reptile*.
5. **C** A *bed* is a small area of planted ground in a *garden*. A *plot* is a piece of land in a *cemetery*.
6. **D** *Migraine* is a condition involving pains in the *head*. *Heartburn* is a condition involving pains in the *stomach*.
7. **D** To *condense* something by definition is to make it more *compact* (solid; dense). To *refine* something by definition is to make it more *pure*.
8. **A** A *tune* that is *catchy* or intriguing sticks in the mind; so does a *slogan* (attention-getting phrase) that is *memorable*.
9. **D** A *hubbub* (uproar; noise) is by definition *noisy*. A *free-for-all* (out-of-control situation; fight with no rules) is by definition *wild*.
10. **A** *Flax* undergoes various processes in the making of *linen*. *Sand* undergoes various processes in the making of *glass*.
11. **C** One *pasteurizes food* to rid it of germs. One *fumigates* an *area* to rid it of pests.
12. **B** To *lie* is more serious than to *fib* (tell a trivial, unimportant lie). To *complain* is more serious than to *quibble* (make a trivial, unimportant complaint).
13. **A** *Copious* or plentiful is the opposite of *scarce*. *Expeditious* or speedy is the opposite of *slow*.
14. **E** To *spruce up clothing* is to neaten its appearance. To *tidy* a *room* is to neaten its appearance.
15. **A** To *abscond* is to *depart* from a place secretly. To *eavesdrop* is to *listen* to a conversation secretly.
16. **C** A *heinous* (shockingly evil) action exhibits *iniquity* (wickedness). An *ingenuous* (simple and childlike) action exhibits *innocence*.
17. **E** *Bees* are kept in an *apiary* (beehouse). *Rabbits* are kept in a *hutch* (coop or pen).
18. **E** A *decorous* (seemly or proper) manner is characterized by *propriety* (appropriateness). A *reserved* (restrained in words and actions) manner is characterized by *reticence* (self-control; restraint).
19. **A** *Implacable* by definition means not capable of being *appeased* or pacified. *Inexplicable* by definition means not capable of being *explained*.
20. **D** Something *evanescent* or fleeting by definition lacks *permanence*. Something *desultory* (without plan, regularity, or purpose) lacks *methodicalness*.

### Analogy Exercise 2

1. **C** Just as *snow melts*, changing state to a liquid, *dew evaporates*, changing state to a vapor or gas.
2. **D** A *blanket* serves as a source of *warmth*. A *lamp* serves as a source of *illumination* or light.
3. **D** An *orthodontist* treats irregularities of the *teeth*. A *dermatologist* treats irregularities of the *skin*.
4. **C** A *blindfold* serves to block someone's sight or *vision*. A *gag* serves to block someone's *speech*.
5. **C** The surface of *marble* is described in terms of its *grain*. The surface of a *fabric* is described in terms of its *texture*.
6. **C** To *book* a *flight* is to engage to travel on that plane. To *reserve* a *table* is to engage to dine at that restaurant.
7. **D** A *muddle* or confused mess is by definition *untidy*. A *snarl* or knot is by definition *tangled*.
8. **B** To *stock* an *aquarium* is to supply it with fish. To *furnish* an *apartment* is to supply it with furniture.
9. **B** The projections on a *saw* are called *teeth*. The projections on a *fork* are called *tines*.
10. **A** By definition, something *anarchic* (disorderly; chaotic) lacks *order*. By definition, something *aimless* (pointless) lacks *purpose*.
11. **A** When you neglect your *appearance*, you come to look *seedy* (shabby). When you neglect your

*health*, you come to look *run-down* (worn-out).

12. **A**    A *patrician* (noble) is a member of the *aristocracy*. A *professor* is a member of the *faculty*.
13. **D**    An *abyss* is an immeasurably deep pit, one far deeper than a mere *gully* or trench. A *tidal wave* is an extraordinarily high wave, one far higher than a mere *ripple*.
14. **E**    A *disadvantage* or drawback that is *insurmountable* by definition cannot be overcome. Likewise, a *barrier* or obstacle that is *insuperable* by definition cannot be overcome.
15. **D**    A *clap* is the noise made by *thunder*. A *report* is the noise made by an *explosion*.
16. **A**    By definition, someone *hoary* (white with age) lacks *youthfulness*. Likewise, by definition someone *somnolent* (sleepy or drowsy) lacks *alertness*.
17. **E**    A *penitent* (repentant person) is by definition *contrite* or remorseful. A *zealot* (excessively devoted enthusiast) is by definition *fanatical*.
18. **C**    A *quip* (clever remark) is by its nature *witty*. A *quibble* (trivial complaint) is by its nature *petty*.
19. **C**    A *philatelist* is a person who collects *stamps*. A *numismatist* is a person who collects *coins*.
20. **D**    To *extract* someone from a *quagmire* is to free him or her from a swamp or bog. To *release* someone from *incarceration* is to free him or her from imprisonment.

## Analogy Exercise 3

1. **D**    *Snow* piles up into a *heap*. *Hay* piles up into a *stack*.
2. **A**    An *ant* is a member of a *colony*. A *goose* is a member of a *flock*.
3. **C**    A *cottage* is a smaller, less expensive house than a *mansion*. A *compact* is a smaller, less expensive car than a *limousine*.
4. **D**    *Mutton* is the meat of a *sheep*. *Veal* is the meat of a *calf*.
5. **B**    The job of a *scribe* was to *write*. The job of a *minstrel* was to *sing*.
6. **C**    To be *ecstatic* (overjoyed) is more extreme than to be simply *joyful*. To be *despairing* (hopelessly gloomy) is more extreme than to be simply *discouraged*.
7. **C**    *Bees* live in a *beehive*. *Termites* live in a *nest*.
8. **D**    To *uproot* a *tree* is to pull it out. To *extract* a *tooth* likewise is to pull it out.
9. **A**    To *satisfy* a *craving* (desire; appetite) is to put an end to it by providing what one craved. To *quench* a *thirst* is to put an end to it by providing what one wanted to drink.
10. **B**    The job of a *recruiter* (person charged with getting new members) is to encourage *enlistments*. The job of a *salesperson* is to encourage *purchases*.
11. **A**    A *jerk* (quick push or pull) is by definition *sudden*. A *shove* (push exerting force) is by definition *forcible*.
12. **E**    Someone *stern* (severe; harsh) is not characterized by *leniency* (mildness; tolerance). Someone *grave* (serious and dignified) is not characterized by *frivolity* (levity; lack of seriousness).
13. **B**    A *gallery* is a division of a *museum*. A *ward* is a division of a *hospital*.
14. **A**    To *extricate* a person from an *entanglement* is to free that person from being tangled up or involved. To *release* a person from *confinement* is to free that person from being shut up or confined.
15. **A**    A *roll* of *wallpaper* is a particular quantity of wallpaper. A *bolt* of *cloth* is a particular quantity of cloth.
16. **D**    A *panhandler* (beggar) asks people for *money*. A *pollster* (person who takes polls) asks people for *opinions*.
17. **A**    To *enslave* someone is to take away that person's *liberty*. To *disenfranchise* someone is to take away that person's *vote*.
18. **A**    A *flyspeck* (something small and insignificant, like a stain made by a fly) is by definition *minute* (extremely small). A *splotch* (shapeless spot) is by definition *irregular*.
19. **A**    A *malcontent* (chronically dissatisfied person) *grumbles* or complains. A *spendthrift* (wasteful, improvident person) *squanders* or spends extravagantly.
20. **B**    Someone *hidebound* (rigid; ultraconservative) lacks *flexibility*. Someone *mercurial* (unpredictably changeable) lacks *stability*.

## Analogy Exercise 4

1. **B** A *sheet* is a single piece of *paper*. A *pane* is a single piece of *glass*.
2. **C** The *steering wheel* directs the course of the *automobile*. The *rudder* directs the course of the *ship*.
3. **C** One must *bake* a *souffle* (dish made from sauce, egg yolks, beaten egg whites, flavoring) before one eats it. Similarly, one must *boil porridge* before one eats it.
4. **D** *Wine* is made from *grapes* that have undergone processing. *Paper* is made from *trees* that have undergone processing.
5. **B** A *megaphone* (device used to intensify the voice) increases your force when you *speak*. A *lever* (bar used to exert pressure) increases your force when you *pry* (raise or pull things apart).
6. **C** By definition, to *deflate* something is to remove or empty it of its *air* or gas. Likewise, to *dehydrate* something is to remove its *water*.
7. **B** Just as a *soapbox* is an improvised platform for an informal *orator*, a *pulpit* is a platform for a *preacher*.
8. **D** *Creases* are lines or ridges made in *paper*. *Furrows* are lines or wrinkles made in the *brow*.
9. **B** An *appraiser* estimates or judges the value of a *building*. A *critic* estimates or judges the value of a *book*.
10. **D** By definition, a *spat* is a petty *quarrel*. Likewise, by definition, a *quibble* is a petty *objection*.
11. **B** If one's *footing* is *secure* or dependable, it should not slip. Likewise, if one's *grasp* is *firm*, it too should not slip.
12. **B** Someone *jittery* (nervous) tends to *fidget* (wiggle; twitch). Someone *touchy* (irritable; ready to take offense) tends to *snap* (make irritable retorts).
13. **A** A *door* allows entrance into a *building*. A *hatch* (small doorway or opening) allows entrance into a *plane*.
14. **D** Someone *willful* (stubbornly self-willed) lacks *obedience*. Someone *fretful* (quick to feel annoyance, worry, impatience) lacks *patience*.
15. **E** A *compact* is a small container that holds *powder*. A *flask* is a small container that holds *liquor*.
16. **A** To make fast a *ship*, one *moors* it (ties it up with cables). To make fast a *horse*, one *tethers* it (ties it up with a rope).
17. **C** Someone *brusque* (rudely curt) exhibits *abruptness*. Someone *servile* (subservient, fawning) exhibits *obsequiousness* (fawning attentiveness).
18. **B** A *nomad* (one of a wandering tribe) is a member of a *band*. An *artist* is a member of a *colony* (group of artists living in close association).
19. **A** A *barnacle* fastens itself to the *hull* of a ship. A *tick* fastens itself to the *skin* of a living creature.
20. **C** An *inadvertent error* is by definition a mistake one did not intend to commit. An *unintended slight* is by definition an insult one did not mean to commit.

## LEVEL C

## Analogy Exercise 1

1. **D** A *cluster* of *grapes* is a group of grapes growing together. A *bunch* of *bananas* is a group of bananas growing together.
2. **C** *Algae* (aquatic plantlike organisms) grow on the surface of *ponds*. *Moss* (nonflowering plants) grows on the surface of *tree trunks*.
3. **B** A *hymn* is a religious *song*. A *sermon* is a religious speech or *address*.
4. **D** The *eagle swoops* (moves in a sweeping fashion) to seize its prey. The *panther springs* (leaps) to seize its prey.
5. **D** By definition, a *shambles* (scene of great confusion or disorder) is not *orderly*. By definition, a *pigsty* (pigpen; dirty place) is not *clean*.

6. **C**   To *clinch* a *deal* is to conclude the deal, to come to terms. To *settle* a *lawsuit* likewise is to conclude the lawsuit, to come to terms.
7. **B**   One *taps* or extracts *sap* from a tree. One *draws* or extracts *blood* from a blood vessel.
8. **B**   One holds a *dagger* by its *hilt* or handle. One holds a *trowel* (hand tool used for spreading, scooping) by its *handle*.
9. **D**   *Din* (loud noise; uproar) is by definition *loud*. A *mob* (large disorderly crowd) is by definition *unruly* (not readily disciplined).
10. **D**   Someone *querulous* (habitually complaining) *grumbles*. Someone *garrulous* (talkative; long-winded) *talks*.
11. **E**   To *bristle* is to exhibit *anger*. To *cower* (cringe) is to exhibit *fear*.
12. **B**   One obtains *limestone* from a *quarry* (open excavation). One obtains *oil* from a *well*.
13. **C**   A *sketch* is a short variety act that appears as part of a *revue*. An *essay* is a short literary piece that appears as part of an *anthology*.
14. **A**   To *allay fear* is to alleviate it, to reduce its intensity. To *slake thirst* is to satisfy it, to reduce its intensity.
15. **A**   Someone *circumspect* or cautious considers the possible *consequences* of his or her acts. Someone *wary* or watchfully prudent considers the possible *dangers* he or she may face.
16. **A**   By definition, someone *craven* (cowardly) lacks *courage*. Likewise, by definition, someone *impotent* (powerless) lacks *power*.
17. **E**   Lost in a *quandary* (state of mental perplexity when faced with a difficult situation), one seeks a *solution*. Lost in a *maze*, one seeks an *exit*.
18. **B**   Someone *impecunious* (penniless) would be a likely inhabitant of a *hovel* (wretched small house or hut). Someone *prosperous* (wealthy) would be a likely inhabitant of a *mansion*.
19. **C**   By definition, a *surreptitious* (sneaky, secret) act is characterized by *stealth* (secrecy). By definition, an *obsequious* (attentively fawning) act is characterized by *servility* (subservience).
20. **B**   *Acrophobia* is defined as a fear of *heights*. *Agoraphobia* is defined as a fear of *crowds*.

## Analogy Exercise 2
1. **B**   The foot of a *camel* is called a *hoof*. The foot of a *dog* is called a *paw*.
2. **D**   The heavy, reverberating sound produced by *thunder* is described as a *roll* of thunder. The heavy, reverberating sound of *traffic* is described as the *rumble* of traffic.
3. **B**   By definition, a *magician conjures* or practices magical arts. By definition, a *prophet predicts* or foretells the future.
4. **A**   To *book* a *reservation* is to arrange to engage in a future activity (a meal at a restaurant, a plane flight). To *place* an *order* is to arrange to make a future purchase.
5. **E**   A *plane* is a tool that *smooths* wood. A *saw* is a tool that *cuts* woods.
6. **E**   The job of an *interpreter* is to *translate*. The job of a *censor* (person who examines books and films for objectionable matter) is to *expurgate* (cut out objectionable matter).
7. **D**   By definition, someone *thin-skinned* is easy to *insult*. By definition, someone *weak-willed* is easy to *sway* or influence.
8. **C**   If *access* to something is *unlimited*, one has complete freedom to make use of it. If *entry* to something is *unrestricted*, one has complete freedom to go into it.
9. **B**   To *excavate* a *tunnel* is to dig that tunnel. To *burrow* a *hole* likewise is to dig that hole.
10. **C**   A group of *weeds* growing together is called a *clump*. A group of *trees* growing together is called a *stand*.
11. **B**   A *portfolio* is a carrying case for *papers*. A *quiver* is a carrying case for *arrows*.
12. **E**   When a *storm abates* or subsides, it lessens in intensity. When a *pressure relaxes*, it too lessens in intensity.
13. **D**   A *syllabus* is the outline of a *course* of study. A *flow chart* is the outline of a *procedure*.
14. **D**   To *bolt food* is to swallow it down hastily. To *guzzle* a *beverage* is to swallow it down hastily as well.

15. **C**   A *poacher* is someone who takes *game* (wild animals) illegally. A *pickpocket* is someone who takes *wallets* illegally.
16. **A**   By definition, *plumage* is the *feathers* of a bird. By definition, *foliage* is the *leaves* of plants.
17. **C**   A *cistern* (artificial reservoir) holds *water*. A *tank* holds *oxygen*.
18. **B**   Someone *disobedient* is not characterized by *compliance* (submissiveness). Someone *inconsistent* (changeable) is not characterized by *dependability*.
19. **B**   To *applaud* is to indicate *approbation* or approval. To *jeer* or make scornful remarks is to indicate *derision* or scorn.
20. **E**   By definition, someone *credulous* or gullible is ready to *believe*. By definition, someone *censorious* (condemnatory) is ready to *criticize*.

## Analogy Exercise 3

1. **B**   A *musician* holds a *recital* (performance) to demonstrate his or her artistry. A *sculptor* holds an *exhibition* to demonstrate his or her artistry.
2. **C**   A *picture* is enclosed in a *frame*. A *diamond* is mounted in a *setting*.
3. **D**   To *clear* a *forest*, one cuts down the trees. To *shave hair*, one cuts off the hair.
4. **E**   Just as a *buoy* (beacon) guides a *ship* safely to harbor, a *runway light* guides a *plane* safely to the landing field.
5. **C**   A *bullet ricochets* or rebounds off a surface. A *ball bounces* off a surface.
6. **C**   By definition, a *packrat accumulates* (collects and hangs on to) miscellaneous unneeded items. By definition, a *miser hoards* (collects and hangs on to) money.
7. **C**   To *cure* something (a disease, problem) is to eliminate it, not simply to *alleviate* or reduce it. To *stop* something is to end it, not simply to *retard* it or slow it down.
8. **A**   A *tepid* liquid is not as hot as one that is *boiling*. A *leisurely* pace is not as slow as one that is *plodding*.
9. **C**   A *company* is a subsidiary division of a *conglomerate* (widely diversified corporation). A *school* (e.g., medical school, school of engineering) is a subsidiary division of a *university*.
10. **B**   An *epicure* is one who has sensitive and discriminating tastes in *food*. A *connoisseur* is one who has sensitive and discriminating tastes in *art*.
11. **E**   A *dowel* is a slender rod in comparison with a *pole*. A *twig* is a slender offshoot of a tree in comparison with a *branch*.
12. **B**   Water *flows* through a *conduit* (channel). Water *slides* down a *chute*.
13. **B**   An *extemporaneous speech* is one made without the use of notes or text. A *freehand drawing* is one that is made without the use of measurements or mechanical aids.
14. **C**   Someone *dauntless* (intrepid; unafraid) by definition is without *fear*. Someone *eager* by definition is without *reluctance*.
15. **D**   Someone *wary* is extremely cautious or *circumspect*. Someone *foolhardy* is extremely *reckless* or careless of consequences.
16. **C**   A *quack* (charlatan; fraud) makes a pretense of possessing *expertise* (know-how; skill). A *hypocrite* makes a pretense of possessing *virtue*.
17. **A**   To *violate* an *agreement* is to break or disregard that agreement. To *abrogate* a *treaty* is to break or annul that treaty.
18. **A**   Someone *crafty* (cunning) is characterized by *shrewdness*. Someone *sagacious* (wise) is characterized by *wisdom*.
19. **D**   A *lexicographer* (dictionary-maker) studies *words*. An *archaeologist* studies *fossils*.
20. **E**   A *quirk* (individual peculiarity) is by definition *idiosyncratic*. A *whim* (caprice; fancy) is by definition *fanciful*.

## Analogy Exercise 4

1. **A**   A *song* is performed by a *vocalist* (singer). A *monologue* (soliloquy) is performed by a *speaker*.
2. **C**   A *diver* launches himself or herself from a *springboard*. A *gymnast* launches himself or herself from a *trampoline*.

3. **C**   When *patients relapse*, they return to their former state of illness. When *converts* (people who adopt a religion) *backslide*, they return to their former state of disbelief.

4. **D**   A *skylight* is an opening in the *roof* of a building that lets in light. A *porthole* is an opening in the *hull* of a ship that lets in light.

5. **B**   A *jigsaw puzzle* is made up of individual *pieces*. A *mosaic* (surface decoration made of inlaid pieces set in patterns) is made up of individual *tiles*.

6. **B**   A *quill* is a sharp bristle or projection that sticks out from the hide of a *porcupine*. A *sticker* is a sharp thorn or projection that sticks out from the vine of a *blackberry* plant.

7. **D**   *Deforestation* or clearing destroys *trees*. *Demolition* or razing destroys *buildings*.

8. **A**   To *distort* an *image* is to twist it out of its true proportion. To *slant* an *account* is to twist it out of its true meaning.

9. **B**   By definition, the *onset* of a *disease* is when the illness starts. Likewise, the *commencement* of *hostilities* is when the fighting starts.

10. **A**   To *chortle* (laugh exultantly) is to show *glee* (jubilantly high spirits; merriment). To *smirk* (smile in a self-satisfied manner) is to show *smugness* (self-satisfaction; complacency).

11. **A**   To *spin* a *yarn* is to tell a tale. Likewise, to *recount* an *anecdote* is to tell a tale.

12. **C**   Someone *seasoned* or mature possesses *experience*. Someone *skilled* or competent possesses *proficiency*.

13. **E**   Just as *cannons roar*, making their loud, rumbling noise, so *bells peal*, making their loud, ringing noise.

14. **B**   A *debater* uses *arguments* to win the debate. A *pugilist* or boxer uses *blows* to win the fight.

15. **C**   A *pirate* seeks to gain *booty* or plunder. An *angler* (person who fishes) seeks to gain a *catch* of fish.

16. **E**   Just as *mendacity* (duplicity; falsehood) is the opposite of *honesty*, *avarice* (greed) is the opposite of *generosity*.

17. **D**   Someone *devout* (religious) exhibits *piety*. Someone *compliant* (yielding) exhibits *submissiveness*.

18. **B**   A *juncture* is a point where something *connects*. A *terminus* is a point where something *ends*.

19. **B**   *Prudery* is excessive *modesty*, modesty carried to an affected extreme. *Stinginess* similarly is excessive *thrift*.

20. **B**   Something *blatant* (obtrusively conspicuous) is characterized by its *obviousness*. Something *noisome* (foul-smelling) is characterized by its *stench* (bad smell).

# PART V

# CRITICAL READING QUESTIONS

# OVERVIEW

SAT I critical reading comprehension questions test your ability to understand what you read—both content and technique. Each verbal section on SAT I will include one or two reading passages of different length, followed by six to twelve questions of assorted types. One passage on the test will be **narrative**: a passage from a novel, a short story, an autobiography, or a personal essay. One will deal with the **sciences** (including medicine, botany, zoology, chemistry, physics, geology, astronomy); another with the **humanities** (including art, literature, music, philosophy, folklore); a third, with the **social sciences** (including history, economics, sociology, government.) Some of the above passages may be what the College Board calls **argumentative**; these passages present a definite point of view on a subject. One passage most likely will be "**ethnic**" in content: whether it is a history passage, a personal narrative, or a passage on music, art, or literature, it will deal with concerns of a particular minority group.

The verbal sections fall into three basic patterns.

The 30-question section has 15 critical reading questions. It contains 2 reading passages on separate topics:

1 400- to 500-word reading passage, followed by 5 to 7 questions, depending on the passage's length;
1 500- to 600-word reading passage, followed by 8 to 10 questions.

The 35-question section has 12 critical reading questions. It contains 1 800–900 word reading passage.

The 13-question section has only critical reading questions. It contains 1 pair of reading passages on related topics.
They total 800–900 words, and are followed by:
4 to 5 critical reading questions on Passage 1;
4 to 5 critical reading questions on Passage 2;
3 to 4 critical reading questions comparing the two passages.

The questions that come after each passage are not arranged in order of difficulty. They are arranged to suit the way the passage's content is organized. (A question based on information found at the beginning of the passage will come before a question based on information at the passage's end.)

# TIPS ON HANDLING CRITICAL READING QUESTIONS

**TIP 1**
## TRY TO ANTICIPATE WHAT THE PASSAGE IS ABOUT

As you read the italicized introductory material preceding the passage and tackle the passage's opening sentences, try to anticipate what the passage will be about. Ask yourself who or what the author is talking about. Recollect what else you may have read about the topic. You'll be in a better position to understand what you read.

**TIP 2**
## PICK YOUR QUESTIONS TO ANSWER

On verbal sections with two reading passages, head straight for the passage that appeals to you more. It is hard to concentrate when you read about something wholly unfamiliar to you. Give yourself a break. First tackle the reading passage that interests you or deals with topics in which you are well grounded. Then move on to the other passage. You'll do better that way.

Similarly, when you're ready to answer questions on the passage, consider taking a quick glance at *all* the questions on that passage and starting off with answering the ones you feel you can handle easily. Check out the questions with answer choices that are only two or three words long. (Usually these are vocabulary-in-context questions, or questions on attitude or tone.) Answer them. Then focus on the longer, more difficult questions.

If you are stumped by a tough reading question, don't automatically skip the other questions on that passage. The reading comprehension questions following each passage are not arranged in order of difficulty. They tend to be arranged sequentially: questions on paragraph 1 come before questions on paragraph 2. So look over all the questions on the passage. That tough question may be just one question away from one that's easy for you.

Recognize the questions to bear down on as opposed to the questions to skip. Spot the most time-consuming questions; then, decide whether any given time-consumer is one you should skip. Questions containing the word EXCEPT in capital letters tend to be tricky; they may be ones to take a pass on. Similarly, the following sorts of questions may take a lot of time:

- ones that ask about the author's underlying assumptions;
- ones that ask what additional information would help to clarify points in the passage;
- ones that compare or contrast two passages in great detail;
- ones with extremely lengthy answer choices.

You may decide you want to skip one or more of them.

However...*try to answer all the questions* on one passage before you move on to the second. Often, working through one or two questions will provide you with information you can use in answering other questions on that passage.

Whenever you skip from question to question, or from passage to passage, *be sure you're filling in the right spaces on your answer sheet.*

**TIP 3**
## READ PURPOSEFULLY: PASSAGE, QUESTIONS, AND ANSWER CHOICES

As you work through the passage, try to identify what *kind* of writing this is, what *techniques* are being used, who its intended *audience* may be, and what *feeling* (if any) the author has toward this subject. Try to retain names, dates, and places for quick reference later. In particular, try to remember where in the passage the author makes *major* points. Underline key words, if you like, or indicate main ideas with a star (*) or arrow. Then, when you start looking for a phrase or sentence to justify your answer, you may be able to save time by going back to that section of the passage immediately without having to reread the whole thing.

Read as rapidly as you can with understanding, but do not force yourself. Do not worry about the time element. If you worry about not finishing the test, you will begin to take shortcuts and miss correct answers in your haste.

Figure out whether it ever helps you to read the questions before you read through the passage. Our general advice is, first read the passage; then read the questions. We find most students do better tackling reading exercises in this way. However, in dealing with an extra-long, 800-word reading passage, you may want to try skimming the questions *before* you read the passage to get a sense of what you should be on the lookout for.

Use the practice exercises at the end of this chapter to find out whether or not the "questions first" approach works for you. Select an 800-word passage and skim the questions on it. Next, read the passage and answer the questions. Check your answers. Then think over your experience.

- Did you get through the passage and all 12 questions in 15 minutes or less?
- Did you answer a reasonable number of questions correctly?
- Did you feel in control as you started to read the passage, or did you feel as if you had a jumble of question words dancing around in your head?
- Did you feel that skimming the questions in advance slowed you down too much and wasted your time?

Try another 800-word passage, this time reading the passage first. Consider how you did on this passage. Then decide what's right for you.

In answering questions, don't just settle for the first answer choice that looks good. Read each answer choice and compare what it says to the actual words of the passage. When you come to an answer choice that contradicts the information in the passage or that doesn't answer the question being asked, cross it out.

## TIP 4
## GO BACK TO THE PASSAGE TO DOUBLE-CHECK YOUR ANSWER CHOICE

When you tackle the questions, *go back to the passage* to verify your choice of answer. Do not rely on your memory alone, and, above all, do not ignore the passage and just answer questions on the basis of other things you've read. Remember, the questions are asking you about what *this* author has to say about the subject, not about what some other author you once read said about it in another book.

Use the line references in the questions to be sure you've gone back to the correct spot in the passage. The reading passages on SAT I tend to be longer than those on the old SAT. Fortunately, all the lines are numbered, and the questions often refer you to specific lines in the passage by number. It takes less time to locate a line number than to spot a word or phrase. Use the line numbers to orient yourself in the text.

## TIP 5
## TACKLE THE PAIRED PASSAGES ONE PASSAGE AT A TIME

If the new double passage section has you worried, relax. It's not that formidable, especially if you deal with it our way. The double reading passage is found in a separate verbal section, all on its own. First you'll see a few lines in italics introducing both passages. Then will come the two passages. Their lines will be numbered as if they were one *enormous* passage: if **Passage 1** ends on line 42, **Passage 2** will begin on line 43. However, they are two separate passages and you should tackle them one at a time. Remember, the questions are organized sequentially: questions about **Passage 1** will come before questions about **Passage 2**. So, do things in order. *First* read Passage 1; then jump straight to the questions and answer all those based on Passage 1. Most of the time, the Passage 1 questions will immediately follow the excerpts. Once in a great while, one or two questions that refer to both passages will precede the questions about Passage 1. Don't get sidetracked. Skip the questions referring to both passages and focus on those based on Passage 1. *Next* read Passage 2; then answer all the questions based on Passage 2. *Finally*, tackle the three or four questions that refer to *both* passages. Go back to both passages as needed.

# CRITICAL READING EXERCISES

To develop your ability to handle critical reading questions, work your way through the following four exercises. Each exercise contains a full test's worth of reading passages and questions: one 400-word passage followed by 6 questions, one 550-word passage followed by 9 questions, one 800-word passage followed by 12 questions, plus one pair of passages followed by 13 questions. The passages have been taken from published sources—the same sort of published sources tapped by the makers of SAT I. Warning: These exercises are graded in difficulty. Although the questions don't necessarily get harder the further you go, the reading passages definitely do. Go all the way. Even if you do less well on Level C than you did on Level A, look on every error as an opportunity to learn. Reread all the passages you found difficult. Review all the vocabulary words that you didn't know. Remember, these passages and questions are *all* comparable to the ones on SAT I.

After completing each exercise, see how many questions you answered correctly. (The correct answers are given on page 158.)

Then *read those answer explanations.*

## LEVEL A

Most high school students feel comfortable interpreting reading passages on this level of difficulty. Consider the reading passages that follow to be a warm-up for the harder excerpts to come.

## Exercise 1

Directions: Each passage below is followed by questions based on its content. Answer the questions on the basis of what is stated or implied in the passage and in any introductory material that may be provided.

**Questions 1–5 are based on the following passage.**

*The following passage is taken from a review of a general survey of the natural and physical sciences published in 1964.*

"Idle speculation" has no place in science, but "speculation" is its very lifeblood, a well-known physicist believes.

Line    "The more fundamental and far-reaching a
(5)    scientific theory is, the more speculative it is
likely to be," Dr. Michael W. Ovenden, author
and lecturer at the University of Glasgow,
Scotland, states in his book "Life in the
Universe." Dr. Ovenden says it is erroneous to
(10)    believe that science is only concerned with

"pure facts," for mere accumulation of facts is
a primitive form of science. A mature science
tries to arrange facts in significant patterns to
see relationships between previously unrelated
(15)    aspects of the universe.

A theory that does not suggest new ways
of looking at the universe is not likely to make
an important contribution to the development
of science. However, it is also important that
(20)    theories are checked by new experiments and
observations.

Dr. Ovenden discusses recent discoveries
in biology, chemistry and physics that give
clues to the possibility of life in the solar sys-
(25)    tem and other star systems. He discusses conditions on Mars, Venus, Jupiter and Saturn, and
considers whether or not the same conditions

may be found on planets of other stars.

Only the planets Venus, Earth, and Mars
(30) lie within the temperature zone, about
75,000,000 miles wide, in which life can exist.
Venus is covered by a dense layer of clouds
which permits no observation of the surface,
and the surface temperature of the planet is
(35) not known.

Mars is colder than Earth, the average
temperature being about minus 40 degrees
Fahrenheit, compared with plus 59 degrees
Fahrenheit as the average for Earth. However,
(40) near the Mars poles during the summer season, temperatures may rise to as much as 70
degrees Fahrenheit, whereas winter temperatures may fall to minus 130 degrees
Fahrenheit.
(45) Because of the extreme difference in the
Martian seasons, the only life-forms expected
to exist, without a built-in temperature control
such as warm-blooded animals and humans
have, are those which would stay inactive
(50) most of the year. These life-forms may be a
kind of vegetation that opens its leaves to the
sun in the daytime, stores water and closes its
leaves in the night for protection against the
cold.
(55) Attempts have been made to detect in the
spectrum of the dark markings on Mars the
absorption lines due to chlorophyll. So far the
test has not succeeded. But the infrared spectrum of the Martian markings has been found
(60) to be very similar to the spectrum of Earth
vegetation when studied at high altitudes.

1. The word "idle" in line 1 most nearly means

    (A) resting
    (B) lazy
    (C) empty
    (D) lethargic
    (E) leisurely

2. "Speculation is [science's] very lifeblood"
   (line 2) means that scientists

    (A) are gamblers at heart
    (B) must concern themselves with provable
        facts
    (C) must understand all forms of science
    (D) must form opinions about the data they
        gather
    (E) must keep abreast of new developments

3. According to lines 12–15, a mature science

    (A) concerns itself exclusively with gathering
        and recording facts
    (B) dismisses speculative thinking as overly
        fanciful
    (C) connects hitherto unlinked phenomena in
        meaningful ways
    (D) subordinates speculative thought to the
        accumulation of facts
    (E) differentiates between hypotheses and
        speculation

4. The similarity between the infrared spectrum
   of the Martian markings and the Earth spectrum from high altitudes suggests

    (A) the value of speculative thinking
    (B) the absence of chlorophyll on Mars
    (C) a possibility that Mars has vegetation
    (D) that Mars' surface has been cultivated
    (E) the effect of cold on the color of the
        spectrum

5. The author does all of the following EXCEPT

    (A) make an approximation
    (B) use a metaphor
    (C) state a resemblance
    (D) make a conjecture
    (E) deny a contradiction

**Questions 6–15 are based on the following
passage.**

*The following passage is taken from* The Souls of
Black Folk, *W. E. B. Du Bois's classic study of the
African-American's struggle in this country.*

Once upon a time I taught school in the
hills of Tennessee, where the broad dark vale
of the Mississippi begins to roll and crumple
Line to greet the Alleghanies. I was a Fisk student
(5) then, and all Fisk men thought that Tennessee
was theirs alone, and in vacation time they sal-
lied forth in lusty bands to meet the county
school-commissioners. Young and happy, I too
went, and I shall not soon forget that summer,
(10) seventeen years ago.

First, there was a Teachers' Institute at the
county-seat; and there distinguished guests of
the superintendent taught the teachers frac-
tions and spelling and other mysteries—white

(15) teachers in the morning, Negroes at night. A picnic now and then, and a supper, and the rough world was softened by laughter and song. I remember how—but I wander.

There came a day when all the teachers (20) left the Institute and began the hunt for schools. I learn from hearsay (for my mother was mortally afraid of firearms) that the hunting of ducks and bears and men is wonderfully interesting, but I am sure that the man who has (25) never hunted a country school has something to learn of the pleasures of the chase. I see now the white, hot roads lazily rise and fall and wind before me under the burning July sun; I feel the deep weariness of heart and (30) limb as ten, eight, six miles stretch relentlessly ahead; I feel my heart sink heavily as I hear again and again, "Got a teacher? Yes." So I walked on and on—horses were too expensive—until I had wandered beyond railways, (35) beyond stage lines, to a land of "varmints" and rattlesnakes, where the coming of a stranger was an event, and men lived and died in the shadow of one blue hill.

Sprinkled over hill and dale lay cabins and (40) farmhouses, shut out from the world by the forests and the rolling hills toward the east. There I found at last a little school. Josie told me of it; she was a thin, homely girl of twenty, with a dark-brown face and thick, hard hair. I (45) had crossed the stream at Watertown, and rested under the great willows; then I had gone to a little cabin where Josie was resting on her way to town. The gaunt farmer made me welcome, and Josie, hearing my errand, told me (50) anxiously that they wanted a school over the hill; that but once since the war had a teacher been there; that she herself longed to learn—and thus she ran on, talking fast and loud, with much earnestness and energy.

(55) Next morning I crossed the tall, round hill, plunged into the wood, and came out at Josie's home. The father was a quiet, simple soul, calmly ignorant, with no touch of vulgarity. The mother was different—strong, bustling, (60) and energetic, with a quick, restless tongue, and an ambition to live "like folks." There was a crowd of children. Two growing girls; a shy midget of eight; John, tall, awkward, and eighteen; Jim, younger, quicker, and better-look- (65) ing; and two babies of indefinite age. Then

there was Josie herself. She seemed to be the center of the family: always busy at service, or at home, or berry-picking; a little nervous and inclined to scold, like her mother, yet faithful, (70) too, like her father. I saw much of this family afterwards, and grew to love them for their honest efforts to be decent and comfortable, and for their knowledge of their own ignorance. There was with them no affectation. (75) The mother would scold the father for being so "easy"; Josie would roundly berate the boys for carelessness; and all knew that it was a hard thing to dig a living out of a rocky side-hill.

6. The passage as a whole is best characterized as
   (A) an example of the harsh realities of searching for employment
   (B) a description of the achievements of a graduate of a prestigious school
   (C) an analysis of teacher education in a rural setting
   (D) a reminiscence of a memorable time in one man's life
   (E) an illustration of the innocence and gullibility of youth

7. Lines 21–24 suggest that the author had no firsthand knowledge of hunting living creatures because
   (A) he had too much sympathy for the hunter's prey to become a hunter himself
   (B) his studies had left him no time for recreational activities
   (C) small arms weapons had been forbidden in his home
   (D) hunting was an inappropriate activity for teachers
   (E) his mother had once been wounded by a gunshot

8. To the author, his journey through the Tennessee countryside seemed to be all of the following EXCEPT
   (A) gratifying
   (B) interminable
   (C) tiring
   (D) carefree
   (E) discouraging

9. The "stage lines" mentioned by the author in line 35 refer to

(A) phases of personal growth
(B) theatrical directions
(C) horse-drawn transportation
(D) cultural divisions
(E) train stations

10. The author sets the word *varmints* in quotation marks for which of the following reasons?

(A) He wishes to indicate he is referring to an authority.
(B) He is unsure of the correct spelling of the term.
(C) He recognizes them as hunted creatures.
(D) He is using the word colloquially.
(E) He is defining it as a technical term.

11. The author's attitude toward his school-hunting days is predominantly one of

(A) exasperation
(B) nostalgia
(C) bitterness
(D) self-reproach
(E) amusement

12. The passage suggests that Josie's interest on meeting the author was

(A) magnified by her essentially gregarious nature
(B) sufficiently strong to make her act uncharacteristically
(C) prompted by her need for distractions on the long road to town
(D) intensified by her desire to gain an education
(E) motivated by her longing to escape her impoverished home

13. By saying she wished to live "like folks" (line 61), Josie's mother primarily emphasizes

(A) apprehension about sinking to the level of mere brutes
(B) an expanding greed for material possessions
(C) impatience with people who think themselves too good for their fellows
(D) a longing for her entire family to better themselves
(E) an unfortunate inclination toward conformity

14. The word "roundly" in line 76 means

(A) circuitously
(B) bluntly
(C) approximately
(D) resonantly
(E) fondly

15. The author most likely remembers Josie and her family primarily with feelings of

(A) measured regret
(B) grudging condescension
(C) grateful veneration
(D) outright curiosity
(E) distinct affection

**Questions 16–27 are based on the following passage.**

*The book from which the following passage was taken explains architectural methods both past and present.*

The ancient Chinese believed that in the features of the natural landscape one could glimpse the mathematically precise order of
*Line* the universe and all the beneficial and harmful
(5) forces that were harmoniously connected according to the principle of the Tao—the Way. This was not a question of metaphor; the topography did not represent good or evil; it really *was* good or evil. Under these circum-
(10) stances, locating a building in the landscape became a decision of momentous proportions that could affect an individual and his family for generations to come. The result was *feng-shui*, which means "wind and water," and
(15) which was a kind of cosmic surveying tool. Its coherent, scientific practice dates from the Sung dynasty (960–1126), but its roots are much older than that. It was first used to locate grave sites—the Chinese worshiped their
(20) ancestors, who, they believed, influenced the good fortune of their descendants. Eventually it began to be used to locate the homes of the living; and, indeed, the earliest book on *feng-shui*, published during the Han dynasty (202
(25) B.C.–A.D. 220). was entitled *The Canon of the Dwellings.*

*Feng-shui* combined an intricate set of related variables that reflected the three great

religions of China—Taoism, Buddhism, and
(30) Confucianism. First were the Taoist principles
of yang and yin—male and female. The five
Buddhist planets corresponded to the five elements, the five directions (north, south, west,
east, and center), and the five seasons (the
(35) usual four and midsummer). *Feng-shui*
employed the sixty-four epigrams of the *I-
Ching*, a classic manual of divination popular-
ized by Confucius, and also made use of the
astrological signs: the constellations were
(40) divided into four groups: the Azure Dragon
(east), the Black Tortoise (north), the White
Tiger (west), and the Red Bird (south).

The first task of the geomancer, who was
called *feng-shui hsien sheng*, or "doctor of the
(45) vital force," was to detect the presence of each
of these variables in the natural landscape.
Hilly ground represented the Dragon; low
ground was the Tiger: the ideal was to have
the Dragon on the left and the Tiger on the
(50) right (hence, to face south). In a predominantly hilly area, however, a low spot was a good
place to build; in flatter terrain, heights were
considered lucky. The best site was the junction between the Dragon and the Tiger, which
(55) is why the imperial tombs around Beijing are
so beautifully situated, just where the valley
floor begins to turn into mountain slopes.

The shape of mountain peaks, the presence of boulders, and the direction of streams
(60) all incorporated meanings that had to be
unraveled. Often simple observation did not
suffice, and the Chinese had to resort to external aids. The mariner compass was a Chinese
invention, but the *feng-shui* compass served a
(65) different purpose. It resembled a large, flat,
circular platter. In the center, like the bull's-
eye of a dartboard, was a magnetic needle,
surrounded by eighteen concentric circles.
Each ring represented a different factor and
(70) was inscribed with the constellations, odd and
even numbers, the planets and the elements,
the seasons, the hexagrams, the signs of the
zodiac, the solar orbit, and so on. With the aid
of the compass, the geomancer could discover
(75) the existence of these variables even when
they were not visible to the naked eye.

It might appear that *feng-shui* made man
the victim of fate, but this is not the case. For
one thing, there was a moral dimension to the
(80) belief; and to gain the full benefit of an auspi-

ciously placed home, the family itself had to
remain honest and upright. Moreover, the geomancer's job was not only to identify bad and
good sites but also to advise on how to miti-
(85) gate evil influences or to improve good ones.
Trees could be planted to camouflage undesir-
able views; streams could be rerouted;
mounds could be built up or cut down. It is no
accident that the greatest Chinese art of all is
(90) gardening.

Many villages in China have a grove of
trees or bamboo behind them, and a pond in
front. The function of these picturesque features is not as landscaping embellishment, or
(95) at least it is not only that; they are intended to
fend off evil influences. The pagodas that can
still be seen built on the tops of hills and
mounds serve the same purpose. When visiting some recently built farmhouses in the
(100) county of Wuqing, I noticed that the entrances
to some of the courtyards were screened by a
wall that forced the visitor to wind his way
around it, as in a maze or an obstacle course.
But the purpose of the *ying-pei*, as the Chinese
(105) walls are called, is not to prevent the passerby
from looking in. These are "spirit walls" and
are meant to keep out asomatous[1] trespassers.
The *ying-pei* is not an isolated superstition,
like lucky horseshoes in the West; it too is part
(110) of *feng-shui*.

---

[1]Lacking a body; ghostly; spirit-like.

16. The passage suggests that the ancient Chinese

    (A) are not clearly understood by modern-day
        thinkers
    (B) were preoccupied with death
    (C) did not understand the basic physical prin-
        ciples that govern the universe
    (D) behaved in a peaceful manner
    (E) conducted their lives according to a
        well-defined philosophy

17. As described in the passage, *feng-shui* is a
    practice that

    (A) has spread throughout the world
    (B) is used to locate building sites
    (C) is widely used near the water's edge
    (D) most people consider a foolish superstition
    (E) is used to determine the appearance of
        buildings

18. According to the passage, the Tao apparently

(A) originated about a thousand years ago
(B) is a kind of metaphor
(C) is a way of viewing the world
(D) is a prescription for a happy life
(E) is a moral code that guides human behavior

19. Based on the passage, *feng-shui* seems to have developed as a practice mainly because the Chinese believed in

(A) the sayings of Confucius
(B) life after death
(C) astrology
(D) providing for future generations
(E) original sin

20. The best definition of a "geomancer" (line 43) is one who

(A) knew how to provide spiritual counsel
(B) understood religion
(C) could read and interpret the terrain
(D) guided people in the wilderness
(E) served as a medium between the living and the dead

21. The principles of *feng-shui* suggest that the best terrain on which to build a house is

(A) partly flat and partly hilly
(B) a river valley
(C) mountainous
(D) where mountains meet the sea
(E) rugged with lots of trees

22. The author compares the center of a *feng-shui* compass to bull's-eye of a dartboard (lines 66–67) in order to

(A) suggest that *feng-shui* is like a game
(B) clarify the appearance of the compass
(C) indicate that *feng-shui* is a complex art
(D) explain that it is extremely difficult to find ideal building sites
(E) belittle the art of *feng-shui*

23. The author of the passage implies that the city of Beijing was deliberately built

(A) near mountains
(B) on a large bay
(C) at the confluence of two rivers
(D) to maximize the sun's light and warmth
(E) close to ancient burial places

24. According to the passage, an ideally-situated home

(A) assures happiness to the family living there
(B) is no guarantee of good fortune
(C) empowered families to ward off sickness and disease
(D) helps a family establish financial security
(E) keeps families together

25. The author calls gardening the "greatest" art in China (line 89) because

(A) Chinese gardens are usually very beautiful
(B) the best gardeners in the world come from China
(C) gardening is a popular pastime in China
(D) Chinese gardens contain symbolic meanings
(E) the Chinese know how to grow exotic plants and flowers

26. Which of the following best describes the author's attitude toward *feng-shui*?

(A) Mild skepticism
(B) Surprise
(C) Awe and wonder
(D) Amused mockery
(E) Intellectual curiosity

27. To repel evil spirits a family believing in *feng-shui* is likely to pay attention to all of the following EXCEPT

(A) the distance to their home of large rock formations
(B) the accessibility of the main entrance
(C) the placement of trees around the house
(D) the color of their house
(E) the appearance of nearby mountains

**Questions 28–40 are based on the following pair of passages.**

*The following passages discuss problems of being poor in America. The first is an excerpt from a best-selling study of a Puerto Rican family, written by an anthropologist in the 1960s. The second is an excerpt from a speech given at a Florida school in 1965.*

**Passage 1**

Low wages, chronic unemployment and underemployment lead to low income, lack of property ownership, absence of savings,
Line absence of food reserves in the home, and a
(5) chronic shortage of cash. These conditions reduce the possibility of effective participation in the larger economic system. And as a response to these conditions we find in the culture of poverty a high incidence of pawning
(10) personal goods, borrowing from local money-lenders at usurious rates of interest, sponta-neous informal credit devices organized by neighbors, the use of secondhand clothing and furniture, and the pattern of frequent buying of
(15) small quantities of food many times a day as the need arises.

People with a culture of poverty produce very little wealth and receive very little in return. They have a low level of literacy and
(20) education, usually do not belong to labor unions, are not members of political parties, generally do not participate in the national welfare agencies, and make very little use of banks, hospitals, department stores, museums
(25) or art galleries. They have a critical attitude toward some of the basic institutions of the dominant classes, hatred of the police, mis-trust of government and those in high position, and a cynicism which extends even to the
(30) church. This gives the culture of poverty a high potential for protest and for being used in political movements aimed against the exist-ing social order.

People with a culture of poverty are aware
(35) of middle-class values, talk about them and even claim some of them as their own, but on the whole they do not live by them. Thus it is important to distinguish between what they say and what they do. For example, many will
(40) tell you that marriage by law, by the church, or by both, is the ideal form of marriage, but few

will marry. To men who have no steady jobs or other sources of income, who do not own property and have no wealth to pass on to their
(45) children, who are present-time oriented and who want to avoid the expense and legal diffi-culties involved in formal marriage and divorce, free unions or consensual marriage make a lot of sense. Women will often turn
(50) down offers of marriage because they feel it ties them down to men who are immature, punishing and generally unreliable. Women feel that consensual union gives them a better break; it gives them some of the freedom and
(55) flexibility that men have. By not giving the fathers of their children legal status as hus-bands, the women have a stronger claim on their children if they decide to leave their men. It also gives women exclusive rights to a
(60) house or any other property they may own.

**Passage 2**

You ask me what is poverty? Listen to me. Here I am, dirty, smelly, and with no "proper" underwear on and with the stench of my rot-ting teeth near you. I will tell you. Listen to
(65) me. Listen without pity. I cannot use your pity. Listen with understanding. Put yourself in my dirty, worn-out ill-fitting shoes, and hear me.

Poverty is getting up every morning from a dirt- and illness-stained mattress. The sheets
(70) have long since been used for diapers. Poverty is living in a smell that never leaves. This is a smell of urine, sour milk, and spoiling food sometimes joined with the strong smell of long-cooked onions. Onions are cheap. If you
(75) have smelled this smell, you did not know how it came. It is the smell of the outdoor privy. It is the smell of young children who cannot walk the long dark way in the night. It is the smell of the mattresses where years of
(80) "accidents" have happened. It is the smell of the milk which has gone sour because the refrigerator long has not worked, and it costs money to get it fixed. It is the smell of rotting garbage. I could bury it, but where is the shov-
(85) el? Shovels cost money.

Poverty is always being tired. I have always been tired. They told me at the hospital when the last baby came that I had chronic anemia caused from poor diet, a bad case of
(90) worms, and that I needed a corrective opera-tion. I listened politely—the poor are always

polite. The poor always listen. They don't say
that there is no money for iron pills, or better
food, or worm medicine. The idea of an opera-
(95) tion is frightening and costs so much that, if I
had dared, I would have laughed. . . .
    Poverty is looking into a black future.
Your children won't play with my boys. They
will turn to other boys who steal to get what
(100) they want. I can already see them behind the
bars of their prison instead of behind the bars
of my poverty. Or they will turn to the freedom of alcohol or drugs, and find themselves
enslaved. And my daughter? At best, there is
(105) for her a life like mine. . . Poverty is an acid
that drips on pride until all pride is worn away.
Poverty is a chisel that chips on honor until
honor is worn away. Some of you say that you
would do *something* in my situation, and
(110) maybe you would, for the first week or the
first month, but for year after year after year?
    I have come out of my despair to tell you
this. Remember I did not come from another
place or another time. Others like me are all
(115) around you. Look at us with an angry heart,
anger that will help you help me. Anger that
will let you tell of me. The poor are always
silent. Can you be silent too?

28. A defining characteristic of poverty, according
    to the author of Passage 1, is that poor people

    (A) lack the imagination to lift themselves out
        of poverty
    (B) lack the skills to find decent jobs
    (C) are constantly in a state of crisis
    (D) are somewhat responsible for their own
        poverty
    (E) are isolated from the mainstream of society

29. The author of Passage 1 uses the phrase "cul-
    ture of poverty" to suggest that

    (A) causes of poverty have been carefully stud-
        ied and analyzed
    (B) poor people often take pride in their
        poverty
    (C) for some people poverty has become a pre-
        vailing way of life
    (D) poor people share a common background
    (E) there are several levels and classifications
        of poor people

30. By asserting that the culture of poverty can be
    used by political movements (lines 30–33), the
    author is

    (A) predicting an uprising by the poor
    (B) citing a reason for eliminating poverty
    (C) cautioning the middle class to beware of
        the poor
    (D) criticizing the motives of politicians
    (E) alluding to a particular historical event

31. The author's point about the need to "distinguish
    between what [poor people] say and what they
    do" (lines 37–39) is meant to suggest that

    (A) poor people are often hypocritical
    (B) lying is part of the culture of poverty
    (C) the poor are often unable to change the
        conditions of their lives
    (D) the poor are fooling themselves
    (E) poverty causes people to have illusions

32. A conclusion to be drawn from the discussion of
    marriage in Passage 1 is that men and women in
    the culture of poverty

    (A) avoid legalized marriages for practical and
        economic reasons
    (B) prefer to be independent
    (C) cannot afford to marry and raise a family
    (D) do not trust each other to be faithful hus-
        bands and wives
    (E) consider themselves unworthy of legal
        marriage

33. The comparison between the "bars of their prison"
    and the "bars of my poverty" (lines 101–102) is
    meant to suggest that the speaker believes that

    (A) her sons must choose between a life of
        crime and a life of poverty
    (B) escaping from poverty is more difficult
        than escaping from prison
    (C) her sons can escape from poverty but not
        from prison
    (D) crime results from poverty
    (E) poverty and imprisonment are similar

34. Evidence in Passage 2 suggests that the speak-
    er lives

    (A) on an isolated farm
    (B) in an urban slum
    (C) in a housing project
    (D) in the country
    (E) near a big city

35. The primary emotion conveyed by the speaker in Passage 2 is
   (A) jealousy
   (B) resentment
   (C) discouragement
   (D) hopelessness
   (E) resignation

36. When the speaker says "the poor always listen" (line 92) and "the poor are always silent" (lines 117–118) she is implying that poor people
   (A) feel intimidated by authority
   (B) cannot express themselves articulately
   (C) prefer to keep to themselves
   (D) suffer from powerlessness
   (E) don't want to antagonize other people

37. The main intent of the speaker in Passage 2 is to
   (A) convey information about poverty to the audience
   (B) enrage the audience
   (C) arouse the audience to action
   (D) define poverty
   (E) describe real differences between the rich and the poor

38. Compared to Passage 1, Passage 2 is more likely to evoke an emotional response from the reader because
   (A) it uses shocking language
   (B) it is written in first person singular
   (C) the speaker shows intense emotion
   (D) it repeatedly uses the word *poverty*
   (E) the audience is being addressed as "you"

39. In discussing poverty, the authors of both passages seem to agree that poverty
   (A) cannot be clearly defined
   (B) means more than lack of money
   (C) is more widespread than most people think
   (D) cannot be eliminated
   (E) weakens the fabric of society

40. Passage 2 illustrates the contention in Passage 1 that the poor
   (A) suffer from a chronic shortage of cash
   (B) mistrust the government
   (C) have a low level of literacy and education
   (D) rely on neighbors to borrow money
   (E) make little use of banks, hospitals and department stores

# Exercise 2

> Directions: Each passage below is followed by questions based on its content. Answer the questions on the basis of what is <u>stated</u> or <u>implied</u> in the passage and in any introductory material that may be provided.

## Questions 1–7 are based on the following passage.

*The following passage, taken from a memoir by a Japanese-American writer, describes the conflicts she felt as she grew up living in two cultures and trying to meet two very different sets of expectations.*

Whenever I succeeded in the *Hakujin* world, my brothers were supportive, whereas Papa would be disdainful, undermined by my
Line obvious capitulation to the ways of the West. I
(5) wanted to be like my Caucasian friends. Not only did I want to look like them, I wanted to act like them. I tried hard to be outgoing and socially aggressive and act confidently, like my girlfriends. At home I was careful not to
(10) show these personality traits to my father. For him it was bad enough that I did not even look Japanese: I was too big, and I walked too assertively. My behavior at home was never calm and serene, but around my father I still
(15) tried to be as Japanese as I could.

As I passed puberty and grew more interested in boys, I soon became aware that an Oriental female evoked a certain kind of interest from males. I was still too young to under-
(20) stand how or why an Oriental female fascinated Caucasian men, and of course, far too young to see then that it was a form of "not seeing." My brothers would warn me, "Don't trust the *Hakujin* boys. They only want one
(25) thing. They'll treat you like a servant and expect you to wait on them hand and foot. They don't even know how to be nice to you." My brothers never dated Caucasian girls. In fact, I never really dated Caucasian boys until
(30) I went to college. In high school, I used to sneak out to dances and parties where I would meet them. I wouldn't even dare to think what Papa would do if he knew.

What my brothers were saying was that I
(35) should not act toward Caucasian males as I did

toward them. I must not "wait on them" or allow them to think I would, because they wouldn't understand. In other words, be a Japanese female around Japanese men and act
(40) as a *Hakujin* around Caucasian men. The double identity within a "double standard" resulted not only in confusion for me of my role, or roles, as a female, but also in who or what I was racially. With the admonitions of my
(45) brothers lurking deep in my consciousness, I would try to be aggressive, assertive and "come on strong" toward Caucasian men. I mustn't let them think I was submissive, passive, and all-giving like Madame Butterfly.
(50) With Asian males I would tone down my natural enthusiasm and settle into patterns instilled in me through the models of my mother and sisters. I was not comfortable in either role.

1. The author's father reacted negatively to her successes in the Caucasian world because

   (A) he wanted her older sisters to be more successful than she was
   (B) his expectations were that she could do even better than he had done
   (C) he realized worldly success alone could not make her happy
   (D) he envied her for having opportunities that he had never known
   (E) he felt her Westernization was costing him his authority over her

2. The author most likely uses the Japanese word *Hakujin* to stand for Caucasians because

   (A) she knows no other word with that meaning
   (B) her brothers insisted that she address white boys in that way
   (C) she enjoys showing off her knowledge of exotic terminology
   (D) that is how her immediate family referred to them
   (E) it is a term that indicates deep respect

3. The father of the author expected her to be

   (A) tranquil and passive
   (B) subservient to Caucasian males
   (C) successful in the *Hakujin* way
   (D) increasingly independent and aggressive
   (E) open about going to school dances

4. By describing the white boys' fascination with Oriental women as "not seeing" (lines 22–23), the author primarily wishes to convey that

   (A) the white boys were reluctant to date their Oriental classmates or see them socially
   (B) they had no idea what she was like as an individual human being
   (C) the boys were too shy to look the girls in the eye
   (D) the boys could not see her attractions because she was too large to meet Japanese standards of beauty
   (E) love is nearsighted, if not blind

5. By a "double identity within a 'double standard'" (lines 40–41) the author primarily means

   (A) she had one standard while her brothers had another
   (B) she had one standard while her mother had another
   (C) she was Japanese at home and *Hakujin* outside the home
   (D) she was too assertive at school to be passive at home
   (E) she felt like a double agent, betraying both sides

6. As used in lines 48–49, the figure of Madame Butterfly can best be described as

   (A) a model the author sought to emulate
   (B) the pattern the author's brothers wished her to follow
   (C) a particularly generous *Hakujin*
   (D) a role the author eventually found comfortable
   (E) an ethnic stereotype

7. The author's reaction to the roles she was required to adopt was primarily one of

   (A) indifference
   (B) despair
   (C) bemusement
   (D) outrage
   (E) unease

**Questions 8–15 are based on the following passage.**

*The following excerpt is taken from a standard text on the history of Mexican art.*

Pre-Spanish history in Mexico is riddled with lacunae or gaps. All that can be stated with certainty is that, quite independent of any
*Line* European or Oriental influence, peoples
(5) speaking different languages and at various stages of cultural development gradually created a civilization in Mexico which, by the tenth century, already knew the use of certain metals. This civilization has left us temples,
(10) palaces, tombs, ball-courts, images of its gods, ritual masks and funeral urns, mural paintings and codices, jewelry and personal ornaments, pottery for household and religious uses, weapons and primitive tools. All these do not
(15) belong to the same epoch, style, or culture, but together they form a rich and varied aggregation which is, nevertheless, homogeneous and comparable to Chinese art of the two thousand years from Confucius to the Ming dynasty.
(20) Pre-Spanish art in Mexico served a religious function. It was not content to copy the external world, whose visible forms were for it no more than an outward testimony of great inner forces. It created original compositions,
(25) using real elements with an almost musical freedom. It is not a crude art; they are mistaken who see in its bold simplifications or wayward conceptions an inability to overcome technical difficulties. The ancient Mexican
(30) artist was deliberate and skillful, and, though never led by a merely descriptive aim, he often lingered over his subjects with realistic and minutely observant pleasure. One marvels at his plastic feeling and at his powers of dec-
(35) orative composition.

   The Mayas achieved in sculpture a placid and austere beauty of proportion and sensitiveness in modeling which has rarely been surpassed. The works of the Totonacs reveal a
(40) people of keen sensibility and varied means of expression. Their grace and tranquil, formal beauty, their plastic rhythm and interpretation of psychological values place their makers among the creators of purest art. Aztec works
(45) rival the sober and vigorous solidity of great Egyptian sculpture, which they surpass in

human intensity. The colossal statue of
Coatlicue shows that equilibrium between a
maximum richness of detail and an assertion
(50) of plastic structure which, centuries later, is
again to be found in the Mexican baroque.
    In its finest works, Mexican sculpture
equals the masterpieces of any other period.
The plastic feeling of these mysterious people
(55) led them to solutions that are surprising in
their modernity. There are Tarascan statuettes
that anticipate the essential and drastic simplicity of Brancusi, and Totonac masks that
recall the poignant mortality which haunted
(60) Lehmbruck. The reclining figure of Chac-
mool seems to forecast the lines of "The
Mountains" by the English sculptor, Henry
Moore. The ancient Mexicans tried sculptural
caricature also, and even sought to reproduce
(65) color effects plastically. These people have left
us, as Robert Fry affirms, "more masterpieces
of pure sculpture than the whole of
Mesopotamia, or than the majority of modern
European civilizations."

8. The word "riddled" in line 1 most nearly
means
(A) puzzled
(B) questioned
(C) interpreted
(D) sifted
(E) filled

9. The author stresses that our knowledge of pre-
Spanish civilization in Mexico is
(A) incomplete
(B) homogeneous
(C) academic
(D) graphic
(E) paradoxical

10. Which of the following statements best
expresses the main idea of the passage?
(A) Religion dominated early Mexican art.
(B) The artists of ancient Mexico excelled
chiefly in decoration.
(C) Mexican art surpasses European and Asian
art.
(D) Many masterpieces exist among pre-
Spanish Mexican art works.
(E) Modern Mexican art cannot equal pre-
Spanish Mexican art.

11. The author implies that distortions in ancient
Mexican art were
(A) reparable
(B) deliberate
(C) beautiful
(D) caused by inferior tools
(E) inflicted at a later date

12. The statement in lines 33–35 ("One marvels …
decorative composition") is best interpreted as
conveying
(A) skepticism about the ancient Mexican
artist's commitment to decorative art
(B) distrust of the plastic, synthetic quality of
purely decorative art
(C) perplexity about how the pre-Spanish artist
could have achieved his level of technical skill
(D) admiration for both the artist's technical
expertise and artistic sensibility
(E) a desire to study the origins of Mexican art
further

13. The word "modeling" in line 38 most nearly
means
(A) posing for artists
(B) imitating the work of others
(C) displaying fashions
(D) being good examples
(E) shaping objects

14. In the last paragraph, the author probably men-
tions Brancusi, Lehmbruck, and Henry Moore
in order to
(A) prove that he is acquainted with the works
of modern artists
(B) show that their works were influenced by
Mexican art
(C) explain that good art has universal appeal
(D) add a note of irony to his argument
(E) relate Mexican art to more familiar works
of art

15. It can be inferred from the passage that much
of ancient Mexican art depicted
(A) abstract patterns
(B) landscapes
(C) people
(D) still life
(E) pure color

**Questions 16–27 are based on the following passage.**

*The following passage is an excerpt from a historical study, done in the 1980s, of the relationship between the press and each American president from George Washington to Ronald Reagan.*

In the shifting relationship between the press and the presidency over nearly two centuries, there has remained one primary con-
Line stant—the dissatisfaction of one with the
(5) other. No president has escaped press criticism, and no president has considered himself fairly treated. The record of every administration has been the same, beginning with mutual protestations of goodwill, ending with recrimi-
(10) nations and mistrust.

This is the best proof we could have that the American concept of a free press in a free society is a viable idea, whatever defects the media may have. While the Founding Fathers
(15) and their constituencies did not always agree on the role the press should play, there was a basic consensus that the newspaper (the only medium of consequence at the time) should be the buffer state between the rulers and the ruled.
(20) The press could be expected to behave like a watchdog, and government at every level, dependent for its existence on the opinions of those it governed, could expect to resent being watched and having its shortcomings, real or
(25) imaginary, exposed to the public view.

Reduced to such simple terms, the relationship of the presidents to the press since George Washington's first term is understandable only as an underlying principle. But this
(30) basic concept has been increasingly complicated by the changing nature of the presidency, by the individual nature of presidents, by the rise of other media, especially television, and by the growing complexity of beliefs
(35) about the function of both press and government.

In surveying nearly two centuries of this relationship, it is wise to keep in mind an axiom of professional historians—that we
(40) should be careful not to view the past in terms of our own times, and make judgments accordingly. Certain parallels often become obvious, to be sure, but to assert what an individual president should or should not have

(45) done, by present standards, is to violate historical context. Historians occasionally castigate each other for this failing, and in the case of press and government, the danger becomes particularly great because the words them-
(50) selves—"press" and "government," even "presidency"—have changed in meaning so much during the past two hundred years.

Recent scholarship, for example, has emphasized that colonial Americans believed
(55) in a free press, but not at all in the sense that we understand it today. Basic to their belief was the understanding, which had prevailed since the invention of the printing press in the fifteenth century, that whoever controlled the
(60) printing press was in the best position to control the minds of men. The press was seen at once as an unprecedented instrument of power, and the struggle to control it began almost as soon as the Gutenberg (or Mazarin)
(65) Bible appeared at Mainz in 1456, an event which meant that, for the first time, books could be reproduced exactly and, more important, that they could be printed in quantity.

Two primary centers of social and politi-
(70) cal power—the state and the church—stood to benefit most from the invention of the printing press. In the beginning it was mutually advantageous for them to work together; consequently it was no accident that the first
(75) printing press on the North American continent was set up in Mexico City in 1539 by Fray Juan Zumarraga, first Catholic bishop of that country. It gave the church an unprecedented means of advancing conversion, along
(80) with the possibility of consolidating and extending its power, thus providing Catholic Spain with the same territorial advantages that would soon be extended elsewhere in the Americas.

(85) When British colonies were established in North America during the early part of the seventeenth century, it was once again a religious faith, this time Protestant, that brought the first printing press to what is now the
(90) United States. But while colonial printing in Central and South America remained the province of the Catholics for some time and was used primarily for religious purposes, in North America secular publishing became an
(95) adjunct of a church-dominated press almost at once and was soon dominant.

It is part of American mythology that the nation was "cradled in liberty" and that the colonists, seeking religious freedom, immedi-
(100) ately established a free society, but the facts are quite different. The danger of an uncontrolled press to those in power was well expressed by Sir William Berkeley, governor of Virginia, when he wrote home to his superi-
(105) ors in 1671: "I thank God there are no free schools nor printing, and I hope we shall not have these hundred years; for learning has brought disobedience, and heresy, and sects into the world, and printing has divulged
(110) them, and libels against the best government, God keep us from both." There are those in twentieth-century America who would say "Amen" to Berkeley's view of printing and "libels against the best government."

16. According to the passage, all American presidents have experienced

 (A) disappointment with the quality of their press coverage
 (B) goodwill from some reporters in the press corps
 (C) alternating periods of antagonism and harmony with the press
 (D) hostility between themselves and the press
 (E) having untruthful reports published about themselves

17. Conflict between the president and the press indicates that

 (A) the press publishes the truth even when it hurts the president
 (B) freedom of the press is alive and well in the United States
 (C) presidents have traditionally had little respect for the press
 (D) the press is made up mostly of critics and cynics
 (E) friendly reporters are rarely assigned to cover the president

18. In the early days of the country, the function of the press was to

 (A) interpret the government's actions for the people
 (B) carefully observe and report on the work of all elected officials

 (C) serve as a conduit of information between the government and the people
 (D) preserve, protect, and defend the Bill of Rights, especially freedom of the press
 (E) mold public opinion

19. Since the early days the relationship between the president and the press has been altered by all of the following EXCEPT

 (A) the term of office has remained four years
 (B) the position of "Press Secretary" has been created
 (C) presidents hold televised news conferences
 (D) U.S presidents are expected to be world leaders
 (E) an increasingly large number of news people cover the president

20. The author of the passage cautions the reader about judging presidents of the distant past because

 (A) press reports of their day cannot be trusted
 (B) modern scholars have revised history
 (C) we can't fully grasp the context of the past
 (D) second-guessing is unfair to former presidents
 (E) history is an imprecise science

21. In colonial America, the phrase "free press" (line 55) meant that

 (A) the same newspapers were published throughout the thirteen colonies
 (B) the press influenced what people thought and did
 (C) aside from the Bible, newspapers were the colonists' favorite reading material
 (D) very few people could afford to own a printing press
 (E) the government was less powerful than the press

22. The passage implies that before the invention of the printing press

 (A) most people were illiterate
 (B) people depended for their news on word-of-mouth
 (C) governments played a less influential role in people's lives
 (D) news about the government traveled more slowly
 (E) the civil and church authorities were virtually the same

23. The notion that it was "no accident" (line 74) that Juan Zumarraga set up the first printing press in North America means that

   (A) the church ordered Zumarraga to set up a printing press
   (B) Zumarraga worked as an agent of the Spanish government
   (C) printing holy bibles raised funds for the church
   (D) the church quickly saw that the printing press could help spread the word of God
   (E) Zumarraga advocated the improvement of the printing press

24. In contrast to printing in South America, printing in North America

   (A) was less politically-oriented
   (B) was founded by the Catholic church
   (C) was dominated by religion
   (D) began earlier in the history of the New World
   (E) quickly became less religious in nature

25. The author refers to Sir William Berkeley as an example of a colonist who

   (A) was loyal to the English crown
   (B) was appointed rather than elected to his office
   (C) held the church above other institutions
   (D) advocated religious tolerance
   (E) inspired confidence in the press

26. Americans who might say "Amen" to Berkeley's views (line 112), are likely to believe

   (A) that limits should be set on freedom of the press
   (B) in the exercise of complete religious freedom for all
   (C) in a *laissez-faire* type of government
   (D) in the separation of church and state
   (E) that extremism in defense of freedom is not justified

27. The passage suggests that issues of a free press

   (A) pertain only to the United States
   (B) have been intertwined with matters concerning the separation of church and state
   (C) still raise controversy in the United States
   (D) are clearly discussed in the Constitution of the United States
   (E) originated during George Washington's administration

**Questions 28–40 are based on the following pair of passages.**

*The following passages are excerpts from the writings of two naturalists with a deep affection for the American wilderness. The first is about the Grand Canyon, the second, about the Sonoran Desert in the state of Arizona.*

**Passage 1**

      Those who have long and carefully studied the Grand Canyon of the Colorado do not hesitate for a moment to pronounce it by far
Line the most sublime of all earthly spectacles. If
(5) its sublimity consisted only in its dimensions, it could be sufficiently set forth in a single sentence. It is more than 200 miles long, from 5 to 12 miles wide, and from 5,000 to 6,000 feet deep. There are in the world valleys which
(10) are longer and a few which are deeper. There are valleys flanked by summits loftier than the palisades of the Kaibab. Still the Grand Canyon is the sublimest thing on earth. It is not so alone by virtue of its magnitudes, but
(15) by virtue of the whole—its *ensemble*.
      The common notion of a canyon is that of a deep, narrow gash in the earth, with nearly vertical walls, like a great and neatly cut trench. There are hundreds of chasms in the
(20) Plateau Country which answer very well to this notion. Many of them are sunk to frightful depths and are fifty to a hundred miles in length. Some are exceedingly narrow, as the canyons of the forks of the Virgen, where the
(25) overhanging walls shut out the sky. Some are intricately sculptured, and illuminated with brilliant colors; others are picturesque by reason of their bold and striking sculpture. A few of them are most solemn and impressive by
(30) reason of their profundity and the majesty of their walls. But, as a rule, the common canyons are neither grand nor even attractive. Upon first acquaintance they are curious and awaken interest as a new sensation, but they
(35) soon grow tiresome for want of diversity, and become at last mere bores. The impressions they produce are very transient, because of their great simplicity, and the limited range of ideas they present.
(40)      It is perhaps in some respects unfortunate that the stupendous pathway of the Colorado River through the Kaibabs was ever called a

canyon, for the name identifies it with a baser conception. But the name presents as wide a
(45) range of signification as the word *house*. The log cabin of the rancher, the painted and vine-clad cottage of the mechanic, the home of the millionaire, the places where parliaments assemble, and the grandest temples of
(50) worship, are all houses. Yet the contrast between St. Mark's and the rude dwelling of the frontiersman is not greater than that between the chasm of the Colorado and the trenches in the rocks which answer to the ordi-
(55) nary conception of a canyon. So is the chasm an expansion of the simple type of drainage channels peculiar to the Plateau Country. To the conception of its vast proportions must be added some notion of its intricate plan, the
(60) nobility of its architecture, its colossal buttes, its wealth of ornamentation, the splendor of its colors, and its wonderful atmosphere. All of these attributes combine with infinite complexity to produce a whole which at first
(65) bewilders and at length overpowers.

## Passage 2

Last Saturday before dusk, the summer's 114 degree heat broke to 79 within an hour. A fury of wind whipped up, pelting houses with dust, debris, and gravel. Then a scatter of rain
(70) came, as a froth of purplish clouds charged across the skies. As the last of the sun's light dissipated, we could see Baboquivari Peak silhouetted on a red horizon, lightning dancing around its head.
(75) The rains came that night—they changed the world.
Crusty dry since April, the desert floor softened under the rain's dance. Near the rain-pocked surface, hundreds of thousands of
(80) bloodroot amaranth are popping off their seedcoats and diving toward light. Barren places will soon be shrouded in a veil of green.
Desert arroyos are running again, muddy water swirling after a head of suds, dung, and
(85) detritus. Where sheetfloods pool, buried animals awake, or new broods hatch. At dawn, dark egg-shaped clouds of flying ants hover over ground, excited in the early morning light.
In newly filled waterholes, spadefoot
(90) toads suddenly congregate. The males bellow. They seek out mates, then latch onto them with their special nuptial pads. The females

spew out egg masses into the hot murky water. For two nights, the toad ponds are wild with
(95) chanting while the Western spadefoot's burnt-peanut-like smell looms thick in the air.
A yellow mud turtle crawls out of the drenched bottom of an old adobe borrow pit where he had been buried through the hot dry
(100) spell. He plods a hundred yards over to a floodwater reservoir and dives in. He has no memory of how many days it's been since his last swim, but the pull of the water—*that* is somehow familiar.
(105) This is the time when the Papago Indians of the Sonoran Desert celebrate the coming of the rainy season moons, the *Jujkiabig Mamsad,* and the beginning of a new year.
Fields lying fallow since the harvest of the
(110) winter crop are now ready for another planting. If sown within a month after summer solstice, they can produce a crop quick enough for harvest by the Feast of San Francisco, October 4.
When I went by the Madrugada home in
(115) Little Tucson on Monday, the family was eagerly talking about planting the flashflood field again. At the end of June, Julian wasn't even sure if he would plant this year—no rain yet, too hot to prepare the field, and hardly
(120) any water left in their *charco* catchment basin.
Now, a fortnight later, the pond is nearly filled up to the brim. Runoff has fed into it through four small washes. Sheetfloods have swept across the field surface. Julian imagines
(125) big yellow squash blossoms in his field, just another month or so away. It makes his mouth water.
Once I asked a Papago youngster what the desert smelled like to him. He answered with
(130) little hesitation:
"The desert smells like rain."
His reply is a contradiction in the minds of most people. How could the desert smell like rain, when deserts are, by definition, places
(135) which lack substantial rainfall?
The boy's response was a sort of Papago shorthand. Hearing Papago can be like tasting a delicious fruit, while sensing that the taste comes from a tree with roots too deep to fathom.
(140) The question had triggered a scent—creosote bushes after a storm—their aromatic oils released by the rains. His nose remembered being out in the desert, overtaken: *the desert smells like rain.*

28. Passage 1 indicates that the Grand Canyon is "the sublimest thing on earth" (line 13) because of its

    (A) size
    (B) geologic formations
    (C) mysterious beauty
    (D) overall appearance
    (E) stature among the world's natural wonders

29. Passage 1 implies that visitors to the Grand Canyon are most likely to be

    (A) enthusiastic at first but quick to seek fresh wonders
    (B) astonished by the Grand Canyon's incomparable size
    (C) overwhelmed by the canyon's variety of features
    (D) awestruck by the agelessness of the place
    (E) impressed by the mixture of colors and rock formations

30. The author thinks that the Grand Canyon should not have been called a "canyon" because

    (A) it is far too big for a canyon
    (B) most canyons have vertical walls
    (C) it is made up of several unconnected parts
    (D) the Grand Canyon transcends the common notion of the word
    (E) it was not formed the way most other canyons were

31. One can infer from the passage that Saint Mark's (line 51) is:

    (A) a large church
    (B) an ornate structure
    (C) an archaeological ruin
    (D) a holy shrine
    (E) a tourist attraction

32. Relating the Grand Canyon to "drainage channels" (lines 56–57) helps the author make the point that

    (A) large canyons at one time were very small
    (B) flowing water is necessary in canyon formation
    (C) the Grand Canyon is in a class by itself
    (D) canyons change perpetually in Plateau Country
    (E) the canyons of Plateau Country are unique

33. According to Passage 2, rainshowers in the desert

    (A) soak instantly into the earth
    (B) are usually preceded by thunder
    (C) promote the growth of vegetation
    (D) force birds from their nests
    (E) keep the land cool enough for comfortable human habitation

34. The word "dissipated" (line 72) most nearly means

    (A) squandered
    (B) distributed
    (C) separated
    (D) vanished
    (E) indulged

35. The author's attitude toward the coming of the rains is best described as

    (A) respect for the rains' destructive powers
    (B) awe of their revitalizing effects
    (C) appreciation of the rains' practical utility
    (D) puzzlement at the rains' delayed arrival
    (E) skepticism of their ultimate influence

36. The author of Passage 2 identifies the spadefoot toad by all of the following characteristics EXCEPT

    (A) its relative size
    (B) the time of day it is particularly active
    (C) its manner of propagating offspring
    (D) the sound it makes as its mating call
    (E) its characteristic odor

37. According to the author, the Papago youngster's description of the desert's smell (line 131) would strike most readers as apparently

    (A) incontrovertible
    (B) literal
    (C) tentative
    (D) paradoxical
    (E) hypothetical

38. In contrast to the author of Passage 2, the author of Passage 1 relies almost exclusively on his sense(s) of

    (A) sight and sound
    (B) sight and smell
    (C) sight only
    (D) smell only
    (E) sound only

39. The author of Passage 2 most obviously differs
from the author of Passage 1 in that he

(A) views nature more like a poet than a scientist
(B) includes information about his personal
experiences
(C) uses figurative language
(D) is more respectful of nature's wonders
(E) includes more geological information

40. The two passages differ in that Passage 1 is

(A) abstract, whereas Passage 2 is concrete
(B) practical, whereas Passage 2 is speculative
(C) analytical, whereas Passage 2 is didactic
(D) cynical, whereas Passage 2 is earnest
(E) resigned, whereas Passage 2 is argumenta-
tive

## LEVEL B

Most high school students have some difficulty comprehending reading passages on this level. Consider
the reading passages that follow to be a good sample of the mid-range prose excerpts you will face on SAT I.

## Exercise 1

Directions: Each passage below is followed by questions based on its content. Answer the questions on
the basis of what is stated or implied in the passage and in any introductory material that may be
provided.

**Questions 1–6 are based on the following
passage.**

*In the following passage, author Peter Matthiessen
considers Native American spirituality.*

We can no longer pretend—as we did for
so long—that Indians are a primitive people:
no, they are a traditional people, that is, a
Line "first" or "original" people, a primal people,
(5) the inheritors of a profound and exquisite wisdom distilled by long ages on this earth. The
Indian concept of earth and spirit has been
patronizingly dismissed as simple hearted
"naturalism" or "animism," when in fact it
(10) derives from a holistic vision known to all
mystics and great teachers of the most venerated religions of the world.
      This universal and profound intuitive
knowledge may have come to North America
(15) with the first peoples to arrive from Asia,
although Indians say it was the other way
around, that the assumption of white historians
that a nomadic people made a one-way journey across the Bering Strait from Asia and
(20) down into America, and never attempted to
travel the other way, makes little sense. Today
most Indians believe that they originated on

this continent: at the very least, there was travel in both directions. (In recent years, this the-
(25) ory has been given support by a young anthropologist who, on the basis of stone tools and
skull measurements as well as pictographs and
cave drawings, goes so far as to suggest that
the Cro-Magnon—the first truly modern
(30) men—who came out of nowhere to displace
the Neanderthals in Eurasia perhaps 40,000
years ago were a pre-Indian people from
North America.) According to the Hopi, runners were sent west across the Bering Strait as
(35) messengers and couriers, and information was
exchanged between North America and
Eurasia in very early times, long before
European history had begun.
      The Old Way—what the Lakota call
(40) *wouncage*, "our way of doing"—is very consistent throughout the Indian nations, despite
the great variety of cultures. The Indian cannot
love the creator and desecrate the earth, for
Indian existence is not separable from the nat-
(45) ural world. It is not a matter of "worshiping
nature," as anthropologists suggest: to worship
nature, one must stand apart from it and call it
"nature" or the "human habitat" or "the environment." For the Indian, there is no separa-
(50) tion. Man is an aspect of nature, and nature

itself is a manifestation of primordial religion. Even the word "religion" makes an unnecessary separation, and there is no word for it in the Indian tongues. Nature is the "Great Mysterious," (55) the "religion before religion," the profound intuitive apprehension of the true nature of existence attained by sages of all epochs: the whole universe is sacred, man is the whole universe, and the religious ceremony is life itself, the miracu- (60) lous common acts of every day.

1. To the author, the distinction between the words *primitive* and *primal* (lines 1–4) is that

(A) where the former is excessively positive, the latter is neutral in significance
(B) while the latter is often used metaphorically, the former is not
(C) the latter reinforces the notion of Indian barbarism that is implicit in the former
(D) while the former has some negative connotations, the latter has neutral or positive ones
(E) the former came into common use earlier than the latter did

2. The author most likely used quotation marks around certain words in the last sentence of the first paragraph (lines 6–12) because

(A) they are quotations from another work
(B) they are slang
(C) they come from another language
(D) he disagrees with their application here
(E) he wishes to emphasize their appropriateness

3. Which of the following is the most accurate statement about the second paragraph of the passage?

(A) It develops the idea of the first paragraph.
(B) It is a digression from the author's argument.
(C) It provides examples to illustrate the points made in the first paragraph.
(D) It provides a logical introduction to the third paragraph.
(E) It is full of totally unsupported assumptions.

4. The author's attitude toward Indian religion is one of

(A) respect
(B) idolatry
(C) condemnation
(D) pity
(E) indifference

5. The word "apprehension" in line 56 means

(A) capture
(B) foreboding
(C) understanding
(D) achievement
(E) approval

6. By calling the common acts of every day miraculous, Matthiessen is being

(A) paradoxical
(B) allusive
(C) sarcastic
(D) analytical
(E) apologetic

## Questions 7–15 are based on the following passage.

*The following passage, written by a zoological anthropologist, is an excerpt from a field-research study into the organization and behavior of chimpanzee society.*

Many primates live in an organized troop in which all ages and both sexes are included, and in which members always move compactly Line together as a stable social unit. There is a (5) ranking hierarchy among troop males, although the strictness with which the hierarchy is enforced varies. The ranking relationship is recognized among them and the hierarchy functions to ameliorate conflict. The high- (10) est-ranking male or males defend, control, and lead the troop; the strong social bond among members and their safety is maintained.

On the other hand, chimpanzees lack a stable social troop. Even members of a region- (15) al population, who are acquainted with each other, rarely move en masse but move in temporarily formed parties that usually consist of less than ten animals. Such parties maintain associative and friendly contact through their (20) rich vocal and behavioral communication. Chimpanzee society ensures the free and independent movement of each individual based on highly developed individuality without the restriction of either territoriality or hierarchy. (25) On the other hand, a chimpanzee enjoys the benefits of group life in that it can avoid the enemy and find fruits with less effort.

Although there is a loose dominant and subordinate relationship among individuals, (30) chimpanzees are rarely placed under the restraint of the ranking hierarchy. The rigidly organized troop characteristic of most primates must be an adaptation for avoiding enemies like man and carnivores and for defense (35) against these enemies. In this context, a group of monkeys is more likely to survive than a single individual. The group provides a social mechanism for survival. Females and young monkeys, especially a female with a baby, (40) must be protected by others. As their food, fruits, nuts, leaves, and some kinds of insects, is scattered in a wide area in the natural habitat, a dominant animal does not control the entire food source, nor does a subordinate ani- (45) mal starve when the former is satiated. An important problem in the rigid hierarchical social organization is that each animal must adjust its movements and behaviors to those of the troop. A rigidly organized troop cannot be (50) maintained when individuals do not subordinate their personal desires for the good of troop unity or solidarity. The flexible social organization of the chimpanzee may be one resolution of this problem. This kind of social (55) organization may be one of the original factors raising individuality to the level of personality. Chimpanzees have not rejected group life, but they have rejected individual uniformity and the pressure of a dominance hierarchy.

(60)     That experienced big males can appropriately cope with critical situations as the leader, and that followers appropriately react to the leader's behavior, prove that chimpanzee society is not a simple chaotic gathering but a (65) developed society based on highly developed psychological processes and individuality. The identity of fellow chimpanzees is formed in the mind of those chimpanzees who utilize the same range. The size of the regional popula- (70) tion must be restricted by the upper limit of members that an animal can identify and have friendly relations with. Another factor restricting population size must be environmental conditions, that is, the volume and the distribu- (75) tion of food and shelter and the geophysical condition of the habitat. The latter may influence the moving pattern, moving range, and the grouping pattern of each individual and group of individuals. Chimpanzees form (80) regional populations even in continuous habitats such as those found in the Budongo Forest.

7. In many primate troops, the social hierarchy consists of

(A) females only
(B) males only
(C) males of all ages
(D) females of all ages
(E) both males and females of all ages

8. According to the passage, primate societies are

(A) generally unstable
(B) flexible
(C) extremely competitive
(D) dominated by adult males
(E) frequently in conflict with each other

9. The author believes that primates establish strong bonds within a troop in order to

(A) protect the members of the troop
(B) facilitate food-gathering
(C) establish loyalty to the group
(D) keep other troops from encroaching on their territory
(E) teach the youngest members how to survive

10. Unlike other primates, chimpanzees

(A) are not bound to troops
(B) lack a strict hierarchy within their troops
(C) share the raising of their young
(D) are hostile to chimpanzees from alien populations
(E) form troops that consist of fewer than ten members

11. The author compares chimpanzees to other primates mainly to emphasize the point that

(A) chimpanzees are more easily trained than other kinds of monkeys
(B) great variations in behavior exist among primates of different species
(C) chimpanzees are different
(D) all primates have man as their common enemy
(E) primate behavior is well-understood

12. The passage implies that chimpanzees are more human-like than other primates because

(A) the basic unit of chimpanzee society is the family
(B) they know how to express their emotions
(C) each chimpanzee has a distinct personality
(D) they learn from their mistakes
(E) loyalty to the group takes precedence over individuality

13. As described in the passage, the major difference between a rigid and a flexible social structure among primates is

(A) the ability of each to withstand predators
(B) the frequency of communication among members
(C) the distances a member may travel from the main group
(D) the amount of individual freedom afforded to members
(E) the relative size of the main group

14. According to the passage, the chimpanzee population in a given area is partly determined by

(A) dominant chimpanzee males
(B) the proximity of humans
(C) predators
(D) the size of the food supply
(E) the degree of compatibility between troops of chimpanzees

15. The author cites the Budongo Forest (line 81) as an example of a place where

(A) chimpanzee troops have distinctive personalities
(B) troops of chimpanzees have formed a melting pot
(C) several species of primates co-exist
(D) geophysical conditions are conducive to large troops of chimpanzees
(E) regional populations of chimpanzees have developed

## Questions 16–27 are based on the following passage.

*The following passage, taken from a historical study of war, discusses a research project undertaken to determine the real causes of war.*

There has been no lack of theories on the cause of war. But we do lack theories that hold up when tested against the facts of history.
Line This deficiency of all existing theories has led
(5) a group of scholars to try to reverse the typical way of arriving at an explanation for war. Instead of coming up with a theory and then looking for the evidence, they have decided to look first at the evidence. Their first undertak-
(10) ing was to collect the most precise information possible about wars, their length, destructiveness, and participants. But before they could do even this they needed careful definitions of terms, so it would be clear which events
(15) belonged in the category of "war," when a state could be considered "participating in a war," what in fact a "state" was, and so on. Like all definitions, theirs were somewhat arbitrary, but they carefully justified their
(20) choices and, more important, they drew up their definitions first, before arriving at their conclusions so that they could not be accused of defining events in a way that would prove their presuppositions.
(25)     After agreeing on definitions, they set out to collect data. Even though they confined themselves to wars fought in the last 150 years, they encountered difficulties in getting precise information on items such as the number of
(30) casualties. Nevertheless, they argue, their results are better than any that preceded them. These basic facts about wars they published in a handbook, *The Wages of War 1865–1965*, edited by two leaders of the project, J. David
(35) Singer and Melvin Small. Even though this is only the beginning of the project, it already provides some answers to questions about wars. You might hear a street corner preacher tell you that the end of the world is at hand,
(40) because the number of wars is increasing just as the Bible prophesies. If you want to check the validity of such an assertion, you could turn to *The Wages of War* and answer the question using the best available data.

*(45)*     The next step in the project is to identify conditions or events that seem to be associated with wars. They are not looking for explanations, but just for correlations, that is, items that usually accompany each other. It is for *(50)* this reason that they have named their project "The Correlates of War." Starting with their collection of data on wars, they could examine the hypothesis of Woodrow Wilson that autocracies are the cause of wars. If this were true, *(55)* then autocracies would fight other autocracies and democracies might fight autocracies in defense but democracies would never fight democracies. After defining "democracy" in a way that could be measured (for example, the *(60)* frequency with which officeholders change office), they would see if any of the wars they had identified in the last 150 years had been fought between two countries clearly identifiable as democracies. If they could find no *(65)* such wars, they could say there was a *correlation* between democracy and peace. It would not yet be a *proof* that autocracies cause war. There could be other explanations—the world might contain only one or two democracies. *(70)* But a correlation would be an important first step.

The Correlates of War project is just entering this second stage. It will be some time before a full theory appears. Even when the *(75)* project does produce a theory of war (if it finds evidence to warrant such a theory), it may not provide the final word on the subject. Any such project must make decisions early in the research, such as what counts as a war and *(80)* what does not. These decisions can crucially affect the outcome, even though it might not be evident for a long time that they will. Here is an example of this problem. The Correlates of War project counts the wars fought by *(85)* Prussia under Bismarck as three separate wars because each stopped before the next one started. On the other hand, Hitler's belligerent moves against neighboring countries in 1939 and 1940 (Poland, Denmark, Belgium, France, *(90)* Norway) are counted as only one war because they took place in rapid succession. If these data are used in specific ways, they could "demonstrate" that Bismarck was more war-like than Hitler. For some purposes this might *(95)* be satisfactory but not for others.

Another problem is revealed by this example. Because the Danes capitulated to the Germans in 1940, that encounter is not listed as a war at all. Because the Belgians did resist, *(100)* that is counted as part of World War II. But the difference between these two situations was not the willingness of Germany to fight but the willingness of Germany's victim to resist. What is measured, then, is not so much the *(105)* willingness of states to go to war (which may be the most important phenomenon to explain) but the willingness of other states to resist aggression. In spite of such objections, however, the Correlates of War project is an *(110)* important effort, in many ways superior to earlier studies on the causes of war.

16. The goal of the research project described in the passage is to
   (A) put an end to war once and for all
   (B) develop a new theory about the causes of war
   (C) correct errors in history books about the causes of war
   (D) reverse the method customarily used to study wars
   (E) compare and contrast several important wars

17. Historians participating in the study have devised new research methods because
   (A) evidence becomes harder to find as time goes on
   (B) past assumptions are being challenged by a new, younger generation of historians
   (C) professional historians are divided into two groups—theoreticians and practitioners
   (D) historians continually revise history as new evidence comes to light
   (E) existing theories fail to coincide with facts

18. By calling the scholars' definitions of terms "somewhat arbitrary" (lines 18–19), the author of the passage is suggesting that
   (A) the procedures used in the study were sloppy
   (B) the scholars should have used dictionary definitions
   (C) too much effort was wasted on defining terms
   (D) the scholars had no better alternatives
   (E) writing precise definitions was not important to the study

19. The author of the passage commends the researchers for

    (A) not being discouraged by the vast amount of factual information on war
    (B) devising a new theory about the causes of war
    (C) thoroughly surveying all the previous theories about the subject
    (D) defining their terms as objectively as possible
    (E) keeping personal bias out of their study

20. The author uses the example of the street corner preacher (line 38) in order to make the point that

    (A) many Americans are ignorant about history
    (B) you should not trust the word of people who speak on street corners
    (C) facts speak louder than opinions
    (D) ancient wars described in the Bible were not included in the study
    (E) the Bible is not a reliable source of historical information

21. After collecting factual data about wars, the scholars devoted themselves to studying

    (A) the political and social conditions that have often led to war
    (B) democracies and autocracies
    (C) the effectiveness of wartime propaganda
    (D) the important figures (e.g., Wilson, Hitler) associated with various wars
    (E) what caused the actual outbreak of hostilities

22. The study described in the passage has derived its name "The Correlates of War" from

    (A) the name of the theory on which the study is based
    (B) a common explanation of the causes of war
    (C) the title of an important book on the subject
    (D) the researchers' expectations that they would find numerous correlations
    (E) the research method used by the participants

23. According to the author, a potential weakness of the study is that

    (A) the limits of the study are not clearly defined
    (B) the correlations may be misinterpreted
    (C) other historians will not accept the findings of the study
    (D) the present study ignores previous studies of the same subject
    (E) most correlations are unreliable

24. The author of the passage implies that research studies like "The Correlates of War"

    (A) are an essential function of the academic world
    (B) add immeasurably to the world's fund of knowledge
    (C) may fail to produce definitive results
    (D) inspire scholars to continue work in the field
    (E) serve as a valuable resource for policy makers

25. The author compares the warlike qualities of Bismarck and of Hitler in order to illustrate that

    (A) researchers generally prove whatever they want
    (B) research design and procedure may invalidate the findings
    (C) "The Correlates of War" project is notorious for its faulty research techniques
    (D) the preliminary findings of "The Correlates of War" project are invalid
    (E) evidence in historical research is subject to distortion and manipulation

26. The author seems to think that "The Correlates of War" project

    (A) is being carried out by hard-working researchers
    (B) is a formidable challenge for the researchers
    (C) has the potential to prevent future wars
    (D) will ultimately contribute to our understanding of war
    (E) is the best of its kind

27. Which pair of adjectives best describes the author's overall feelings about "The Correlates of War" project?

    (A) amazed and astonished
    (B) scornful and cynical
    (C) optimistic and hopeful
    (D) resentful and bitter
    (E) casual and indifferent

**Questions 28–40 are based on the following pair of passages.**

*Pablo Picasso was probably the most influential painter of the twentieth century. In the first passage, written by Picasso himself, the artist explains his views on art. The second passage discusses Cubism, the type of modern art originated by Picasso.*

## Passage 1

I can hardly understand the importance given to the word *research* in connection with modern painting. In my opinion to search
Line means nothing in painting. To find, is the
(5) thing. Nobody is interested in following a man who, with his eyes fixed on the ground, spends his life looking for the pocketbook that fortune should put in his path. The one who finds something no matter what it might be, even if
(10) his intention were not to search for it, at least arouses our curiosity, if not our admiration.

Among the several sins that I have been accused of committing, none is more false than the one that I have, as the principal objec-
(15) tive in my work, the spirit of research. When I paint, my object is to show what I have found and not what I am looking for. In art intentions are not sufficient and, as we say in Spanish: love must be proved by facts and not by rea-
(20) sons. What one does is what counts and not what one had the intention of doing.

We all know that Art is not truth. Art is a lie that makes us realize truth, at least the truth that is given us to understand. The artist must
(25) know the manner whereby to convince others of the truthfulness of his lies. If he only shows in his work that he has searched, and researched, for the way to put over lies, he would never accomplish anything.
(30) The idea of research has often made painting go astray, and made the artist lose himself in mental lucubrations[1]. Perhaps this has been the principal fault of modern art. The spirit of research had poisoned those who have not
(35) fully understood all the positive and conclusive elements in modern art and has made them attempt to paint the invisible and, therefore, the unpaintable.

They speak of naturalism in opposition to
(40) modern painting. I would like to know if anyone has ever seen a natural work of art. Nature

and art, being two different things, cannot be the same thing. Through art we express our conception of what nature is not.

---
[1]Meditation; study.

## Passage 2

(45) Cubism, with Picasso and Braque at its head, rejected the conventional notions of beauty. Discarding the world of perspectives and naturalism, they put in their place a new world obeying only the laws of the artist's
(50) inner vision. Picasso succeeded in freeing the technique of painting from its slavish adherence to the description of nature, and he gave it new laws of harmony and balance. This break with the past had far-reaching conse-
(55) quences. From now on the painter became a free creator, a poet.

Through the break in the wall, poetry crept into painting, with all that is unusual, miraculous, and disturbing. Things around us
(60) which do not seem worthy of the artist's glance, things often considered ugly, were revealed in Picasso's pictures in their most ordinary essence but also in a new, extraordinary significance.
(65) "I put into my pictures all the things I enjoy," said Picasso, and so he does, with his pipe, glass, packet of tobacco, and guitar. He is tireless in seeking to define the forms of these objects and their essential volume, trans-
(70) forming them into poetic images, and treating them freely and naturally as in daily life. In this connection André Breton wrote of Picasso: "It rested with a failure of the will of this man, and what we are concerned about
(75) would have been at least postponed, if not utterly lost." To which Paul Eluard added: "Yes, for this man held in his hands the fragile key to the problem of reality. He sought to see what he sees, to set vision free, to attain sight.
(80) He achieved this."

Picasso considers art a process that is never completed; he studies the problem that interests him over and over again, from different angles. Thus he does not create pictures in
(85) the conventional, picture-gallery sense of the word; he does not seek, but finds, in the words of the aphorism attributed to him. The elemental side of his talent never allows him to rest content with what he has achieved. He is

(90) always interested exclusively in the present, in the picture on which he is working. "Everything must be done anew, and not just patched up," he says, and these words sum up his programme.

(95)   The constant creativity which has no regard for the nature of anything he has painted before gives Picasso the freedom to move at will in the boundless spaces of free expression. It gives him the freedom to draw on all (100) sources of inspiration for the most varied motifs, opening up all spheres of culture, contemporary, distant, or historic.

   Thus this restless, disturbing spirit, one of the most truthful witnesses to the conflict-torn (105) century we live in, goes again and again into the attack on the gates of the unknown. Each new development in his art does more than merely increase the number of pictures he has painted: it turns against his very work itself, (110) testing the foundations on which it rests. Picasso confounds his followers and turns inside out the aesthetic principles he himself has just established.

28. To Picasso, the author of Passage 1, the man who spends his life "with his eyes fixed on the ground" (lines 5–6) represents those artists who

(A) don't appreciate modern art
(B) try hard but have no artistic talent
(C) contemplate their subjects too much before painting
(D) paint only to make money
(E) study the works of the great masters

29. The sentence "When I paint, my object is to show what I have found and not what I am looking for" (lines 15–17) is

(A) a digression from the main point of the passage
(B) a denial of an accusation
(C) an explanation of one of "several sins" (line 12)
(D) a paraphrase of what art critics have said about Picasso
(E) a false statement that the author intends to disprove

30. The statement that "Art is not truth" (line 22) implies

(A) artists are liars and are basically untrustworthy
(B) we should not take art too seriously
(C) art gives us more than truth; it gives us understanding
(D) we should be prepared to suspend our disbelief when we view art
(E) we must accept the idea that truth comes in many forms

31. To Picasso, the most successful art is that which

(A) shows what the artist has seen
(B) reveals what the artist has found
(C) arouses our curiosity but not our admiration
(D) accurately portrays the subject
(E) conceals the artist's techniques

32. As used in Passage 1, "naturalism" in art (line 39) refers to

(A) realism
(B) a school of contemporary art
(C) pre-twentieth-century painting
(D) outdoor paintings
(E) paintings using colors found only in nature

33. The aspect of Picasso's art that is emphasized in Passage 2 is his

(A) profundity
(B) enormous output of work
(C) innovations
(D) technical achievement
(E) appeal to art lovers

34. Passage 2 implies that prior to Picasso, artists

(A) were held back by the social customs of the day
(B) were rarely encouraged to experiment
(C) were dependent on patrons for success
(D) adhered to strict rules of art
(E) restricted their paintings to one acceptable style

35. According to Passage 2 Picasso broke painting tradition in all of the following ways EXCEPT by

(A) ignoring the need for harmony and balance
(B) expanding the subject matter of paintings
(C) throwing out the rules of perspective
(D) expressing himself more freely
(E) discarding the need for realistic painting

36. The statement that "everything must be done anew, and not just patched up" (lines 91–93) suggests that Picasso believes that

(A) artists should practice leaving well enough alone
(B) artists can benefit from their mistakes
(C) bad pictures need more than just patching up
(D) spontaneity is lost when artists start tinkering with their pictures
(E) patching a picture restricts artists' freedom of expression

37. The author of Passage 2 seems to believe that Picasso is not only an energetic artist but also

(A) an observer of the politics of his time
(B) a social revolutionary
(C) a bold experimenter
(D) an inspiration to other artists
(E) an intellectual

38. Eluard's view that Picasso sought to "attain sight" (line 79) coincides with Picasso's statement in Passage 1 that

(A) "to search means nothing" (lines 3–4)
(B) "my object is to show what I have found" (line 16)
(C) "what one does is what counts" (line 20)
(D) "art is a lie" (lines 22–23)
(E) "nature and art . . . cannot be the same thing" (lines 41–43)

39. Both Passage 1 and Passage 2 describe Picasso as an artist who

(A) transforms objects into "poetic images" (line 70)
(B) "does not seek, but finds" (line 86)
(C) is never "content with what he has achieved" (line 89)
(D) attacks the "gates of the unknown" (line 106)
(E) "confounds his followers" (line 111)

40. Compared to Passage 2, Passage 1 is

(A) less controversial
(B) more up-to-date
(C) more argumentative
(D) more historical
(E) less personal

## LEVEL C

Most high school students have trouble following reading passages at this level of difficulty. Consider the excerpts that follow as a chance for you to acquaint yourself with the toughest prose that occurs on SAT I.

## Exercise 1

Directions: Each passage below is followed by questions based on its content. Answer the questions on the basis of what is stated or implied in the passage and in any introductory material that may be provided.

**Questions 1–7 are based on the following passage.**

*The following passage is taken from* Cranford, *Elizabeth Gaskell's nineteenth-century novel set in a small English town.*

In the first place, in Cranford all the holders of houses, at least those above a certain rent, are women. If a married couple come to
Line  settle in the town, somehow the gentleman
(5)  disappears; he is either fairly frightened to death by being the only man in the Cranford evening parties, or is accounted for by being

with his regiment, his ship, or closely engaged in business all the week in the great neighbor-
(10) ing commercial town of Drumble, distant only twenty miles on a railroad. In short, whatever does become of the gentlemen, they are not at Cranford. What could they do if they were there? The surgeon has his round of thirty
(15) miles, and sleeps at Cranford; but every man cannot be a surgeon. For keeping the trim gardens full of choice flowers without a weed to speck them; for frightening away little boys who look wistfully at the said flowers through
(20) the railings; for rushing out at the geese that occasionally venture into the gardens if the gates are left open; for deciding all questions of literature and politics without troubling themselves with unnecessary reasons or argu-
(25) ments; for obtaining clear and correct knowledge of everybody's affairs in the parish; for keeping their neat maid-servants in admirable order; for kindness (somewhat dictatorial) to the poor, and real tender good offices to each
(30) other whenever they are in distress—the ladies of Cranford are quite sufficient. "A man," as one of them observed to me once, "is so in the way in the house!" Although the ladies of Cranford know all each other's proceedings,
(35) they are exceedingly indifferent to each other's opinions. Indeed, as each has her own individuality, not to say eccentricity, pretty strongly developed, nothing is so easy as verbal retaliation; but, somehow, goodwill reigns
(40) among them to a considerable degree.
　　　The Cranford ladies have only an occasional little quarrel, spurted out in a few peppery words and angry jerks of the heads; just enough to prevent the even tenor of their lives
(45) from becoming too flat. Their dress is very independent of fashion; as they observe, "What does it signify how we dress here at Cranford, where everybody knows us?" And if they go from home, their reasoning is equally
(50) cogent, "What does it signify how we dress here, where nobody knows us?" The materials of their clothes are, in general, good and plain, and most of them are nearly as scrupulous as Miss Tyler, of cleanly memory; but I will
(55) answer for it, the last gigot, the last tight and scanty petticoat in wear in England, was seen in Cranford—and seen without a smile.

1. The passage can best be described as

(A) an argument in favor of the supremacy of women
(B) a laudatory depiction of a vanishing way of life
(C) an illustration of the virtues of female independence
(D) an analysis of the reasons for the dearth of males
(E) a humorous portrait of the residents of a town

2. According to the passage, the men of Cranford are primarily distinguished by their

(A) docility
(B) awkwardness
(C) absence
(D) cowardice
(E) aloofness

3. The word "offices" in line 29 refers to

(A) places of employment
(B) daily religious ceremonies
(C) rooms in which household work is performed
(D) acts done on behalf of others
(E) positions of authority

4. The narrator's attitude toward the ladies of Cranford is primarily one of

(A) abiding suspicion
(B) wistful nostalgia
(C) bitter sarcasm
(D) gentle mockery
(E) fervent enthusiasm

5. The scrupulous Miss Tyler (lines 53–54) most likely was noted for her

(A) chaste behavior
(B) spotless attire
(C) wholesome outlook
(D) precise memory
(E) humorless disposition

6. Lines 55–56 suggest that "the last gigot" is

(A) a type of covered carriage
(B) an outmoded article of apparel
(C) a modish kind of fabric
(D) a subject too grave to evoke a smile
(E) a meticulous elderly woman

7. To the narrator, the ladies of Cranford seem to be all of the following EXCEPT

   (A) idiosyncratic
   (B) benevolent
   (C) overbearing
   (D) submissive
   (E) inquisitive

**Questions 8–15 are based on the following passage.**

*The following passage from a 1984* Scientific American *article reveals the ocean depths to be the home of strong, tumultuous currents.*

"It was a dark and stormy night."
This much-parodied opening line from a Victorian novel accurately describes condi-
*Line* tions 4,800 meters below sea level at the base
(5) of the continental rise 450 miles off the coast of New England in the middle of September, 1979. It is always dark, of course, at depths below 1,000 meters. The instruments we had moored some weeks earlier at the much
(10) greater depth, at the base of the Scotian Rise, revealed the presence of a storm that lasted for about a week. The forces on the moored instruments equaled those that above sea level would be generated by a fresh gale of
(15) between 34 and 40 knots.
Such an energetic event three miles below the ocean surface came as a revelation to those who grew up believing the abyss was a region as calm as it was dark. The notion of
(20) a tranquil abyss had been so generally held that many investigators were initially reluc-
tant to accept the evidence for strong currents and storms in the deep sea. The first argument for the existence of such currents came
(25) from theory. Cold water is denser than warm water, and models of ocean circulation showed that the sinking of cold water near the poles should generate strong, deep and steady currents flowing toward the Equator.
(30) Subsequent observations not only confirmed the presence of the deep currents but also dis-
closed the existence of eddies on the western side of ocean basins that can be some 300 times as energetic as the mean current.
(35) Photographs of the sea floor underlying the

deep currents also revealed extensive graded beds indicative of the active transport of sediment. The final evidence for dynamic activity at great depths came from direct measure-
(40) ments of currents and sediments in the North Atlantic carried out in the HEBBLE[1] program.
Before we describe the HEBBLE find-
ings in some detail let us briefly review the
(45) sources and sinks of deep-sea sediments and the forces that activate the global patterns of ocean circulation. The sediments that end up on the ocean floor are of two main types. One component is the detritus[2] whose source
(50) is the weathering of rocks on continents and islands. This detritus, together with decaying vegetable matter from land plants, is carried by rivers to the edge of the continent and out onto the continental shelf, where it is picked
(55) up by marine currents. Once the detritus reaches the edge of the shelf it is carried to the base of the continental rise by gravita-
tional processes. A significant amount of ter-
restrial material is also blown out to sea in
(60) subtropical regions by strong desert winds. Every year some 15 billion tons of continen-
tal material reaches the outlets of streams and rivers. Most of it is trapped there or on the continental shelves; only a few billion
(65) tons escapes into the deep sea.
The second major component arriving at the sea floor consists of the shells and skele-
tons of dead microscopic organisms that flourish and die in the sunlit waters of the
(70) top 100 meters of the world's oceans. Such biological material contributes to the total inventory at the bottom about three billion tons per year. Rates of accumulation are governed by rates of biological productivity,
(75) which are controlled in part by surface cur-
rents. Where surface currents meet they are said to converge, and where they part they are said to diverge. Zones of divergence of major water masses allow nutrient-rich deep-
(80) er water to "outcrop" at the sunlit zone where photosynthesis and the resulting fixa-
tion of organic carbon take place. Such belts of high productivity and high rates of accumulation are normally around the major
(85) oceanic fronts (such as the region around the Antarctic) and along the edges of major

currents (such as the Gulf Stream off New England and the Kuroshio currents off Japan). Nutrient-rich water also outcrops in a (90) zone along the Equator, where there is a divergence of two major, wind-driven gyres.

---

[1] Naval research program known as the High-Energy Benthic Boundary-Layer Experiment.

[2] Debris; fragmented rock particles.

8. The primary purpose of the passage is to

   (A) contrast surface currents with marine currents
   (B) question the methods of earlier investigators
   (C) demonstrate the benefits of the HEBBLE program
   (D) describe a replicable laboratory experiment
   (E) summarize evidence supporting oceanic circulation

9. The quotation at the beginning of the passage (line 1) is cited chiefly to illustrate

   (A) the popularity of conventional Victorian literature
   (B) the author's intent to parody the HEBBLE experiment
   (C) problems in finding appropriate openings for technical articles
   (D) noteworthy physical characteristics of the ocean depths
   (E) the difficulty of determining one's location underwater at night

10. Which of the following best describes the attitude of many scientists when they first encountered the theory that strong currents are at work in the deeps?

    (A) Somber resignation
    (B) Measured approbation
    (C) Marked skepticism
    (D) Academic detachment
    (E) Active espousal

11. According to the passage, the earliest data supporting the idea that the sea depths were dynamic rather than placid came from

    (A) underwater photographic surveys
    (B) the activities of the HEBBLE program
    (C) analysis of North Atlantic sea-bed sediments
    (D) direct measurement of undersea currents
    (E) models showing how hot and cold water interact

12. As defined in the passage, the second type of deep-sea sediment consists of which of the following?

    I. Minute particles of rock
    II. Fragmentary shells
    III. Wind-blown soil

    (A) I only
    (B) II only
    (C) I and II only
    (D) I and III only
    (E) I, II, and III

13. This passage most likely would be of particular interest to

    (A) navigators of sailing vessels
    (B) students of global weather patterns
    (C) current passengers on ocean liners
    (D) designers of sea-floor structures
    (E) researchers into photosynthesis

14. In the passage the authors do all of the following EXCEPT

    (A) approximate an amount
    (B) refer to a model
    (C) give an example
    (D) propose a solution
    (E) support a theory

15. The style of the passage can best be described as

    (A) oratorical
    (B) epigrammatic
    (C) expository
    (D) digressive
    (E) metaphorical

**Questions 16–27 are based on the following passage.**

*The following passage, written by a university professor, is from a scholarly book about how international monetary policy contributes to the world's problems.*

What is money? That is not so simple a question as might appear. In fact, money can only be defined in terms of the functions it Line performs—that is, by the need it fulfills. As (5) Sir Ralph Hawtrey once noted, "Money is one of those concepts which, like a teaspoon or an umbrella, but unlike an earthquake or a butter-

cup, are definable primarily by the use or purpose which they serve." Money is anything,
(10) regardless of its physical or legal characteristics, that customarily and principally performs
certain functions.

Three such functions are usually specified,
corresponding to the three basic needs served
(15) by money—the need for a *medium of
exchange*, the need for a *unit of account*, and
the need for a *store of value*. Most familiar is
the first, the function of a medium of
exchange, whereby goods and services are
(20) paid for and contractual obligations dis-
charged. In performing this role the key
attribute of money is general acceptability in
the settlement of debt. The second function of
money, that of a unit of account, is to provide
(25) a medium of information—a common denom-
inator or *numeraire* in which good and services may be valued and debts expressed. In
performing this role, money is said to be a
"standard of value" or "measure of value" in
(30) valuing goods and services and a "standard of
deferred payment" in expressing debts. The
third function of money, that of a store of
value, is to provide a means of holding wealth.

The development of money was one of the
(35) most important steps in the evolution of
human society, comparable, in the words of
one writer, "with the domestication of animals, the cultivation of the land, and the har-
nessing of power." Before money there was
(40) only barter, the archetypical economic transaction, which required an inverse double coincidence of wants in order for exchange to occur.
The two parties to any transaction each had to
desire what the other was prepared to offer.
(45) This was an obviously inefficient system of
exchange, since large amounts of time had to
be devoted to the necessary process of search
and bargaining. Under even the most elemental circumstances, barter was unlikely to
(50) exhaust all opportunities for advantageous
trade:

Bartering is costly in ways too numerous
to discuss. Among others, bartering
requires an expenditure of time and the
(55) use of specialized skills necessary for
judging the commodities that are being
exchanged. The more advanced the specialization in production and the more

complex the economy, the costlier it will
(60) be to undertake all the transactions necessary to make any given good reach its
ultimate user by using barter.

The introduction of generalized exchange
intermediaries cut the Gordian knot of barter
(65) by decomposing the single transaction of
barter into separate transactions of sale and
purchase, thereby obviating the need for a
double coincidence of wants. This served to
facilitate multilateral exchange; the costs of
(70) transactions reduced, exchange ratios could be
more efficiently equated with the demand and
supply of goods and services. Consequently,
specialization in production was promoted and
the advantages of economic division of labor
(75) became attainable—all because of the development of money.

The usefulness of money is inversely proportional to the number of currencies in circulation. The greater the number of currencies,
(80) the less is any single money able to perform
efficiently as a lubricant to improve resource
allocation and reduce transactions costs.
Diseconomies remain because of the need for
multiple price quotations (diminishing the
(85) information savings derived from money's
role as unit of account) and for frequent currency conversions (diminishing the stability
and predictability of purchasing power derived
from money's roles as medium of exchange
(90) and store of value). In all national societies,
there has been a clear historical tendency to
limit the number of currencies, and eventually
to standardize the domestic money on just a
single currency issued and managed by the
(95) national authorities. The result has been a
minimization of total transaction costs within
nation-states.

Between nation-states, however, costs of
transactions remain relatively high, because
(100) the number of currencies remains high. Does
this suggest that global efficiency would be
maximized if the number of currencies in the
world were minimized? Is this the optimal
organizational principle for international mon-
(105) etary relations? Not necessarily. It is true that
total transactions costs, other things being
equal, could be minimized by standardizing on
just a single global money. "On the basis of
the criterion of maximizing the usefulness of

*(110)* money, we should have a single world currency." But there are other criteria of judgment as
well; economic efficiency, as I have indicated,
is a multi-variate concept. And we shall soon
see that the costs of a single world currency or
*(115)* its equivalent, taking full account of both the
microeconomic and macroeconomic dimen-
sions of efficiency, could easily outweigh the
single microeconomic benefit of lower transaction costs. As Charles Kindleberger has
*(120)* written: "The case for international money is
the general case for money. [But] it may well
be that the costs of an international money are
so great that the world cannot afford it."

16. The author of the passage asks the reader,
"What is money?" in order to

(A) challenge the reader by asking an unan-
swerable question
(B) make the reader feel uncomfortable
(C) test the reader's intelligence
(D) introduce an unfamiliar definition of the
word
(E) feign ignorance

17. The explanation of the three functions of
money (lines 13–33)

(A) is a section of a controversial economic
theory
(B) is common knowledge among informed
people
(C) breaks new ground in economic thinking
(D) is a comprehensive analysis of monetary
policy
(E) is valid for only some kinds of money

18. According to the passage, money meets three
needs:

I.   medium of exchange
II.  unit of account
III. store of value

The sticker price of a new car in the dealer's
showroom is an example of

(A) II only
(B) III only
(C) Partly I and partly III
(D) Partly II and partly III
(E) Partly I and partly II

19. By calling barter "the archetypical economic
transaction," the author is saying that barter

(A) is obsolete
(B) is both a theory and a real-life activity
(C) is a model for economic exchanges
(D) is a primitive form of exchange
(E) usually satisfies all the parties involved in
a deal

20. According to the passage, the chief shortcoming of barter is that

(A) making deals is too time-consuming
(B) three- or four-way deals are virtually
impossible
(C) down payments cannot be used
(D) neither party to a bartering agreement is
ever fully satisfied
(E) no one could ever make a profit

21. The reference to the "Gordian knot" (line 64)
suggests that the author thinks that

(A) barter was inherently too slow
(B) it was difficult to change the barter system
to a monetary system
(C) the economist, Gordon, deserves credit for
introducing the monetary system
(D) most people lack the skill to accurately
determine the value of commodities
(E) barter restricts the free exchange of goods
and services

22. Based on the passage, a monetary system has all
of the following advantages over barter EXCEPT

(A) a double coincidence of wants is eliminated
(B) the cost of doing business is lower
(C) supply and demand determine the cost of
goods and services
(D) a greater division of labor is possible
(E) opportunities of advantageous trade are
reduced

23. The author believes that a large number of currencies in circulation

(A) leads to an unstable money supply
(B) reduces the efficiency of the international
economy
(C) makes international travel more complex
(D) requires the creation of a central monetary
authority
(E) widens the gap between rich nations and
poor nations

24. According to the passage, standardizing the currency of a nation is likely to result in

(A) a reduction in the cost of monetary transactions
(B) a short period of inflation
(C) an increase of money in circulation
(D) greater confidence in the banking system
(E) increased international stature

25. By responding "Not necessarily" to the questions posed in lines 100–105, the author is suggesting that

(A) a solution to the problem is still years away
(B) advocates of minimizing the number of currencies are seriously mistaken
(C) many nations resist the creation of a single world currency
(D) the most obvious solution is not the best solution
(E) the simplest solution is the one that will work

26. To improve the efficiency of the international monetary system, the author supports

(A) increasing the world's gold supply
(B) setting limits on the amount of money being exchanged
(C) lowering tariffs between nations
(D) creating a single worldwide currency
(E) reducing transaction costs

27. The author of the passage draws which of the following conclusions about the creation of a worldwide currency?

(A) It may cause more problems than it will solve.
(B) Discussing it further is pointless.
(C) Reducing transaction costs must precede the creation of a worldwide currency.
(D) Proposals for such a currency must provide for a reduction of transaction costs.
(E) It is an ideal never to be attained.

**Questions 28–40 are based on the following pair of passages.**

*The following passages discuss* This Side of Paradise, *F. Scott Fitzgerald's autobiographical first novel, written when the author was in his early twenties. Both passages are excerpts from essays by literary critics.*

**Passage 1**

The defects of *This Side of Paradise* should not blind the reader to its importance in Fitzgerald's career. It marked his movement,
Line clumsy and pasted together as the novel often
(5) is, from a clever short-story writer and would-be poet to an ambitious novelist. All his life he was to think of himself primarily as a novelist, to save his best work for his novels, to plunder his published short stories for usable
(10) material for them. If he achieved nothing else in this first novel, he had at least taken his scattered literary effusions and his undescribed experiences, sifted them, shaped and reshaped them, often looked at them ironically, and fashioned
(15) them into a sustained narrative. Compared with the material he took directly from his *Nassau Lit* stories, the writing had improved greatly. In many rewritten passages, *This Side of Paradise* shows Fitzgerald moving to that freshness of
(20) language which became his identifying mark.

The novel took the bold step that Fitzgerald needed: it confirmed his ideas about the importance of his feelings and about his ability to put them down. It helped Fitzgerald thrash out
(25) those "ideas still in riot" that he attributes to Amory [the novel's main character] at the close of the book: his ideas about love and women, about the Church, about his past, about the importance of *being* as contrasted with *doing*.
(30) Though it borrowed heavily from the many writers to whom he was attracted, the book still has Fitzgerald's own stamp: the naiveté and honesty that is part of "the stamp that goes into my books so that people can read it blind like
(35) Braille." If Amory is not as honest with himself as Fitzgerald's later characters can be, it is chiefly from a lack of perception rather than from a deliberate desire to deceive.

Finally, though Fitzgerald placed his twin
(40) hopes of money and the girl in the book's great success, the book is not merely contrived to achieve these aims. The badness in it is not that of the professional who shrewdly calculates his effects; it is that of the ambitious amateur writer
(45) who produces what seems to him to be witty, fresh, and powerful prose. It is a much better book than *The Romantic Egotist*, the version he finished before he left Princeton. For Fitzgerald at twenty-three, it was the book he wanted to
(50) write, the book he could write, and the book

that did get written. Before it even reached its audience, Fitzgerald had found his craft.

## Passage 2

It has been said by a celebrated person that to meet F. Scott Fitzgerald is to think of a stu-
(55) pid old woman with whom someone has left a diamond; she is extremely proud of the dia- mond and shows it to everyone who comes by, and everyone is surprised that such an ignorant old woman should possess so valuable a jewel;
(60) for in nothing does she appear so inept as in the remarks she makes about the diamond.

The person who invented this simile did not know Fitzgerald very well and can only have seen him, I think, in his more diffident or
(65) uninspired moods. The reader must not sup- pose that there is any literal truth in the image. Scott Fitzgerald is, in fact, no old woman, but a very good-looking young man, nor is he in the least stupid, but, on the contrary, exhilarat-
(70) ingly clever. Yet there *is* a symbolic truth in the description quoted above; it is true that Fitzgerald has been left with a jewel which he doesn't know quite what to do with. For he has been given imagination without intellectu-
(75) al control of it; he has been given the desire for beauty without an aesthetic ideal; and he has been given a gift for expression without very many ideas to express.

Consider, for example, the novel—*This*
(80) *Side of Paradise*—with which he founded his reputation. It has almost every fault and defi- ciency that a novel can possibly have. It is not only highly imitative but it imitates an inferior model. Fitzgerald, when he wrote the book,
(85) was drunk with Compton Mackenzie, and it sounds like an American attempt to rewrite *Sinister Street*. Now, Mackenzie, in spite of his gift for picturesque and comic invention and the capacity for pretty writing that he says he
(90) learned from Keats, lacks both the intellectual force and the emotional imagination to give body and outline to the material which he secretes in such enormous abundance. With the seeds he took from Keats's garden, one of the
(95) best-arranged gardens in England, he enflore- ated [generated flowers] so profusely that he blotted out the path of his own. Michael Fane, the hero of *Sinister Street*, was swamped in the forest of descriptions; he was smothered by
(100) creepers and columbines. From the time he

went up to Oxford, his personality began to grow dimmer, and, when he last turned up (in Belgrade) he seemed quite to have lost his identity. As a consequence, Amory Blaine, the
(105) hero of *This Side of Paradise*, had a very poor chance of coherence: Fitzgerald did endow him, to be sure, with a certain emotional life which the phantom Michael Fane lacks; but he was quite as much a wavering quantity in a
(110) phantasmagoria of incident that had no domi- nating intention to endow it with unity and force. In short, one of the chief weaknesses of *This Side of Paradise* is that it is really not *about* anything: its intellectual and moral con-
(115) tent amounts to little more than a gesture—a gesture of indefinite revolt. The story itself, furthermore, is very immaturely imagined: it is always just verging on the ludicrous. And finally, *This Side of Paradise* is one of the most
(120) illiterate books of any merit ever published (a fault which the publisher's proofreader seems to have made no effort to remedy). Not only is it ornamented with bogus ideas and faked liter- ary references, but it is full of literary words
(125) tossed about with the most reckless inaccuracy.

28. The author of Passage 1 thinks that *This Side of Paradise* demonstrates Fitzgerald's ability to

    (A) compose both long stories and short novels
    (B) write short stories
    (C) include poetic language in his writing
    (D) tell a long story
    (E) edit his own writing

29. The author of Passage 1 believes that Fitzgerald's reputation as a writer rests on

    (A) his original use of words
    (B) his compelling narratives
    (C) the suspensefulness of his plots
    (D) his use of irony
    (E) using bits and pieces to create coherent stories

30. Passage 1 suggests that Amory, the main char- acter of *This Side of Paradise*,

    (A) is a serious and responsible person
    (B) is a thinly disguised version of Fitzgerald
    (C) represents all that Fitzgerald admired
    (D) symbolizes what Fitzgerald wanted to be
    (E) is a composite of people that Fitzgerald knew

31. By hoping that people could read his books "blind like Braille" (lines 34–35), Fitzgerald meant that his writing was

    (A) vivid and sensual
    (B) deep and full of meaning
    (C) sophisticated and subtle
    (D) plain and direct
    (E) truthful and innocent

32. Throughout Passage 1, the writing of Fitzgerald is characterized as

    (A) egotistical
    (B) immature
    (C) phony
    (D) optimistic
    (E) deceptively easy to read

33. The author of Passage 2 relates the anecdote of the old woman and the diamond in order to

    (A) disturb Fitzgerald's readers
    (B) belittle Fitzgerald as a writer
    (C) clarify a mistaken view of Fitzgerald
    (D) suggest that Fitzgerald is preoccupied with wealth
    (E) explain an aspect of Fitzgerald's personality

34. The author's assertion that "Fitzgerald has been left with a jewel which he doesn't know quite what to do with" (lines 73–74) most nearly means that

    (A) Fitzgerald's exceptional talent as a writer needs polishing
    (B) Fitzgerald should take more writing courses
    (C) Fitzgerald's writing needs better editing
    (D) Fitzgerald will probably become a best-selling author
    (E) Fitzgerald is destined to become one of the great American writers

35. According to the author of Passage 2, *Sinister Street* can best be described as

    (A) highly inferior to *This Side of Paradise*
    (B) more engrossing than *This Side of Paradise*
    (C) a pale imitation of *This Side of Paradise*
    (D) an unfortunate model for *This Side of Paradise*
    (E) more realistic than *This Side of Paradise*

36. The author of Passage 2 bases much of his criticism of *Sinister Street* on the grounds that

    (A) the book's hero is sadly over-emotional
    (B) its flowery prose overshadows its hero's story
    (C) it deals with a conventional subject
    (D) the book lacks wit and inventiveness
    (E) the novel will fail to interest most readers

37. *This Side of Paradise* is called "illiterate" (line 120) because it

    (A) is incoherent
    (B) uses slang
    (C) lacks substance
    (D) contains many errors
    (E) is trite

38. The authors of Passage 1 and Passage 2 agree that *This Side of Paradise*

    (A) suggests that Fitzgerald is a talented writer
    (B) is the worst of Fitzgerald's novels
    (C) is a blot on Fitzgerald's career
    (D) should have been rewritten
    (E) will have a wide audience despite its flaws

39. According to both Passage 1 and Passage 2, a major flaw of *This Side of Paradise* is its

    (A) one-dimensional characters
    (B) long-winded descriptions
    (C) moralizing
    (D) excessive wordiness
    (E) lack of artistic focus

40. Based on evidence found in Passage 1 and Passage 2, when were the two passages apparently written?

    (A) Both passages were written at about the same time, immediately after the publication of *This Side of Paradise*.
    (B) Both passages were written long after the publication of *This Side of Paradise*.
    (C) Both passages were written sometime between the publication of *This Side of Paradise* and the publication of Fitzgerald's next novel.
    (D) Passage 1 was written long after the publication of *This Side of Paradise*; Passage 2 was written shortly afterward.
    (E) Passage 1 was written shortly after the publication of *This Side of Paradise*; Passage 2 was written long afterward.

# ANSWERS TO CRITICAL READING EXERCISES

## LEVEL A

### Critical Reading Exercise 1

| | | | | | | | | | |
|---|---|---|---|---|---|---|---|---|---|
| 1. C | 5. E | 9. C | 13. D | 17. B | 21. A | 25. D | 29. C | 33. E | 37. C |
| 2. D | 6. D | 10. D | 14. B | 18. C | 22. B | 26. E | 30. B | 34. D | 38. C |
| 3. C | 7. C | 11. B | 15. E | 19. D | 23. A | 27. D | 31. C | 35. D | 39. B |
| 4. C | 8. D | 12. D | 16. E | 20. C | 24. B | 28. E | 32. A | 36. D | 40. A |

### Critical Reading Exercise 2

| | | | | | | | | | |
|---|---|---|---|---|---|---|---|---|---|
| 1. E | 5. C | 9. A | 13. E | 17. B | 21. B | 25. C | 29. B | 33. C | 37. D |
| 2. D | 6. E | 10. D | 14. E | 18. B | 22. C | 26. A | 30. D | 34. D | 38. C |
| 3. A | 7. E | 11. B | 15. C | 19. A | 23. D | 27. C | 31. B | 35. B | 39. B |
| 4. B | 8. E | 12. D | 16. D | 20. C | 24. E | 28. D | 32. A | 36. A | 40. A |

## LEVEL B

### Critical Reading Exercise 1

| | | | | | | | | | |
|---|---|---|---|---|---|---|---|---|---|
| 1. D | 5. C | 9. A | 13. D | 17. E | 21. A | 25. B | 29. B | 33. C | 37. C |
| 2. D | 6. A | 10. A | 14. D | 18. D | 22. E | 26. E | 30. C | 34. D | 38. B |
| 3. B | 7. B | 11. C | 15. E | 19. D | 23. B | 27. C | 31. B | 35. A | 39. B |
| 4. A | 8. D | 12. C | 16. B | 20. C | 24. C | 28. C | 32. A | 36. E | 40. C |

## LEVEL C

### Critical Reading Exercise 1

| | | | | | | | | | |
|---|---|---|---|---|---|---|---|---|---|
| 1. E | 5. B | 9. D | 13. D | 17. B | 21. B | 25. D | 29. A | 33. C | 37. D |
| 2. C | 6. B | 10. C | 14. D | 18. A | 22. E | 26. E | 30. B | 34. A | 38. A |
| 3. D | 7. D | 11. E | 15. C | 19. C | 23. B | 27. A | 31. E | 35. D | 39. E |
| 4. D | 8. E | 12. B | 16. D | 20. A | 24. A | 28. D | 32. B | 36. B | 40. D |

# ANSWER EXPLANATIONS

## LEVEL A

### Critical Reading Exercise 1

1. **C**  Ovenden clearly approves of speculation (pondering; evolving theories by taking a fresh look at a subject or concept). However, he approves of purposeful speculation, speculation that has as its goal the discovery of new ways of looking at the universe. Pointless, idle, *empty* speculation or woolgathering he finds unscientific.

2. **D**  By asserting that "(s)peculation is [science's] very lifeblood," Ovenden says that science cannot exist without speculation. Scientists *must* speculate, must evolve theories, must *form opinions about the data they gather.*

3. **C**  A mature science tries "to see relationships between previously unrelated aspects of the universe," that is, to connect *hitherto unlinked phenomena in* significant patterns or *meaningful ways.*

4. **C**  The similarities of the spectrums suggest the possibility of vegetation on Mars.

5. **E**  Use the process of elimination to find the correct answer to this question.

    The author *makes an approximation*: he indicates the temperature zone in which life can exist is "about [*approximately*] 75,000,000 miles wide." Therefore, you can eliminate (A).

    The author *uses a metaphor*: he implicitly compares speculation to blood. Therefore, you can eliminate (B).

    The author *states a resemblance*: in the last sentence of the passage, he says "the infrared spectrum of the Martian markings has been found to be very similar to the spectrum of Earth vegetation." Therefore, you can eliminate (C).

    The author *makes a conjecture* about the sort of life-forms "without a built-in temperature control" that might exist on Mars: in the last sentence of the next-to-last paragraph, he conjectures (guesses; speculates) they "may be a form of vegetation" that closes its leaves at night. Therefore, you can eliminate (D).

    Only (E) is left. At no time does the author *deny a contradiction*. The correct answer is (E).

6. **D**  As the comment "I shall not soon forget that summer" (line 9) suggests, in this passage Du Bois shares his memories or *reminiscences* of what was *a memorable time* in his life.

7. **C**  To "learn from hearsay" is to learn not from one's own personal experience but from the comments of others. Why did Du Bois have to learn about the pleasures of hunting from hearsay and not from experiences? The comment in parentheses suggests the reason. His mother was terrified of guns. Therefore, we can assume that he had no chance to learn about hunting because *small arms weapons had been forbidden in his home.*

8. **D**  Use the process of elimination to answer this question.

    Is Du Bois's journey through the countryside *gratifying* to him? Yes; he enjoys "the pleasures of the chase." Therefore, you can eliminate (A).

    Does his journey seem *interminable* to him? Yes; the "miles stretch relentlessly ahead," never letting up. Therefore, you can eliminate (B).

    Is his journey *tiring* to him? Yes; he feels "deep weariness of heart and limb." Therefore, you can eliminate (C).

    Does his hunt for a school feel *discouraging* to him? Yes; he feels "his heart sink heavily" as he hears there is no job opening. Therefore, you can eliminate (E).

Is his journey a *carefree* one? No; throughout his journey he has the ongoing anxiety about when and where he will find a job. The correct answer is (D).

9.  **C**    Note the context in which *stage lines* appears. Du Bois has "wandered beyond railways, beyond stage lines" to the back country. The parallel structure suggests that stage lines, like railways, has to do with *transportation*, in this case with the *horse-drawn* form of transportation that took over when travelers went beyond the railroad's extent.

10. **D**    To indicate he finds himself way out in the back country, Du Bois adopts a *colloquial*, down-home manner of speech, referring to pests or vermin as *varmints*, a term he would not customarily use.

11. **B**    Looking back on those memorable "pleasures of the chase," Du Bois clearly feels *nostalgia* for days gone by.

12. **D**    Immediately on learning why Du Bois is in the vicinity, Josie "anxiously," eagerly tells him all about a potential school, stressing how "she herself longed to learn." Living in the backwoods, Josie would have been interested in meeting any stranger. However, her interest in meeting this stranger was increased when she learned his errand; that is, it was *intensified by her desire to gain an education*.

13. **D**    Making "honest efforts to be decent and comfortable," scolding her husband and children if they do not work to improve their lot and live "like folks," Josie's mother shows her *longing for her entire family to better themselves*.

14. **B**    In scolding her brothers roundly, Josie is being *blunt* or plainspoken.

15. **E**    The author "grew to love" this family. Clearly, he regards them with *distinct affection*.

16. **E**    The ancient Chinese view of life is described in the opening lines of the passage. People believed in the "mathematically precise order of the universe" and in the "forces that were harmoniously connected." In other words, life was structured *according to a well-defined philosophy*.

17. **B**    By defining *feng-shui* as a "kind of cosmic surveying tool" (line 15), the author is saying that it *is used to locate building sites*.

18. **C**    As described in lines 1–9 of the passage, the Tao *is a way of viewing the world*.

19. **D**    The main reason for the development of *feng-shui* is to "affect an individual and his family for generations to come" (lines 12–13). Evidently, the Chinese believed in *providing for future generations*.

20. **C**    The function of a geomancer, according to lines 43–46, was to *read and interpret the terrain*.

21. **A**    Based on lines 47–57, the best building sites were located between the Dragon (hilly ground) and the Tiger (low ground), that is, on terrain that is *partly flat and partly hilly*.

22. **B**    Because the *feng-shui* compass is an elaborate instrument with a complicated design, the author compares its center to a familiar dartboard in order to *clarify its appearance* for the reader.

23. **A**    Lines 54–57 of the passage describe the setting of Beijing. The city is located where the valley floor begins to slope upward to the *mountains*.

24. **B**    The use of *feng-shui* in selecting a homesite is intended to protect the residents from misfortune. The family, according to lines 77–83, must also be moral and upright because *feng-shui* gives *no guarantees of good fortune*.

25. **D**    Believers in *feng-shui* attentively care for the gardens surrounding their homes, since each of its features contributes to the well-being of the home and *contains symbolic meanings*.

26. **E**    The author describes *feng-shui* objectively, as though the concept has aroused his *intellectual curiosity*.

27. **D**    Adherents of *feng-shui* heed the presence of boulders (line 59), design proper access to the main entrance of the house (lines 100–108), consider the placement of trees (line 86) and the shape of nearby mountains (line 58). Only *the color of the house* is not mentioned.

28. **E**    The passage states that the condition of poor people reduces the "possibility of . . . participation in the larger economic system," made up, for example, of labor unions, political parties, and welfare agencies. Nonparticipation *isolates the poor from the mainstream of society*.

29. **C**    A "culture" may be defined as a group of people sharing a specific set of beliefs and values, customs, and traditions. The phrase "culture of poverty," therefore, signifies a group for whom poverty *has become a prevailing way of life*.

30. **B** By pointing out that the potential for protest and for being used in political movements resides in the culture of poverty, the author is indirectly citing *a reason for eliminating poverty* from our society.

31. **C** People in the culture of poverty, despite their intentions, cannot live up to the middle-class values they espouse mainly because they are *unable to change the conditions of their lives* as much as they may wish to.

32. **A** The discussion of marriage contains several *practical and economic* reasons why poor men and women avoid legal marriages. Men, for one, don't want "expense and legal difficulties." Women want to maintain "exclusive rights to a house or any other property."

33. **E** The metaphor suggests the similarity between *poverty and imprisonment.*

34. **D** Because the speaker talks about the smell of the outdoor privy and about burying the garbage in the ground, she appears to live *in the country*. However, she worries about her sons being influenced by bad companions. Thus, she is unlikely to live on an isolated farm (where her sons would not have other boys living nearby to influence them).

35. **D** Although all the listed emotions are evident in the passage, *hopelessness* and despair are prevalent. Near the end, the speaker actually says, "I have come out of my despair to tell you this."

36. **D** The silence of the poor reaffirms their sense of despair. They feel *powerless* to alter their condition. Therefore, they listen but don't say anything.

37. **C** The last paragraph summarizes the speaker's intent—*to arouse the audience into action:* "Look at us with an angry heart, anger that will help you help me."

38. **C** Each of the choices describes Passage 2. The quality of the passage to which the audience is most likely to respond, however, is that the speaker herself *shows such intense emotion.*

39. **B** Both authors show that poverty *means far more than lack of money.* Passage 1 stresses the whole "culture of poverty." Passage 2 highlights the smells, the weariness, and the hopelessness that accompany poverty.

40. **A** The speaker in Passage 2 says she has had no money to fix the refrigerator, to buy a shovel, to purchase iron pills, and so forth. Each of these is an example of something that results from a *chronic shortage of cash.*

## Critical Reading Exercise 2

1. **E** Her father scorned her successes in the world outside the home because he felt "undermined by" her clear surrender or "capitulation to the ways of the West." She had given in to Western ways, disobeying his wishes. Thus, *he felt her Westernization was costing him his authority over her.*

2. **D** In her Japanese home, her immediate family (including her Westernized brothers) customarily referred to Caucasians by using the Japanese term *Hakujin*. In explaining the conflicts she experienced as someone caught between two cultures, she uses the Japanese term for its authenticity.

3. **A** The author was careful not to show her aggressiveness and assertiveness to her father because these traits were unacceptable to him. He expected his daughter not to be outgoing and aggressive but to be *tranquil* (calm; serene) *and passive* (submissive; not initiating action).

4. **B** "Not seeing" refers to the white boys' inability to see the author as she truly was. Instead of seeing the actual Japanese-American adolescent girl, with her worries about fitting in with her friends and her embarrassment about her father's conservatism, they saw a stereotypical Oriental *geisha*, someone straight out of a paperback fantasy. Clearly, *they had no idea what she was like as an individual human being.*

5. **C** The term "double standard" generally refers to male-female roles, and to the different expectations society has for male and female behavior. In referring to her "double identity within a 'double standard,'" the author indicates that being Japanese at home and *Hakujin* outside the home influenced the way she defined herself as a woman.

6. **E** *Madame Butterfly*, the heroine of the opera of that name, is a classic example of submissive, obedient Japanese womanhood. Thus, over the years, she has grown from a simple literary figure to become (like Stowe's Uncle Tom, or Puzo's Godfather) *an ethnic stereotype.*

7. **E**  The last sentence of the passage states that the author "was not comfortable in either role" she had to play. In other words, her reaction to these roles was primarily one of discomfort or *unease*.

8. **E**  To be riddled with lacunae (that is, gaps or holes) is to be permeated with holes, *filled* with holes, the way a sieve is full of holes.

9. **A**  There are major gaps in our knowledge of pre-Spanish history in Mexico. Thus, our knowledge is *incomplete*.

10. **D**  Use the process of elimination to answer this question.

   While the passage states art in the period "served a religious function," the passage stresses the art itself, not the religious basis for the art. Therefore, you can eliminate (A).

   Though the early Mexican artists excelled in decorative composition, they created sculptures that went far beyond mere decoration. Therefore, you can eliminate (B).

   The author states Mexican art "is comparable to" great Chinese art, rivals Egyptian art, foreshadows modern European art. He does not say it exceeds or surpasses European and Asian art. Therefore, you can eliminate (C).

   The author never discusses modern Mexican art. Therefore, you can eliminate (E).

   Throughout the passage, particularly in the final two paragraphs, the author cites masterpiece after masterpiece of pre-Spanish Mexican art. The correct answer is (D).

11. **B**  The author insists that the "bold simplifications or wayward conceptions" of early Mexican art were the result of creative decisions made by skilled artists and not the unfortunate consequences of sloppy technique. Thus, these supposed distortions were *deliberate* (intentional).

12. **D**  In marveling at the artist's plastic feeling, the author is awed by the sculptor's feel for carving and shaping works of art. In other words, the author feels *admiration for both the artist's technical expertise and artistic sensibility*.

13. **E**  The passage is discussing the Mexican artists' gift for sculpture, for fashioning or *shaping objects* into works or art. That is the sense in which *modeling* is used here.

14. **E**  The author has just been discussing the "surprising . . . modernity" of early Mexican sculpture. He indicates these works "anticipate" more modern, and therefore *more familiar* to the reader, works by Brancusi, Lehmbruck, and Moore.

15. **C**  The emphasis on sculpture (masks, reclining figures, statuettes) suggests that much of Mexican art depicted *people*.

16. **D**  The first paragraph of the passage says that the administration of every president has ended with "recriminations and mistrust." Presidents, like everyone else, hate to be criticized in public. Therefore, they all have experienced *hostility between themselves and the press*.

17. **B**  Conflict between the president and the press is the "best proof" (line 11) that *freedom of the press is alive and well in the United States*.

18. **B**  In the days of the Founding Fathers, there was an expectation that the press would act "like a watchdog" (lines 20–21) that would *carefully observe and report on the work of all elected officials*.

19. **A**  The relationship between the press and the presidency has become increasingly complicated by changes in the nature of the presidency (lines 26–36), including the creation of the position of Press Secretary and the fact that the president is a world leader. The press itself now includes television, and reporters from all over the world cover the president. What hasn't altered the relationship between the press and the president is the fact that *the term of office has remained four years*.

20. **C**  The author advises the reader (lines 40–41) "not to view the past in terms of our own times" because to do so violates the historical context. In other words, *we can't fully grasp the context of the past*.

21. **B**  Basic to the beliefs of the colonists was that "whoever controlled the printing press was in the best position to control the minds of men" (lines 59–61), which meant that *the press influenced what people thought and did*.

22. **C**  The printing press endowed authorities of the church and state with unparalleled power to control the thoughts and actions of the people. Prior to Gutenberg's invention, then, *governments played a less influential role in people's lives*.

23. **D**  Early on, both the church and the state realized the power inherent in the printing press. It was to their mutual advantage to have a printing press set up in South America as quickly as possible.

Using the printing press, the state gained control of territory, and the church *spread the word of God.*

24. **E**  The passage says that in North America secular publishing "was soon dominant" (line 95). In other words, printing *quickly became less religious in nature.*

25. **C**  The quotation by Berkeley suggests that the governor of Virginia took a dim view of anti-church activities, including printing anything that criticized the church. Evidently, he *held the church above other institutions,* including the government he served.

26. **A**  Those who agree with Berkeley would support his general view that *there should be limits set on freedom of the press.*

27. **C**  The passage says that some twentieth-century people agree with Berkeley's sentiments about the free press. Issues of free press, even today *raise controversy in the United States.*

28. **D**  In the last sentence of the first paragraph the author explains why the Grand Canyon is the "sublimest thing on earth." It is sublime "by virtue of the whole—its *ensemble,*" or its *overall appearance.*

29. **B**  The first paragraph implies that the *Grand Canyon's incomparable size* is what is likely to impress a visitor. Only after long and careful study do observers begin to understand that the canyon has more to offer than magnitude. The distinctive quality of its overall appearance—its *ensemble,* in the author's words—lends it majesty.

30. **D**  Lines 16–39 explain the author's view that the *Grand Canyon transcends the common notion of the word* canyon. The Grand Canyon is markedly different from other places we call *canyons.*

31. **B**  To heighten the contrast between the Grand Canyon and ordinary canyons, the author makes a contrast between St. Mark's and a "rude (that is, crude) dwelling" on the frontier. Since a frontier dwelling is apt to be primitive and unadorned, this suggests that St. Mark's must be a refined, *ornate structure.*

32. **A**  The passage calls the Grand Canyon an "expansion of the simple type of drainage channels peculiar to Plateau Country," implying that *large canyons at one time were very small.* Earlier in the passage the author cited the example of a huge building. It, too, is an expansion—an enlargement of a small house.

33. **C**  As described in the third paragraph, the rain *promotes the growth of vegetation,* described as "a veil of green." The rain also prepares the ground "for another planting."

34. **D**  The last of the sun's light dissipates or *vanishes* as darkness falls.

35. **B**  To the author, the coming of the rains changes the world, transforming the desert into a *revitalized* landscape filled with creatures mating and giving birth. This transformation fills him with *awe.*

36. **A**  Several distinctive qualities of the spadefoot toad are mentioned. The toads chant throughout the night. The female toads "spew out egg masses" as they reproduce. The male toads "bellow," in their characteristic mating call. Their characteristic "burnt-peanut-like" odor fills the air. Only the *relative size* of the toad is not mentioned in the passage.

37. **D**  To most people, the youngster's reply "is a contradiction." In other words, it seems *paradoxical* to them that a desert could smell like rain.

38. **C**  In describing the Grand Canyon, the author uses only his sense of *sight.*

39. **B**  The author of Passage 2 writes in the first person. He recounts his *personal experiences* with rainshowers, with toads and turtles, and with members of the Papago tribe. The author of Passage 1, on the other hand, while equally passionate about his subject, removes himself from the writing. Both authors write poetically, using figures of speech, and both respect nature's wonders. The author of Passage 2 clearly includes far less geological data than does the author of Passage 1.

40. **A**  Except for the facts and figures of the first paragraph, Passage 1 lacks the *concrete* details of Passage 2. The author of Passage 1 writes in more *abstract* language about the nature of canyons and the uniqueness of the Grand Canyon. Passage 2, in contrast, is filled with specific down-to-earth images of the sights and sounds of the desert, from the "veil of green" of nascent vegetation to the incessant chanting of the spadefoot toads.

## LEVEL B

### Critical Reading Exercise 1

1. **D**   To pretend that Indians are a primitive people is to choose to see them as unlettered and barbaric. To view them as a "first" or primal people is to choose to see them as linked to ancient truths. Thus, to the author, the distinction between "primitive" and "primal" is that *while the former has some negative connotations, the latter has neutral or positive ones.*

2. **D**   Matthiessen rejects those who would patronizingly dismiss Indian spirituality as simple hearted (or simpleminded) in any way. Thus, he puts *animism* and *naturalism* in quotes because *he disagrees with their being applied* to something as profound as the Indian concept of earth and spirit.

3. **B**   In the first and third paragraphs, Matthiessen is making assertions about the nature of Indian spirituality. In the second paragraph, however, he moves away from the subject of religion to exploring various theories of Indian origins in North America. Thus, the second paragraph is a *digression from the argument* made in the opening and closing paragraphs of the passage.

4. **A**   Refusing to adopt a patronizing or condescending attitude toward Indian religion, comparing it to the most venerated or revered religions of the world, Matthiessen clearly views Indian religion with *respect.*
      (B) is incorrect. Though Matthiessen has great respect for Indian religion, his attachment to it is not so immoderate as to be termed *idolatry* (giving absolute religious devotion to something that is not actually God, for example, a physical object or man-made image).

5. **C**   Sages in their wisdom *understand* or apprehend the universe's true nature.

6. **A**   A miracle is by definition an act or event so extraordinary that it seems a manifestation of God's supernatural power. Thus, to call the ordinary, common acts of every day miraculous is to be self-contradictory or *paradoxical.*

7. **B**   Lines 4–5 of the passage say that the hierarchy consists of the troop's *males.*

8. **D**   Lines 9–11 of the passage say that in primate troops, males "defend, control, and lead the troop." Therefore, the troops are *dominated by adult males.*

9. **A**   The passage says that the strong social bond in the troop is maintained for safety (line 12). Therefore, it is meant to *protect the members of the troop.*

10. **A**   According to lines 13–14, "chimpanzees lack a stable social troop." Rather, they form temporary groups (lines 16–17). Therefore, unlike other primates, chimpanzees *are not bound to troops.*

11. **C**   The second paragraph of the passage contrasts the social organization of chimpanzees and social organization of other primates. Clearly, *chimpanzees are different.*

12. **C**   The discussion of chimpanzee social organization (lines 21–24) implies that each chimpanzee develops *a distinct personality.*

13. **D**   The flexible social organization of chimpanzees, discussed in lines 52–59, "raises individuality" and rejects "individual uniformity," traits that foster *the amount of individual freedom afforded to members.*

14. **D**   Population size, according to lines 72–76, is partly controlled by *the size of the food supply.*

15. **E**   The Budongo Forest is called a "continuous habitat" (line 80) in which several "regional populations" of chimpanzees have developed.

16. **B**   The opening paragraph of the passage describes the goal of the project. The project's objective is not to use a new research method but to use a different technique in order to *develop a new theory about the causes of war.*

17. **E**   The reason given in lines 4–6 for reversing the customary research method is that *existing theories fail to coincide with facts.*

18. **D**   Although the phrase has a negative ring, the author explains that all definitions are "somewhat arbitrary." Therefore, *the scholars had no better alternatives.*

19. **D** The author takes pains to describe the care with which the researchers defined the terms of the study. Of particular note is that the researchers drew up their definitions "before arriving at their conclusions" (lines 21–22) so that they would keep *personal bias out of their study.*

20. **C** By looking up the assertions of the street corner preacher in *The Wages of War,* one can check the facts. Ultimately, the author is suggesting, *facts speak louder than opinions.*

21. **A** The next step taken by the researchers was "to identify conditions or events… associated with wars" (lines 45–47) because of the assumption that there have been certain *political and social conditions that have often led to war.*

22. **E** The basic premise of the study is that there may be correlations of conditions or events that often lead to war. Seeking correlations is the basic *research method used by the participants* in the study.

23. **B** The author argues that correlations do not necessarily constitute proof (lines 66–69). With so many variables at play in the conditions and events leading to war, *correlations may be misinterpreted.*

24. **C** Lines 74–77 raise the possibility that the project may find that there is insufficient evidence to warrant a theory of war. In other words, in spite of the participants' best intentions, the findings *may fail to produce definitive results.*

25. **B** The discussion of Bismarck and Hitler (lines 83–94) is presented as an example of a potential problem. Because of faulty design (e.g., a definition of *war*), one or more conclusions can be dead wrong. Consequently, the *design and procedure may invalidate the findings.*

26. **E** Despite problems and flaws in "The Correlates of War" project, the author still maintains—in the last lines of the passage—that the study is *the best of its kind.*

27. **C** Regardless of his doubts about some research techniques being used by the scholars engaged in the project, the author takes a generally positive position regarding the outcomes of the project. He is largely *optimistic and hopeful.*

28. **C** The man "with his eyes fixed to the ground" is the artist who "searches." To Picasso, the search means nothing in painting. *Artists who contemplate their subjects too much* before painting may have good intentions, but they are likely to fail. After all, results, not intentions, count.

29. **B** Picasso's statement is a *denial of the accusation* that the principal objective of his work is "the spirit of research," discussed in lines 12–15.

30. **C** The idea that art *gives us more than truth, that it gives us understanding* is made clear by the thought that "art is a lie that makes us realize truth, at least the truth that is given us to understand" (lines 22–24).

31. **B** Picasso says that his object in art is to show what he has found, not what he was looking for. Therefore, in Picasso's opinion a successful piece of art *reveals what the artist has found.*

32. **A** The word "naturalism" in this context means *realism.* Realists in art, as the name suggests, try to recreate as realistically as they can three-dimensional objects on a two-dimensional surface, an impossible undertaking in Picasso's view. As he writes, "Nature and art . . . cannot be the same thing."

33. **C** Much of the passage describes Picasso's *innovations,* such as "freeing the technique of painting from its slavish adherence to the description of nature" and making the painter "a free creator, a poet."

34. **D** The passage explains that once Picasso burst onto the art scene, the *strict rules of art* no long applied. Among other things, Picasso broke with such past traditions as "obeying only the laws of the artist's inner vision" and painting with "slavish adherence to the description of nature."

35. **A** Picasso gave painting "new laws of harmony and balance," but he was careful not to *ignore the need for harmony and balance.*

36. **E** The notion that *patching a picture restricts artists' freedom of expression* is supported by the paragraph beginning on line 95. When an artist has "no regard for the nature of anything he painted before," he has the "freedom to move at will in the boundless spaces of free expression."

37. **C** Throughout the passage, but particularly in the last paragraph, Picasso is portrayed as a *bold experimenter.* For example, the author says Picasso tested the foundations on which his own art rested.

38. **B** Eluard's phrase reminds us of Picasso's statement in Passage 1 that "*my object is to show what I have found.*" In other words, Picasso wants to see objects anew, with fresh eyes, or to "attain sight."

39. **B** Both passages allude to Picasso's "aphorism," that the artist "*does not seek, but finds*": In Passage 1, see the first paragraph; in Passage 2, see lines 86–87.

40. **C**  Passage 2 is an appreciation of Picasso as artist. Throughout Passage 1, Picasso defends himself from false accusations and clarifies misconceptions about art. The tone of Passage 1, therefore, is more contentious, *more argumentative* than the tone of Passage 2.

## LEVEL C

## Critical Reading Exercise 1

1. **E**  Both paragraphs *humorously portray the female residents* of Cranford, describing their idiosyncrasies of dress and behavior at length.

2. **C**  In stating that "whatever does become of the gentlemen, they are not at Cranford," the author indicates that the gentlemen are distinguished chiefly by their *absence.*

3. **D**  The "tender good offices [performed for] each other whenever they are in distress" are the kind *acts done* by the good ladies of Cranford *on behalf of others* needing their help.

4. **D**  In showing both the eccentricities and the virtues that characterize the ladies of Cranford, the author exhibits an attitude that is *mocking*, but only *gently* so.

5. **B**  Note the context in which the author refers to "Miss Tyler, of cleanly memory." The author has just been talking about the unfashionable attire of Cranford ladies, emphasizing that their clothes are made of good (that is, long-lasting) material. The Cranford ladies wear their clothes for years, but they are scrupulous about keeping them clean. In this they resemble Miss Tyler, known for her *spotless attire.*

6. **B**  Since the bulk of the last paragraph concerns the ladies' eccentricities of dress and indifference to current fashion, it can be inferred that "the last gigot" most likely is *an outmoded article of apparel* worn well after its time by the unfashionable ladies of Cranford.

7. **D**  Arbitrarily ready to decide issues "without troubling themselves with unnecessary reasons," dictatorial or overbearing to their dependents, and quite able to do without men, the ladies of Cranford do not seem in the least *submissive* (yielding).

8. **E**  By providing background on how the theory of a dynamic abyss came to take hold in the scientific community and on how the forces that activate the global patterns of ocean currents actually work, the passage serves to *summarize evidence supporting oceanic circulation.*

9. **D**  In stating that the quote "accurately describes conditions" in the depths, the author indicates he is using the quote primarily to illustrate *noteworthy physical characteristics* (darkness; turbulence) of the depths.

10. **C**  The opening sentence states that "many investigators were initially reluctant" to accept the evidence in favor of this controversial hypothesis. Committed to the belief that the depths of the ocean were calm ("the notion of the tranquil abyss"), these scientists at first viewed the idea that the abyss could be dynamic with *marked skepticism* (distinct doubt).

11. **E**  The passage states that the *first* argument for the existence of dynamic currents in the deeps came from theory, based on "models of ocean circulation" involving the tendency of cold water to sink.

12. **B**  Both minute particles of rock and grains of wind-blown soil belong to the first type of sediment discussed ("detritus whose source is the weathering of rocks on continents and islands"). Only the *fragmentary shells* of dead microscopic organisms belong to the second type.

13. **D**  Because they need to take into account the effects of strong sea-floor currents on the structures they plan to build, *designers of sea-floor structures* are most likely to be interested in this particular article.

14. **D**  The authors approximate an amount ("about three billion tons per year"), refer to a model of ocean circulation, give several examples ("such as the..."), and list evidence to support a theory. They never *propose a solution* to a problem.

15. **C**  The authors are objective and factual. Their style can best be described as *espository* (explanatory).

16. **D** The author asks this question, not because readers don't know what money is, but because he wishes the reader to consider a definition different from the usual one. By the end of the paragraph the author *introduces an unfamiliar* (to most readers) *definition of the word.*

17. **B** At the beginning of the second paragraph the author writes that "Three such functions are usually specified," which amounts to saying that these three functions are *common knowledge among informed people.*

18. **A** The sticker price on a car informs prospective buyers of the cost, or value, of the car. Therefore, the sticker price qualifies as *a unit of account,* as defined in lines 23–27.

19. **C** The definition of "archetype" is a pattern or model on which others are based. Consequently, barter is *a model for economic exchanges.*

20. **A** In line 46 the author says that bartering required "large amounts of time." The expenditure of time is reiterated in lines 53–54. Clearly, the chief shortcoming of barter is that *making deals was too time-consuming.*

21. **B** A Gordian knot, an allusion to an ancient Greek myth, has come to refer to anything which is difficult to untie or unravel. Hence, it was *difficult to change the barter system to a monetary system.*

22. **E** The passage cites several advantages of money over barter: the double coincidence of wants is eliminated by a monetary system (lines 63–68); when money is the medium of exchange, the cost of doing business is lower (lines 68–70); supply and demand determine the cost of goods and services (70–72)—a basic principle of economics; and in a monetary system a greater division of labor is possible (72–75), which increases efficiency.
    Only (E), *opportunities of advantageous trade are reduced,* is not mentioned in the passage.

23. **B** According the passage, "the usefulness of money is inversely proportional to the number of currencies in circulation" (lines 77–79). That is, a large number of currencies *reduces the efficiency of the international economy.*

24. **A** Line 96 of the passage indicates that one of the benefits of a single national currency is a *reduction in the cost of monetary transactions.*

25. **D** After citing several reasons for streamlining the international economy by reducing the number of currencies, the next logical step is to create a single world currency. The author, however, demurs from proposing that step because, as the remainder of the passage explains, *the most obvious solution is not the best solution.*

26. **E** The one most desirable benefit to be derived from a single world currency, which the author reiterates throughout the discussion, is *reducing transaction costs.*

27. **A** The conclusion to be drawn from all the arguments about a single world currency, particularly the high cost of introducing a single standard, is that *it may cause more problems than it will solve.*

28. **D** Passage 1 says that in *This Side of Paradise,* Fitzgerald managed to turn a mass of diverse material "into a sustained narrative" (line 15), indicating that Fitzgerald knew how to *tell a long story.*

29. **A** Passage 1 says that "freshness of language" (lines 19–20) is Fitzgerald's "identifying mark." In other words, Fitzgerald built his reputation on *his original use of words.*

30. **B** The author of Passage 1 claims that *This Side of Paradise* helped "Fitzgerald thrash out those 'ideas still in riot' that he attributes to Amory" (lines 24–27). Amory, therefore, seems to be a *thinly disguised version of Fitzgerald himself*—a young man trying to find himself and make sense of life.

31. **E** In Passage 1, Fitzgerald's words are quoted in the context of a discussion of the "naiveté and honesty" of his work. The quotation confirms that Fitzgerald's writing is characteristically *truthful and innocent.*

32. **B** The entire passage describes the problems of Fitzgerald's *immature* writing. In comparison to the writing in Fitzgerald's earlier work, the writing in *This Side of Paradise* had "improved greatly" (line 17). Nevertheless, the author of the passage still regarded Fitzgerald as an "ambitious amateur" (line 44).

33. **C** The paragraph following the anecdote rebuts *a mistaken view of Fitzgerald.* Lines 63–71 portray Fitzgerald as anything but a "stupid old woman."

34. **A**   The "jewel" refers to Fitzgerald's exceptional talent with words. Talent is not enough, however. *Fitzgerald's talent needed polishing.*

35. **D**   Stating that *This Side of Paradise* "is not only highly imitative but...imitates an inferior model" (lines 82–84), the author indicates that *Sinister Street* was an *unfortunate* choice for a *model* on which Fitzgerald might base his book.

36. **B**   The author describes how the hero of *Sinister Street* is "swamped in the forest of descriptions" (lines 98–99). The author of the novel uses so many flowery descriptive phrases that the reader cannot keep track of the novel's plot. In other words, his pretty writing or *flowery prose overshadows* the novel's *hero's story.*

37. **D**   One reason, among others explained in lines 121–125, that the author calls Fitzgerald's novel "illiterate" is that it *contains many errors* that should have been caught by the publisher's proofreader.

38. **A**   Despite the flaws of *This Side of Paradise*, the authors of both passages apparently recognize *Fitzgerald's talent as a writer.* More specifically, Passage 1 concludes with the words that "Fitzgerald had found his craft." Passage 2 says that Fitzgerald has "imagination" (line 74) and a "gift for expression" (line 77).

39. **E**   Passage 1 describes *This Side of Paradise* as "clumsy and pasted together" (line 4). Passage 2 says the book has "no dominating intention to endow it with unity and force" (lines 110–112). Both criticisms refer to the book's *lack of artistic focus.*

40. **D**   Passage 1 was written long after Fitzgerald became an important literary figure, long after his death, in fact. The author speaks of Fitzgerald in the past tense: "All his life he was to think of himself . . ." (lines 6–10), etc. Passage 2 discusses Fitzgerald as a figure on the contemporary scene: "Scott Fitzgerald is, in fact, . . . a very good-looking young man . . ." (lines 67–68). It also suggests that *This Side of Paradise* illustrates Fitzgerald's talent as a writer, but that his work still needs improvement. The evidence in both passages shows that *Passage 1 was written long after the publication of* This Side of Paradise, *and Passage 2 was written shortly afterward.*

# PART VI

# BUILDING YOUR VOCABULARY

Overview

Tips

SAT I High-Frequency
  Word List

# OVERVIEW

Recognizing the meaning of words is essential to comprehending what you read. The more you stumble over unfamiliar words in a text, the more you have to take time out to look up words in your dictionary, the more likely you are to wind up losing track of what the author has to say.

To succeed in college, you must develop a college-level vocabulary. You must familiarize yourself with technical words in a wide variety of fields, mastering each field's special vocabulary. You must learn to use these words, and re-use them until they become second nature to you. The time you put in now learning vocabulary-building techniques for SAT I will pay off later on, and not just on the SAT.

This section provides you with a fundamental tool that will help you build your vocabulary: Barron's SAT I High-Frequency Word List.

No matter how little time you have before you take SAT I, you can familiarize yourself with the sort of vocabulary you will be facing on the test.

Look over the words on our SAT I High-Frequency Word List: each of these words, ranging from everyday words such as *abstract* and *objective* to less-commonly known ones such as *abstruse* and *iconoclast*, has appeared (as answer choices or as question words) from five to thirty times on SAT and SAT I tests published through 1996. Notice that the words have been divided into groups of ten so you won't be overwhelmed.

Not only will looking over the SAT I High-Frequency Word List reassure you that you do know some SAT-type words, but it also will help you on the actual day of the test. These words have turned up on recent tests: some of them may turn up on the test you take. Look over these words. Review any of them that are unfamiliar to you. Try using these words on your parents and friends. Then, if they do turn up on your test, feel confident: your knowledge of them will help you come up with the correct answer or eliminate an incorrect answer choice.

# TIPS ON BUILDING YOUR VOCABULARY

## READ WIDELY TO DEVELOP YOUR FEELING FOR WORDS

There is only one effective long-range strategy for vocabulary building: READ.

Read—widely and well. Sample different fields—physics, art history, political science, geology—and different styles. Extensive reading is the one sure way to make your vocabulary grow and to develop your feeling for words.

The Sunday edition of *The New York Times* contains special sections on science, literature, and the arts. Tuesday's edition contains a special science section as well. *The Washington Post* and *The Christian Science Monitor* offer excellent coverage of the arts and sciences, as well as current events.

Try to develop an interest in as many fields as you can. Sample some of the quality magazines: *The New Yorker, Smithsonian, Scientific American, Natural History, Harper's, Newsweek, Time*. In these magazines, you'll find articles on the whole range of fields touched on by SAT I. If you take time to acquaint yourself with the contents of these magazines, you'll soon be in command of an expanding vocabulary.

## USE MEMORY TRICKS TO KEEP NEW WORDS IN YOUR ACTIVE VOCABULARY

Reading widely does not always help you remember the words you read. You may have the words in your passive vocabulary and be able to recognize them when you see them in a particular context and yet be unable to define them clearly or think of additional contexts for them.

Remembering words takes work. It also takes wit. You can spend hours memorizing dictionary definitions and get no place. Try capitalizing on your native intelligence by thinking up mnemonic devices—memory tricks—to help you remember new words.

Consider the word *hovel*. A hovel is a dirty, mean house. How can you remember that? Hovel rhymes with shovel. You need to shovel out the hovel to live in it. Rhymes can help you remember what words mean.

Now consider the word *hover*. To hover is to hang fluttering in the air or to wait around. Can rhyme help you here? Hover rhymes with cover. That doesn't seem to work. However, take another look at hover. Cut off the letter *h* and you're left with the word *over*. If a helicopter hovers over an accident, it hangs in the air; if a mother hovers over a sick child, she waits around. Hidden little words can help you remember bigger words.

Try the hidden word trick with a less familiar word than hover. Take the word *credulous*. Credulous means gullible or easily fooled. A credulous person will give money to someone who wants to sell him the Brooklyn Bridge. Now look closely at credulous. What little word is hidden within it? The hidden word is *red*. What happens when a person finds out he's been taken for a fool? Often, the poor fool turns red. Credulous, red in the face. There's your memory trick.

## WORK THROUGH THE SAT I HIGH-FREQUENCY WORD LIST TO EXPAND YOUR COLLEGE-LEVEL VOCABULARY

Take time to acquaint yourself specifically with the sorts of words you must know to do well on SAT I. Follow the procedures outlined below in order to work through the SAT I High-Frequency List most profitably.

1. Select a list of ten words.
2. Allot a definite time each day for the study of a list.
3. Devote at least half an hour to each list.
4. First go through the list looking at the short, simple-looking words (7 letters at most). Mark those you don't know. In studying, pay particular attention to them.
5. Go through the list again looking at the longer words. Pay particular attention to words with more than one meaning and familiar-looking words that have unusual definitions that come as a surprise to you. Study these secondary definitions.
6. List unusual words on index cards that you can shuffle and review from time to time. (Study no more than 5 cards at a time.)
7. Use the illustrative sentences as models and make up new sentences of your own.
8. In making up new sentences, use familiar examples and be concrete: the junior high school band tuning up sounds *discordant*; in *Beauty and the Beast*, until Belle tames him, the Beast has a *volatile* temper.

For each word, the following is provided:

1. The word (printed in heavy type).
2. Its part of speech (abbreviated).
3. A brief definition.
4. A sentence illustrating the word's use.
5. Whenever appropriate, related words are provided, together with their parts of speech.

The word list is arranged in alphabetical order.

# SAT I HIGH-FREQUENCY WORD LIST

## Word List 1

**abate**   V. subside or moderate. Rather than leaving immediately, they waited for the storm to *abate*. abatement, N.

**aberrant**   ADJ. abnormal or deviant. Given the *aberrant* nature of the data, we came to doubt the validity of the entire experiment.

**abject**   ADJ. wretched; lacking pride. On the streets of New York the homeless live in *abject* poverty, huddling in doorways to find shelter from the wind.

**abrasive**   ADJ. rubbing away; tending to grind down. Just as *abrasive* cleaning powders can wear away a shiny finish, *abrasive* remarks can wear away a listener's patience. abrade, V.

**absolute**   ADJ. complete; totally unlimited; certain. Although the King of Siam was an *absolute* monarch, he did not want to behead his unfaithful wife without *absolute* evidence of her infidelity.

**abstain**   V. refrain; withhold from participation. After considering the effect of alcohol on his athletic performance, he decided to *abstain* from drinking while he trained for the race. abstinence, N.

**abstract**   ADJ. theoretical; not concrete; nonrepresentational. To him, hunger was an *abstract* concept; he had never missed a meal.

**abstruse**   ADJ. obscure; profound; difficult to understand. She carries around *abstruse* works of philosophy, not because she understands them but because she wants her friends to think she does.

**acclaim**   V. applaud; announce with great approval. The NBC sportscasters *acclaimed* every American victory in the Olympics and lamented every American defeat. acclamation, acclaim, N.

**accolade**   N. award of merit. In the world of public relations, a "Clio" is the highest *accolade* an advertising campaign can receive.

## Word List 2

**acknowledge**   V. recognize; admit. Although I *acknowledge* that the Beatles' tunes sound pretty dated nowadays, I still prefer them to the "gangsta" rap songs my brothers play.

**acquiesce**   V. assent; agree without protesting. When we asked her to participate in the play, she immediately *acquiesced*. acquiescence, N.; acquiescent, ADJ.

**acrimonious**   ADJ. bitter in words or manner. The candidate attacked his opponent in highly *acrimonious* terms. acrimony, N.

**acute**   ADJ. quickly perceptive; keen; brief and severe. The *acute* young doctor realized immediately that the gradual deterioration of her patient's once-*acute* hearing was due to a chronic illness, not an *acute* one.

**adapt**   V. alter; modify. Some species of animals have become extinct because they could not *adapt* to a changing environment.

**address**   V. direct a speech to; deal with or discuss. Due to *address* the convention in July, Brown planned to *address* the issue of low-income housing in his speech.

**adherent**   N. supporter; follower. In the wake of the scandal, the senator's one-time *adherents* quietly deserted him.

**adjacent**   ADJ. neighboring; adjoining. You will find questions based on this reading passage located on the *adjacent* page.

**adroit**   ADJ. skillful; nimble. The juggler's admirers particularly enjoyed his *adroit* handling of difficult balancing tricks.

**adulation**   N. flattery; admiration. The rock star relished the *adulation* she received from her groupies and yes-men.

## Word List 3

**adversary**   N. opponent. The young wrestler struggled to overcome his *adversary*.

**adverse**   ADJ. unfavorable; hostile. The recession had a highly *adverse* effect on Father's investment portfolio: he lost so much money that he could no longer afford the butler and the upstairs maid. **adversity**, N.

**advocate** V. urge; plead for. Noted abolitionists such as Frederick Douglass and Sojourner Truth *advocated* the eradication of the Southern institution of slavery. also N.

**aesthetic** ADJ. artistic; dealing with or capable of appreciation of the beautiful. The beauty of Tiffany's stained glass appealed to Esther's *aesthetic* sense. **aesthete**, N.

**affable** ADJ. easily approachable; warmly friendly. Accustomed to cold, aloof supervisors, Nicholas was amazed at how *affable* his new employer was.

**affinity** N. natural liking; kinship; similarity. Octavia felt an immediate *affinity* for the folk dancers she met; their love of dance was hers as well.

**affirmation** N. positive assertion; confirmation; solemn pledge by one who refuses to take an oath. Despite Tom's *affirmations* of innocence, Aunt Polly still suspected he had eaten the pie.

**aggressor** N. attacker. Before you punish both boys for fighting, see whether you can determine which one was the *aggressor*.

**alienate** V. make hostile; separate. Heather's attempts to *alienate* Amy from Ellen failed because the two friends had complete faith in one another.

**alleviate** V. relieve. The doctor's reassuring remarks *alleviated* June's fears for the baby; though he'd been born prematurely, he was rapidly gaining weight and could go home in a couple of weeks.

## Word List 4

**allure** V. entice; attract. *Allured* by the song of the sirens, the helmsman steered the ship toward the reef. also N.

**aloof** ADJ. apart; reserved; standoffish. His classmates thought James was a snob because, instead of joining in their conversations, he remained silent and *aloof*.

**altruistic** ADJ. unselfishly generous; concerned for others. In providing tutorial assistance and college scholarships for hundreds of economically disadvantaged youths, Eugene Lang performed a truly *altruistic* deed. **altruism**, N.

**ambiguous** ADJ. unclear or doubtful in meaning. The proctor's *ambiguous* instructions thoroughly confused us; we didn't know which

columns we should mark and which we should leave blank. **ambiguity**, N.

**ambivalence** N. the state of having contradictory or conflicting emotional attitudes. Torn between loving her parents one minute and hating them the next, she was confused by the *ambivalence* of her feelings. **ambivalent**, ADJ.

**ameliorate** V. improve; make more satisfactory. Carl became a union organizer because he wanted to join the fight to *ameliorate* the working conditions in the factory.

**amend** V. correct; change, generally for the better. Hoping to *amend* his circumstances, Luong left Vietnam for the United States.

**amorphous** ADJ. formless; lacking shape or definition. As soon as we have decided on our itinerary, we shall send you a copy; right now, our plans are still *amorphous*.

**ample** ADJ. abundant. Bond had *ample* opportunity to escape. Why did he let us catch him?

**anarchist** N. person who seeks to overturn the established government; advocate of abolishing authority. Denying she was an *anarchist*, Katya maintained she wished only to make changes in our government, not to destroy it entirely. **anarchy**, N.

## Word List 5

**anecdote** N. short account of an amusing or interesting event. Rather than make concrete proposals for welfare reform, President Ronald Reagan told *anecdotes* about poor people who became wealthy despite their impoverished backgrounds.

**anguish** N. acute pain; extreme suffering. Visiting the site of the explosion, the governor wept to see the *anguish* of the victims and their families.

**animosity** N. active enmity. By advocating cuts in campaign spending and limits on congressional powers, the reform candidate almost seemed to invite the *animosity* of the party's leaders.

**antagonistic** ADJ. hostile; opposed. Despite his lawyers' best efforts to stop him, the angry prisoner continued to make *antagonistic* remarks to the judge. **antagonism**, N.

**antiquated** ADJ. old-fashioned; obsolete. Philip had grown so accustomed to editing his articles on word processors that he thought typewriters were too *antiquated* for him to use.

**antithesis**  N. contrast; direct opposite of or to. Good is the *antithesis* of evil, innocence the *antithesis* of guilt.

**apathy**  N. lack of caring; indifference. A firm believer in democratic government, she could not understand the *apathy* of people who never bothered to vote. apathetic, ADJ.

**apocryphal**  ADJ. untrue; made up. To impress his friends, Ted invented *apocryphal* tales of his adventures in the big city.

**appease**  V. pacify or soothe; relieve. Tom and Jody tried to *appease* their crying baby by offering him one toy after another. However, they couldn't calm him down until they *appeased* his hunger by giving him a bottle.

**appreciate**  V. be thankful for; increase in worth; be thoroughly conscious of. Little Orphan Annie truly *appreciated* the stocks Daddy Warbucks gave her, which *appreciated* in value considerably over the years.

## Word List 6

**apprehension**  N. fear; discernment; capture. The tourist refused to drive his rental car through downtown Miami because he felt some *apprehension* that he might be carjacked.

**arable**  ADJ. fit for growing crops. The first settlers wrote home glowing reports of the New World, praising its vast acres of *arable* land ready for the plow.

**arbitrary**  ADJ. unreasonable or capricious; randomly selected without any reason; based solely on one's unrestricted will or judgment. The coach claimed the team lost because the umpire made some *arbitrary* calls.

**arbitrate**  V. act as judge. Because both sides had confidence in her sense of fairness, she was called upon to *arbitrate* the dispute that threatened to divide the committee.

**archaic**  ADJ. antiquated. "Methinks," "thee," and "thou" are *archaic* words that are no longer part of our standard vocabulary.

**ardor**  N. heat; passion; zeal. Katya's *ardor* was catching; soon all her fellow demonstrators were busily making posters and handing out flyers, inspired by her enthusiasm for the cause. ardent, ADJ.

**arid**  ADJ. dry; barren. The cactus has adapted to survive in an *arid* environment.

**arrogance**  N. pride; haughtiness. Convinced that Emma thought she was better than anyone else in the class, Ed rebuked her for her *arrogance*.

**articulate**  ADJ. effective; distinct. Her *articulate* presentation of the advertising campaign impressed her employers so much that they put her in charge of the project. also V.

**ascendancy**  N. controlling influence. Leaders of religious cults maintain *ascendancy* over their followers by methods that can verge on brainwashing.

## Word List 7

**ascetic**  ADJ. practicing self-denial; austere. The wealthy, self-indulgent young man felt oddly drawn to the *ascetic* life led by members of some monastic orders. also N.

**aspire**  V. seek to attain; long for. Because he *aspired* to a career in professional sports, Philip enrolled in a graduate program in sports management. aspiration, N.

**assessment**  N. evaluation; judgment. Your SAT I score plays a part in the admission committee's *assessment* of you as an applicant.

**assuage**  V. ease or lessen (pain); satisfy (hunger); soothe (anger). Jilted by Jane, Dick tried to *assuage* his heartache by indulging in ice cream. One gallon later, he had *assuaged* his appetite but not his grief.

**astute**  ADJ. wise; shrewd. Expecting Miss Marple to be a woolly-headed old lady, Inspector Craddock was startled by the *astute* observations she made.

**asylum**  N. place of refuge; safety. Fleeing persecution, the political refugee sought *asylum* in the United States.

**atrophy**  V. waste away. After three months in a cast, Stan's biceps had *atrophied* somewhat; however, he was sure that if he pumped iron for a while he would soon build it up.

**attentive**  ADJ. considerate; thoughtful; paying attention. Thuy is very *attentive* to her Vietnamese-speaking parents, acting as their interpreter and helping them deal with American society.

**audacious**  ADJ. daring; bold. Audiences cheered as Luke Skywalker and Princess Leia made their *audacious*, death-defying leap to freedom, escaping Darth Vader's troops. audacity, N.

**augment**  V. increase; add to. Beth *augmented* her inadequate salary by selling Tupperware at parties at friends' homes.

## Word List 8

**austerity** N. sternness; severity; strict economy; lack of luxuries. The bishops charged with conducting the heresy inquiry were a solemn, somewhat forbidding group; their demeanor reflected their *austerity*.

**authentic** ADJ. genuine. The art expert was able to distinguish the *authentic* Van Gogh painting from the forged copy. authenticate, V.

**authoritarian** ADJ. favoring or exercising total control; nondemocratic. Forced to obey the dictates of the *authoritarian* regime, the people had no control over their own destiny. also N.

**autonomous** ADJ. self-governing. Although the University of California at Berkeley is just one part of the state university system, in many ways Cal Berkeley is *autonomous*, for it runs several programs that are not subject to outside control. autonomy, N.

**aversion** N. firm dislike. Their mutual *aversion* was so great that they refused to speak to one another.

**banal** ADJ. hackneyed; commonplace; trite. Was it Pendleton's stale plot or his cliché-ridden dialogue that made his play seem so *banal*? banality, N.

**bane** N. cause of ruin. Lack of public transportation is the *bane* of urban life.

**belie** V. contradict; give a false impression. His coarse, hard-bitten exterior *belied* his inner sensitivity.

**belittle** V. disparage; make fun of. Parents should not *belittle* their children's early attempts at drawing, but should encourage their efforts.

**belligerent** ADJ. quarrelsome. Whenever he had too much to drink, he became *belligerent* and tried to pick fights with strangers.

## Word List 9

**benevolent** ADJ. generous; charitable. Mr. Fezziwig was a *benevolent* employer who wished to make Christmas merrier for young Scrooge and his other employees.

**benign** ADJ. kindly; favorable; not malignant. Though her *benign* smile and gentle bearing made Miss Marple seem a sweet little old lady, in reality she was a tough-minded, shrewd observer of human nature.

**bequeath** V. leave to someone by a will; hand down. Although Maud had intended to *bequeath* the family home to her nephew, she died before changing her will. bequest, N.

**biased** ADJ. slanted; prejudiced. Because the judge played golf regularly with the district attorney's father, we feared he might be *biased* in the prosecution's favor. bias, N.

**bland** ADJ. soothing; mild; dull. Unless you want your stomach lining to be eaten away, stick to a *bland* diet. blandness, N.

**blasphemy** N. irreverence; sacrilege; cursing. In my father's house, the Dodgers were the holiest of holies; to cheer for another team was to utter words of *blasphemy*. blasphemous, ADJ.

**bolster** V. support; reinforce. The debaters amassed file boxes full of evidence to *bolster* their arguments.

**braggart** N. boastful person. I wouldn't mind Bob's being such a *braggart* if I felt he'd done anything worth bragging about.

**brawn** N. muscular strength; sturdiness. It takes *brawn* to become a champion weight-lifter. brawny, ADJ.

**brevity** N. conciseness; briefness. *Brevity* is essential when you send a telegram or cablegram; you are charged for every word.

## Word List 10

**buttress** V. support; prop up. The attorney came up with several far-fetched arguments in a vain attempt to *buttress* his weak case. also N.

**cacophonous** ADJ. discordant; inharmonious. Do the students in the orchestra enjoy the *cacophonous* sounds they make when they're tuning up? I don't know how they can stand the racket. cacophony, N.

**cajole** V. coax; wheedle. Diane tried to *cajole* her father into letting her drive the family car. cajolery, N.

**candor** N. frankness. The *candor* with which Gene spoke during the job interview impressed us all; it was clear he held nothing back. candid, ADJ.

**capricious** ADJ. fickle; incalculable. The storm was *capricious*, changing its course constantly.

**categorical** ADJ. without exceptions; unqualified; absolute. Though the captain claimed he was never, never sick at sea, he finally had to qualify his *categorical* denial: he was "hardly ever" sick at sea.

**causal** ADJ. implying a cause-and-effect relationship. The psychologist maintained there was a *causal* relationship between the nature of one's early childhood experiences and one's adult personality. causality, N.

**censorious** ADJ. critical. *Censorious* people delight in casting blame.

**censure** V. blame; criticize. The senator was *censured* for his inappropriate behavior. also N.

**certitude** N. certainty. Though there was no *certitude* of his getting the job, Lou thought he had a good chance of doing so.

## Word List 11

**charlatan** N. quack; pretender to knowledge. When they realized that the Wizard didn't know how to get them back to Kansas, Dorothy and her companions were indignant that they'd been duped by a *charlatan*.

**choreography** N. art of representing dances in written symbols; arrangement of dances. Merce Cunningham has begun to use a computer in designing *choreography*: a software program allows him to compose arrangements of possible moves and immediately view them onscreen.

**chronicle** V. report; record (in chronological order). The gossip columnist was paid to *chronicle* the latest escapades of socially prominent celebrities. also N.

**civil** ADJ. having to do with citizens or the state; courteous and polite. Although Internal Revenue Service agents are *civil* servants, they are not always *civil* to suspected tax cheats.

**clamor** N. noise. The *clamor* of the children at play outside made it impossible for her to take a nap. also V.

**clemency** N. disposition to be lenient; mildness, as of the weather. Why did the defense lawyer look pleased when his case was sent to Judge Bland's chambers? Bland was known for her *clemency* toward first offenders.

**coercion** N. use of force to get someone's compliance. They forced him to obey, but only by using great *coercion*. coerce, V.

**compelling** ADJ. overpowering; irresistible in effect. The prosecutor presented a well-reasoned case, but the defense attorney's *compelling* arguments for leniency won over the jury.

**compliance** N. readiness to yield; conformity in fulfilling requirements. When I give an order, I expect *compliance*, not defiance. The design

for the new school had to be in *compliance* with the local building code. comply, V.

**composure** N. mental calmness. Even the latest crisis at work failed to shake Nancy's *composure*.

## Word List 12

**compress** V. close; squeeze; contract. She *compressed* the clothes into a tight bundle.

**concede** V. admit; yield. Despite all the evidence Monica had assembled, Mark refused to *concede* that she was right.

**conciliatory** ADJ. reconciling; appeasing; amiable. Hoping to end the coldness that had grown between them, he wrote a *conciliatory* note. conciliate, V.

**concise** ADJ. brief and compact. When you define a new word, be *concise*: the shorter the definition, the easier it is to remember.

**conclusive** ADJ. convincing; decisive. We have *conclusive* evidence that proves her innocence.

**concur** V. agree in opinion. Justice O'Connor wrote a minority opinion because she did not *concur* with the reasoning of her fellow justices.

**condone** V. overlook voluntarily; forgive. Although she had excused Huck for his earlier escapades, Widow Douglas refused to *condone* his latest prank.

**confirm** V. corroborate; verify; support. I have several witnesses who will *confirm* my account of what happened.

**conflagration** N. great fire. In the *conflagration* that followed the 1906 earthquake, much of San Francisco burned to the ground.

**conformity** N. agreement or compliance; actions in agreement with prevailing social customs. In *conformity* with the by-laws of the Country Dance and Song Society, I am submitting a petition nominating Susan Murrow as president of the society.

## Word List 13

**confront** V. face; challenge. All I ask is the chance to *confront* my accusers face to face.

**conscientious** ADJ. scrupulous; careful. A *conscientious* editor, she checked every definition for its accuracy.

**consistency** N. absence of contradictions; dependability; uniformity; degree of thickness.

Holmes judged puddings and explanations on their *consistency*: he liked his puddings without lumps and his explanations without improbabilities.

**consolidation** N. merger; combination. The *consolidation* of the two firms went smoothly; they merged without a hitch.

**conspicuous** ADJ. easily seen; noticeable; striking. Janet was *conspicuous* both for her red hair and for her height.

✓**contagion** N. infection. Fearing *contagion*, they took great steps to prevent the spread of the disease.

**contemporary** N. person belonging to the same period. Though Charlotte Bronte and George Eliot were *contemporaries*, the two novelists depicted their Victorian world in markedly different ways. also ADJ.

**contempt** N. scorn; disdain. Brave but unimaginative, he had nothing but *contempt* for cowards. contemptuous, ADJ.

✓**contend** V. struggle; compete; assert earnestly. Sociologist Harry Edwards *contends* that young African-American athletes are exploited by some college recruiters.

✓**contentious** ADJ. quarrelsome. Disagreeing violently with the referees' ruling, the coach became so *contentious* that they threw him out of the game.

## Word List 14

**contract** V. compress or shrink; make a pledge; catch a disease. Warm metal expands; cold metal *contracts*.

✓**converge** V. approach; tend to meet; come together. African-American men from all over the United States *converged* on Washington to take part in the historic Million Man march.

✓**conviction** N. strongly held belief. Nothing could shake his *conviction* that she was innocent. (secondary meaning)

**cordial** ADJ. gracious; heartfelt. Our hosts greeted us at the airport with a *cordial* welcome and a hearty hug.

**corroborate** V. confirm; support. Though Huck was quite willing to *corroborate* Tom's story, Aunt Polly knew better than to believe either of them.

**corrosion** N. destruction by chemical action. The *corrosion* of the girders supporting the bridge took place so gradually that no one suspected any danger until the bridge suddenly collapsed. corrode, V.

**credibility** N. believability. Because the candidate had made some pretty unbelievable promises, we began to question the *credibility* of everything he said.

✓**credulity** N. belief on slight evidence; gullibility; naivete. Con artists take advantage of the *credulity* of inexperienced investors to swindle them out of their savings. credulous, ADJ.

**crescendo** N. increase in the volume or intensity, as in a musical passage; climax. I love it when a piece of music suddenly shifts its mood, dramatically switching from a muted, contemplative passage to a *crescendo* with blaring trumpets and clashing cymbals.

**cryptic** ADJ. mysterious; hidden; secret. Martin loved to act mysterious, making *cryptic* comments no one could understand.

## Word List 15

✓**cursory** ADJ. casual; hastily done. Because a *cursory* examination of the ruins indicates the possibility of arson, we believe the insurance agency should undertake a more extensive investigation of the fire's cause.

✓**curtail** V. shorten; reduce. When Elton asked Cher for a date, she said she was really sorry she couldn't go out with him, but her dad had ordered her to *curtail* her social life.

✓**cynic** N. one who is skeptical or distrustful of human motives. A born *cynic*, Sidney was suspicious whenever anyone gave him a gift "with no strings attached." cynical, ADJ.

**daunt** V. intimidate; frighten. "Boast all you like of your prowess. Mere words cannot *daunt* me," the hero answered the villain.

**dawdle** V. loiter; waste time. We have to meet a deadline so don't *dawdle*; just get down to work.

**debilitate** V. weaken; enfeeble. Michael's severe bout of the flu *debilitated* him so much that he was too tired to go to work for a week.

✓**debunk** V. expose something as nonsensical or false. I have gathered enough evidence to *debunk* the legend that Billy the Kid was a heroic, Robin Hood-like figure.

**decorum** N. propriety; orderliness and good taste in manners. Even the best-mannered students have trouble behaving with *decorum* on the last day of school. decorous, ADJ.

**defame** V. harm someone's reputation; malign. If you try to *defame* my good name, my lawyers will see you in court. defamation, N.

**deference** N. courteous regard for another's wish. In *deference* to the minister's request, please do not take photographs during the wedding service.

## Word List 16

**defiance** N. refusal to yield; resistance. When John reached the "terrible two's," he responded to every parental request with howls of *defiance*. defy, V.

**degenerate** V. become worse; deteriorate. As the fight dragged on, the champion's style *degenerated* until he could barely keep on his feet.

**degrade** V. lower in rank or dignity; debase. Some secretaries object to fetching the boss a cup of coffee because they feel it *degrades* them to do such lowly tasks.

**deliberate** V. consider; ponder. Offered the new job, she asked for time to *deliberate* before she told them her decision.

**delineate** V. portray; depict; sketch. Using only a few descriptive phrases, Austen *delineates* the character of Mr. Collins so well that we can predict his every move. delineation, N.

**denounce** V. condemn; criticize. The reform candidate *denounced* the corrupt city officers for having betrayed the public's trust. denunciation, N.

**deny** V. contradict; refuse. Do you *deny* his story, or do you support what he says? denial, N.

**depict** V. portray; describe. Some newspaper accounts *depicted* the movie star as a reclusive prima donna; others portrayed her as a sensitive artist harassed by the media.

**deplore** V. regret strongly; express grief over. Although I *deplore* the disintegration of the modern family, I understand that not every marriage can be saved.

**depravity** N. corruption; wickedness. Even Romans who had grown accustomed to perversions and immorality during Tiberius's reign were shocked by the *depravity* of the emperor Caligula.

## Word List 17

**deprecate** V. express disapproval of; protest against; belittle. A firm believer in old-fash-

ioned courtesy, Miss Post *deprecated* the modern tendency to address new acquaintances by their first names. deprecatory, ADJ.

**deride** V. ridicule; make fun of. The critics *derided* his pretentious dialogue and refused to consider his play seriously. derision, N.

**derivative** ADJ. unoriginal; derived from another source. Although her early poetry was clearly *derivative* in nature, the critics felt she had promise and eventually would find her own voice.

**desecrate** V. profane; violate the sanctity of. Shattering the altar and trampling the holy objects underfoot, the invaders *desecrated* the sanctuary.

**despondent** ADJ. depressed; gloomy. To the concern of his parents, William became seriously *despondent* after he broke up with Jan. despondency, N.

**despot** N. tyrant; harsh, authoritarian ruler. How could a benevolent king turn overnight into a *despot*?

**detached** ADJ. emotionally removed; calm and objective; indifferent. A psychoanalyst must maintain a *detached* point of view and stay uninvolved with her patients' personal lives. detachment, N. (secondary meaning)

**deterrent** N. something that discourages; hindrance. Does the threat of capital punishment serve as a *deterrent* to potential killers? deter, V.

**detrimental** ADJ. harmful; damaging. The candidate's acceptance of major financial contributions from a well-known racist ultimately proved *detrimental* to his campaign, for he lost the backing of many of his early grassroots supporters. detriment, N.

**devious** ADJ. roundabout; erratic; not straightforward. His plan was so *devious* that it was only with great difficulty we could follow its shifts and dodges.

## Word List 18

**didactic** ADJ. teaching; instructional. Pope's lengthy poem *An Essay on Man* is too *didactic* for my taste: I dislike it when poets turn preachy and moralize.

**diffuse** ADJ. wordy; rambling; spread out. If you pay authors by the word, you tempt them to produce *diffuse* manuscripts rather than concise ones.

**digression** N. wandering away from the subject.

Nobody minded when Professor Renoir's lectures wandered away from their official theme; his *digressions* were always more fascinating than the topic of the day. digress, V.

**diligence** N. steadiness of effort; persistent hard work. Her employers were greatly impressed by her *diligence* and offered her a partnership in the firm. diligent, ADJ.

**dilute** V. make less concentrated; reduce in strength. She preferred to *dilute* her coffee with milk.

**diminution** N. lessening; reduction in size. Old Jack was as sharp at eighty as he had been at fifty; increasing age led to no *diminution* of his mental acuity.

**disband** V. dissolve; disperse. The chess club *disbanded* after its disastrous initial season.

✓**discerning** ADJ. mentally quick and observant; having insight. Though no genius, the star was sufficiently *discerning* to tell her true friends from the countless phonies who flattered her.

**disclose** V. reveal. Although competitors offered him bribes, he refused to *disclose* any information about his company's forthcoming product. disclosure, N.

**discordant** ADJ. not harmonious; conflicting. Nothing is quite so *discordant* as the sound of a junior high school orchestra tuning up. discord, N.

## Word List 19

**discredit** V. defame; destroy confidence in; disbelieve. The campaign was highly negative in tone; each candidate tried to *discredit* the others.

**discriminating** ADJ. able to see differences; prejudiced. A superb interpreter of Picasso, she was sufficiently *discriminating* to judge the most complex works of modern art. (secondary meaning) discrimination, N.

✓**discursive** ADJ. digressing; rambling. As the lecturer wandered from topic to topic, we wondered what if any point there was to his *discursive* remarks.

**disdain** V. view with scorn or contempt. In the film *Funny Face*, the bookish heroine *disdained* fashion models for their lack of intellectual interests. also N.

✓**disinclination** N. unwillingness. Some mornings I feel a great *disinclination* to get out of bed.

✓**disinterested** ADJ. unprejudiced. Given the judge's political ambitions and the lawyers' financial interest in the case, the only *disinterested* person in the courtroom may have been the court reporter.

**dismantle** V. take apart. When the show closed, they *dismantled* the scenery before storing it.

**dismiss** V. put away from consideration; reject. Believing in John's love for her, she *dismissed* the notion that he might be unfaithful. (secondary meaning)

✓**disparage** V. belittle. Do not *disparage* any donation, no matter how small it may be; every penny counts, and these little gifts mean a lot.

✓**disparate** ADJ. basically different; unrelated. Unfortunately, Tony and Tina have *disparate* notions of marriage: Tony sees it as a carefree extended love affair, while Tina sees it as a solemn commitment to build a family and a home.

## Word List 20

**disparity** N. difference; condition of inequality. Their *disparity* in rank made no difference at all to the prince and Cinderella.

**dispassionate** ADJ. calm; impartial. Known in the company for his cool judgment, Bill could impartially examine the causes of a problem, giving a *dispassionate* analysis of what had gone wrong, and go on to suggest how to correct the mess.

**dispel** V. drive away; scatter; cause to vanish. The bright sunlight eventually *dispelled* the morning mist.

**disperse** V. cause to break up; scatter. The police fired tear gas into the crowd to *disperse* the protesters.

**disputatious** ADJ. argumentative; fond of arguing. Convinced he knew more than his lawyers, Alan was a *disputatious* client, ready to argue about the best way to conduct the case.

✓**disseminate** V. distribute; spread; scatter (like seeds). By their use of the Internet, propagandists have been able to *disseminate* their pet doctrines to new audiences around the globe.

✓**dissent** V. disagree. In the recent Supreme Court decision, Justice O'Connor *dissented* from the majority opinion. also N.

**dissipate** V. squander; waste; scatter. He is a fine artist, but I fear he may *dissipate* his gifts if he keeps wasting his time on such trivial pursuits.

**dissonance**  N. dissonance. Composer Charles Ives often used *dissonance*—clashing or unresolved chords—for special effects in his musical works.

**dissuade**  V. advise against. Tom could not *dissuade* Huck from running away from home. dissuasion, N.

## Word List 21

**distant**  ADJ. reserved or aloof; cold in manner. His *distant* greeting made me feel unwelcome from the start. (secondary meaning)

**divergent**  ADJ. differing; deviating. Since graduating from medical school, the two doctors have taken *divergent* paths, one going on to, become a nationally prominent surgeon, the other dedicating himself to a small family practice in his home town. divergence, N.

**diverse**  ADJ. differing in some characteristics; various. The professor suggested *diverse* ways of approaching the assignment and recommended that we choose one of them. diversity, N.

**diversion**  N. act of turning aside; pastime. After studying for several hours, he needed a *diversion* from work. divert, V.

**divulge**  V. reveal. No lover of gossip, Charlotte would never *divulge* anything that a friend told her in confidence.

**document**  V. provide written evidence. She kept all the receipts from her business trip in order to *document* her expenses for the firm. also N.

**dogmatic**  ADJ. opinionated; arbitrary; doctrinal. We tried to discourage Doug from being so *dogmatic*, but never could convince him that his opinions might be wrong.

**dormant**  ADJ. sleeping; lethargic; latent. At fifty her long-*dormant* ambition to write flared up once more; within a year she had completed the first of her great historical novels.

**dubious**  ADJ. doubtful; questionable. Many critics of SAT I contend the test is of *dubious* worth.

**duplicity**  N. double-dealing; hypocrisy. When Tanya learned that Mark had been two-timing her, she was furious at his *duplicity*.

## Word List 22

**dutiful**  ADJ. respectful; obedient. The *dutiful* child grew up to be a conscientious adult, aware of her civic obligations.

**ebb**  V. recede; lessen. His fortunes began to *ebb* during the Recession. also, N.

**eccentric**  ADJ. odd; whimsical; irregular. The comet passed close by the earth in its *eccentric* orbit.

**eclectic**  ADJ. selective in choosing from a variety of sources. The reviewers praised the new restaurant's *eclectic* selection of dishes, which ranged from Oriental stir fries to French ragouts and stews.

**eclipse**  V. darken; extinguish; surpass. The new stock market high *eclipsed* the previous record set in 1995.

**effervescent**  ADJ. exuberant; bubbly and excited. Nothing depressed Amy for long; she was so naturally *effervescent* that she was soon as high-spirited as ever. effervesce, V.

**egotistical**  ADJ. excessively self-centered; self-important; conceited. Typical *egotistical* remark: "But enough of this chit-chat about you and your little problems. Let's talk about what's really important: *Me!*"

**elaboration**  N. addition of details; intricacy. Tell what happened simply, without any *elaboration*. elaborate, V.

**elated**  ADJ. overjoyed; in high spirits. Grinning from ear to ear, Bonnie Blair was clearly *elated* by her fifth Olympic gold medal. elation, N.

**eloquence**  N. expressiveness; persuasive speech. The crowds were stirred by Martin Luther King's *eloquence*. eloquent, ADJ.

## Word List 23

**elusive**  ADJ. evasive; baffling; hard to grasp. Trying to pin down exactly when the contractors would be finished remodeling the house, Nancy was frustrated by their *elusive* replies. elude, V.

**embellish**  V. adorn; ornament. The costume designer *embellished* the leading lady's ball gown with yards and yards of ribbon and lace.

**emulate**  V. imitate; rival. In a brief essay, describe a person you admire, someone whose virtues you would like to *emulate*.

**endorse**  V. approve; support. Everyone waited to see which one of the rival candidates for the city council the mayor would *endorse*. endorsement, N. (secondary meaning)

**enduring**  ADJ. lasting; surviving. Keats believed in the *enduring* power of great art, which would outlast its creators' brief lives.

✓**enervate**   V. weaken. She was slow to recover from her illness; even a short walk to the window would *enervate* her. enervation, N.

✓**engender**   V. cause; produce. To receive praise for real accomplishments *engenders* self-confidence in a child.

**enhance**   V. advance; improve. You can *enhance* your chances of being admitted to the college of your choice by learning to write well; an excellent essay can *enhance* any application.

**enigma**   N. puzzle; mystery. "What *do* women want?" asked Dr. Sigmund Freud. Their behavior was an *enigma* to him.

**enmity**   N. ill will; hatred. At Camp David President Carter labored to bring an end to the *enmity* that prevented Egypt and Israel from living in peace.

## Word List 24

✓**enumerate**   V. list; mention one by one. Huck hung his head in shame as Miss Watson *enumerated* his many flaws.

✓**ephemeral**   ADJ. short-lived; fleeting. Its adult stage lasting less than two days, the mayfly is by definition an *ephemeral* creature.

**epic**   N. long heroic poem, or similar work of art. Kurosawa's film *Seven Samurai* is an *epic* that portrays the struggle of seven warriors to destroy a band of robbers. also ADJ.

✓**epicure**   N. connoisseur of food and drink. *Epicures* patronize this restaurant because it features exotic wines and dishes. epicurean, ADJ.

**episodic**   ADJ. loosely connected; divided into incidents; occurring at intervals. Though he tried to follow the plot of *Gravity's Rainbow*, John found the novel too *episodic*; he enjoyed individual passages, but had trouble following the work as a whole.

✓**equanimity**   N. calmness of temperament; composure. Even the inevitable strains of caring for an ailing mother did not disturb Bea's *equanimity*.

✓**equivocal**   ADJ. ambiguous; intentionally misleading. Rejecting the candidate's *equivocal* comments on tax reform, the reporters pressed him to say where he stood on the issue. equivocate, V.

**erratic**   ADJ. odd; unpredictable; wandering. Investors become anxious when the stock market appears *erratic*.

**erroneous**   ADJ. mistaken; wrong. I thought my answer was correct, but it was *erroneous*.

✓**erudite**   ADJ. learned; scholarly. Though his fellow students thought him *erudite*, Paul knew he would have to spend many years in serious study before he could consider himself a scholar.

## Word List 25

✓**esoteric**   ADJ. hard to understand; known only to the chosen few. *New Yorker* short stories often include *esoteric* allusions to obscure people and events: the implication is, if you are in the in-crowd, you'll get the reference; if you come from Cleveland, you won't.

✓**espouse**   V. adopt; support. She was always ready to *espouse* a worthy cause.

**esteem**   V. respect; value; judge. Though I reject Ezra Pound's politics, I *esteem* him for his superb poetry and his acute literary criticism.

✓**ethereal**   ADJ. light; heavenly; unusually refined. In Shakespeare's *The Tempest*, the spirit Ariel is an *ethereal* creature, too airy and unearthly for our mortal world.

**eulogy**   N. expression of praise, often on the occasion of someone's death. Instead of delivering a spoken *eulogy* at Genny's memorial service, Jeff sang a song he had written in her honor.

✓**euphemism**   N. mild expression used in place of an unpleasant one. Until recently, many Southern Americans avoided the word *bull* in polite speech, replacing it by a *euphemism*, such as *he-cow* or *male beast*.

✓**euphonious**   ADJ. pleasing in sound. *Euphonious* even when spoken, the Italian language is particularly pleasing to the ear when sung. euphony, N.

**euphoria**   N. feeling of great happiness and well-being (sometimes exaggerated). Delighted with her SAT scores, sure that the university would accept her, Allison was filled with *euphoria*. euphoric, ADJ.

✓**evanescent**   ADJ. fleeting; vanishing. Brandon's satisfaction in his new job was *evanescent*, for he immediately began to notice its many drawbacks. evanescence, N.

✓**exacerbate**   V. worsen; embitter. The latest bombing *exacerbated* England's already existing bitterness against the IRA, causing the prime minister to break off the peace talks abruptly.

## Word List 26

✓**exacting**   ADJ. extremely demanding. Cleaning the ceiling of the Sistine Chapel was an *exacting* task, one that demanded extremely meticulous care on the part of the restorers. exaction, N.

**exalt**   V. raise in rank or dignity; praise. The actor Alec Guinness was *exalted* to the rank of knighthood by the queen.

**execute**   V. put into effect; carry out. The choreographer wanted to see how well Margaret could *execute* a pirouette. (secondary meaning) execution, N.

**exemplary**   ADJ. serving as a model; outstanding. At commencement the dean praised Ellen for her *exemplary* behavior as class president.

**exemplify**   V. serve as an example of; embody. For a generation of balletgoers, Rudolf Nureyev *exemplified* the ideal of masculine grace.

✓**exhaustive**   ADJ. thorough; comprehensive. We have made an *exhaustive* study of all published SAT tests and are happy to share our research with you.

✓**exhume**   V. dig out of the ground; remove from the grave. Could evidence that might identify the serial killer have been buried with his victim? To answer this question, the police asked the authorities for permission to *exhume* the victim's body.

✓**exonerate**   V. acquit; exculpate. The defense team feverishly sought fresh evidence that might *exonerate* their client.

✓**expedient**   ADJ. suitable to achieve a particular end; practical; politic. A pragmatic politician, he was guided by what was *expedient* rather than by what was ethical. expediency, N.

**expedite**   V. hasten. Because we are on a tight schedule, we hope you will be able to *expedite* the delivery of our order.

## Word List 27

**expertise**   N. specialized knowledge; expert skill. Although she is knowledgeable in a number of fields, she was hired for her special *expertise* in computer programming.

**explicit**   ADJ. totally clear; definite; outspoken. Don't just hint around that you're dissatisfied: be *explicit* about what's bothering you.

✓**exploit**   N. deed or action, particularly a brave deed. Raoul Wallenberg was noted for his *exploits* in rescuing Jews from Hitler's forces.

✓**exploit**   V. make use of, sometimes unjustly. Cesar Chavez fought attempts to *exploit* migrant farmworkers in California. exploitation, N.

**expository**   ADJ. explanatory; intended to explain. The manual that came with my VCR was no masterpiece of *expository* prose: its explanations were so garbled that I couldn't even figure out how to rewind a tape.

✓**extant**   ADJ. still in existence. I'd hoped to buy a copy of Margaret Dean Smith's facsimile of *The Dancing Master*. Unfortunately, all the copies *extant* are in libraries or private collections; none are for sale.

**extol**   V. praise; glorified. The president *extolled* the astronauts, calling them the pioneers of the Space Age.

✓**extraneous**   ADJ. not essential; superfluous. No wonder Ted can't think straight! His mind is so cluttered up with *extraneous* trivia, he can't concentrate on the essentials.

✓**extricate**   V. free; disentangle. The fox could not *extricate* itself from the trap.

**exuberance**   N. overflowing abundance; joyful enthusiasm; flamboyance; lavishness. I was bowled over by the *exuberance* of Amy's welcome. What an enthusiastic greeting!

## Word List 28

✓**facile**   ADJ. easily accomplished; ready or fluent; superficial. Words came easily to Jonathan: he was a *facile* speaker and prided himself on being ready to make a speech at a moment's notice.

**facilitate**   V. help bring about; make less difficult. Rest and proper nourishment should *facilitate* the patient's recovery.

**fallacious**   ADJ. false; misleading. Paradoxically, *fallacious* reasoning does not always yield erroneous results: even though your logic may be faulty, the answer you get may nevertheless be correct. fallacy, N.

**fanaticism**   N. excessive zeal; extreme devotion to a belief or cause. When Islamic fundamentalists demanded the death of Salman Rushdie because his novel questioned their faith, world opinion condemned them for their *fanaticism*.

✓**fastidious**   ADJ. difficult to please; squeamish. Bobby was such a *fastidious* eater that he would eat a sandwich only if his mother first cut off every scrap of crust.

**feasible**    ADJ. practical. Is it *feasible* to build a new stadium for the Yankees on New York's West Side? Without additional funding, the project is clearly unrealistic.

**fervor**    N. glowing ardor; intensity of feeling. At the protest rally, the students cheered the strikers and booed the dean with equal *fervor*.

**fickle**    ADJ. changeable; faithless. As soon as Romeo saw Juliet, he forgot all about his old girlfriend Rosaline. Was Romeo *fickle*?

**figurative**    ADJ. not literal, but metaphorical; using a figure of speech. "To lose one's marbles" is a *figurative* expression; if you're told that Jack has lost his marbles, no one expects you to rush out to buy him a replacement set.

**flagrant**    ADJ. conspicuously wicked; blatant; outrageous. The governor's appointment of his brother-in-law to the State Supreme Court was a *flagrant* violation of the state laws against nepotism (favoritism based on kinship).

## Word List 29

**flippant**    ADJ. lacking proper seriousness. When Mark told Mona he loved her, she dismissed his earnest declaration with a *flippant* "Oh, you say that to all the girls!" flippancy, N.

**florid**    ADJ. ruddy; reddish; flowery. If you go to Florida and get a sunburn, your complexion will look *florid*.

**fluctuate**    V. waver; shift. The water pressure in our shower *fluctuates* wildly; you start rinsing yourself off with a trickle, and two minutes later, you think you're going to drown.

**foolhardy**    ADJ. rash; heedless. Don't be *foolhardy*. Get some advice from experienced people before you strike out on your own.

**foresight**    N. ability to foresee future happenings; prudence. A wise investor, she had the *foresight* to buy land just before the current real estate boom.

**forestall**    V. prevent by taking action in advance. By setting up a prenuptial agreement, the prospective bride and groom hoped to *forestall* any potential arguments about money in the event of a divorce.

**forsake**    V. desert; abandon; renounce. No one expected Gauguin to *forsake* his wife and children and run off to Tahiti.

**forthright**    ADJ. outspoken; frank. Never afraid to call a spade a spade, she was perhaps too *forthright* to be a successful party politician.

**fortuitous**    ADJ. accidental; by chance. Though he pretended their encounter was *fortuitous*, he'd actually been hanging around her usual haunts for the past two weeks.

**foster**    V. rear; encourage; nurture. According to the legend, Romulus and Remus were *fostered* by a she-wolf who raised them as if they were her cubs. also ADJ.

## Word List 30

**founder**    V. fail completely; sink. After hitting the submerged iceberg, the *Titanic* started taking in water rapidly and soon *foundered*.

**founder**    N. person who establishes (an organization, business). Among those drowned when the *Titanic* sank was the *founder* of the Abraham & Straus department store.

**frail**    ADJ. weak. The sickly child seemed too *frail* to lift the heavy carton.

**frivolous**    ADJ. lacking in seriousness; self-indulgently carefree; relatively unimportant. Though Nancy enjoyed Bill's *frivolous*, lighthearted companionship, she sometimes wondered whether he could ever be serious. frivolity, N.

**frugality**    N. thrift; economy. In economically hard times, those who do not learn to practice *frugality* risk bankruptcy. frugal, ADJ.

**fundamental**    V. basic; primary; essential. The committee discussed all sorts of side issues without ever getting down to addressing the *fundamental* problem.

**furtive**    ADJ. stealthy; sneaky. Noticing the *furtive* glance the customer gave the diamond bracelet on the counter, the jeweler wondered whether he had a potential shoplifter on his hands.

**futile**    ADJ. ineffective; fruitless. Why waste your time on *futile* pursuits?

**galvanize**    V. stimulate by shock; stir up; revitalize. News that the prince was almost at their door *galvanized* the ugly stepsisters into a frenzy of combing and primping.

**garbled**    ADJ. mixed up; jumbled; distorted. A favorite party game involves passing a whispered message from one person to another, till, by the time it reaches the last player, the message is totally *garbled*.

## Word List 31

**garrulous** ADJ. loquacious; wordy; talkative. My Uncle Henry can out-talk any three people I know. He is the most *garrulous* person in Cayuga County.

**genre** N. particular variety of art or literature. Both a short story writer and a poet, Langston Hughes proved himself equally skilled in either *genre.*

**germane** ADJ. pertinent; bearing upon the case at hand. The judge would not allow the testimony to be heard by the jury because it was not *germane* to the case.

**glacial** ADJ. like a glacier; extremely cold. Never a warm person, when offended John could seem positively *glacial.*

**glib** ADJ. fluent; facile; slick. Keeping up a steady patter to entertain his customers, the kitchen gadget salesman was a *glib* speaker, never at a loss for a word.

**glutton** N. someone who eats too much; greedy person. Who is the *glutton* who ate up all the chocolate chip cookies I made for dessert? gluttonous, ADJ.

**gorge** N. small, steep-walled canyon. The whitewater rafting guide warned us about the rapids farther downstream, where the river cut through a narrow *gorge.*

**grandiose** ADJ. pretentious; high-flown; ridiculously exaggerated; impressive. The aged matinee idol still had *grandiose* notions of his supposed importance in the theatrical world.

**gratify** V. please. Amy's success in her new job *gratified* her parents.

**gratuitous** ADJ. given freely; unwarranted; unprovoked. Who asked you to comment? We don't need any *gratuitous* criticism from someone who has no business dissing us.

## Word List 32

**gravity** N. seriousness. We could tell we were in serious trouble from the *gravity* of the principal's expression. (secondary meaning) grave, ADJ.

**gregarious** ADJ. sociable. Typically, partygoers are *gregarious*; hermits are not.

**grievance** N. cause of complaint. When her supervisor ignored her complaint, she took her *grievance* to the union.

**grudging** ADJ. unwilling; reluctant; stingy. We received only *grudging* support from the mayor despite his earlier promises of aid.

**guile** N. deceit; duplicity; wiliness; cunning. Iago uses considerable *guile* to trick Othello into believing that Desdemona has been unfaithful.

**gullible** ADJ. easily deceived. Overly *gullible* people have only themselves to blame if they fall for scams repeatedly. As the saying goes, "Fool me once, shame on you. Fool me twice, shame on *me.*"

**hackneyed** ADJ. commonplace; trite. When the reviewer criticized the movie for its *hackneyed* plot, we agreed; we had seen similar stories hundreds of times before.

**hallowed** ADJ. blessed; consecrated. Although the dead girl's parents had never been active churchgoers, they insisted that their daughter be buried in *hallowed* ground.

**hamper** V. obstruct. The new mother didn't realize how much the effort of caring for an infant would *hamper* her ability to keep an immaculate house.

**harass** V. annoy by repeated attacks; torment. When he could not pay his bills as quickly as he had promised, he was *harassed* by his creditors.

## Word List 33

**hardy** ADJ. sturdy; robust; able to stand inclement weather. We asked the gardening expert to recommend particularly *hardy* plants that could withstand our harsh New England winters.

**haughtiness** N. pride; arrogance. When she realized that Darcy believed himself too good to dance with his inferiors, Elizabeth took great offense at his *haughtiness.*

**hedonist** N. one who believes that pleasure is the sole aim in life. A thoroughgoing *hedonist*, he considered only his own pleasure and ignored any claims others had on his money or time.

**heed** V. pay attention to; consider. We hope you *heed* our advice and get a good night's sleep before the test. also N.

**heresy** N. opinion contrary to popular belief; opinion contrary to accepted religion. Galileo's assertion that the earth moved around the sun directly contradicted the religious teachings of his day; as a result, he was tried for *heresy.* heretic, N.

**heterodox**   ADJ. unorthodox; unconventional. To those who upheld the belief that the earth did not move, Galileo's theory that the earth circled the sun was disturbingly *heterodox*.

**heterogeneous**   ADJ. dissimilar; mixed. This year's entering class is a remarkably *heterogeneous* body: it includes students from forty different states and twenty-six foreign countries, some the children of billionaires, others the offspring of welfare families.

**heyday**   N. time of greatest success; prime. In their *heyday*, the San Francisco Forty-Niners won the Super Bowl two years running.

**hiatus**   N. gap; interruption in duration or continuity; pause. During the summer *hiatus*, many students try to earn enough money to pay their tuition for the next school year.

**hierarchy**   N. arrangement by rank or standing; authoritarian body divided into ranks. To be low man on the totem pole is to have an inferior place in the *hierarchy*.

## Word List 34

**hindrance**   N. block; obstacle. Stalled cars along the highway present a *hindrance* to traffic that tow trucks should remove without delay. hinder, V.

**hoard**   V. stockpile; accumulate for future use. Whenever there are rumors of a food shortage, many people are tempted to *hoard* food. also N.

**homogeneous**   ADJ. of the same kind. Because the student body at Elite Prep was so *homogeneous*, Sara and James decided to send their daughter to a school that offered greater cultural diversity.

**hone**   V. sharpen. Determined to get a good shave, Ed *honed* his razor with great care.

**hostility**   N. unfriendliness; hatred. Children often feel *hostility* toward the new baby in the family.

**humane**   ADJ. marked by kindness or consideration. It is ironic that the *Humane* Society sometimes must show its compassion toward mistreated animals by killing them to put them out of their misery.

**husband**   V. use sparingly; conserve; save. Marathon runners must *husband* their energy so that they can keep going for the entire distance.

**hyperbole**   N. exaggeration; overstatement. As far as I'm concerned, Apple's claims about the new computer are pure *hyperbole*: no machine is that good!

**hypocritical**   ADJ. pretending to be virtuous; deceiving. Believing Eddie to be interested only in his own advancement, Greg resented his *hypocritical* posing as a friend. hypocrisy, N.

**hypothetical**   ADJ. based on assumptions or hypotheses; supposed. Suppose you are accepted by Harvard, Stanford, and Brown. Which one would you choose to attend? Remember, this is only a *hypothetical* situation. hypothesis, N.

## Word List 35

**iconoclast**   N. one who attacks cherished traditions. A born *iconoclast*, Jean Genet deliberately set out to shock conventional theatergoers with his radical plays.

**idiosyncrasy**   N. individual trait, usually odd in nature; eccentricity. One of Richard Nixon's little *idiosyncracies* was his liking for ketchup on cottage cheese. One of Hannibal Lecter's little *idiosyncrasies* was his liking for human flesh.

**ignominy**   N. deep disgrace; shame or dishonor. To lose the ping-pong match to a trained chimpanzee! How could Rollo stand the *ignominy* of his defeat?

**illicit**   ADJ. illegal. The defense attorney maintained that her client had never performed any *illicit* action.

**illuminate**   V. brighten; clear up or make understandable; enlighten. Just as a lamp can *illuminate* a dark room, a perceptive comment can *illuminate* a knotty problem.

**illusory**   ADJ. deceptive; not real. Unfortunately, the costs of running the lemonade stand were so high that Tom's profits proved *illusory*.

**imbalance**   N. lack of balance or symmetry; disproportion. Because of the great *imbalance* between the number of males and females invited, the dance was unsuccessful.

**immaculate**   ADJ. spotless; flawless; absolutely clean. Ken and Jessica were wonderful tenants and left the apartment in *immaculate* condition when they moved out.

**immune**   ADJ. resistant to; free or exempt from. Fortunately, Florence had contracted chicken pox as a child and was *immune* to it when her baby broke out in spots.

**immutable**   ADJ. unchangeable. All things change over time; nothing is *immutable*.

## Word List 36

**impair** V. injure; hurt. Drinking alcohol can *impair* your ability to drive safely; if you're going to drink, don't drive.

**impartial** ADJ. not biased; fair. As members of the jury, you must be *impartial*, showing no favoritism to either party but judging the case on its merits.

**impassive** ADJ. without feeling; imperturbable; stoical. Refusing to let the enemy see how deeply shaken he was by his capture, the prisoner kept his face *impassive*.

**impeccable** ADJ. faultless. The uncrowned queen of the fashion industry, Diana was acclaimed for her *impeccable* taste.

**impecunious** ADJ. without money. Though Scrooge claimed he was too *impecunious* to give alms, he easily could have afforded to be charitable.

• **impede** V. hinder; block; delay. A series of accidents *impeded* the launching of the space shuttle.

**impel** V. drive or force onward. A strong feeling of urgency *impelled* her; if she failed to finish the project right then, she knew that she would never get it done.

**imperceptible** ADJ. unnoticeable; undetectable. Fortunately, the stain on the blouse was *imperceptible* after the blouse had gone through the wash.

**imperious** ADJ. domineering; haughty. Jane rather liked a man to be masterful, but Mr. Rochester seemed so bent on getting his own way that he was actually *imperious*!

• **impervious** ADJ. impenetrable; incapable of being damaged or distressed. The carpet salesman told Simone that his most expensive brand of floor covering was warranted to be *impervious* to ordinary wear and tear.

## Word List 37

**impetuous** ADJ. violent; hasty; rash. "Leap before you look" was the motto suggested by one particularly *impetuous* young man.

**implement** V. put into effect; supply with tools. The mayor was unwilling to *implement* the plan until she was sure it had the governor's backing. also N.

**implication** N. something hinted at or suggested. When Miss Watson said she hadn't seen her purse since the last time Jim was in the house, the *implication* was that she suspected Jim had taken it. imply, V.

**implicit** ADJ. understood but not stated. Jack never told Jill he adored her; he believed his love was *implicit* in his actions.

**implore** V. beg. He *implored* her to give him a second chance.

**impoverished** ADJ. poor. The loss of their ancestral farm left the family *impoverished* and without hope.

**impregnable** ADJ. able to fight off an attack; unconquerable; invulnerable. Despite the British attempts to force her to recant, Joan of Arc's faith that God had told her to save France proved to be *impregnable*.

**impromptu** ADJ. without previous preparation; off the cuff; on the spur of the moment. The judges were amazed that she could make such a thorough, well-supported presentation in an *impromptu* speech.

**inadvertently** ADV. by oversight; carelessly or unintentionally. He *inadvertently* omitted to answer two questions on the examination.

**inane** ADJ. silly; senseless. There's no point to what you're saying. Why are you bothering to make such *inane* remarks?

## Word List 38

**inaugurate** V. start; initiate; install in office. The airline decided to *inaugurate* its new route to the Far East with a special reduced fare offer. inaugural, ADJ.

**incarcerate** V. imprison. Which is better, to execute a serial killer or to *incarcerate* that person for life?

**incense** V. enrage; infuriate. Cruelty to defenseless animals *incensed* Kit.

**incentive** N. spur; motive. Mike's strong desire to outshine his big sister was all the *incentive* he needed to do well in school.

**incessant** ADJ. uninterrupted; unceasing. In a famous TV commercial, the frogs' *incessant* croaking goes on and on until eventually it turns into a single word: "Bud-weis-er."

**incidental** ADJ. not essential; minor. The scholarship covered his major expenses at college and some of his *incidental* expenses as well.

**incite** V. arouse to action; goad; motivate; induce to exist. In a fiery speech, Mario *incited* his fellow students to go out on strike to protest the university's anti-affirmative-action stand.

**incline**   N. slope; slant. The architect recommended that the nursing home's ramp be rebuilt because its *incline* was too steep for wheelchairs.

**inclined**   ADJ. tending or leaning toward; bent. Though I am *inclined* to be skeptical, the witness's manner *inclines* me to believe his story. also V.

**inclusive**   ADJ. tending to include all. The comedian turned down the invitation to join the Players' Club, saying any club that would let him in was too *inclusive* for him.

## Word List 39

**incoherent**   ADJ. unintelligible; muddled; illogical. The bereaved father sobbed and stammered, his words becoming almost *incoherent* in his grief. incoherence, N.

**incongruous**   ADJ. not fitting; absurd. Dave saw nothing *incongruous* about wearing sneakers with his tuxedo; he couldn't understand why his date took one look at him and started to laugh. incongruity, N.

**inconsequential**   ADJ. insignificant; unimportant. Brushing off Ali's apologies for having broken the wineglass, Tamara said, "Don't worry about it; it's *inconsequential*."

**incontrovertible**   ADJ. indisputable; not open to question. Unless you find the evidence against my client absolutely *incontrovertible*, you must declare her not guilty of this charge.

**incorrigible**   ADJ. uncorrectable. Though Widow Douglass hoped to reform Huck, Miss Watson called him *incorrigible* and said he would come to no good end.

**indefatigable**   ADJ. tireless. Although the effort of taking out the garbage tired Wayne out for the entire morning, when it came to partying, he was *indefatigable*.

**indict**   V. charge. The district attorney didn't want to *indict* the suspect until she was sure she had a strong enough case to convince a jury. indictment, N.

**indifferent**   ADJ. unmoved; lacking concern. Because she felt no desire to marry, she was *indifferent* to his constant proposals.

**indigenous**   ADJ. native. Cigarettes are made of tobacco, one of the *indigenous* plants the early explorers found in the New World.

**indigent**   ADJ. poor; destitute. Someone who is truly *indigent* can't even afford to buy a pack of cigarettes. (Don't mix up *indigent* and *indigenous*. See previous sentence.)

## Word List 40

**indiscriminate**   ADJ. choosing at random; confused. Disapproving of her son's *indiscriminate* television viewing, Shirley decided to restrict him to watching educational programs.

**indolent**   ADJ. lazy. Couch potatoes lead an *indolent* life lying back on their Lazyboy recliners watching TV. indolence, N.

**indomitable**   ADJ. unconquerable; unyielding. Focusing on her game despite all her personal problems, tennis champion Steffi Graf proved she had an *indomitable* will to win.

**indubitable**   ADJ. unable to be doubted; unquestionable. Auditioning for the chorus line, Molly was an *indubitable* hit: the director fired the leading lady and hired Molly in her place!

**induce**   V. persuade; bring about. After the quarrel, Tina said nothing could *induce* her to talk to Tony again. inducement, N.

**indulge**   V. humor; treat leniently. Parents who constantly *indulge* their children by giving in to their every whim may thoroughly spoil them.

**industrious**   ADJ. diligent; hard-working. If you are *industrious* and apply yourself to your assignments, you will do well in college. industry, N.

**ineffectual**   ADJ. not effective; weak. Because the candidate failed to get across his message to the public, his campaign was *ineffectual*.

**inept**   ADJ. unsuited; absurd; incompetent. The *inept* glovemaker was all thumbs.

**inequity**   N. unfairness. In demanding equal pay for equal work, women protest the basic *inequity* of a system that gives greater financial rewards to men.

## Word List 41

• **inert**   ADJ. inactive; lacking power to move. "Get up, you lazybones," Tina cried to Tony, who lay in bed *inert*.

• **inexorable**   ADJ. relentless; unyielding; implacable. Ignoring the defense attorney's pleas for clemency, the judge was *inexorable*, giving the convicted felon the maximum punishment allowed by law.

• **infamous**   ADJ. notoriously bad. Charles Manson and the Jeffrey Dahmer are both *infamous* killers.

**infer** V. deduce; conclude. From the students' glazed looks, it was easy for me to *infer* that they were bored out of their minds.

**infiltrate** V. pass into or through; penetrate (an organization) sneakily. In order to be able to *infiltrate* enemy lines at night without being seen, the scouts darkened their faces and wore black coveralls. infiltrator, N.

**infinitesimal** ADJ. exceedingly small; so small as to be almost nonexistent. Making sure everyone was aware she was on an extremely strict diet, Melanie said she would have only an *infinitesimal* sliver of pie.

**infraction** N. violation (of a rule or regulation); breach. When Dennis Rodman butted heads with that referee, he committed a clear *infraction* of NBA rules.

**ingenious** ADJ. clever; resourceful. Kit admired the *ingenious* way that her computer keyboard opened up to reveal the built-in CD-ROM below. ingenuity, N.

**ingrate** N. ungrateful person. That *ingrate* Bob sneered at the tie I gave him.

**inherent** ADJ. firmly established by nature or habit; intrinsic. Elaine's *inherent* love of justice caused her to champion people whom she thought society had treated unfairly.

## Word List 42

**inimical** ADJ. unfriendly; hostile; harmful; detrimental. I've always been friendly to Martha. Why is she so *inimical* to me?

**initiate** V. begin; originate; receive into a group. The college is about to *initiate* a program in reducing math anxiety among students.

**injurious** ADJ. harmful. Smoking cigarettes can be *injurious* to your health.

**innate** ADJ. inborn. Mozart's parents soon recognized young Wolfgang's *innate* talent for music.

**innocuous** ADJ. harmless. An occasional glass of wine with dinner is relatively *innocuous* and should have no ill effect.

**innovation** N. change; introduction of something new. Although Richard liked to keep up with all the latest technological *innovations*, he didn't always abandon tried and true techniques in favor of something new. innovate, V.

**inopportune** ADJ. untimely; poorly chosen. A rock concert is an *inopportune* setting for a quiet conversation.

**insatiable** ADJ. not easily satisfied; greedy. Lexy's passion for new clothes is *insatiable*; she can shop till she literally drops.

**insightful** ADJ. discerning; perceptive. Sol thought he was very *insightful* about human behavior, but he hadn't a clue why people acted the way they did.

**insinuate** V. hint; imply; creep in. When you said I looked robust, were you trying to *insinuate* I'm getting fat?

## Word List 43

**insipid** ADJ. lacking in flavor; dull. Flat prose and flat ginger ale are equally *insipid*: both lack sparkle.

**insolvent** ADJ. bankrupt; unable to repay one's debts. Although young Lord Widgeon was *insolvent*, he had no fear of being thrown into debtors' prison, for he was sure that if his creditors pressed him for payment his wealthy parents would repay what he owed.

**instigate** V. urge; start; provoke. Rumors of police corruption led the mayor to *instigate* an investigation into the department's activities.

**insularity** N. narrow-mindedness; isolation. The *insularity* of the islanders manifested itself in their suspicion of anything foreign. insular, ADJ.

**insuperable** ADJ. insurmountable; unbeatable. Faced by almost *insuperable* obstacles, the members of the underground maintained their courage and will to resist.

**insurgent** ADJ. rebellious. Because the *insurgent* forces had occupied the capital and had gained control of the railway lines, several of the war correspondents covering the uprising predicted a rebel victory.

**intangible** ADJ. not material; not able to be perceived by touch; vague; elusive. Emotions are *intangible*, and yet we know that we feel love and hate, though we cannot grasp them in our hands.

**integral** ADJ. complete; necessary for completeness. Physical education is an *integral* part of our curriculum; a sound mind and a sound body are complementary.

**integrity** N. uprightness; wholeness. Lincoln, whose personal *integrity* has inspired millions, fought a civil war to maintain the *integrity* of the Republic, that these United States might remain undivided for all time.

**intermittent**    ADJ. periodic; on and off. The outdoor wedding reception had to be moved indoors to avoid the *intermittent* showers that fell on and off all afternoon.

## Word List 44

**intervene**    V. come between. Rachel tried to *intervene* in the quarrel between her two sons.

**intimidate**    V. frighten. I'll learn karate and then those big bullies won't be able to *intimidate* me any more.

• **intractable**    ADJ. unruly; stubborn; unyielding. Charlie Brown's friend Pigpen was *intractable*: he absolutely refused to take a bath.

• **intransigence**    N. refusal of any compromise; stubbornness. When I predicted that the strike would be over in a week, I didn't expect to encounter such *intransigence* from both sides. intransigent, ADJ.

• **intrepid**    ADJ. fearless. For her *intrepid* conduct nursing the wounded during the war, Florence Nightingale was honored by Queen Victoria.

**intricate**    ADJ. complex; knotty; tangled. Eric spent many hours designing mazes so *intricate* that none of his classmates could solve them. intricacy, N.

• **intrinsic**    ADJ. essential; inherent; built-in; natural. Although my grandmother's china has little *intrinsic* value, I shall always treasure it for the memories it evokes.

**introspective**    ADJ. looking within oneself. Though young Francis of Assisi led a wild and worldly life, even he had *introspective* moments during which he examined his soul.

**intuition**    N. immediate insight; power of knowing without reasoning. Even though Tony denied that anything was wrong, Tina trusted her *intuition* that something was bothering him. intuitive, ADJ.

**inundate**    V. overwhelm; flood; submerge. This semester I am *inundated* with work. You should see the piles of paperwork flooding my desk.

## Word List 45

**invert**    V. turn upside down or inside out. When he *inverted* his body in a handstand, he felt the blood rush to his head.

• **irascible**    ADJ. irritable; easily angered. Miss Minchin's *irascible* temper intimidated the younger schoolgirls, who feared she'd burst into a rage at any moment.

**ironic**    ADJ. relating to a contradiction between an event's expected result and its actual outcome; sarcastic. It is *ironic* that his success came when he least wanted it.

• **irrational**    ADJ. illogical; lacking reason; insane. Many people have such an *irrational* fear of snakes that they panic at the sight of a harmless garter snake.

**irrelevant**    ADJ. not applicable; unrelated. No matter how *irrelevant* the patient's mumblings may seem, they give us some indications of what he has on his mind.

• **irreproachable**    ADJ. blameless; impeccable. Homer's conduct at the office party was *irreproachable*; even Marge didn't have anything bad to say about how he behaved.

• **irresolute**    ADJ. uncertain how to act; weak. She had no respect for him because he seemed weak-willed and *irresolute*.

**irreverence**    N. lack of proper respect. Some audience members were amused by the *irreverence* of the comedian's jokes about the Pope; others felt offended by his lack of respect for their faith. irreverent, ADJ.

• **jargon**    N. language used by a special group; technical terminology; gibberish. The computer salesmen at the store used a *jargon* of their own that we simply couldn't follow; we had no idea what they were jabbering about.

• **jocular**    ADJ. said or done in jest; joking. Please do not take my *jocular* remarks seriously.

## Word List 46

• **judicious**    ADJ. sound in judgment; wise. At a key moment in his life, Tom made a *judicious* investment that was the foundation of his later wealth.

**justification**    N. good or just reason; defense; excuse. The jury found him guilty of the more serious charge because they could see no possible *justification* for his actions.

**kindle**    V. start a fire; inspire. Her teacher's praise *kindled* a spark of hope inside Maya.

**labyrinth**    N. maze. Hiding from Indian Joe, Tom and Becky soon lost themselves in the *labyrinth* of secret underground caves.

• **laconic**    ADJ. brief and to the point. Many of the characters portrayed by Clint Eastwood are *laconic* types: strong men of few words.

- **lament** V. grieve; express sorrow. Even advocates of the war *lamented* the loss of so many lives in combat. lamentation, N.
- **languish** V. lose animation; lose strength. Left at Miss Minchin's school for girls while her father went off to war, Sarah Crewe refused to *languish*; instead, she hid her grief and actively befriended her less fortunate classmates.
- **lassitude** N. languor; weariness. After a massage and a long soak in the hot tub, I gave in to my growing *lassitude* and lay down for a nap.
- **laud** V. praise. The NFL *lauded* Boomer Esiason's efforts to raise money to combat cystic fibrosis. laudable, laudatory, ADJ.
- **legacy** N. a gift made by a will. Part of my *legacy* from my parents is an album of family photographs.

## Word List 47

**lethargic** ADJ. drowsy; dull. The stifling classroom made Sarah *lethargic*: she felt as if she were about to nod off.

**levity** N. lack of seriousness; lightness. Stop giggling and wriggling around in your seats: such *levity* is inappropriate in church.

**liability** N. drawback; debts. Her lack of an extensive vocabulary was a *liability* that she was able to overcome.

**list** V. tilt; lean over. That flagpole should be absolutely vertical; instead, it *lists* to one side. (secondary meaning)

**listlessness** N. lack in spirit or energy. We had expected him to be full of enthusiasm and were surprised by his *listlessness*.

**loathe** V. detest. Booing and hissing, the audience showed how much they *loathed* the wicked villain.

**lofty** ADJ. very high. Barbara Jordan's fellow students used to tease her about her *lofty* ambitions.

**loquacious** ADJ. talkative. Though our daughter barely says a word to us these days, put a phone in her hand and you'll see how *loquacious* she really is: our phone bills are out of sight!

**lucid** ADJ. easily understood; clear; intelligible. Ellen made an excellent teacher: her explanations of technical points were *lucid* enough for a child to grasp.

**lurid** ADJ. wild; sensational; graphic; gruesome. Do the *lurid* cover stories in the *Enquirer* actually attract people to buy that trashy tabloid?

## Word List 48

**magnanimous** ADJ. generous. Philanthropists by definition are *magnanimous*; misers, by definition, are not. magnanimity, N.

**magnate** N. person of prominence or influence. Growing up in Pittsburgh, Annie Dillard was surrounded by the mansions of the great steel and coal *magnates* who set their mark on that city.

**maladroit** ADJ. clumsy; bungling. How *maladroit* it was of me to mention seeing you out partying last night! From the look on his face, I take it that your boyfriend thought you were otherwise occupied.

**malevolent** ADJ. wishing evil. Iago is a *malevolent* villain who takes pleasure in ruining Othello.

**malice** N. hatred; spite. Jealous of Cinderella's beauty, her wicked stepsisters expressed their *malice* by forcing her to do menial tasks.

**malign** V. speak evil of; bad-mouth; defame. Her hatred of her ex-husband ran so deep that she *maligned* anyone who even casually dated him.

**marred** ADJ. damaged; disfigured. She had to refinish the *marred* surface of the table. mar, V.

**martinet** N. rigid disciplinarian; strict military officer. No talking at meals! No mingling with the servants! Miss Minchin was a *martinet* who insisted that the schoolgirls in her charge observe each regulation to the letter.

**materialism** N. preoccupation with physical comforts and things. By its nature, *materialism* is opposed to idealism, for where the materialist emphasizes the needs of the body, the idealist emphasizes the needs of the soul.

**meager** ADJ. scanty; inadequate. His salary was far too *meager* for him to afford to buy a new car.

## Word List 49

**meander** V. wind or turn in its course. Needing to stay close to a source of water, he followed every twist and turn of the stream as it *meandered* through the countryside.

**medley** N. mixture. The band played a *medley* of Gershwin tunes.

**meek** ADJ. quiet and obedient; spiritless. Can Lois Lane see through Superman's disguise and spot the superhero hiding behind the guise of *meek*, timorous Clark Kent?

**melancholy** ADJ. gloomy; morose; blue. To Eugene, stuck in his small town, a train whistle was a *melancholy* sound, for it made him think of all the places he would never get to see.

**mercenary** ADJ. interested in money or gain. Andy's every act was prompted by *mercenary* motives: his first question was always "What's in it for me?"

**mercurial** ADJ. capricious; changing; fickle. Quick as quicksilver to change, he was *mercurial* in nature and therefore erratic.

**merger** N. combination (of two business corporations). When the firm's president married the director of financial planning, the office joke was that it wasn't a marriage, it was a *merger*.

**methodical** ADJ. systematic. An accountant must be *methodical* and maintain order among his financial records.

**meticulous** ADJ. excessively careful; painstaking; scrupulous. Martha Stewart was a *meticulous* housekeeper, fussing about each and every detail that went into making up her perfect home.

**minute** ADJ. extremely small. The twins resembled one another closely; only *minute* differences set them apart.

## Word List 50

**misanthrope** N. one who hates mankind. In *Gulliver's Travels*, Swift portrays an image of humanity as vile, degraded beasts; for this reason, some critics consider him a *misanthrope*.

**misconstrue** V. interpret incorrectly; misjudge. She took the passage seriously rather than humorously because she *misconstrued* the author's ironic tone.

**miserly** ADJ. stingy; mean. The *miserly* old man greedily counted the gold coins he had hoarded over the years.

**misnomer** N. wrong name; incorrect designation. His tyrannical conduct proved to us all that his nickname, King Eric the Just, was a *misnomer*.

**mitigate** V. appease; moderate. Nothing Jason did could *mitigate* Medea's anger; she refused to forgive him for betraying her.

**mollify** V. soothe. The airline customer service representative tried to *mollify* the angry passenger by offering her a seat in first class.

**momentous** ADJ. very important. When Marie and Pierre Curie discovered radium, they had no idea of the *momentous* impact their discovery would have upon society.

**monotony** N. sameness leading to boredom. He took a clerical job, but soon grew to hate the *monotony* of his daily routine. monotonous, ADJ.

**morbid** ADJ. given to unwholesome thought; moody; characteristic of disease. This *morbid* dwelling on cancer is unhealthy; quit sitting around brooding and get your mind on more pleasant topics.

**morose** ADJ. ill-humored; sullen; melancholy. Forced to take early retirement, Bill acted *morose* for months; then, all of a sudden, he shook off his sullen mood and was his usual cheerful self.

## Word List 51

**mundane** ADJ. worldly as opposed to spiritual. Uninterested in philosophical or spiritual discussions, Tom talked only of *mundane* matters such as the daily weather forecast or the latest basketball results.

**munificent** ADJ. very generous. The Annenberg Trust made a *munificent* gift to the city that supported art programs in the public schools. munificence, N.

**mutability** N. ability to change in form; fickleness. Going from rags to riches, and then back to rags again, the bankrupt financier was a victim of the *mutability* of fortune.

**muted** ADJ. silent; muffled; toned down. In the funeral parlor, the mourners' voices had a *muted* quality. mute, V.

**naivete** N. quality of being unsophisticated; simplicity; artlessness; gullibility. Touched by the *naivete* of sweet, convent-trained Cosette, Marius pledges himself to protect her innocence. naive, ADJ.

**nebulous** ADJ. vague; hazy; cloudy. After twenty years, she had only a *nebulous* memory of her grandmother's face.

**nefarious** ADJ. very wicked. The villain's crimes, though various, were one and all *nefarious*.

**nonchalance** N. indifference; lack of concern; composure. The first time they performed at the club, all the guys tried to look cool and unconcerned, but none of them could match Dale's *nonchalance*; you would have thought he'd been onstage for years.

**nonentity** N. person of no importance; nonexistence. Don't dismiss William as a *nonentity*; in his quiet way, he's very important to the firm.

**nostalgia**   N. homesickness; longing for the past. My grandfather seldom spoke of life in the old country; he had little patience with *nostalgia*. nostalgic, ADJ.

## Word List 52

**notoriety**   N. disrepute; ill fame. To the starlet, any publicity was good publicity: if she couldn't have a good reputation, she'd settle for *notoriety*. notorious, ADJ.

**novelty**   N. something new; newness. The computer is no longer a *novelty* around the office. novel, ADJ.

**novice**   N. beginner. Even a *novice* at word processing can get started writing letters right away by following these simple directions.

**nuance**   N. shade of difference in meaning or color. Jody has an extraordinary eye for color. She can look at a painting and see *nuances* in the paint that are indistinguishable to me.

**nullify**   V. to make invalid; void; abolish. Once the contract was *nullified*, it no longer had any legal force.

**nurture**   V. nourish; educate; foster. The Head Start program attempts to *nurture* pre-kindergarten children so that they will do well when they enter public school. also N.

**obdurate**   ADJ. stubborn. The manager was *obdurate* in refusing to discuss the workers' grievances.

**objective**   ADJ. not influenced by emotions; fair. Even though he was her son, she tried to be *objective* about his behavior. objectivity, N.

**objective**   N. goal; aim. A degree in medicine was her ultimate *objective*.

**obliterate**   V. destroy completely. The explosion *obliterated* the facade of the Federal Building, gutting it completely.

## Word List 53

**oblivion**   N. obscurity; forgetfulness. After a brief period of popularity, Hurston's works fell into *oblivion*; no one bothered to reprint them, or even to read them any more.

**oblivious**   ADJ. inattentive or unmindful; wholly absorbed. Deep in her book, Nancy was *oblivious* to the noisy squabbles of her brother and his friends.

**obscure**   ADJ. dark; vague; unclear. Even after I read the poem a fourth time, its meaning was still *obscure*. obscurity, N.

**obscure**   V. darken; make unclear. At times he seemed purposely to *obscure* his meaning, preferring mystery to clarity.

**obsequious**   ADJ. slavishly attentive; servile; fawning; sycophantic. Why are some waiters in fancy restaurants so *obsequious*? What makes them think I want people fawning all over me?

**obsessive**   ADJ. related to thinking about something constantly; preoccupying. Ballet, which had been a hobby, began to dominate his life; his love of dancing became *obsessive*.

**obstinate**   ADJ. stubborn; hard to control or treat. We tried to persuade him to give up smoking, but he was *obstinate* and refused to change.

**obtuse**   ADJ. blunt; stupid. What can you do with somebody who's so *obtuse* that he can't even tell that you're insulting him?

**officious**   ADJ. meddlesome; excessively pushy in offering one's services. After the long flight, Jill just wanted to nap, but the *officious* bellboy was intent on showing her all the special features of the deluxe suite.

**ominous**   ADJ. threatening. Those clouds are *ominous*; they suggest a severe storm is on the way.

## Word List 54

**opaque**   ADJ. dark; not transparent. The *opaque* window shade kept the sunlight out of the room. opacity, N.

**opportunist**   N. individual who sacrifices principles for expediency by taking advantage of circumstances. Forget about ethics! He's such an *opportunist* that he'll vote in favor of any deal that will give him a break.

**optimist**   N. person who looks on the good side. The pessimist says the glass is half-empty; the *optimist* says it is half-full.

**optional**   ADJ. not compulsory; left to one's choice. I was impressed by the range of *optional* accessories for my laptop computer that were available. option, N.

**opulence**   N. extreme wealth; luxuriousness; abundance. The glitter and *opulence* of the ballroom took Cinderella's breath away. opulent, ADJ.

**ornate**   ADJ. excessively or elaborately decorated. The furnishings of homes shown on *Lifestyles of the Rich and Famous* tend to be highly *ornate*.

**ostentatious** ADJ. showy; pretentious; trying to attract attention. Trump's latest casino in Atlantic City is the most *ostentatious* gambling palace in the East: it easily outglitters its competitors. ostentation, N.

**pacifist** N. one opposed to force; antimilitarist. During the war, *pacifists*, though they refused to bear arms, nevertheless served in the front lines as ambulance drivers and medical corpsmen.

**painstaking** ADJ. showing hard work; taking great care. The new high-frequency word list is the result of *painstaking* efforts on the part of our research staff.

**palliate** V. ease pain; make less severe or offensive. If we cannot cure this disease at present, we can, at least, try to *palliate* it. palliation, N.

## Word List 55

**paltry** ADJ. insignificant; petty; trifling. One hundred dollars for a genuine imitation Rolex watch! Lady, this is a *paltry* sum to pay for such a high-class piece of jewelry.

**paradigm** N. model; example; pattern. Pavlov's experiment in which he trains a dog to salivate on hearing a bell is a *paradigm* of the conditioned-response experiment in behavioral psychology.

**paradox** N. something apparently contradictory in nature; statement that looks false but is actually correct. Richard presents a bit of a *paradox*, for he is a card-carrying member of both the National Rifle Association and the relatively pacifist American Civil Liberties Union.

**paragon** N. model of perfection. Her fellow students disliked Lavinia because Miss Minchin always pointed her out as a *paragon* of virtue.

**parochial** ADJ. narrow in outlook; provincial; related to parishes. Although Jane Austen writes novels set in small rural communities, her concerns are universal, not *parochial*.

**parody** N. humorous imitation; spoof; takeoff; travesty. The show *Forbidden Broadway* presents *parodies* spoofing the year's new productions playing on Broadway.

**parry** V. ward off a blow; deflect. Unwilling to injure his opponent in such a pointless clash, Dartagnan simply tried to *parry* his rival's thrusts.

**parsimony** N. stinginess; excessive frugality. Silas Marner's *parsimony* did not allow him to indulge himself in any luxuries.

**partial** ADJ. incomplete. In this issue we have published only a *partial* list of contributors because we lack space to acknowledge everyone.

**partial** ADJ. biased; having a liking for something. I am extremely *partial* to chocolate eclairs. partiality, N.

**partisan** ADJ. one-sided; prejudiced; committed to a party. On certain issues of conscience, she refused to take a *partisan* stand. also N.

## Word List 56

**passive** ADJ. not active; acted upon. Mahatma Gandhi urged his followers to pursue a program of *passive* resistance rather than resorting to violence and acts of terrorism.

**paucity** N. scarcity; lack. They closed the restaurant because the *paucity* of customers meant that it was a losing proposition to operate.

**pedantic** ADJ. showing off learning; bookish. Leavening his decisions with humorous, down-to-earth anecdotes, Judge Wapner was a pleasant contrast to the typical *pedantic* legal scholar. pedant, N.

**penchant** N. strong inclination; liking. Dave has a *penchant* for taking risks: one semester he went steady with three girls, two of whom were stars on the school karate team.

**pensive** ADJ. dreamily thoughtful; thoughtful with a hint of sadness; contemplative. The *pensive* lover gazed at the portrait of his beloved and deeply sighed.

**perceptive** ADJ. insightful; aware; wise. Although Maud was a generally *perceptive* critic, she had her blind spots: she could never see flaws in the work of her friends.

**perfunctory** ADJ. superficial; not thorough; lacking interest, care, or enthusiasm. The auditor's *perfunctory* inspection of the books failed to spot many obvious errors.

**peripheral** ADJ. marginal; outer. We lived, not in central London, but in one of those *peripheral* suburbs that spring up on the outskirts of a great city. periphery, N.

**perjury** N. false testimony while under oath. Rather than lie under oath and perhaps be indicted for *perjury*, the witness chose to take the Fifth Amendment, refusing to answer any questions on the grounds that he might incriminate himself.

**pernicious** ADJ. very destructive. The Athenians

argued that Socrates's teachings had a *pernicious* effect on young and susceptible minds; therefore, they condemned him to death.

## Word List 57

**perpetuate**  V. make something last; preserve from extinction. Some critics attack *The Adventures of Huckleberry Finn* because they believe Twain's book *perpetuates* a false image of African-Americans in this country.

**perturb**  V. disturb greatly. The thought that electricity might be leaking out of the empty light bulb sockets *perturbed* my aunt so much that at night she crept about the house screwing fresh bulbs in the vacant spots.

**pervasive**  ADJ. pervading; spread throughout every part. Despite airing them for several hours, Martha could not rid her clothes of the *pervasive* odor of mothballs that clung to them. pervade, v.

**pessimism**  N. belief that life is basically bad or evil; gloominess. Considering how well you have done in the course so far, you have no real reason for such *pessimism* about your final grade.

**petty**  ADJ. trivial; unimportant; very small. She had no major complaints about his work, only a few *petty* quibbles that were almost too minor to state.

**petulant**  ADJ. touchy; peevish. If you'd had hardly any sleep for three nights and people kept phoning and waking you up, you'd sound pretty *petulant*, too.

**phenomena**  N. observable facts; subjects of scientific investigation. We kept careful records of the *phenomena* we noted in the course of these experiments.

**philanthropist**  N. lover of mankind; doer of good. In his role as *philanthropist* and public benefactor, John D. Rockefeller, Sr., donated millions to charity; as an individual, however, he was a tight-fisted old man.

**pious**  ADJ. devout; religious. The challenge for church people today is how to be *pious* in the best sense, that is, to be devout without becoming hypocritical or sanctimonious. piety, N.

**pitfall**  N. hidden danger; concealed trap. Her parents warned young Sophie against the many *pitfalls* that lay in wait for her in the dangerous big city.

## Word List 58

**pithy**  ADJ. concise; meaningful; substantial; meaty. Some of Whoopi Goldberg's one-liners at the Oscar Awards were *pithy* and to the point: they packed a wallop, but were short and sweet.

**pivotal**  ADJ. crucial; key; vital. The new "smart weapons" technology played a *pivotal* role in the quick resolution of the war with Iraq.

**placate**  V. pacify; conciliate. The store manager tried to *placate* the angry customer, offering to replace the damaged merchandise or to give back her money right away.

**plagiarize**  V. steal another's ideas and pass them off as one's own. The teacher could tell that the student had *plagiarized* parts of his essay; she could recognize whole paragraphs straight from *Barron's Book Notes*.

**platitude**  N. trite remark; commonplace statement. In giving advice to his son, old Polonius expressed himself only in *platitudes*; every word out of his mouth was a commonplace.

**plausible**  ADJ. having a show of truth but open to doubt; specious. Your mother made you stay home from school because she needed you to program the VCR? I'm sorry, you'll have to come up with a more *plausible* excuse than that.

**pliant**  ADJ. flexible; easily influenced. Pinocchio's disposition was *pliant*; he was like putty in his tempters' hands.

**plight**  N. condition, state (especially a bad state or condition); predicament. Many people feel that the federal government should do more to alleviate the *plight* of the homeless.

**poignancy**  N. quality of being deeply moving; keenness of emotion. Watching the tearful reunion of the long-separated mother and child, the social worker was touched by the *poignancy* of the scene. poignant, ADJ.

**polemical**  ADJ. aggressive in verbal attack; disputatious. Alexis was a master of *polemical* rhetoric; she should have worn a T-shirt with the slogan "Born to Debate."

## Word List 59

**pomposity**  N. self-important behavior; acting like a stuffed shirt. Although the commencement speaker had some good things to say, we had to laugh at his *pomposity* and general air of parading his own dignity. pompous, ADJ.

**ponderous** ADJ. weighty; unwieldy. Sol's humor lacked the light touch; his jokes were always *ponderous*.

**porous** ADJ. full of pores; like a sieve. Dancers like to wear *porous* clothing because it allows the ready passage of water and air.

**potent** ADJ. powerful; persuasive; greatly influential. The jury was swayed by the highly *potent* testimony of the crime's sole eyewitness. potency, N.

**pragmatic** ADJ. practical (as opposed to idealistic); concerned with the practical worth or impact of something. This coming trip to France should provide me with a *pragmatic* test of the value of my conversational French class.

**prattle** V. babble. Baby John *prattled* endlessly about his cats and his ball and his bottle of juice.

**precarious** ADJ. uncertain; risky. Saying the stock would be a *precarious* investment, Tom advised me against purchasing it.

**precedent** N. something preceding in time that may be used as an authority or guide for future action. If I buy you a car for your sixteenth birthday, your brothers will want me to buy them cars when they turn sixteen, too; I can't afford to set such an expensive *precedent*.

**precipitate** ADJ. rash; premature; hasty; sudden. Though I was angry enough to resign on the spot, I had enough sense to keep myself from quitting a job in such a *precipitate* fashion.

**precipitous** ADJ. steep; overhasty. This hill is difficult to climb because it is so *precipitous*; one slip, and our descent will be *precipitous* as well.

## Word List 60

**preclude** V. make impossible; eliminate. The fact that the band was already booked to play in Hollywood on New Year's Eve, *precluded* their accepting the New Year's Eve gig in London they were offered.

**precocious** ADJ. advanced in development. Listening to the grown-up way the child discussed serious topics, we couldn't help remarking how *precocious* she was. precocity, N.

**predecessor** N. former occupant of a post. I hope I can live up to the fine example set by my late *predecessor* in this office.

**predilection** N. partiality; preference. Although I have written all sorts of poetry over the years, I have a definite *predilection* for occasional verse.

**preeminent** ADJ. outstanding; superior. The king traveled to Boston because he wanted the *preeminent* surgeon in the field to perform the operation.

**premise** N. assumption; postulate. Because Jack had based his argument upon a faulty *premise*, his opponent cheerfully pointed out the holes in his logic.

**preposterous** ADJ. absurd; ridiculous. When he tried to downplay his youthful experiments with marijuana by saying he hadn't inhaled, we all thought, "What a *preposterous* excuse!"

**prestige** N. impression produced by achievements or reputation. Did Rockefeller become a philanthropist because he was innately generous or because he hoped to gain social *prestige* by donating to popular causes?

**pretentious** ADJ. ostentatious; pompous; making unjustified claims; overly ambitious. None of the other prize winners are wearing their medals; isn't it a bit *pretentious* of you to wear yours?

**prevalent** ADJ. widespread; generally accepted. A radical committed to social change, Reed had no patience with the conservative views *prevalent* in the America of his day.

## Word List 61

**problematic** ADJ. doubtful; unsettled; questionable; perplexing. Given the many areas of conflict still awaiting resolution, the outcome of the peace talks remains *problematic*.

**proclivity** N. inclination; natural tendency. Watching the two-year-old voluntarily put away his toys, I was amazed by his *proclivity* for neatness.

**procrastinate** V. postpone; delay or put off. Looking at four years of receipts and checks he still had to sort through, Bob was truly sorry he had *procrastinated* for so long and not finished filing his taxes long ago.

**prodigal** ADJ. wasteful; reckless with money. Don't be so *prodigal* spending my money; when you've earned some money, you can waste it as much as you want! also N.

**prodigious** ADJ. marvelous; enormous. Watching the champion weight lifter heave the weighty barbell to shoulder height and then boost it overhead, we marveled at his *prodigious* strength.

**prodigy**   N. marvel; highly gifted child. Menuhin was a *prodigy*, performing wonders on his violin when he was barely eight years old.

**profane**   V. violate; desecrate; treat unworthily. The members of the mysterious Far Eastern cult sought to kill the British explorer because he had *profaned* the sanctity of their holy goblet by using it as an ashtray. also ADJ.

**profligate**   N. dissipated; wasteful; wildly immoral. Although surrounded by wild and *profligate* companions, she nevertheless managed to retain some sense of decency.

**profound**   ADJ. deep; not superficial; complete. Freud's remarkable insights into human behavior caused his fellow scientists to honor him as a *profound* thinker. profundity, N.

**profusion**   N. overabundance; lavish expenditure; excess. At the wedding feast, food and drink was served in such *profusion* that the goodies piled on the tables almost overflowed onto the floor.

## Word List 62

**proliferation**   N. rapid growth; spread; multiplication. Times of economic hardship inevitably encourage the *proliferation* of countless get-rich-quick schemes. proliferate, V.

**prolific**   ADJ. abundantly fruitful. My editors must assume I'm a *prolific* writer: they expect me to revise six books this year!

**prologue**   N. introduction (to a poem or play). In the *prologue* to *Romeo and Juliet*, Shakespeare introduces the audience to the feud between the Montagues and the Capulets.

**prophetic**   ADJ. foretelling the future. I have no magical *prophetic* powers; when I predict what will happen, I base my predictions on common sense. prophesy, V.

**propitious**   ADJ. favorable; fortunate; advantageous. Chloe consulted her horoscope to see whether Tuesday would be a *propitious* time to dump her boyfriend.

**propriety**   N. fitness; correct conduct. Miss Manners counsels her readers so that they may behave with due *propriety* in any social situation and not embarrass themselves.

**prosaic**   ADJ. dull and unimaginative; matter-of-fact; factual. Though the ad writers had come up with a wildly imaginative campaign to pub-

licize the new product, the head office rejected it for a more *prosaic*, ordinary approach.

**protract**   V. prolong. Seeking to delay the union members' vote, the management team tried to *protract* the negotiations endlessly.

**provincial**   ADJ. pertaining to a province; limited in outlook; unsophisticated. As *provincial* governor, Sir Henry administered the Queen's law in his remote corner of Canada. Caught up in local problems, out of touch with London news, he became sadly *provincial*.

**provisional**   ADJ. tentative. Edward's appointment was *provisional*; he needed the approval of the board of directors before it would be made permanent.

## Word List 63

**provocative**   ADJ. arousing anger or interest; annoying. In a typically *provocative* act, the bully kicked sand into the weaker man's face.

**proximity**   N. nearness. Blind people sometimes develop a compensatory ability to sense the *proximity* of objects around them.

**prudent**   ADJ. cautious; careful. A miser hoards money not because he is *prudent* but because he is greedy. prudence, N.

**pugnacity**   N. combativeness; disposition to fight. "Put up your dukes!" he cried, making a fist to show his *pugnacity*.

**pungent**   ADJ. stinging; sharp in taste or smell; caustic. The *pungent* odor of ripe Limburger cheese appealed to Simone but made Stanley gag.

**purse**   V. pucker; contract into wrinkles. Miss Watson *pursed* her lips to show her disapproval of Huck's bedraggled appearance.

**qualified**   ADJ. limited; restricted. Unable to give the candidate full support, the mayor gave him only a *qualified* endorsement. (secondary meaning)

**quandary**   N. dilemma. When both Harvard and Stanford accepted Laura, she was in a *quandary* as to which school she should attend.

**quell**   V. extinguish; put down; quiet. Miss Minchin's demeanor was so stern and forbidding that she could *quell* any unrest among her students with one intimidating glance.

**querulous**   ADJ. fretful; whining. Even the most agreeable toddlers can begin to act *querulous* if they miss their nap.

## Word List 64

**quiescent**   ADJ. at rest; dormant; temporarily inactive. After the great eruption, fear of Mount Etna was great; people did not return to cultivate its rich hillside lands until the volcano had been *quiescent* for a full two years.

**ramble**   V. wander aimlessly (physically or mentally). Listening to the teacher *ramble*, Judy wondered whether he'd ever get to his point.

**rancor**   N. bitterness; hatred. Let us forget our *rancor* and join together in a new spirit of friendship and cooperation.

**rant**   V. rave; talk excitedly; scold; make a grandiloquent speech. When he heard that I'd totaled the family car, Dad began to *rant* at me like a complete madman.

**ratify**   V. approve formally; verify. Before the treaty could go into effect, it had to be *ratified* by the president.

**raucous**   ADJ. harsh and shrill; disorderly and boisterous. The *raucous* crowd of New Year's Eve revelers got progressively noisier as midnight drew near.

**raze**   V. destroy completely. Spelling is important: to raise a building is to put it up; to *raze* a building is to tear it down.

**rebuttal**   N. refutation; response with contrary evidence. The defense lawyer confidently listened to the prosecutor sum up his case, sure that she could answer his arguments in her *rebuttal*.

**recalcitrant**   ADJ. obstinately stubborn; determined to resist authority; unruly. Which animal do you think is more *recalcitrant*, a pig or a mule?

**recant**   V. disclaim or disavow; retract a previous statement; openly confess error. Those who can, keep true to their faith; those who can't, *recant*.

## Word List 65

**receptive**   ADJ. quick or willing to receive ideas, suggestions, etc. Adventure-loving Huck Finn proved a *receptive* audience for Tom's tales of buried treasure and piracy.

**recluse**   N. hermit; loner. Disappointed in love, Miss Emily became a *recluse*; she shut herself away in her empty mansion and refused to see another living soul. reclusive, ADJ.

**recount**   V. narrate or tell; count over again. A born storyteller, my father loved to *recount* anecdotes about his early years in New York.

**rectify**   V. set right; correct. You had better send a check to *rectify* your account before American Express cancels your credit card.

**redundant**   ADJ. superfluous; repetitious; excessively wordy. In your essay, you unnecessarily repeat several points; try to be less *redundant* in future. redundancy, N.

**refute**   V. disprove. The defense called several respectable witnesses who were able to *refute* the false testimony of the prosecution's sole witness.

**relegate**   V. banish to an inferior position; delegate; assign. After Ralph dropped his second tray of drinks that week, the manager swiftly *relegated* him to a minor post cleaning up behind the bar.

**relevant**   ADJ. pertinent; referring to the case in hand. How *relevant* Virginia Woolf's essays are to women writers today! It's as if Woolf in the 1930s foresaw our current literary struggles. relevancy, N.

**relinquish**   V. give up something with reluctance; yield. Denise never realized how hard it would be for her to *relinquish* her newborn son to the care of his adoptive parents.

**relish**   V. savor; enjoy. Watching Peter enthusiastically chow down, I thought, "Now there's a man who *relishes* a good dinner!" also N.

## Word List 66

**remorse**   N. guilt; self-reproach. The murderer felt no *remorse* for his crime.

**renegade**   N. deserter; traitor. Because he had abandoned his post and joined forces with the Indians, his fellow officers considered the hero of *Dancing with Wolves* a *renegade*. also ADJ.

**renounce**   V. forswear; repudiate; abandon; discontinue. Joan of Arc refused to *renounce* her testimony even though she knew she would be burned at the stake as a witch.

**replete**   ADJ. filled to the brim or to the point of being stuffed; abundantly supplied. The movie star's memoir was *replete* with juicy details about the love life of half of Hollywood.

**replicate**   V. reproduce; duplicate. To the chagrin of the scientists, they were unable to *replicate* the results of their controversial experiment.

**reprehensible**   ADJ. deserving blame. Shocked by the viciousness of the bombing, politicians of every party uniformly condemned the terror-ists' *reprehensible* deed.

**repress** V. restrain; hold back; crush; suppress. Anne's parents tried to curb her impetuosity without *repressing* her boundless high spirits.

**reprimand** V. reprove severely; rebuke. Every time Ermengarde made a mistake in class, she was afraid that Miss Minchin would *reprimand* her and tell her father how badly she was doing in school. also N.

**reproach** V. express disapproval. He never could do anything wrong without imagining how the look on his mother's face would *reproach* him afterwards. reproachful, ADJ.

**reprove** V. censure; rebuke. The principal severely *reproved* the students whenever they talked in the halls.

## Word List 67

**repudiate** V. disown; disavow. On separating from Tony, Tina announced that she would *repudiate* all debts incurred by her soon-to-be ex-husband.

**repulsion** N. act of driving back; distaste. The *repulsion* of the enemy forces was not accom-plished bloodlessly; many of the defenders were wounded in driving the enemy back. repel, V.

**rescind** V. cancel. Because of the public outcry against the new taxes, the senator proposed a bill to *rescind* the unpopular financial measure.

**resentment** N. indignation; bitterness; displea-sure. The Danish court was aware of Hamlet's *resentment* of his mother's hasty remarriage.

**reserve** N. self-control; formal but distant man-ner. Although some girls were attracted by Mark's air of *reserve*, Judy was put off by it, for she felt his aloofness indicated a lack of openness. reserved, ADJ.

**resigned** ADJ. unresisting; patiently submissive. *Resigned* to his downtrodden existence, Bob Cratchit was too meek to protest Scrooge's bul-lying.

**resolve** N. determination. Nothing could shake his *resolve* that his children would receive the best education that money could buy. resolved, ADJ.

**respite** N. interval of relief; time for rest; delay in punishment. After working nonstop on this project for three straight months, I need a *respite*!

**resplendent** ADJ. dazzling; glorious; brilliant. While all the adults were commenting how glorious the emperor looked in his *resplendent* new clothes, one little boy was heard to say, "But he's naked!"

**restraint** N. controlling force; control over one's emotions. Amanda dreamed of living an inde-pendent life, free of all parental *restraints*.

## Word List 68

**retaliation** N. repayment in kind (usually for bad treatment). When the bully kicked sand in the slender boy's face, he didn't expect any *retaliation* from his wimpy-looking victim. retaliate, V.

**reticent** ADJ. reserved; uncommunicative; inclined to be silent. Fearing his competitors might get advance word about his plans from talkative staff members, Hughes preferred *reti-cent* employees to loquacious ones.

**retiring** ADJ. modest; shy. Given Susan's *retir-ing* personality, no one expected her to take up public speaking; surprisingly enough, she became a star of the school debate team.

**retract** V. withdraw; take back. When I saw how Fred and his fraternity brothers had trashed the frat house, I decided to *retract* my offer to let them use our summer cottage for the weekend. retraction, N.

**reverent** ADJ. respectful. The young acolyte's *reverent* attitude was appropriate in a house of worship.

**rhetorical** ADJ. pertaining to effective commu-nication; insincere in language. To win his audience, the speaker used every *rhetorical* trick in the book.

**rigorous** ADJ. severe; harsh; demanding; exact. Disliked by his superiors, the officer candidate in *An Officer and a Gentleman* went through an extremely *rigorous* training program.

**robust** ADJ. vigorous; strong. After pumping iron and taking karate for six months, the little old lady was far more *robust* in health and could break a plank with her fist.

**rudimentary** ADJ. not developed; elementary; crude. Although my grandmother's English vocabulary was limited to a few *rudimentary* phrases, she always could make herself under-stood.

**sagacious** ADJ. perceptive; shrewd; having insight. Mr. Bond, that was not a particularly *sagacious* move on your part. I had not expected such a foolish trick from a smart fellow like you. sagacity, N.

## Word List 69

**sanction**   V. approve; ratify. Nothing will convince me to *sanction* the engagement of my daughter to such a worthless young man.

**sanctuary**   N. refuge; shelter; shrine; holy place. The tiny attic was Helen's *sanctuary* to which she fled when she had to get away from the rest of her family.

**sarcasm**   N. scornful remarks; stinging rebuke. Though Ralph tried to ignore the mocking comments of his supposed friends, their *sarcasm* wounded him deeply.

**satirical**   ADJ. mocking. The humor of cartoonist Gary Trudeau often is *satirical*; through the comments of the Doonesbury characters, Trudeau ridicules political corruption and folly.

**saturate**   V. soak thoroughly. *Saturate* your sponge with water until it can't hold any more.

**savory**   ADJ. tasty; pleasing, attractive, or agreeable. Julia Child's recipes enable amateur chefs to create *savory* delicacies for their guests.

**scanty**   ADJ. meager; insufficient. Thinking his helping of food was *scanty*, Oliver Twist asked for more.

**scoff**   V. mock; ridicule. He *scoffed* at dentists until he had his first toothache.

**scrupulous**   ADJ. conscientious; extremely thorough. I'm very happy to recommend Adam as an employee because he's always been highly *scrupulous* about doing a good job whenever he's worked for me.

**scrutinize**   V. examine closely and critically. Searching for flaws, the sergeant *scrutinized* every detail of the private's uniform.

## Word List 70

**seclusion**   N. isolation; solitude. One moment she loved crowds; the next, she sought *seclusion*. secluded, ADJ.

**sectarian**   ADJ. relating to a religious faction or sub-group; narrow-minded; limited. Far from being broad-minded, the religious leader was intolerant of new ideas, paying attention only to purely *sectarian* interests. sect, N.

**sedentary**   ADJ. requiring sitting. Disliking the effect of her *sedentary* occupation on her fig-

ure, Stacy decided to work out at the gym every other day.

**sequester**   V. isolate; retire from public life; segregate; seclude. Banished from his kingdom, the wizard Prospero *sequestered* himself on a desert island.

**serenity**   N. calmness; placidity. The sound of air raid sirens pierced the *serenity* of the quiet village of Pearl Harbor.

**servile**   ADJ. slavishly submissive; fawning; cringing. Constantly fawning on his employer, Uriah Heep was a *servile* creature.

**sever**   V. cut; separate. The released prisoner wanted to begin a new life and *sever* all connections with his criminal past.

**severity**   N. harshness; intensity; austerity; rigidity. The newspaper editorials disapproved of the *severity* of the sentence.

**shrewd**   ADJ. clever; astute. A *shrewd* investor, he took clever advantage of the fluctuations of the stock market.

**singular**   ADJ. unique; extraordinary; odd. Though the young man tried to understand Father William's *singular* behavior, he still found it odd that the old man incessantly stood on his head. singularity, N.

## Word List 71

**skeptical**   ADJ. doubting; suspending judgment until one has examined the evidence supporting a point of view. I am *skeptical* about the new health plan; I want some proof that it can work. skepticism, N.

**slacken**   V. slow up; loosen. As they passed the finish line, the runners *slackened* their pace.

**slander**   N. defamation; utterance of false and malicious statements. Considering the negative comments politicians make about each other, it's a wonder that more of them aren't sued for *slander*. also V.

**slothful**   ADJ. lazy. The British word "layabout" is a splendid descriptive term for someone *slothful*: What did the lazy bum do? He lay about the house all day.

**slovenly**   ADJ. untidy; careless in work habits. Unshaven, sitting around in his bathrobe all afternoon, Gus didn't seem to care about the *slovenly* appearance he presented.

**solemnity**   N. seriousness; gravity. The minister was concerned that nothing should disturb the *solemnity* of the marriage service.

**solicit** V. request earnestly; seek. Knowing she needed to have a solid majority for the budget to pass, the mayor telephoned all the members of the city council to *solicit* their votes.

**solitude** N. state of being alone; seclusion. Much depends on how much you like your own company. What to one person seems fearful isolation, to another is blessed *solitude*.

**soluble** ADJ. able to be dissolved; able to be explained. Sherlock Holmes took the *soluble* powder and dissolved it into a seven percent solution.

**somber** ADJ. gloomy; depressing; dark; drab. From the doctor's grim expression, I could tell he had *somber* news.

## Word List 72

**sparse** ADJ. not thick; thinly scattered; scanty. He had moved from the densely populated city to the remote countryside where the population was *sparse*.

**spendthrift** N. someone who wastes money. Easy access to credit encourages people to turn into *spendthrifts* who shop till they drop.

**spontaneity** N. lack of premeditation; naturalness; freedom from constraint. When Betty and Amy met, Amy impulsively hugged her roommate-to-be, but Betty drew back, unprepared for such *spontaneity*. spontaneous, ADJ.

**sporadic** ADJ. occurring irregularly. Although you can still hear *sporadic* outbursts of laughter and singing outside, the big Halloween parade has passed; the party's over till next year.

**spurious** ADJ. false; counterfeit. Unaccustomed to the design of the new hundred-dollar bills, many storekeepers rejected them as *spurious*.

**spurn** V. reject; scorn. The heroine *spurned* the villain's advances.

**squalor** N. filth; degradation; dirty, neglected state. Rusted, broken-down cars in its yard, trash piled up on the porch, tar paper peeling from the roof, the shack was the picture of *squalor*.

**squander** V. waste. If you *squander* your allowance on candy and comic books, you won't have any money left to buy the new box of crayons you want.

**stagnant** ADJ. motionless; stale; dull. Mosquitoes commonly breed in ponds of *stagnant* water. stagnate, V.

**stanza** N. division of a poem. Do you know the last *stanza* of "The Star-Spangled Banner"?

## Word List 73

**static** ADJ. unchanging; lacking development. Nothing had changed at home; life was *static*. stasis, N.

**steadfast** ADJ. loyal; unswerving. Penelope was *steadfast* in her affections, faithfully waiting for Ulysses to return from his wanderings.

**stoic** ADJ. impassive; unmoved by joy or grief. I wasn't particularly *stoic* when I had my flu shot; I squealed like a stuck pig. also N.

**strident** ADJ. loud and harsh; insistent. We could barely hear the speaker over the *strident* cries of the hecklers.

**strut** N. pompous walk; swagger. Colonel Blimp's *strut* as he marched about the parade ground revealed him for what he was: a pompous buffoon. also V.

**stupefy** V. make numb; stun; amaze. Disapproving of drugs in general, Laura refused to take sleeping pills or any other medicine that might *stupefy* her.

**subdued** ADJ. less intense; quieter. In the hospital visitors spoke in a *subdued* tone of voice for fear of disturbing the patients.

**submissive** ADJ. yielding; timid. Crushed by his authoritarian father, Will had no defiance left in him; he was totally *submissive* in the face of authority.

**subordinate** ADJ. occupying a lower rank; inferior; submissive. Bishop Proudie's wife expected all the *subordinate* clergy to behave with great deference to the wife of their superior.

**subside** V. settle down; descend; grow quiet. The doctor assured us that the fever would eventually *subside*.

## Word List 74

**substantial** ADJ. ample; solid; in essentials. The scholarship represented a *substantial* sum of money.

**substantiate** V. establish by evidence; verify; support. These endorsements from satisfied customers *substantiate* our claim that Barron's *How to Prepare for SAT I* is the best SAT-prep book on the market.

**subtlety** N. perceptiveness; ingenuity; delicacy. Never obvious, she expressed herself with such *subtlety* that her remarks went right over the heads of most of her audience. subtle, ADJ.

**succinct**   ADJ. brief; terse; compact. Don't bore your audience with excess verbiage: be *succinct*.

**supercilious**   ADJ. arrogant; condescending; patronizing. The *supercilious* headwaiter sneered at customers whom he thought did not fit in at a restaurant catering to an ultra-fashionable crowd.

**superfluous**   ADJ. excessive; overabundant; unnecessary. Please try not to include so many *superfluous* details in your report; just give me the facts. superfluity, N.

**supersede**   V. cause to be set aside; replace; make obsolete. Bulk mailing postal regulation 326D *supersedes* bulk mailing postal regulation 326C. If, in bundling your bulk mailing, you continue to follow regulation 326C, your bulk mailing will be returned to you stamped "REFUSED BY POSTAL SERVICE."

**supplant**   V. replace; usurp. Did the other woman actually *supplant* Princess Diana in Prince Charles's affections, or did Charles never love Diana at all?

**suppress**   V. crush; subdue; inhibit. After the armed troops had *suppressed* the rebellion, the city was placed under martial law.

**surmount**   V. overcome. I know you can *surmount* any difficulties that may stand in the way of your getting an education.

## Word List 75

**surpass**   V. exceed. Her SAT I scores *surpassed* our expectations.

**surreptitious**   ADJ. secret; furtive; sneaky; hidden. Hoping to discover where his mom had hidden the Christmas presents, Timmy took a *surreptitious* peek into the master bedroom closet.

**susceptible**   ADJ. impressionable; easily influenced; having little resistance, as to a disease; receptive to. Said the patent medicine man to the extremely *susceptible* customer: "Buy this new miracle drug, and you will no longer be *susceptible* to the common cold."

**sustain**   V. experience; support; nourish. Stuart *sustained* such a severe injury that the doctors feared he would be unable to work to *sustain* his growing family.

**swindler**   N. cheat. She was gullible and trusting,

an easy victim for the first *swindler* who came along.

**sycophant**   N. servile flatterer; bootlicker; yes man. Fed up with the toadies and brownnosers who made up his entourage, the star cried, "Get out, all of you! I'm sick to death of *sycophants*!"

**symmetry**   N. arrangement of parts so that balance is obtained; congruity. Something lopsided by definition lacks *symmetry*.

**taciturn**   ADJ. habitually silent; talking little. The stereotypical cowboy is a *taciturn* soul, answering lengthy questions with a "Yep" or "Nope."

**taint**   V. contaminate; cause to lose purity; modify with a trace of something bad. Fighting to preserve her good name, Desdemona wondered what had occurred to *taint* her reputation.

**tangential**   ADJ. peripheral; only slightly connected; digressing. Despite Clark's attempts to distract her with *tangential* remarks, Lois kept on coming back to her main question: why couldn't he come out to dinner with Superman and her?

## Word List 76

**tangible**   ADJ. able to be touched; real; palpable. Although Tom did not own a house, he had several *tangible* assets—a car, a television, a PC—that he could sell if he needed cash.

**tantamount**   ADJ. equivalent in effect or value. Though Rudy claimed his wife was off visiting friends, his shriek of horror when she walked into the room was *tantamount* to a confession that he believed she was dead.

**tedious**   ADJ. boring; tiring. The repetitious nature of work on the assembly line made Martin's job very *tedious*. tedium, N.

**temper**   V. moderate; tone down or restrain; toughen (steel). Not even her supervisor's grumpiness could *temper* Nancy's enthusiasm for her new job.

**tenacity**   N. firmness; persistence. Jean Valjean could not believe the *tenacity* of Inspector Javert. All Valjean had done was to steal a loaf of bread, and the inspector had pursued him doggedly for twenty years!

**tentative**   ADJ. provisional; experimental; doubtful. Your *tentative* proposal sounds feasible; let me know when the final details are worked out.

**termination**   N. end. Because of the unexpected

*termination* of his contract, he urgently needed a new job.

**terse** ADJ. concise; abrupt; pithy. There is a fine line between speech that is *terse* and to the point and speech that is too abrupt.

**threadbare** ADJ. worn through till the threads show; shabby and poor. The poor adjunct professor hid the *threadbare* spots on his jacket by sewing leather patches on his sleeves.

**thrive** V. prosper; flourish. Despite the impact of the recession on the restaurant trade, Philip's cafe *thrived*.

## Word List 77

**tirade** N. extended scolding; denunciation; harangue. The cigar smoker went into a bitter *tirade* denouncing the anti-smoking forces that had succeeded in banning smoking from most planes and restaurants.

**torpor** N. lethargy; sluggishness; dormancy. Throughout the winter, nothing aroused the bear from his *torpor*: he would not emerge from hibernation until spring.

**torrent** N. rushing stream; flood. Day after day of heavy rain saturated the hillside until the water ran downhill in *torrents*. torrential, ADJ.

**tractable** ADJ. docile; easily managed. Although Susan seemed a *tractable* young woman, she had a stubborn streak of independence that occasionally led her to defy the powers-that-be when she felt they were in the wrong.

**transcendent** ADJ. surpassing; exceeding ordinary limits; superior. For the amateur chef, dining at the four-star restaurant was a *transcendent* experience: the meal surpassed his wildest dreams.

**transient** ADJ. momentary; temporary; staying for a short time. Lexy's joy at finding the perfect Christmas gift for Phil was *transient*; she still had to find presents for Roger, Laura, Allison, and Uncle Bob.

**transparent** ADJ. easily detected; permitting light to pass through freely. Bobby managed to put an innocent look on his face; to his mother, however, his guilt was *transparent*.

**trepidation** N. fear; nervous apprehension. If you've never seen an SAT test, it's natural for you to feel some *trepidation* when you take the exam; if you're familiar with the test, however, you've got a much better chance of staying calm.

**trifling** ADJ. trivial; unimportant. Why bother going to see a doctor for such a *trifling*, everyday cold?

**trite** ADJ. hackneyed; commonplace. The *trite* and predictable situations in many television programs turn off many viewers, who respond by turning off their sets.

## Word List 78

**trivial** ADJ. unimportant; trifling. Too many magazines ignore newsworthy subjects and feature *trivial* affairs. trivia, N.

**turbulence** N. state of violent agitation. Warned of approaching *turbulence* in the atmosphere, the pilot told the passengers to fasten their seat belts.

**tyranny** N. oppression; cruel government. Frederick Douglass fought against the *tyranny* of slavery throughout his entire life.

**undermine** V. weaken; sap. The recent corruption scandals have *undermined* many people's faith in the city government.

**uniformity** N. sameness; monotony. After a while, the *uniformity* of TV situation comedies becomes boring. uniform, ADJ.

**universal** ADJ. characterizing or affecting all; present everywhere. At first, no one shared Christopher's opinions; his theory that the world was round was met with *universal* disdain.

**unkempt** ADJ. disheveled; uncared for in appearance. Jeremy hated his neighbor's *unkempt* lawn: he thought its neglected appearance had a detrimental effect on neighborhood property values.

**unobtrusive** ADJ. inconspicuous; not blatant. The secret service agents in charge of protecting the president tried to be as *unobtrusive* as possible.

**unprecedented** ADJ. novel; unparalleled. For a first novel, Margaret Mitchell's novel *Gone with the Wind* was an *unprecedented* success.

**unwarranted** ADJ. unjustified; groundless; undeserved. We could not understand Martin's *unwarranted* rudeness to his mother's guests.

## Word List 79

**usurp** V. seize another's power or rank. The revolution ended when the victorious rebel general succeeded in his attempt to *usurp* the throne.

**vacillate**   V. waver; fluctuate. Uncertain which suitor she ought to marry, the princess *vacillated*, saying now one, now the other. vacillation, N.

**vehement**   ADJ. forceful; impetuous; with marked vigor. "Give me liberty or give me death," he cried, with *vehement* ardor.

**venerate**   V. revere. In Tibet today, the common people still *venerate* their traditional spiritual leader, the Dalai Lama.

**veracity**   N. truthfulness. Trying to prove Anita Hill a liar, Senator Spector repeatedly questioned her *veracity*.

**verbose**   ADJ. wordy. We had to make some major cuts in Senator Foghorn's speech because it was far too *verbose*.

**viable**   ADJ. practical or workable; capable of maintaining life. The plan to build a new baseball stadium, though missing a few details, is *viable* and stands a good chance of winning popular support.

**vilify**   V. slander. Waging a highly negative campaign, the candidate attempted to *vilify* his opponent's reputation.

**vindicate**   V. clear from blame; exonerate; justify or support. The lawyer's goal was to *vindicate* her client and prove him innocent on all charges. The critics' extremely favorable reviews *vindicate* my opinion that *The Madness of King George* is a brilliant movie.

**vindictive**   ADJ. out for revenge; malicious. Divorce sometimes brings out a *vindictive* streak in people; when Tony told Tina he was getting a divorce, she poured green Jello into his aquarium and turned his tropical fish into dessert.

## Word List 80

**virtuoso**   N. highly skilled artist. The child prodigy Yehudi Menuhin grew into a *virtuoso* whose violin performances thrilled millions. virtuosity, N.

**virulent**   ADJ. extremely poisonous; hostile; bitter. Laid up with an extremely *virulent* case of measles, he blamed his doctors because his recovery took so long. In fact, he became quite *virulent* on the subject of the quality of modern medical care.

**volatile**   ADJ. changeable; explosive; evaporating rapidly. The political climate today is extremely *volatile*: no one can predict what the electorate will do next. Maria Callas's temper was extremely *volatile*: the only thing you could predict was that she was sure to blow up. Acetone is an extremely *volatile* liquid: it evaporates instantly.

**voluble**   ADJ. fluent; glib; talkative. An excessively *voluble* speaker suffers from logorrhea: he runs off at the mouth a lot!

**voluminous**   ADJ. bulky; large. Despite her family burdens, she kept up a *voluminous* correspondence with her friends.

**vulnerable**   ADJ. susceptible to wounds. His opponents could not harm Achilles, who was *vulnerable* only in his heel.

**whimsical**   N. capricious; fanciful. He dismissed his generous gift to his college as a sentimental fancy, an old man's *whimsical* gesture. whimsy, N.

**willful**   ADJ. intentional; headstrong; stubbornly set on getting one's way. Donald had planned to kill his wife for months; clearly, her death was a case of deliberate, *willful* murder, not a crime of passion committed by a hasty, *willful* youth unable to foresee the consequences of his deeds.

**withhold**   V. refuse to give; hold back. The NCAA may *withhold* permission for academically-underprepared athletes to participate in intercollegiate sports as freshmen.

**zealot**   N. fanatic; person who shows excessive zeal. Though Glenn was devout, he was no *zealot*; he never tried to force his beliefs on his friends.

# PART VII

# TESTS FOR PRACTICE

Verbal Reasoning Test 1
Verbal Reasoning Test 2
Verbal Reasoning Test 3

## ANSWER SHEET FOR VERBAL REASONING TEST 1

Remove answer sheet by cutting on dotted line.

### Section 1

1. Ⓐ Ⓑ Ⓒ Ⓓ Ⓔ
2. Ⓐ Ⓑ Ⓒ Ⓓ Ⓔ
3. Ⓐ Ⓑ Ⓒ Ⓓ Ⓔ
4. Ⓐ Ⓑ Ⓒ Ⓓ Ⓔ
5. Ⓐ Ⓑ Ⓒ Ⓓ Ⓔ
6. Ⓐ Ⓑ Ⓒ Ⓓ Ⓔ
7. Ⓐ Ⓑ Ⓒ Ⓓ Ⓔ
8. Ⓐ Ⓑ Ⓒ Ⓓ Ⓔ
9. Ⓐ Ⓑ Ⓒ Ⓓ Ⓔ
10. Ⓐ Ⓑ Ⓒ Ⓓ Ⓔ
11. Ⓐ Ⓑ Ⓒ Ⓓ Ⓔ
12. Ⓐ Ⓑ Ⓒ Ⓓ Ⓔ
13. Ⓐ Ⓑ Ⓒ Ⓓ Ⓔ
14. Ⓐ Ⓑ Ⓒ Ⓓ Ⓔ
15. Ⓐ Ⓑ Ⓒ Ⓓ Ⓔ
16. Ⓐ Ⓑ Ⓒ Ⓓ Ⓔ
17. Ⓐ Ⓑ Ⓒ Ⓓ Ⓔ
18. Ⓐ Ⓑ Ⓒ Ⓓ Ⓔ
19. Ⓐ Ⓑ Ⓒ Ⓓ Ⓔ
20. Ⓐ Ⓑ Ⓒ Ⓓ Ⓔ
21. Ⓐ Ⓑ Ⓒ Ⓓ Ⓔ
22. Ⓐ Ⓑ Ⓒ Ⓓ Ⓔ
23. Ⓐ Ⓑ Ⓒ Ⓓ Ⓔ
24. Ⓐ Ⓑ Ⓒ Ⓓ Ⓔ
25. Ⓐ Ⓑ Ⓒ Ⓓ Ⓔ
26. Ⓐ Ⓑ Ⓒ Ⓓ Ⓔ
27. Ⓐ Ⓑ Ⓒ Ⓓ Ⓔ
28. Ⓐ Ⓑ Ⓒ Ⓓ Ⓔ
29. Ⓐ Ⓑ Ⓒ Ⓓ Ⓔ
30. Ⓐ Ⓑ Ⓒ Ⓓ Ⓔ

### Section 2

1. Ⓐ Ⓑ Ⓒ Ⓓ Ⓔ
2. Ⓐ Ⓑ Ⓒ Ⓓ Ⓔ
3. Ⓐ Ⓑ Ⓒ Ⓓ Ⓔ
4. Ⓐ Ⓑ Ⓒ Ⓓ Ⓔ
5. Ⓐ Ⓑ Ⓒ Ⓓ Ⓔ
6. Ⓐ Ⓑ Ⓒ Ⓓ Ⓔ
7. Ⓐ Ⓑ Ⓒ Ⓓ Ⓔ
8. Ⓐ Ⓑ Ⓒ Ⓓ Ⓔ
9. Ⓐ Ⓑ Ⓒ Ⓓ Ⓔ
10. Ⓐ Ⓑ Ⓒ Ⓓ Ⓔ
11. Ⓐ Ⓑ Ⓒ Ⓓ Ⓔ
12. Ⓐ Ⓑ Ⓒ Ⓓ Ⓔ
13. Ⓐ Ⓑ Ⓒ Ⓓ Ⓔ
14. Ⓐ Ⓑ Ⓒ Ⓓ Ⓔ
15. Ⓐ Ⓑ Ⓒ Ⓓ Ⓔ
16. Ⓐ Ⓑ Ⓒ Ⓓ Ⓔ
17. Ⓐ Ⓑ Ⓒ Ⓓ Ⓔ
18. Ⓐ Ⓑ Ⓒ Ⓓ Ⓔ
19. Ⓐ Ⓑ Ⓒ Ⓓ Ⓔ
20. Ⓐ Ⓑ Ⓒ Ⓓ Ⓔ
21. Ⓐ Ⓑ Ⓒ Ⓓ Ⓔ
22. Ⓐ Ⓑ Ⓒ Ⓓ Ⓔ
23. Ⓐ Ⓑ Ⓒ Ⓓ Ⓔ
24. Ⓐ Ⓑ Ⓒ Ⓓ Ⓔ
25. Ⓐ Ⓑ Ⓒ Ⓓ Ⓔ
26. Ⓐ Ⓑ Ⓒ Ⓓ Ⓔ
27. Ⓐ Ⓑ Ⓒ Ⓓ Ⓔ
28. Ⓐ Ⓑ Ⓒ Ⓓ Ⓔ
29. Ⓐ Ⓑ Ⓒ Ⓓ Ⓔ
30. Ⓐ Ⓑ Ⓒ Ⓓ Ⓔ
31. Ⓐ Ⓑ Ⓒ Ⓓ Ⓔ
32. Ⓐ Ⓑ Ⓒ Ⓓ Ⓔ
33. Ⓐ Ⓑ Ⓒ Ⓓ Ⓔ
34. Ⓐ Ⓑ Ⓒ Ⓓ Ⓔ
35. Ⓐ Ⓑ Ⓒ Ⓓ Ⓔ

### Section 3

1. Ⓐ Ⓑ Ⓒ Ⓓ Ⓔ
2. Ⓐ Ⓑ Ⓒ Ⓓ Ⓔ
3. Ⓐ Ⓑ Ⓒ Ⓓ Ⓔ
4. Ⓐ Ⓑ Ⓒ Ⓓ Ⓔ
5. Ⓐ Ⓑ Ⓒ Ⓓ Ⓔ
6. Ⓐ Ⓑ Ⓒ Ⓓ Ⓔ
7. Ⓐ Ⓑ Ⓒ Ⓓ Ⓔ
8. Ⓐ Ⓑ Ⓒ Ⓓ Ⓔ
9. Ⓐ Ⓑ Ⓒ Ⓓ Ⓔ
10. Ⓐ Ⓑ Ⓒ Ⓓ Ⓔ
11. Ⓐ Ⓑ Ⓒ Ⓓ Ⓔ
12. Ⓐ Ⓑ Ⓒ Ⓓ Ⓔ
13. Ⓐ Ⓑ Ⓒ Ⓓ Ⓔ

# 1 1 1 1 1 1 1 1 1 1 1 1

# VERBAL REASONING TEST 1
## Section 1

TIME—30 MINUTES
30 QUESTIONS

For each of the following questions, select the best answer from the choices provided and fill in the appropriate circle on the answer sheet.

Directions: Each sentence below has one or two blanks, each blank indicating that something has been omitted. Beneath the sentence are five words or sets of words labeled A through E. Choose the word or set of words that, when inserted in the sentence, best fits the meaning of the sentence as a whole.

Example:

Medieval kingdoms did not become constitutional republics overnight; on the contrary, the change was ____.

(A) unpopular
(B) unexpected
(C) advantageous
(D) sufficient
(E) gradual

Ⓐ Ⓑ Ⓒ Ⓓ ●

1. Because the salt used to de-ice highways in snowbelt states is highly ____ , it can turn the reinforcing bars in the concrete on highways, bridges, and parking garages into rusty mush.

   (A) adhesive
   (B) obvious
   (C) diluted
   (D) corrosive
   (E) profitable

2. Before the 1960s, African-American cartoonists labored mostly without mainstream recognition, their work ____ African-American magazines, journals, and newspapers.

   (A) confined to
   (B) unconscious of
   (C) irrelevant to
   (D) unacceptable to
   (E) derided by

3. Although the book might satisfy Bloom's hard-core fans, it is ____ by its monotonous citations and its ____ style.

   (A) marred...slipshod
   (B) warped...elegant
   (C) enhanced...impeccable
   (D) unified...laconic
   (E) annotated...exhaustive

4. Calculation and planning informed the actress's every word and gesture: there was not a ____ moment in her entire performance.

   (A) spontaneous
   (B) tasteful
   (C) histrionic
   (D) lethargic
   (E) poignant

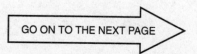

GO ON TO THE NEXT PAGE

**1   1 1 1 1 1 1 1 1 1 1**

5. None of her students minded when Professor Rivera's lectures wandered away from their official theme; her _____ were always more fascinating than the topic of the day.

    (A) summaries
    (B) digressions
    (C) intimations
    (D) metaphors
    (E) imprecations

6. Sociobiology, the study of the biological and evolutionary basis of social behavior, is a _____ discipline, part biology and part sociology, that requires an understanding of both fields.

    (A) summary
    (B) hybrid
    (C) prolific
    (D) hypothetical
    (E) pedantic

7. Though Widow Douglass hoped to reform Huck, her sister Miss Watson _____ him _____ and said he would come to no good end.

    (A) called…amendable
    (B) declared…qualified
    (C) pronounced…incorrigible
    (D) proclaimed…optimistic
    (E) professed…cured

8. By nature he was a _____, demanding that his subordinates respond to orders _____.

    (A) pessimist…positively
    (B) dissident…noncommittally
    (C) martinet…promptly
    (D) despot…magnanimously
    (E) virtuoso…obsequiously

9. Critics point out that, far from moving _____ closer to its goals, the field of behavioral genetics is _____ the same problems that have always plagued it.

    (A) intermittently…composed of
    (B) dramatically…divorced from
    (C) inexorably…mired in
    (D) steadily…acclaimed for
    (E) uniformly…enhanced by

GO ON TO THE NEXT PAGE

# 1   1   1   1   1   1   1   1   1   1   1   1

Directions: Each question below consists of a related pair of words or phrases, followed by five pairs of words or phrases labeled A through E. Select the pair that best expresses a relationship similar to that expressed in the original pair.

Example:

CRUMB : BREAD ::

(A) ounce : unit
(B) splinter : wood
(C) water : bucket
(D) twine : rope
(E) cream : butter

Ⓐ ● Ⓒ Ⓓ Ⓔ

10. EGG : CHICKEN ::

(A) litter : kitten
(B) bulb : tulip
(C) hay : horse
(D) hive : bee
(E) tree : woodpecker

11. LOCKER : CLOTHING ::

(A) graveyard : tombstones
(B) freezer : cold
(C) quarry : marble
(D) well : bucket
(E) vault : valuables

12. LAUNCH : PRODUCT ::

(A) jettison : cargo
(B) moor : vessel
(C) modify : invention
(D) initiate : enterprise
(E) consume : resource

13. GLUTTON : MODERATION ::

(A) braggart : performance
(B) prophet : message
(C) sophisticate : ambition
(D) miser : generosity
(E) paragon : knowledge

14. SHARD : POTTERY ::

(A) stitch : embroidery
(B) rim : saucer
(C) knife : cutlery
(D) trowel : bricklaying
(E) splinter : glass

15. ENIGMA : PUZZLING ::

(A) comment : cryptic
(B) reproof : critical
(C) contradiction : surprising
(D) quandary : resolved
(E) argument : unsound

GO ON TO THE NEXT PAGE ⇒

1     1   1   1   1   1   1   1   1   1   1   1

Directions: Each passage below is followed by questions based on its content. Answer the questions on the basis of what is <u>stated</u> or <u>implied</u> in that passage and in any introductory material that may be provided.

**Questions 16–21 are based on the following passage.**

*The style of the renowned modern artist Pablo Picasso changed radically in the course of his long career, as he reacted to new artistic stimuli and fresh ways of seeing the world. In this excerpt from a survey of Picasso's art, the critic Alfred Barr considers the impact of Black African art on Picasso's work, in particular on his painting* Les Demoiselles d'Avignon (The Girls of Avignon).

Traditionally, *Les Demoiselles d'Avignon* was indeed supposed to have been influenced by African Negro sculpture, but Picasso has since
Line denied this, affirming that although he was
(5) much interested in Iberian[1] sculpture he had no knowledge of Negro art while he was working on *Les Demoiselles*. Only later in 1907, he states, did he discover Negro sculpture.

Quite recently however, Picasso has
(10) assured us that the two right-hand figures of *Les Demoiselles* were completed some time after the rest of the composition. It seems possible therefore that Picasso's memory is incomplete and that he may well have painted
(15) or repainted the astonishing heads of these figures *after* his discovery of African sculpture, just as only a year before, stimulated by Iberian sculpture, he had repainted the head of Gertrude Stein's portrait months after he had
(20) completed the rest of the picture...

The discovery and appreciation of African Negro sculpture among the artists of Paris in the early 1900s is still a somewhat confused story. It seems probable that as early as 1904
(25) Vlaminck began to take an interest in this hitherto neglected art. Shortly afterwards he introduced Derain to his new enthusiasm, and before long Derain and his fellow *fauve*[2] Matisse began to form collections. Vlaminck's

(30) admiration lay more in the romantic and exotic values of the masks and fetishes but Derain and Matisse found in them unhackneyed aesthetic values involving the bold distortion and structural reorganization of natural forms.
(35) It is strange that Picasso, who had met Matisse by 1906, should have been unaware of African art until the middle of 1907 when, as he says, he discovered it for himself almost accidentally while leaving the gallery of his-
(40) toric sculpture in the Trocadero. However, the discovery, he affirms, was a "revelation" to him and he began immediately to make use of it. Whatever general stimulation the *fauves* had got from African art there is little specific
(45) trace of it in their painting. But several of Picasso's works of 1907–08 incorporate African forms and possibly colors to such an extent that the title "Negro Period" has hitherto been applied to his art of this time, includ-
(50) ing *Les Demoiselles d'Avignon*. Actually, Iberian sculpture continued to interest him and often its forms were fused (and by critics confused) with those of the Congo and the Guinea Coast.
(55) For instance the *Woman in Yellow* has long been considered one of the important paintings of Picasso's Negro Period but it now seems clear that this hieratically impressive figure is related to Iberian bronzes even more
(60) closely than are the three earlier figures of *Les Demoiselles d'Avignon* which it resembles in style. As Sweeney has pointed out, the face and pose are remarkably similar to an archaic votive figure from Despenaperros. The ocher
(65) color and striated patterns, however, may have been suggested by Negro art. More African in

GO ON TO THE NEXT PAGE ➔

1    1    1    1    1    1    1    1    1    1    1    1

form is the *Head*, which may have been inspired by the almond-shaped masks of the Ivory Coast or French Congo.

---

[1] The term Iberian refers to the peninsula in southwest Europe that is made up of Spain and Portugal.

[2] The *fauves* were a group of twentieth-century French artists noted for vivid colors and striking contrasts.

16. The opening paragraph suggests that Picasso would have agreed with which of the following statements?

(A) In painting *Les Demoiselles d'Avignon*, he was directly inspired by black art.
(B) In painting *Les Demoiselles d'Avignon*, he may have been indirectly influenced by African sculpture.
(C) In painting *Les Demoiselles d'Avignon*, he explicitly copied Iberian models.
(D) In painting *Les Demoiselles d'Avignon*, he may have been influenced by ancient Spanish art.
(E) In painting *Les Demoiselles d'Avignon*, he lost interest in Iberian sculpture.

17. As shown in lines 12–20, Picasso reacted to new artistic stimuli by

(A) attempting to reproduce them faithfully
(B) deciding to come back to his artistic roots
(C) rethinking already completed works of art
(D) begining to collect inspiring examples
(E) forgetting his earlier influences

18. In the second paragraph, the author

(A) poses a question
(B) refutes a misapprehension
(C) makes a hypothesis
(D) cites the testimony of authorities
(E) contrasts two unlike situations

19. According to lines 35–40, Picasso first became acquainted with African art

(A) through another artist
(B) on a trip to Africa
(C) through an art historian
(D) in an art gallery
(E) in a book of reproductions

20. The term "applied to" (line 49) most likely means

(A) spread on
(B) credited to
(C) placed in contact with
(D) used to designate
(E) requested as

21. We can infer from lines 62–64 that Despenaperros is most likely

(A) a town on the Ivory Coast of Africa
(B) the name of a young French girl from Avignon
(C) a contemporary artist known to Picasso
(D) a location on the Iberian peninsula
(E) the name of a village near Avignon

**Questions 22–30 are based on the following passage.**

*Taken from the writings of Benjamin Franklin, the following excerpt, published in 1784, demonstrates Franklin's attitude toward the so-called "savages" of North America and reveals something of what these Native Americans thought about the white men and women who had come to their land.*

GO ON TO THE NEXT PAGE

1     1     1     1     1     1     1     1     1     1     1     1

Savages we call them, because their manners differ from ours, which we think the perfection of civility; they think the same of
Line theirs.
(5)     Perhaps, if we could examine the manners of different nations with impartiality, we should find no people so rude as to be without rules of politeness, nor any so polite as not to have some remains of rudeness.
(10)     The Indian men, when young, are hunters and warriors; when old, counselors, for all their government is by counsel of the sages; there is no force, there are no prisons, no officers to compel obedience or inflict punish-
(15) ment. Hence they generally study oratory, the best speaker having the most influence. The Indian women till the ground, dress the food, nurse and bring up the children, and preserve and hand down to posterity the memory of
(20) public transactions. These employments of men and women are accounted natural and honorable. Having few artificial wants, they have abundance of leisure for improvement by conversation. Our laborious manner of life,
(25) compared with theirs, they esteem slavish and base; and the learning, on which we value ourselves, they regard as frivolous and useless.
    An instance of this occurred at the treaty of Lancaster, in Pennsylvania, in the year
(30) 1744, between the government of Virginia and the Six Nations. After the principal business was settled, the commissioners from Virginia acquainted the Indians by a speech that there was at Williamsburg a college, with a fund for
(35) educating Indian youth; and that, if the Six Nations would send down half a dozen of their young lads to that college, the government would take care that they should be well provided for, and instructed in all the learning of
(40) the white people. It is one of the Indian rules of politeness not to answer a public proposition the same day that it is made; they think that it would be treating it as a light matter, and that they show it respect by taking time to
(45) consider it, as of a matter important. They therefore deferred their answer till the day following; when their speaker began by express-

ing their deep sense of the kindness of the Virginia government in making them that
(50) offer, saying:
    "We know that you highly esteem the kind of learning taught in those colleges, and that the maintenance of our young men, while with you, would be very expensive to you. We are
(55) convinced, therefore, that you mean to do us good by your proposal, and we thank you heartily. But you, who are wise, must know that different nations have different conceptions of things; and you will therefore not take
(60) it amiss, if our ideas of this kind of education happen not to be the same as yours. We have had some experience of it. Several of our young people were formerly brought up at the colleges of the northern provinces: they were
(65) instructed in all your sciences; but when they came back to us they were bad runners, ignorant of every means of living in the woods, unable to bear cold or hunger. They knew neither how to build a cabin, take a deer, nor kill
(70) an enemy, spoke our language imperfectly, were therefore neither fit for hunters, warriors, nor counselors; they were totally good for nothing.
    We are, however, not the less obliged by
(75) your kind offer, though we decline accepting it; and, to show our grateful sense of it, if the gentlemen of Virginia will send us a dozen of their sons, we will take care of their education, instruct them in all we know, and make *men* of
(80) them."

22. According to Franklin, Indian leaders maintain their authority by means of their

(A) warlike ability
(B) skill as hunters
(C) verbal prowess
(D) personal wealth
(E) punitive capacity

GO ON TO THE NEXT PAGE ⟹

# 1   1 1 1 1 1 1 1 1 1 1 1

23. The word "dress" in line 17 means

 (A) clothe
 (B) adorn
 (C) medicate
 (D) straighten
 (E) prepare

24. Franklin attributes the amount of leisure time for conversing available to the Indians to

 (A) their greater efficiency and productivity
 (B) the amount of hard labor performed by Indian women
 (C) their relative indolence compared to whites
 (D) their simpler, more natural lifestyle
 (E) the degree of their general gregariousness

25. Franklin's purpose in quoting this speech is primarily to

 (A) demonstrate the natural oratorical abilities of Indians
 (B) condemn the Virginians' failure to recruit Indian students for their schools
 (C) give an example of the Indian viewpoint on the benefits of white civilization
 (D) describe a breakdown in communications between Indians and whites
 (E) advocate the adoption of Indian educational techniques

26. The Indians' chief purpose in making the speech seems to be to

 (A) tactfully refuse a friendly gesture
 (B) express their opinions on equality
 (C) gratify their intended audience
 (D) describe native American customs
 (E) request funds to start their own school

27. According to this passage, the Indians' idea of education differs from that of the gentlemen of Virginia in that the Indians

 (A) also believe in the education of young women
 (B) have different educational goals
 (C) teach different branches of science
 (D) include different aspects of nature
 (E) speak a different language

28. The word "take" in line 69 means

 (A) endure
 (B) transport
 (C) confiscate
 (D) catch
 (E) accept

29. The Indians responsible for the speech would probably agree that they

 (A) have no right to deny Indian boys the opportunity for schooling
 (B) are being insulted by the offer of the commissioners
 (C) know more about the various branches of science than the commissioners do
 (D) have a better way of educating young men than the commissioners do
 (E) should not offer to educate the sons of the gentlemen of Virginia

30. The tone of the speech as a whole is best described as

 (A) aloof but angry
 (B) insistently demanding
 (C) grudgingly admiring
 (D) eager and inquiring
 (E) courteous but ironic

# STOP
**IF YOU FINISH BEFORE TIME IS CALLED, YOU MAY CHECK YOUR WORK ON THIS SECTION ONLY. DO NOT WORK ON ANY OTHER SECTION IN THE TEST.**

2   2   2   2   2   2   2   2   2   2   2

## Section 2

TIME—30 MINUTES
35 QUESTIONS

For each of the following questions, select the best answer from the choices provided and fill in the appropriate circle on the answer sheet.

---

Directions: Each sentence below has one or two blanks, each blank indicating that something has been omitted. Beneath the sentence are five words or sets of words labeled A through E. Choose the word or set of words that, when inserted in the sentence, best fits the meaning of the sentence as a whole.

Example:

Medieval kingdoms did not become constitutional republics overnight; on the contrary, the change was ____.

(A) unpopular
(B) unexpected
(C) advantageous
(D) sufficient
(E) gradual

Ⓐ  Ⓑ  Ⓒ  Ⓓ  ●

---

1. Despite careful restoration and cleaning of the murals in the 1960s, the colors slowly but steadily ____.

   (A) persisted
   (B) embellished
   (C) saturated
   (D) deteriorated
   (E) stabilized

2. After the lonely rigors of writing, Mr. Doyle enjoys the ____ aspects of filmmaking.

   (A) impersonal
   (B) transitory
   (C) narrative
   (D) social
   (E) profitable

3. So important was the textile trade between England and America—____ quantities of indigo and raw-ginned cotton a year going in one direction, millions of yards of printed cotton fabrics in the other—that it ____ right through the American War of Independence.

   (A) immense…innovated
   (B) vast…continued
   (C) illicit…collaborated
   (D) insignificant…diversified
   (E) enormous…ceased

4. Like doctors exploring the mysteries concealed within the human body, astronomers are finding that X rays offer an invaluable means for examining otherwise ____ structures.

   (A) inconsequential
   (B) hidden
   (C) ambivalent
   (D) diseased
   (E) ephemeral

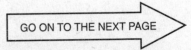

GO ON TO THE NEXT PAGE

5. When trees go dormant in winter, the procedure is anything but ____: it is an active meta-
   bolic process that changes the plant ____.

   (A) sleepy...radically
   (B) pleasant...intermittently
   (C) dynamic...majestically
   (D) overt...openly
   (E) organic...thoroughly

6. As Reginald Machell's lavishly carved throne
   clearly illustrates, California craftsmen were
   not afraid of ____.

   (A) competition
   (B) embellishment
   (C) imitation
   (D) expediency
   (E) antiquity

7. One might dispute the author's handling of
   particular points of Kandinsky's interaction
   with his artistic environment, but her main theses are ____.

   (A) unaesthetic
   (B) incongruous
   (C) untenable
   (D) undecipherable
   (E) irreproachable

8. After reading numbers of biographies recounting dysfunctions and disasters, failed marriages
   and failed careers, Joyce Carol Oates ____ a
   word to ____ the genre: *pathography*, the story
   of diseased lives.

   (A) invented...curtail
   (B) reiterated...criticize
   (C) hypothesized...indict
   (D) dismissed...obscure
   (E) coined...describe

9. Rebuffed by his colleagues, the initially ____
   young researcher became increasingly ____.

   (A) outgoing...withdrawn
   (B) boisterous...excitable
   (C) diligent...tolerant
   (D) theoretical...pragmatic
   (E) tedious...polished

10. Publishers have discovered that black America
    is not a ____ of attitudes and opinions but a
    rich mixture lending itself to numerous expres-
    sions in print.

    (A) concoction
    (B) medley
    (C) monolith
    (D) paradox
    (E) controversy

GO ON TO THE NEXT PAGE

2   2   2   2   2   2   2   2   2   2   2

Directions: Each question below consists of a related pair of words or phrases, followed by five pairs of words or phrases labeled A through E. Select the pair that <u>best</u> expresses a relationship similar to that expressed in the original pair.

Example:

CRUMB : BREAD ::

(A) ounce : unit
(B) splinter : wood
(C) water : bucket
(D) twine : rope
(E) cream : butter

Ⓐ ● Ⓒ Ⓓ Ⓔ

11. NAME TAG : PERSON ::

    (A) medal : soldier
    (B) doorbell : house
    (C) number : telephone
    (D) label : product
    (E) index : book

12. ACTOR : AUDITION ::

    (A) orator : speech
    (B) conductor : orchestra
    (C) composer : score
    (D) applicant : interview
    (E) director : vision

13. TANK : HELIUM ::

    (A) stove : propane
    (B) cask : wine
    (C) lead vest : radium
    (D) balloon : air
    (E) molecule : atom

14. KINDLE : FIRE ::

    (A) incite : riot
    (B) shoot : battle
    (C) raze : building
    (D) kidnap : ransom
    (E) emend : book

15. DISMOUNT : HORSE ::

    (A) disembark : ship
    (B) display : power
    (C) distinguish : identity
    (D) dispel : illusion
    (E) dismiss : charge

16. HUTCH : RABBIT ::

    (A) coop : chicken
    (B) bridle : horse
    (C) litter : cat
    (D) sanctuary : bird
    (E) silo : grain

17. TATTLETALE : REVEAL ::

    (A) swindler : snoop
    (B) judge : lecture
    (C) miser : hoard
    (D) defector : brag
    (E) transient : detour

18. SCALE : FISH ::

    (A) pluck : chicken
    (B) groom : horse
    (C) scurry : mouse
    (D) snare : rabbit
    (E) carve : steak

GO ON TO THE NEXT PAGE

2   2   2   2   2   2   2   2   2   2   2

19. TUSSLE : DUEL ::

   (A) wrestle : compete
   (B) contend : assent
   (C) compliment : disparage
   (D) squabble : debate
   (E) struggle : connive

20. PLOW : FIELD ::

   (A) prime : surface
   (B) weed : flowerbed
   (C) set : table
   (D) fell : tree
   (E) gather : bouquet

21. FRAME : FILM ::

   (A) panel : cartoon
   (B) camera : photograph
   (C) spool : thread
   (D) margin : paper
   (E) watercolors : painting

22. CLAUSTROPHOBIA : CONFINEMENT ::

   (A) neuralgia : nerves
   (B) egomania : self
   (C) hydrophobia : dogs
   (D) kleptomania : stealing
   (E) acrophobia : heights

23. COGNIZANT : AWARENESS ::

   (A) cursory : exhaustion
   (B) restive : impatience
   (C) stimulating : vacillation
   (D) ominous : harshness
   (E) impartial : vilification

GO ON TO THE NEXT PAGE

2   2   2   2   2   2   2   2   2   2   2   2

---

Directions: The passage below is followed by questions based on its content. Answer the questions on the basis of what is stated or implied in the passage and in any introductory material that may be provided.

---

**Questions 24–35 are based on the following passage.**

*The following passage is an excerpt from Henry James's short story "The Pupil." In this section, Pemberton, the young British tutor, describes some of the hasty trips around Europe during which he came to know his pupil, Morgan Moreen, and Morgan's family.*

A year after he had come to live with them Mr. and Mrs. Moreen suddenly gave up the villa at Nice. Pemberton had got used to sud-
Line denness, having seen it practiced on a consid-
(5) erable scale during two jerky little tours—one in Switzerland the first summer, and the other late in the winter, when they all ran down to Florence and then, at the end of ten days, lik-ing it much less than they had intended, strag-
(10) gled back in mysterious depression. They had returned to Nice "for ever," as they said; but this didn't prevent their squeezing, one rainy muggy May night, into a second-class railway-carriage—you could never tell by
(15) which class they would travel—where Pemberton helped them to stow away a won-derful collection of bundles and bags. The explanation of this manoeuvre was that they had determined to spend the summer "in some
(20) bracing place"; but in Paris they dropped into a small furnished apartment—a fourth floor in a third-rate avenue, where there was a smell on the staircase and the *portier*[1] was hateful—and passed the next four months in blank
(25) indigence.
The better part of this forced temporary stay belonged to the tutor and his pupil, who, visiting the Invalides[2] and Notre Dame, the Conciergerie and all the museums, took a hun-
(30) dred rewarding rambles. They learned to know their Paris, which was useful, for they came

back another year for a longer stay, the general character of which in Pemberton's memory today mixes pitiably and confusedly with that
(35) of the first. He sees Morgan's shabby knicker-bockers—the everlasting pair that didn't match his blouse and that as he grew longer could only grow faded. He remembers the par-ticular holes in his three or four pair of colored
(40) stockings.
Morgan was dear to his mother, but he never was better dressed than was absolutely necessary—partly, no doubt, by his own fault, for he was as indifferent to his appearance as a
(45) German philosopher. "My dear fellow, so are you! I don't want to cast you in the shade." Pemberton could have no rejoinder for this—the assertion so closely represented the fact. If however the deficiencies of his own wardrobe
(50) were a chapter by themselves he didn't like his little charge to look too poor. Later he used to say "Well, if we're poor, why, after all, shouldn't we look it?" and he consoled him-self with thinking there was something rather
(55) elderly and gentlemanly in Morgan's disre-pair—it differed from the untidiness of the urchin who plays and spoils his things. He could trace perfectly the degrees by which, in proportion as her little son confined himself to
(60) his tutor for society, Mrs. Moreen shrewdly forbore to renew his garments. She did noth-ing that didn't show, neglected him because he escaped notice, and then, as he illustrated this clever policy, discouraged at home his public
(65) appearances. Her position was logical enough—those members of her family who did show had to be showy.

GO ON TO THE NEXT PAGE

2  2  2  2  2  2  2  2  2  2  2  2

During this period and several others Pemberton was quite aware of how he and his
(70) comrade might strike people; wandering languidly through the Jardin des Plantes[3] as if they had nowhere to go, sitting on the winter days in the galleries of the Louvre, so splendidly ironical to the homeless, as if for the
(75) advantage of the steam radiators. They joked about it sometimes: it was the sort of joke that was perfectly within the boy's compass. They figured themselves as part of the vast vague hand-to-mouth multitude of the enormous city
(80) and pretended they were proud of their position in it—it showed them "such a lot of life" and made them conscious of a democratic brotherhood. If Pemberton couldn't feel a sympathy in destitution with his small com-
(85) panion—for after all Morgan's fond parents would never have let him really suffer—the boy would at least feel it with him, so it came to the same thing. He used sometimes to wonder what people would think they were—to
(90) fancy they were looked askance at, as if it might be a suspected case of kidnapping. Morgan wouldn't be taken for a young patrician with a tutor—he wasn't smart enough— though he might pass for his companion's
(95) sickly little brother. Now and then he had a five-franc piece, and except once, when they bought a couple of lovely neckties, one of which he made Pemberton accept, they laid it out scientifically in old books. This was sure
(100) to be a great day, always spent at the used book stands on the quays, in a rummage of the dusty boxes that garnish the parapets. Such occasions helped them to live, for their books ran low very soon after the beginning of their
(105) acquaintance. Pemberton had a good many in England, but he was obliged to write to a friend and ask him kindly to get some fellow to give him something for them.

---

[1] Hall porter or custodian.

[2] Famous Paris monument; site of the tomb of Napoleon.

[3] Botanical garden.

24. The primary purpose of the passage is to
   (A) denounce the ill treatment of an exceptional child
   (B) describe a boy's reactions to his irresponsible parents
   (C) portray a selfish and unfeeling mother and son
   (D) recount an outsider's impressions of an odd family
   (E) advocate an unusual educational experiment

25. It can be inferred from lines 10–25 that the reason for the Moreens' sudden departure from Nice had to do with
   (A) ill health
   (B) changes in climate
   (C) educational opportunities
   (D) financial problems
   (E) shifts of mood

26. According to lines 17–25, Pemberton's visit to Paris can be described as all of the following EXCEPT
   (A) gratifying
   (B) sudden
   (C) instructive
   (D) elegant
   (E) frugal

27. Lines 30–35 suggest that the narrator is making these comments about Pemberton's travels with the Moreen family
   (A) on Pemberton's return with the Moreens to Nice
   (B) in response to visiting Paris for the first time
   (C) some time after Pemberton's wanderings with the Moreens
   (D) in answer to Morgan's questions about his childhood
   (E) in an effort to write down his memoirs

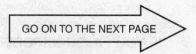

GO ON TO THE NEXT PAGE

28. The tone of Morgan's speech to his tutor (lines 45–46) can best be described as

    (A) apathetic
    (B) bitter
    (C) teasing
    (D) exasperated
    (E) self-righteous

29. The statement that "the deficiencies of his own wardrobe were a chapter by themselves" (lines 49–50) serves to

    (A) indicate the author's intention to cover this topic in a separate chapter
    (B) separate Pemberton's problems from those of Morgan and the rest of the Moreens
    (C) suggest that Pemberton was allotted insufficient closet space by the Moreens
    (D) establish Pemberton's inability to learn to dress himself appropriately
    (E) convey Pemberton's sensitivity about the disreputable state of his clothes

30. According to lines 61–67, Mrs. Moreen most likely ceases to spend money on new clothing for Morgan because

    (A) she and her husband have grown increasingly miserly with the passage of time
    (B) the child is so small for his age that he needs little in the way of clothing
    (C) she is unwilling to offend Pemberton by dressing his pupil in finer garments than Pemberton can afford
    (D) she resents the child and intentionally neglects him, spending money on herself that should be his
    (E) she has only enough money to buy clothes for those family members who must appear in polite society

31. As described in lines 41–67, Mrs. Moreen's approach toward Morgan can best be described as

    (A) stern but nurturing

(B) fond but pragmatic
(C) cruel and unfeeling
(D) tentative but loving
(E) doting and overprotective

32. Morgan and Pemberton regard the "hand-to-mouth multitude" of Paris (lines 77–83) with a sense of

    (A) amusement
    (B) condescension
    (C) indifference
    (D) identification
    (E) resentment

33. The author most likely describes the galleries of the Louvre as "so splendidly ironical to the homeless" because

    (A) homeless and other destitute people are not allowed within the museum
    (B) people in the galleries make sarcastic comments about poorly dressed museum goers
    (C) the Louvre originated as a shelter for the homeless of Paris
    (D) their opulence contrasts so markedly with the poverty of those who lack homes
    (E) the museum does an excellent job of teaching poor people about different styles of life

34. The word "smart" in line 93 means

    (A) intelligent
    (B) painful
    (C) fashionable
    (D) impudent
    (E) resourceful

35. An aspect of Pemberton's character that is made particularly clear in the final paragraph is his

    (A) tendency to joke about serious matters
    (B) longing to have a younger brother
    (C) concern for how he appears to others
    (D) reluctance to accept gifts from Morgan
    (E) pride in his identification with the poor

## STOP

**IF YOU FINISH BEFORE TIME IS CALLED, YOU MAY CHECK YOUR WORK ON THIS SECTION ONLY. DO NOT WORK ON ANY OTHER SECTION IN THE TEST.**

3  3  3  3  3  3  3  3  3  3  3

## Section 3

TIME—15 MINUTES
13 QUESTIONS

For each question in this section, choose the best answer and fill in the appropriate circle on the answer sheet.

Directions: The two passages below are followed by questions based on their content and on the relationship between the two passages. Answer the questions on the basis of what is stated or implied in the passages and in any introductory material that may be provided.

### Questions 1–13 are based on the following passages.

*The following passages concern the learning and behavior of infants during the first months of life. The first passage comes from a popular guide for new parents, the second from a textbook on child development.*

### Passage 1

The two-month-old baby has hardly roused himself from the long night of his first weeks in this world when he is confronted
Line with some of the profound problems of the
(5)  race. We invite him to study the nature of reality, to differentiate self and non-self, and to establish useful criteria in each of these categories. A project of such magnitude in academic research would require extensive labora-
(10) tory equipment and personnel; to be fair about it, it has taken just that to reconstruct the experiments of the infant. And there are few grown and fully accredited scientists who can equal the infant for zeal and energy in sorting
(15) out the raw data in this project. His equipment is limited to his sensory organs, his hands, his mouth, and a primitive memory apparatus.
At two months, as we have seen, he recognizes an object that *we* know to be a human
(20) face and we know to be an object outside himself. But to the baby this is just an image, an image incidentally that he can't differentiate from the mental image, the picture in memory. But this face is one piece in the jigsaw puz-
(25) zle—a key piece, we think. Then gradually in the weeks to come the association of breast or bottle, of hands, voice, a multitude of pleasurable sense experiences begin to cluster around this face and to form the crude image of a
(30) person.
Meantime the infant is conducting a series of complicated experiments in sensory discrimination. We must remember that in the early months he does not discriminate
(35) between his body and other bodies. When he clutches the finger of his mother or his father he doesn't see it as someone else's finger and his behavior indicates that he treats it exactly the same as he does his own finger. It takes
(40) him some time, in fact, to recognize his own hand at sight and to acquire even a rudimentary feeling that this is part of his own body. In the first group of experiments he discovers that the object that passes occasionally in front
(45) of his eyes (which *we* know to be his hand) is the same as the object with visual and taste qualities that he can identify. In another experimental series he discovers that the sensations that accompany the introduction of *this* object
(50) into his mouth are different from those experienced when he takes a nipple into his mouth, or a toy, or his mother's or father's finger.

### Passage 2

Very soon after birth, environmental forces, or response contingencies, begin to
(55) operate in conjunction with the infant's

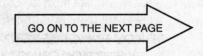

GO ON TO THE NEXT PAGE

built-in response repertoire to produce learned changes in behavior. It will not be long before the baby, instead of awaiting a touch near the mouth to open it, will do so when the bottle or (60) nipple is seen approaching it. Or the head may be turned in the appropriate direction when the baby is placed in the accustomed feeding posture. Such anticipatory gestures symbolize the essence of learning. Such response systems (65) are the classically conditioned or Pavlovian variety, because they involve elicited behavior.

Operant conditioning is in a sense also anticipatory; the infant makes a response presumably in anticipation of receiving a reward. (70) Response consequences serve as reinforcers of the behavior, then, and tend to perpetuate the behavior. Thus an infant who spontaneously makes a sound, which is then followed by an attractive consequence such as sweet fluid or (75) the smiling presence of the mother, will very likely repeat the act with increasing frequency as time (and reinforcement) goes on. Similarly, a response which is followed by an aversive consequence, such as a frightening (80) noise, will tend not to be repeated in the future. The infant thus behaves in accordance with expectations about the availability of positive reinforcers or punishments, based upon past experience.

(85) It must be clear by now that thought begins at birth. There are psychologists who would not want to term the anticipatory gestures just spoken of as thought. Even they, however, would have difficulty pinpointing (90) the stage of development or learning at which the onset of thought occurs. It is perhaps more meaningful to speak of increasing levels of symbolization.

A number of developmental theorists have (95) postulated stages of thought development. While no two systems or theories of cognition or thought development are exactly the same, most are agreed that the baby begins with a primitive appreciation of what is there and (100) what is not, and most agree that early in life what is not there is unimportant to the child. Only with increasing cortical development, cognitive complexity, and experience in sens-

ing, perceiving, and storing information does (105) the child begin to take into consideration the current absence of past stimulation and to consider how things are different or might be different than they are. Such "mental manipulations" occur later and set the stage for very (110) symbolic higher thought processes of which mature persons are capable.

1. By stating that a two-month-old baby confronts "some of the profound problems of the race" (lines 1–5), the author means that the infant

(A) will start to figure out what is real and what is imaginary
(B) is far more intelligent that we may think
(C) begins to understand that dreams are not real
(D) begins to locate its physical boundaries
(E) soon learns to communicate with the world outside itself.

2. The author of Passage 1 compares a baby with a scientist (lines 12–15) in order to make the point that

(A) the infant is tireless in its efforts to understand its environment
(B) the infant uses a form of the scientific method
(C) scientific experimentation is very time-consuming
(D) an infant is a human laboratory
(E) many scientific studies have been done on how infants learn

3. The author of Passage 1 apparently believes that during infancy learning begins with

(A) feeling loved
(B) the baby's senses
(C) images that the infant sees
(D) ideas stored in the infant's memory
(E) repetition of certain sights and sounds

GO ON TO THE NEXT PAGE ⟹

4. The account in Passage 1 of how an infant learns to discriminate between its own body and the body of others suggests that

    (A) all babies follow one of several well-defined patterns
    (B) the sequence is highly structured and precise
    (C) some babies learn more quickly than others
    (D) there are several different theories about how the process works
    (E) male babies learn differently from female babies

5. Based on Passage 1, an important milestone in infant development apparently occurs when a baby learns

    (A) to grasp someone else's finger with its hand
    (B) to remember objects like a mother's face even when the object is out of sight
    (C) that its mother and father have different faces
    (D) that its own hand has a distinctive smell and taste
    (E) that its own hand is different from another person's hand

6. The behavior of infants discussed in the first paragraph of Passage 2 occurs because

    (A) infants feel emotions just as adults do
    (B) every baby responds to the environment in certain predictable ways
    (C) every baby is born with certain instincts
    (D) infants naturally learn to respond to certain stimuli in the environment
    (E) healthy babies do not need to be taught to ingest food

7. The author uses the phrase "classically conditioned" response system (lines 64–66), to mean that infants

    (A) use built-in response contingencies to satisfy their basic needs
    (B) cry when they are hungry
    (C) respond to their environment early in life
    (D) can be trained to learn from their environment
    (E) learn to elicit certain behaviors from their caregivers

8. With regard to an infant's capacity to think, the author of Passage 2 believes that

    (A) newborns are capable of thought
    (B) thought develops even without external stimulation
    (C) real thought does not occur until an infant has had some experience
    (D) the development of memory triggers thought
    (E) all newborns have the same thoughts

9. The author suggests that the term "symbolization" (line 93) be used to refer to

    (A) fright that infants feel after hearing a loud noise
    (B) vivid images in an infant's mind
    (C) the difference between positive and negative reinforcement
    (D) a form of mental activity occurring in an infant
    (E) an infant's memory

10. Passage 2 implies that one can determine the maturity of people's thought processes by

    (A) observing their capacity to think abstractly
    (B) measuring the speed at which their minds work
    (C) checking their rate of intellectual growth
    (D) assessing the size of their memory banks
    (E) evaluating their ability to retain information

11. The authors of both passages agree that early in life a newborn learns

    (A) to manipulate ideas in a primitive form
    (B) to differentiate between things that are not there and things that are
    (C) what to do when it feels discomfort
    (D) to distinguish between behaviors that provide pleasure and behaviors that don't
    (E) to influence the immediate environment

GO ON TO THE NEXT PAGE

3 3 3 3 3 3 3 3 3 3 3

12. Compared to Passage 1, Passage 2 places more emphasis on the
    (A) research being done to understand new-born infants
    (B) parents' role in helping an infant develop
    (C) external indications of an infant's thought patterns
    (D) emotional growth of infants
    (E) psychology of thought development

13. In contrast to the author of Passage 2, the author of Passage 1 describes the development of an infant's thought with greater
    (A) attention to theory
    (B) authority
    (C) seriousness of purpose
    (D) scientific evidence
    (E) accuracy

# STOP

**IF YOU FINISH BEFORE TIME IS CALLED, YOU MAY CHECK YOUR WORK ON THIS SECTION ONLY. DO NOT WORK ON ANY OTHER SECTION IN THE TEST.**

# ANSWER KEY

## Section 1

| | | | | | | | | | |
|---|---|---|---|---|---|---|---|---|---|
| 1. **D** | 4. **A** | 7. **C** | 10. **B** | 13. **D** | 16. **D** | 19. **D** | 22. **C** | 25. **C** | 28. **D** |
| 2. **A** | 5. **B** | 8. **C** | 11. **E** | 14. **E** | 17. **C** | 20. **D** | 23. **E** | 26. **A** | 29. **D** |
| 3. **A** | 6. **B** | 9. **C** | 12. **D** | 15. **B** | 18. **C** | 21. **D** | 24. **D** | 27. **B** | 30. **E** |

## Section 2

| | | | | | | | | | |
|---|---|---|---|---|---|---|---|---|---|
| 1. **D** | 5. **A** | 9. **A** | 13. **B** | 17. **C** | 21. **A** | 24. **D** | 27. **C** | 30. **E** | 33. **D** |
| 2. **D** | 6. **B** | 10. **C** | 14. **A** | 18. **A** | 22. **E** | 25. **D** | 28. **C** | 31. **B** | 34. **C** |
| 3. **B** | 7. **E** | 11. **D** | 15. **A** | 19. **D** | 23. **B** | 26. **D** | 29. **E** | 32. **D** | 35. **C** |
| 4. **B** | 8. **E** | 12. **D** | 16. **A** | 20. **A** | | | | | |

## Section 3

| | | | | | | |
|---|---|---|---|---|---|---|
| 1. **D** | 3. **B** | 5. **E** | 7. **C** | 9. **D** | 11. **B** | 13. **B** |
| 2. **A** | 4. **B** | 6. **D** | 8. **A** | 10. **A** | 12. **E** | |

## ANALYSIS OF TEST RESULTS

### I.  Self-Rating Chart

| | | | | Total |
|---|---|---|---|---|
| **Sentence Completions**<br>Number Correct | Section 1<br>(Questions 1–9)<br>8 | Section 2<br>(Questions 1–10)<br>10 | | 18 |
| **Analogies**<br>Number Correct | Section 1<br>(Questions 10–15)<br>6 | Section 2<br>(Questions 11–23)<br>9 | | 15 |
| **Critical Reading**<br>Number Correct | Section 1<br>(Questions 16–30)<br>13 | Section 2<br>(Questions 24–35)<br>5 | Section 3<br>(Questions 1–13)<br>5 | 23 |

Sentence Completions        Number Correct ___18___
Analogies        Number Correct ___15___
Critical Reasoning        Number Correct ___23___
Subtotal ___56___
*Guessing Penalty:* Subtract 1/4 point for each incorrect answer.    _____
(Do not take off points for questions you left blank.)
TOTAL SCORE ___56.___

### II. Rate Your Performance

| | Sentence Completion/Analogy Score | Reading Score | Total |
|---|---|---|---|
| Excellent | 18–19 Correct | 37–40 | 73–78 |
| Very Good | 14–17 Correct | 27–36 | 55–72 |
| Good | 11–13 Correct | 19–26 | 41–54 |
| Fair | 9–10 Correct | 15–18 | 33–40 |
| Poor | 6–8  Correct | 10–14 | 20–32 |
| Very Poor | 0–5  Correct | 0–9 | 0–19 |

# ANSWER EXPLANATIONS

## SECTION 1

1. **D**  Salt eats away iron bars, turning them into rusty mush, by the process known as corrosion; it is a highly *corrosive* substance.
2. **A**  Until the 1960s, the work of African-American cartoonists was largely limited or *confined* to African-American publications; their cartoons generally did not appear in the mainstream, general press.
3. **A**  The writer is criticizing Bloom's book, which is *marred* (damaged) by its *slipshod* or sloppy style. *Although* is a contrast signal. Its use signals that the writer is *not* satisfied by Bloom's book.
4. **A**  The actress thinks out every move she makes. Consequently, her performance is not *spontaneous* (unplanned, impulsive).
5. **B**  To wander away from one's subject is to *digress*; the students enjoyed the professor's *digressions* or departures from the assigned topic.
6. **B**  Because sociobiology combines aspects of two fields it is a *hybrid* or combined discipline (just as a mule, the offspring of a horse and an ass, is a hybrid animal).
7. **C**  Miss Watson asserts (*pronounces*) that Huck cannot be reformed; she calls him *incorrigible* (uncorrectable). *Though* is a contrast signal. Its use signals that, unlike her widowed sister, Miss Watson has *no* hope of being able to reform Huck.
8. **C**  By definition, a *martinet* (stickler for discipline) would want his subordinates to follow orders *promptly*.
9. **C**  Rather than moving *inexorably* (relentlessly, unstoppably) closer to its goals, the field is stuck or *mired in* its usual problems.
    The phrase "far from" is a contrast signal. Its use signals that the second missing word means the opposite of "moving *inexorably* closer."
10. **B**  Chicken *eggs* develop into *chickens*; tulip *bulbs* develop into *tulips*.
11. **E**  A *locker* is a storage place for *clothing*; a *vault* is a storage place for *valuables*.
12. **D**  To *launch* a *product* is to put it into operation, introducing it to the public. Similarly, to *initiate* or begin an *enterprise* (business venture) is to put it into operation.
13. **D**  A *glutton* (person who eats and drinks to excess) by definition is not noted for *moderation* or restraint; a *miser* (person who hoards money) by definition is not noted for *generosity*.
14. **E**  A *shard* is a broken fragment of *pottery*; a *splinter* is a broken fragment of *glass*.
15. **B**  An *enigma* (mystery; puzzle) is by definition *puzzling*; a *reproof* (rebuke; censure) is by definition *critical*.
16. **D**  Picasso admitted that at the time he was working on *Les Demoiselles* "he was much interested in Iberian" or ancient Spanish sculpture. Thus, *he may have been influenced by ancient Spanish art*.
17. **C**  Picasso had been moved in the past to *rethink completed works*. "Only a year before, stimulated by Iberian sculpture, he had repainted the head of Gertrude Stein's portrait months after he had completed the rest of the picture."
18. **C**  In asserting that Picasso's memory might have been inaccurate and that he might have repainted the heads after his discovery of African sculpture, the author is *making a hypothesis* about what actually took place.
19. **D**  Picasso was in the sculpture galleries of the Trocadero when he ran across African carvings.
20. **D**  The title has been given to this period or *used to designate* it, distinguishing it from his art of earlier times.

21. **D**   The author asserts that experts today agree the *Woman in Yellow* is quite closely related to Iberian bronze statues. To back up this assertion, he cites Sweeney's observation that the *Woman in Yellow* looks remarkably similar to an ancient votive figure from Despenaperros. Thus, it seems most likely that Despenaperros is *a location on the Iberian peninsula* associated with ancient Iberian bronzes.

22. **C**   If "the best speaker" has the most influence in the Indians' counsels, clearly the Indian leaders maintain their authority by means of their *verbal prowess* or skill.

23. **E**   To dress food is to *prepare* it so that it can be cooked.

24. **D**   According to Franklin, they have abundance of leisure because they have "few artificial wants." They work only to satisfy their simple physical needs. Compared to the whites' laborious manner of life, theirs is a *simpler, more natural lifestyle*.

25. **C**   Just before he quotes the speech, Franklin states that the Indians look on the learning of the whites as useless. In recounting this instance of Indian diplomacy, he is *giving an example of the Indian viewpoint on the benefits of white civilization*.

26. **A**   In assuring the commissioners that they recognize both the commissioners' good intentions and wisdom, the Indians are being most diplomatic. However, they are not agreeing to the commissioners' offer. Instead, they are declining or *tactfully refusing* it.

27. **B**   While the education provided the Indians in the colleges of the northern provinces included all the white men's sciences, it did not prepare these young men for life in the woods. Thus, it did not meet the Indian elders' educational goals. It is clear that the Indians and the gentlemen of Virginia *have different educational goals*.

28. **D**   To take a deer in this context is to *catch* it; the speaker is describing how the white man's education fails to prepare young men to become hunters.

29. **D**   The Indians state that a white college education made worthless good-for-nothings out of young Indians. They also assert that they can make men out of the Virginian commissioners' sons. Thus, it seems likely that the Indians would agree that they *have a better way of educating young men than the commissioners do*.

30. **E**   In expressing their gratitude for the offer and thanking the Virginians for their intent, the Indians are being most *courteous*. In making the Virginians an offer they realize the Virginians are unlikely to accept, they are somewhat *ironic* as well.

# SECTION 2

1. **D**   One would expect restoration and cleaning to enhance or improve the murals' colors. Instead, the colors *deteriorated* or grew worse.

2. **D**   In contrast to the loneliness of writing, Mr. Doyle appreciates the *sociability* of working with others on films.

3. **B**   This important trade involving *vast* quantities of textiles was so vital to the economy that not even a war could stop it. Thus, it *continued* or kept on taking place through the Revolutionary War.

4. **B**   The astronomers resemble the doctors in their use of X rays to examine things that are concealed or *hidden*.

5. **A**   The phrase "anything but" signals an extreme degree of contrast. When trees go dormant, the process is decidedly not *sleepy* or sluggish, and the change is extreme or *radical*.

6. **B**   Lavish carvings decorating a throne are a form of *embellishment* (decoration; ornamentation).

7. **E**   "But" signals a contrast. Though one can dispute the way the author treats certain details, one cannot find fault with her main arguments or theses. They are *irreproachable* (flawless; blameless).

8. **E**   Oates has invented or *coined* a new word to *describe* a particular genre.

9. **A**   To be rebuffed is to be rejected or slighted. Being ignored by one's co-workers could make an *outgoing*, sociable person become unsociable and *withdrawn*.

10. **C** By definition, a *monolith* is something solidly uniform, an undifferentiated whole. Black America, however, is a mix of different attitudes and opinions; it is not monolithic at all.

11. **D** A *name tag* identifies a *person*. A *label* identifies a *product*.

12. **D** An *actor* wanting to be considered for a role may have to face an *audition* (tryout). An *applicant* wanting to be considered for a job may have to face an *interview*.

13. **B** *Helium* may be stored in a *tank*. *Wine* may be stored in a *cask*.

14. **A** To *kindle* a *fire* is to start it or bring it into being. To *incite* a *riot* is to start it or bring it into being.

15. **A** To *dismount* is to get off a *horse*. To *disembark* is to get off a *ship*.

16. **A** By definition, a *hutch* is a pen for *rabbits*. By definition, a *coop* is a cage or pen for *chickens*.

17. **C** By definition, a *tattletale reveals* or tells what he or she knows. By definition, a *miser hoards* or saves up what he or she possesses.

18. **A** To *scale* a *fish* is to scrape off its scales. To *pluck* a *chicken* is to pull off its feathers.

19. **D** To *tussle* or scuffle is less formal than to *duel*. To *squabble* or bicker is less formal than to *debate*.

20. **A** One *plows* a *field* to get it ready for planting. One *primes* a *surface* to get it ready for painting.

21. **A** A *frame* is one picture of a series making up a *film*. A *panel* is one picture of a series making up a *cartoon*.

22. **E** By definition, *claustrophobia* is abnormal fear of *confinement*, of being closed in. By definition, *acrophobia* is abnormal fear of *heights*.

23. **B** By definition, someone *cognizant* or conscious of something exhibits *awareness*. By definition, someone *restive* or contrary about something exhibits *impatience*.

24. **D** The tutor, who is not related to the Moreens and is therefore an outsider to the group, is telling the story of his relationship to this unusual family.

25. **D** The Moreens' sudden shifts are apparently motivated by financial problems, for the class they travel in and the apartment they stay in vary with their financial state.

26. **D** Living as he did in a small, uncomfortable apartment and dressing shabbily in threadbare clothes, Pemberton led an *inelegant* life during his visit to Paris.

    Use the process of elimination to answer this question. Pemberton's visit to Paris was *gratifying*; he found his rambles with Morgan rewarding. You can eliminate (A).

    Pemberton's visit to Paris was *sudden*; the Moreens suddenly gave up their villa in Nice and headed for Paris. You can eliminate (B).

    Pemberton's visit to Paris was *instructive*; he and Morgan "learned to know their Paris." You can eliminate (C).

    Pemberton's visit to Paris was *frugal*; he and Morgan seldom had any money, and when they did have some, they were very careful about what they spent it on. You can eliminate (E).

27. **C** Lines 30–35 state that the Moreens "came back another year for a longer stay, the general character of which in Pemberton's memory today mixes pitiably and confusedly with that of the first." The narrator's reference to "Pemberton's memory *today*" indicates that he is speaking *some time after* the events recounted in this tale. The narrator is telling the story of events his friend Pemberton remembers from years past.

28. **C** In telling his tutor that he does not wish to outshine him or cast him in the shade by dressing better than he does, Morgan is affectionately *teasing* Pemberton.

29. **E** To say that something is a chapter by itself is a way of saying that it would take an entire chapter of a book to deal with that subject fully. Thus, Pemberton is asserting that his wardrobe's shortcomings are *major*. Clearly, he is *sensitive about the disreputable state of his clothes*.

30. **E** Mrs. Moreen does not spend money for new clothes for Morgan because he does not make public appearances, that is, does not appear in "polite society." She does spend money on new clothes for the family members who move in polite circles. She loves Morgan and does not neglect him intentionally. This suggests that *she has only enough money to buy clothes for those family members who must appear in polite society*.

31. **B** Mrs. Moreen loves Morgan ("Morgan was dear to his mother"), but she shrewdly refrains from buying him new clothes when she realizes that nobody "important" will see how he is dressed. Her attitude is *fond* (loving) *but pragmatic* (practical).

32. **D**    Morgan and Pemberton consider themselves "part of the vast vague hand-to-mouth multitude of" Paris and feel conscious of being part of a "democratic brotherhood." Thus, on some levels, even if partly in jest, they *identify* with the poor.

33. **D**    Here the irony lies in the *contrast* between the splendors of the great museum and the shabbiness of the poor and homeless who flock to it for shelter and a bit of warmth.

34. **C**    A young patrician is the child of an aristocratic family. Given Morgan's shabby clothing, he does not look smart or *fashionable* enough for people to consider him a member of the aristocracy.

35. **C**    The opening sentence of the final paragraph states that Pemberton was "quite aware of how he and his comrade might strike people." The paragraph then proceeds to give examples of Pemberton's self-consciousness about appearances, as he wonders "what people would think they were" and fancies or imagines they are getting odd looks from people because they are such a mismatched pair. Clearly, the paragraph particularly brings home Pemberton's *concern for how he appears to others*.

# SECTION 3

1. **D**    The phrase refers to the task of differentiating "self and non-self." In other words, the infant begins to *locate its physical boundaries*, learning where its own body ends and the rest of the world begins.

2. **A**    The passage says that few scientists "can equal the infant for zeal and energy." An infant, therefore, is *tireless in its efforts* to figure things out.

3. **B**    Throughout the passage, the author points out the vital role of the *baby's senses* in learning. See, for example, "sensory organs" (lines 15–17), "sense experiences" (lines 25–30), and "sensory discrimination" (lines 31–33).

4. **B**    The infant conducts a step-by-step "series of complicated experiments," which can only be described as *highly structured and precise*.

5. **E**    In lines 47–52 the passage describes the infant's discovery that *its own hand is different from another person's hand*.

6. **D**    The fundamental principle of stimulus-response behavior, which is discussed in the passage, is that organisms, including infants, *naturally learn to respond to certain stimuli* in their environment.

7. **C**    Stimulus-response conditioning is a "classical," universally-acknowledged principle of behavioral psychology. We see evidence of it in newborns when they *respond to their environment early in life*. Pavlov, whose experiments with dogs is widely known, was one of the first scientists to describe the principle.

8. **A**    The author states that *newborns are capable of thought* in lines 85–86.

9. **D**    Because psychologists cannot agree on a precise definition of "thought," the author suggests "symbolization" as an alternative word to describe *the activity that takes place in an infant's mind*.

10. **A**    Mature thought is that which allows the mind to "consider how things are different or might be different than they are." Such speculation demonstrates *a capacity to think abstractly*.

11. **B**    Much of Passage 1 discusses how newborns begin *to differentiate between things that are not there and things that are*. In Passage 2 the author states that "the baby begins with a primitive appreciation of what is there and what is not."

12. **E**    Passage 1 stresses the behavior that a parent might observe as a newborn infant learns to think. Passage 2, on the other hand, focuses on behavior in terms of the *psychology of thought development*.

13. **B**    Passage 2 is written more tentatively. That is, the author recognizes that many assertions regarding infant thought are theoretical and that not all psychologists agree on every theory. In comparison, Passage 1 sounds like the voice of *authority*. This is probably as it should be, for nervous parents want to be told exactly what is going on with their newborns.

## ANSWER SHEET FOR VERBAL REASONING TEST 2

### Section 1

1. Ⓐ Ⓑ Ⓒ Ⓓ Ⓔ
2. Ⓐ Ⓑ Ⓒ Ⓓ Ⓔ
3. Ⓐ Ⓑ Ⓒ Ⓓ Ⓔ
4. Ⓐ Ⓑ Ⓒ Ⓓ Ⓔ
5. Ⓐ Ⓑ Ⓒ Ⓓ Ⓔ
6. Ⓐ Ⓑ Ⓒ Ⓓ Ⓔ
7. Ⓐ Ⓑ Ⓒ Ⓓ Ⓔ
8. Ⓐ Ⓑ Ⓒ Ⓓ Ⓔ
9. Ⓐ Ⓑ Ⓒ Ⓓ Ⓔ
10. Ⓐ Ⓑ Ⓒ Ⓓ Ⓔ
11. Ⓐ Ⓑ Ⓒ Ⓓ Ⓔ
12. Ⓐ Ⓑ Ⓒ Ⓓ Ⓔ
13. Ⓐ Ⓑ Ⓒ Ⓓ Ⓔ
14. Ⓐ Ⓑ Ⓒ Ⓓ Ⓔ
15. Ⓐ Ⓑ Ⓒ Ⓓ Ⓔ
16. Ⓐ Ⓑ Ⓒ Ⓓ Ⓔ
17. Ⓐ Ⓑ Ⓒ Ⓓ Ⓔ
18. Ⓐ Ⓑ Ⓒ Ⓓ Ⓔ
19. Ⓐ Ⓑ Ⓒ Ⓓ Ⓔ
20. Ⓐ Ⓑ Ⓒ Ⓓ Ⓔ
21. Ⓐ Ⓑ Ⓒ Ⓓ Ⓔ
22. Ⓐ Ⓑ Ⓒ Ⓓ Ⓔ
23. Ⓐ Ⓑ Ⓒ Ⓓ Ⓔ
24. Ⓐ Ⓑ Ⓒ Ⓓ Ⓔ
25. Ⓐ Ⓑ Ⓒ Ⓓ Ⓔ
26. Ⓐ Ⓑ Ⓒ Ⓓ Ⓔ
27. Ⓐ Ⓑ Ⓒ Ⓓ Ⓔ
28. Ⓐ Ⓑ Ⓒ Ⓓ Ⓔ
29. Ⓐ Ⓑ Ⓒ Ⓓ Ⓔ
30. Ⓐ Ⓑ Ⓒ Ⓓ Ⓔ

### Section 2

1. Ⓐ Ⓑ Ⓒ Ⓓ Ⓔ
2. Ⓐ Ⓑ Ⓒ Ⓓ Ⓔ
3. Ⓐ Ⓑ Ⓒ Ⓓ Ⓔ
4. Ⓐ Ⓑ Ⓒ Ⓓ Ⓔ
5. Ⓐ Ⓑ Ⓒ Ⓓ Ⓔ
6. Ⓐ Ⓑ Ⓒ Ⓓ Ⓔ
7. Ⓐ Ⓑ Ⓒ Ⓓ Ⓔ
8. Ⓐ Ⓑ Ⓒ Ⓓ Ⓔ
9. Ⓐ Ⓑ Ⓒ Ⓓ Ⓔ
10. Ⓐ Ⓑ Ⓒ Ⓓ Ⓔ
11. Ⓐ Ⓑ Ⓒ Ⓓ Ⓔ
12. Ⓐ Ⓑ Ⓒ Ⓓ Ⓔ
13. Ⓐ Ⓑ Ⓒ Ⓓ Ⓔ
14. Ⓐ Ⓑ Ⓒ Ⓓ Ⓔ
15. Ⓐ Ⓑ Ⓒ Ⓓ Ⓔ
16. Ⓐ Ⓑ Ⓒ Ⓓ Ⓔ
17. Ⓐ Ⓑ Ⓒ Ⓓ Ⓔ
18. Ⓐ Ⓑ Ⓒ Ⓓ Ⓔ
19. Ⓐ Ⓑ Ⓒ Ⓓ Ⓔ
20. Ⓐ Ⓑ Ⓒ Ⓓ Ⓔ
21. Ⓐ Ⓑ Ⓒ Ⓓ Ⓔ
22. Ⓐ Ⓑ Ⓒ Ⓓ Ⓔ
23. Ⓐ Ⓑ Ⓒ Ⓓ Ⓔ
24. Ⓐ Ⓑ Ⓒ Ⓓ Ⓔ
25. Ⓐ Ⓑ Ⓒ Ⓓ Ⓔ
26. Ⓐ Ⓑ Ⓒ Ⓓ Ⓔ
27. Ⓐ Ⓑ Ⓒ Ⓓ Ⓔ
28. Ⓐ Ⓑ Ⓒ Ⓓ Ⓔ
29. Ⓐ Ⓑ Ⓒ Ⓓ Ⓔ
30. Ⓐ Ⓑ Ⓒ Ⓓ Ⓔ
31. Ⓐ Ⓑ Ⓒ Ⓓ Ⓔ
32. Ⓐ Ⓑ Ⓒ Ⓓ Ⓔ
33. Ⓐ Ⓑ Ⓒ Ⓓ Ⓔ
34. Ⓐ Ⓑ Ⓒ Ⓓ Ⓔ
35. Ⓐ Ⓑ Ⓒ Ⓓ Ⓔ

### Section 3

1. Ⓐ Ⓑ Ⓒ Ⓓ Ⓔ
2. Ⓐ Ⓑ Ⓒ Ⓓ Ⓔ
3. Ⓐ Ⓑ Ⓒ Ⓓ Ⓔ
4. Ⓐ Ⓑ Ⓒ Ⓓ Ⓔ
5. Ⓐ Ⓑ Ⓒ Ⓓ Ⓔ
6. Ⓐ Ⓑ Ⓒ Ⓓ Ⓔ
7. Ⓐ Ⓑ Ⓒ Ⓓ Ⓔ
8. Ⓐ Ⓑ Ⓒ Ⓓ Ⓔ
9. Ⓐ Ⓑ Ⓒ Ⓓ Ⓔ
10. Ⓐ Ⓑ Ⓒ Ⓓ Ⓔ
11. Ⓐ Ⓑ Ⓒ Ⓓ Ⓔ
12. Ⓐ Ⓑ Ⓒ Ⓓ Ⓔ
13. Ⓐ Ⓑ Ⓒ Ⓓ Ⓔ

`1` 1 1 1 1 1 1 1 1 1 1 1 `1`

# VERBAL REASONING TEST 2
## Section 1

TIME—30 MINUTES
30 QUESTIONS

For each of the following questions, select the best answer from the choices provided and fill in the appropriate circle on the answer sheet.

---

<u>Directions:</u> Each sentence below has one or two blanks, each blank indicating that something has been omitted. Beneath the sentence are five words or sets of words labeled A through E. Choose the word or set of words that, when inserted in the sentence, <u>best</u> fits the meaning of the sentence as a whole.

Example:

Medieval kingdoms did not become constitutional republics overnight; on the contrary, the change was ____.

(A) unpopular
(B) unexpected
(C) advantageous
(D) sufficient
(E) gradual

Ⓐ Ⓑ Ⓒ Ⓓ ●

---

1. Just as all roads once led to Rome, all blood vessels in the human body ultimately ____ the heart.

    (A) detour around
    (B) shut off
    (C) empty into
    (D) look after
    (E) beat back

2. Supporters of the proposed waterway argue that it will ____ rather than ____ railroad facilities, since the waterway will be icebound during the only months when the railroads can absorb much traffic.

    (A) limit...extend
    (B) build...destroy
    (C) weaken...help
    (D) surpass...equal
    (E) supplement...threaten

3. One of photography's most basic and powerful traits is its ability to give substance to ____, to present precise visual details of a time gone by.

    (A) romance
    (B) premonition
    (C) mysticism
    (D) invisibility
    (E) history

4. Although he was widely celebrated as a radio and motion picture star in the 1940s, George Burns enjoyed his greatest ____ after his return to the screen in the "Oh God" films of the 1980s.

    (A) respite
    (B) collaboration
    (C) renown
    (D) disappointment
    (E) inducement

GO ON TO THE NEXT PAGE →

**1  1  1  1  1  1  1  1  1  1  1**

5. When Doctor Diamond's lab discovered that male and female sex hormones affect the outer layers of the brain in different ways, she was originally ____ to ____ the data because of possible misinterpretations.

   (A) hesitant…release
   (B) proud…distort
   (C) reluctant…assimilate
   (D) inclined…forge
   (E) pleased…locate

6. Despite some personal habits that most people would find repulsive, naked mole rats are ____ housekeepers.

   (A) slovenly
   (B) indifferent
   (C) meticulous
   (D) perfunctory
   (E) repugnant

7. The president was ____ about farm subsidies, nor did he say much about the even more ____ topic of unemployment.

   (A) expansive…interesting
   (B) wordy…important
   (C) uncommunicative…academic
   (D) noncommittal…vital
   (E) enthusiastic…stimulating

8. Biography is a literary genre whose primary ____ is an ability to ____ imaginatively the inner life of a subject on the basis of all the knowable external evidence.

   (A) requisite…reconstruct
   (B) consequence…disregard
   (C) peculiarity…envision
   (D) weapon…undermine
   (E) claim…counteract

9. As more people try to navigate the legal system by themselves, representing themselves in court and drawing up their own wills and contracts, the question arises whether they will be able to ____ judicial ____ without lawyers to guide them.

   (A) await…decisions
   (B) overturn…stipulations
   (C) avoid…quagmires
   (D) forfeit…penalties
   (E) arouse…enmity

GO ON TO THE NEXT PAGE

**1** 1 1 1 1 1 1 1 1 1 1 1 1 **1**

Directions: Each question below consists of a related pair of words or phrases, followed by five pairs of words or phrases labeled A through E. Select the pair that best expresses a relationship similar to that expressed in the original pair.

Example:

CRUMB : BREAD ::

(A) ounce : unit
(B) splinter : wood
(C) water : bucket
(D) twine : rope
(E) cream : butter

Ⓐ ● Ⓒ Ⓓ Ⓔ

10. RESIGN : CHAIRPERSON ::

   (A) abdicate : king
   (B) demote : student
   (C) install : officer
   (D) nominate : candidate
   (E) reelect : governor

11. RUNNERS : SLED ::

   (A) wheels : skateboard
   (B) dancers : stage
   (C) bricks : wall
   (D) chalk : blackboard
   (E) skiers : slope

12. DAMPEN : EAGERNESS ::

   (A) drench : flood
   (B) dominate : mastery
   (C) loosen : confinement
   (D) muffle : sound
   (E) divert : energy

13. ANNOYING : INSUFFERABLE ::

   (A) maddening : outrageous
   (B) nervous : impolite
   (C) chatty : long-winded
   (D) ungainly : graceful
   (E) conceited : apathetic

14. DIGRESSION : TOPIC ::

   (A) detour : itinerary
   (B) prologue : play
   (C) accident : vehicle
   (D) impasse : solution
   (E) reversal : fortune

15. TRUCE : FIGHTING ::

   (A) respite : labor
   (B) convalescence : illness
   (C) reprieve : crime
   (D) cessation : strike
   (E) arbitration : decision

GO ON TO THE NEXT PAGE

**1**   1   1   1   1   1   1   1   1   1   1   1   **1**

---

**Questions 16–21 are based on the following passage.**

*Largely unexplored, the canopy or treetop region of the tropical rain forest is one of the most diverse plant and animal communities on the earth. In this excerpt from a 1984 article on the rain forest canopy, the naturalist Donald R. Perry shares his observations of epiphytes, unusual plants that flourish in this treetop environment.*

The upper story of the rain forest incorporates two-thirds of its volume. This region can be divided arbitrarily into a lower canopy,
Line extending from 10 to 25 meters above the
(5)  ground, an upper canopy, reaching a height of 35 meters, and an emergent zone that encompasses the tops of the tallest trees, which commonly grow to heights of more than 50 meters. The canopy is well-lighted, in contrast
(10)  to the forest understory, which because of thick vegetation above receives only about 1 percent of the sunlight that falls on the treetops. In the canopy all but the smallest of the rain forest trees put forth their leaves, flowers
(15)  and fruit. It also contains many plants that exist entirely within its compass, forming vegetative communities that in number of species and complexity of interactions surpass any others on the earth.
(20)     Among the most conspicuous features of vegetation in the canopy of the tropical rain forest are epiphytes. About 28,000 species in 65 families are known worldwide, 15,500 of them in Central and South America; they
(25)  include species of orchids, bromeliads, and arboreal cacti as well as lower plants such as lichens, mosses, and ferns. Thousands more epiphyte varieties remain unidentified.
The Greek meaning of the word epiphyte
(30)  is "plant that grows on a plant," and they carpet tree trunks and branches. Epiphytes sprout from seeds borne by the wind or deposited by animals, their roots holding tight to the interstices of the bark. Yet they are nonparasitic;
(35)  their hosts provide them with nothing more than a favorable position in the brightly lighted canopy. For nourishment epiphytes depend on soil particles and dissolved minerals carried in rainwater, and on aerial deposits of
(40)  humus. The deposits are the product of organic debris, such as dead leaves from epiphytes and other plants, that lodges among epiphyte roots.
Water is directly available to epiphytes
(45)  only when it rains; other plants have continuous access to moisture trapped in the soil. As a result many epiphytes have developed features that collect and retain rainwater. Some, including orchids and arboreal cacti, have succulent
(50)  stems and leaves, with spongy tissues that store water, as well as waxy leaf coatings that reduce the loss of moisture through transpiration[1]. Many orchids have bulbous stem bases; other families of epiphytes impound water in
(55)  tanks formed by tight rosettes of leaves or in cups shaped by the junctions of broadened petioles[2] and stems. Some species possess absorbent, spongelike root masses that soak up and hold water. Bromeliads, a Central and
(60)  South American family, can hold reserves of several gallons within their cisternlike bases, forming "arboreal swamps" that attract insects of many species, earthworms, spiders, sow bugs, scorpions, tree frogs, and insect eating
(65)  birds.

---

[1] Passage of water through a plant to the atmosphere.
[2] Slender stalks that attach a leaf to the stem.

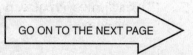
GO ON TO THE NEXT PAGE

1   1   1   1   1   1   1   1   1   1   1

16. In lines 9–13, the author characterizes the floor or understory of the rain forest as relatively

   (A) insignificant
   (B) windy
   (C) thick
   (D) obscure
   (E) voluminous

17. In line 16, "compass" most nearly means

   (A) a curved arc
   (B) an instrument for determining direction
   (C) passageway
   (D) boundaries
   (E) specifications

18. It can be inferred that which of the following is true of epiphytes?

   (A) They lack an adequate root system.
   (B) They cannot draw moisture from tree trunks.
   (C) They are incapable of transpiration.
   (D) They are hard to perceive in the dense rain forest canopy.
   (E) They originated in the Southern Hemisphere.

19. According to lines 46–48, epiphytes are particularly adapted to

   (A) independent growth
   (B) a cloudless environment
   (C) the dissipation of rainwater
   (D) drawing sustenance from a host
   (E) the retention of liquid

20. Epiphytes have direct access to water only when it rains because

   (A) they lack the ability to collect moisture
   (B) the frequency of rain keeps them excessively wet
   (C) the thick canopy protects them from rainstorms
   (D) they lack connections to water in the ground
   (E) dead leaves and other organic debris cover their roots

21. Desert cacti are likely to resemble arboreal cacti most in their

   (A) tolerance of extremes of heat and cold
   (B) dependence on tree trunks for support rather than nourishment
   (C) development of features to cut down the loss of moisture
   (D) lack of roots connecting them to the ground
   (E) absence of variations in size

**Questions 22–30 are based on the following passage.**

*In this excerpt from the novel* A Tale of Two Cities, *Charles Dickens describes the journey of a coach carrying mail and passengers to the seaport town of Dover.*

It was the Dover road that lay, on a Friday night late in November, before the first of the persons with whom this history has business.
*Line* The Dover road lay, as to him, beyond the
(5) Dover mail, as it lumbered up Shooter's Hill. He walked uphill in the mire by the side of the mail, as the rest of the passengers did; not because they had the least relish for walking exercise, under the circumstances, but because
(10) the hill, and the harness, and the mud, and the mail, were all so heavy, that the horses had three times already come to a stop, besides once drawing the coach across the road, with the mutinous intent of taking it back to
(15) Blackheath.
   With drooping heads and tremulous tails, the horses mashed their way through the thick mud, floundering and stumbling between whiles as if they were falling to pieces at the
(20) larger joints. As often as the driver rested them and brought them to a stand, with a wary "Wo-ho! so-ho then!" the near leader violently

GO ON TO THE NEXT PAGE

shook his head and everything upon it—like
an unusually emphatic horse, denying that the
(25) coach could be got up the hill. Whenever the
leader made this rattle, the passenger started,
as a nervous passenger might, and was disturbed in mind.

There was a steaming mist in all the hol-
(30) lows, and it had roamed in its forlornness up
the hill, like an evil spirit, seeking rest and
finding none. A clammy and intensely cold
mist, it made its slow way through the air in
ripples that visibly followed and overspread
(35) one another, as the waves of an unwholesome
sea might do. It was dense enough to shut out
everything from the light of the coachlamps
but these its own workings, and a few yards of
road; and the reek of the laboring horses
(40) steamed into it, as if they had made it all.

Two other passengers, besides the one,
were plodding up the hill by the side of the
mail. All three were wrapped to the cheek-
bones and over the ears, and wore jack-boots.
(45) Not one of the three could have said, from
anything he saw, what either of the other two
was like; and each was hidden under almost as
many wrappers from the eyes of the mind, as
from the eyes of the body, of his two compan-
(50) ions. In those days, travelers were very shy of
being confidential on a short notice, for anyone on the road might be a robber or in league
with robbers. As to the latter, when every post-
ing-house and ale-house could produce some-
(55) body in "the Captain's" pay, ranging from the
landlord to the lowest stable nondescript, it
was the likeliest thing upon the cards. So the
guard of the Dover mail thought to himself,
that Friday night in November, one thousand
(60) seven hundred and seventy-five, lumbering up
Shooter's Hill, as he stood on his own particular perch behind the mail, beating his feet, and
keeping an eye and a hand on the arm-chest
before him, where a loaded blunderbuss lay at
(65) the top of six or eight loaded horse-pistols,
deposited on a substratum of cutlass.

The Dover mail was in its usual genial
position that the guard suspected the passengers, the passengers suspected one another and

(70) the guard, they all suspected everybody else,
and the coachman was sure of nothing but the
horses; as to which cattle he could with a clear
conscience have taken his oath on the two
Testaments that they were not fit for the journey.

22. It can be inferred that the passengers are walking because

(A) they need fresh air and exercise
(B) they are afraid of being robbed
(C) their trip is over
(D) the guard is suspicious of them
(E) the coach cannot carry them uphill

23. In creating an impression of the mail coach's
uphill progress for the reader, the author uses
all of the following devices EXCEPT

(A) description of its surroundings
(B) humorous turns of phrase
(C) contrast with more attractive areas
(D) exaggerated comparisons
(E) references to geographic locations

24. The purpose cited as supporting the argument
that some brute animals are endowed with
Reason most likely is

(A) the driver's intent to use the whip to moti-
vate the horses
(B) the passengers' willingness to walk by the
side of the coach
(C) the horses' determination to turn back to
Blackheath
(D) the traveler's resolve to undertake such a
rugged journey
(E) the guard's aim to quell any manifestations
of mutiny

GO ON TO THE NEXT PAGE

**1    1   1   1   1   1   1   1   1   1   1   1**

25. The passage suggests that the rattle referred to in line 26 most likely was

    (A) the call of the driver to the horses to halt
    (B) the clatter of the wooden wheels upon the cobblestones
    (C) the jangle of the harness when the horse shook his head
    (D) the creaking of the wagon's joints under the strain
    (E) the sound of the coachman using his whip

26. In line 26, the word "started" most nearly means

    (A) began
    (B) jumped
    (C) set out
    (D) went first
    (E) activated

27. In lines 32–36, the author includes the description of the mist primarily to emphasize the

    (A) nearness of the sea
    (B) weariness of the travelers
    (C) gloominess of the surroundings
    (D) transience of the journey
    (E) lateness of the hour

28. The term "the Captain" in line 55 most likely refers to

    (A) the master of a sailing ship
    (B) a police officer
    (C) a highwayman
    (D) an innkeeper or hotel employee
    (E) a town official

29. The attitude of the passengers toward one another shown in lines 67–74 can best be described as

    (A) conspiratorial
    (B) guarded
    (C) benevolent
    (D) resentful
    (E) pugnacious

30. The use of the word "genial" in line 67 is an example of

    (A) understatement
    (B) archaism
    (C) simile
    (D) digression
    (E) irony

## STOP

**IF YOU FINISH BEFORE TIME IS CALLED, YOU MAY CHECK YOUR WORK ON THIS SECTION ONLY. DO NOT WORK ON ANY OTHER SECTION IN THE TEST.**

2 2 2 2 2 2 2 2 2 2 2

## Section 2

TIME—30 MINUTES
35 QUESTIONS
For each of the following questions, select the best answer from the choices provided and fill in the appropriate circle on the answer sheet.

---

Directions: Each sentence below has one or two blanks, each blank indicating that something has been omitted. Beneath the sentence are five words or sets of words labeled A through E. Choose the word or set of words that, when inserted in the sentence, best fits the meaning of the sentence as a whole.

Example:

Medieval kingdoms did not become constitutional republics overnight; on the contrary, the change was ____.

(A) unpopular
(B) unexpected
(C) advantageous
(D) sufficient
(E) gradual

Ⓐ Ⓑ Ⓒ Ⓓ ●

---

1. The museum administration appears to be singularly ____ the comforts of its employees, providing an employee health club, a lending library, and a part-time social worker to help staff members with financial or domestic problems.

    (A) ignorant of
    (B) indifferent to
    (C) attentive to
    (D) exploited by
    (E) uninvolved in

2. China's economic growth curve after reform resembles an airplane taking off, whereas the former Soviet Union's resembles a submarine ____.

    (A) floating
    (B) soaring
    (C) maneuvering
    (D) descending
    (E) veering

3. Trees native to warmer climates are genetically programmed for shorter, milder winters and are therefore ____ to both cold snaps and sudden thaws.

    (A) indifferent
    (B) restricted
    (C) vulnerable
    (D) accessible
    (E) attributed

4. Although, as wife of President John Adams, Abigail Adams sought a greater voice for women, she was not a feminist in the modern sense; she ____ the ____ view of women as "beings placed by providence" under male protection.

    (A) anticipated...current
    (B) regretted...heretical
    (C) distorted...outmoded
    (D) repudiated...radical
    (E) accepted...traditional

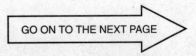
GO ON TO THE NEXT PAGE

2   2   2   2   2   2   2   2   2   2   2

5. An unattractive feature of this memoir is the casually dismissive, often downright ____, comments the author makes about almost all of her former colleagues.

   (A) elegiac
   (B) euphemistic
   (C) objective
   (D) contemptuous
   (E) laudatory

6. There was some stagecraft behind the supposedly ____ moments photographed by Doisneau; in a legal dispute last year, Doisneau ____ that he had paid two models to pose for his famous *The Kiss at the Hotel de Ville*.

   (A) innocent…disproved
   (B) candid…acknowledged
   (C) theatrical…regretted
   (D) affected…intimated
   (E) spontaneous…urged

7. It is all but impossible today to ____ the ferocity with which Russian thinkers at the turn of the century ____ the materialism that had dominated their country's intellectual life since the 1850s.

   (A) forget…relished
   (B) believe…conceded
   (C) grasp…assailed
   (D) emulate…ignored
   (E) challenge…extolled

8. Always less secure in herself than she liked to make out, she too often ____ disagreement as ____ and opposition as treachery.

   (A) rewarded…virtue
   (B) construed…betrayal
   (C) condemned…detachment
   (D) invited…provocation
   (E) interpreted…drollery

9. In prison Malcolm X set himself the task of reading straight through the dictionary; to him, reading was purposeful, not ____.

   (A) deliberate
   (B) retentive
   (C) critical
   (D) desultory
   (E) exhaustive

10. Many scientific discoveries are a matter of ____: Newton was not sitting there thinking about gravity when the apple dropped on his head.

    (A) serendipity
    (B) experimentation
    (C) casuistry
    (D) technology
    (E) principle

GO ON TO THE NEXT PAGE

2 2 2 2 2 2 2 2 2 2 2 2

**Directions:** Each question below consists of a related pair of words or phrases, followed by five pairs of words or phrases labeled A through E. Select the pair that best expresses a relationship similar to that expressed in the original pair.

Example:

CRUMB : BREAD ::

(A) ounce : unit
(B) splinter : wood
(C) water : bucket
(D) twine : rope
(E) cream : butter

Ⓐ ● Ⓒ Ⓓ Ⓔ

11. PEN : SHEEP ::

   (A) litter : piglets
   (B) pack : wolves
   (C) corral : horses
   (D) den : lions
   (E) manger : cattle

12. DISCHARGE : ARMY ::

   (A) revoke : license
   (B) expel : school
   (C) fire : weapon
   (D) inflate : balloon
   (E) launch : campaign

13. SPECTATOR : EXHIBITION ::

   (A) overseer : task
   (B) defendant : trial
   (C) actor : stage
   (D) conductor : bus
   (E) witness : crime

14. KIT : FOX ::

   (A) pack : wolf
   (B) den : lion
   (C) quarry : predator
   (D) cub : bear
   (E) chirp : sparrow

15. BOW : VIOLA ::

   (A) chord : piano
   (B) string : harp
   (C) pick : ukulele
   (D) pedal : organ
   (E) bridge : guitar

16. QUARANTINE : CARRIER ::

   (A) confine : prisoner
   (B) rehabilitate : offender
   (C) lionize : hero
   (D) diagnose : ailment
   (E) dispatch : messenger

17. PERSUASION : SWAY ::

   (A) ignorance : enlighten
   (B) vulnerability : charm
   (C) falsehood : mislead
   (D) determination : waver
   (E) persistence : increase

18. CAREFUL : METICULOUS ::

   (A) sincere : hypocritical
   (B) unreliable : treacherous
   (C) prudent : authentic
   (D) innate : disinclined
   (E) imperious : ostentatious

GO ON TO THE NEXT PAGE

19. SWAMP : WATER ::

    (A) overpower : force
    (B) dam : flood
    (C) kindle : fire
    (D) plow : earth
    (E) lubricate : oil

20. HUTCH : CABINET ::

    (A) newspaper : periodical
    (B) porthole : boat
    (C) latch : door
    (D) star : constellation
    (E) meeting : board

21. DART : SWIFTLY ::

    (A) respond : hastily
    (B) pant : deeply
    (C) saunter : restlessly
    (D) lumber : clumsily
    (E) trudge : purposefully

22. WOODEN : COUNTENANCE ::

    (A) indifferent : success
    (B) hardy : physique
    (C) flat : voice
    (D) unsteady : equilibrium
    (E) immutable : alteration

23. ENTERTAIN : IDEA ::

    (A) amuse : audience
    (B) harbor : suspicion
    (C) console : grief
    (D) invite : guest
    (E) divert : investigation

GO ON TO THE NEXT PAGE

2  2  2  2  2  2  2  2  2  2  2

**Questions 24–35 are based on the following passage.**

*In this excerpt from* The Joy of Music, *the composer and conductor Leonard Bernstein describes the characteristics of the ideal conductor.*

For the qualities that distinguish *great* conductors lie far beyond and above what we have spoken of. We now begin to deal with the
Line intangibles, the deep magical aspect of con-
(5) ducting. It is the mystery of relationships—conductor and orchestra bound together by the tiny but powerful split second. How can I describe to you the magic of the moment of beginning a piece of music? There is only one
(10) possible fraction of a second that feels exactly right for starting. There is a wait while the orchestra readies itself and collects its powers; while the conductor concentrates his whole will and force toward the work in hand; while
(15) the audience quiets down, and the last cough has died away. There is no slight rustle of a program book; the instruments are poised and—bang! That's it. One second later, it is too late, and the magic has vanished.
(20)     This psychological timing is constantly in play throughout the performance of music. It means that a great conductor is one who has great sensitivity to the flow of time; who makes one note move to the next in exactly the
(25) right way and at the right instant. For music, as we said, exists in the medium of time. It is time itself that must be carved up, molded and remolded until it becomes, like a statue, an existing shape and form. This is the hardest to
(30) do. For a symphony is not like a statue, which can be viewed all at once, or bit by bit at leisure, in one's own chosen time. With music, we are trapped in time. Each note is gone as soon as it has sounded, and it never can be
(35) recontemplated or heard again at the particular

instant of rightness. It is always too late for a second look.
    So the conductor is a kind of sculptor whose element is time instead of marble; and
(40) in sculpting it, he must have a superior sense of proportion and relationship. He must judge the largest rhythms, the whole phraseology of a work. He must conquer the form of a piece not only in the sense of form as a mold, but
(45) form in its deepest sense, knowing and controlling where the music relaxes, where it begins to accumulate tension, where the greatest tension is reached, where it must ease up to gather strength for the next lap, where it
(50) unloads that strength.
    These are the intangibles of conducting, the mysteries that no conductor can learn or acquire. If he has a natural faculty for deep perception, it will increase and deepen as he
(55) matures. If he hasn't, he will always be a pretty good conductor. But even the pretty good conductor must have one more attribute in his personality, without which all the mechanics and knowledge and perception are useless; and
(60) that is the power to *communicate* all this to his orchestra—through his arms, face, eyes, fingers, and whatever vibrations may flow from him. If he uses a baton, the baton itself must be a living thing, charged with a kind of elec-
(65) tricity, which makes it an instrument of meaning in its tiniest movement. If he does not use a baton, his hands must do the job with equal clarity. But baton or no baton, his gestures must be first and always meaningful in terms
(70) of the music.
    The chief element in the conductor's technique of communication is the preparation.

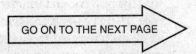

GO ON TO THE NEXT PAGE

2  2  2  2  2  2  2  2  2  2  2

Everything must be shown to the orchestra *before* it happens. Once the player is playing
(75) the note, it is too late. So the conductor always has to be a beat or two ahead of the orchestra . . . And he must hear two things at the same time: what the players are doing at any moment, and what they are about to do a
(80) moment later. Therefore, the basic trick is in the preparatory upbeat. If our conductor is back again on page one of Brahms's *First Symphony*, he must show, in his silent upbeat, the character of the music which is about to
(85) sound. Whether he thinks of it as tense and agitated, or weighty and doom-ridden, his upbeat should show this, in order to enable the orchestra players to respond in kind. It is exactly like breathing: the preparation is like
(90) an inhalation, and the music sounds as an exhalation. We all have to inhale in order to speak, for example; all verbal expression is exhaled. So it is with music: we inhale on the upbeat and sing out a phrase of music, then
(95) inhale again and breathe out the next phrase. A conductor who breathes with the music has gone far in acquiring a technique.

But the conductor must not only make his orchestra play; he must make them want to
(100) play. He must exalt them, lift them, start their adrenaline pouring, either through cajoling or demanding or raging. But however he does it, he must make the orchestra love the music as he loves it. It is not so much imposing his will
(105) on them like a dictator; it is more like projecting his feelings around him so that they reach the last player in the second violin section. And when this happens—when one hundred players share his feelings, exactly, simultane-
(110) ously, responding as one to each rise and fall of the music, to each point of arrival and departure, to each little inner pulse—then there is a human identity of feeling that has no equal elsewhere. It is the closest thing I know
(115) to love itself. On this current of love the conductor can communicate at the deepest levels with his players, and ultimately with his audience. He may shout and rant and curse and insult his players at rehearsal—as some of our
(120) greatest conductors are famous for doing—but

if there is this love, the conductor and his orchestra will remain knit together through it all and function as one.

Well, there is our ideal conductor. And
(125) perhaps the chief requirement of all this is that he be humble before the composer; that he never interpose himself between the music and the audience; that all his efforts, however strenuous or glamorous, be made in the ser-
(130) vice of the composer's meaning—the music itself, which, after all, is the whole reason for the conductor's existence.

24. In the first paragraph, in creating an initial impression of the qualities of the ideal conductor for the reader, the author makes use of

(A) reference to musical notation
(B) contrast to the musicians
(C) comparison with other leaders of ensembles
(D) narration of a sequence of events
(E) allusion to psychological studies

25. The passage is most likely to have been preceded by a discussion of

(A) the deficiencies of conductors whom the author has known
(B) how the conductor relates to the composer
(C) ways in which the orchestra complements the conductor
(D) the technical skills needed to be a reasonably competent conductor
(E) the qualities that transform a conductor into a superior musician

26. The conductor's decision as to the moment when to begin a piece of music can best be described as

(A) tentative
(B) imperceptible
(C) intuitive
(D) trivial
(E) hypothetical

GO ON TO THE NEXT PAGE

2 2 2 2 2 2 2 2 2 2 2

27. In stating that "with music, we are trapped in time," the author is being

(A) resigned
(B) wistful
(C) ironic
(D) figurative
(E) resentful

28. The author mentions sculpting chiefly in order to

(A) place conducting in perspective as one of the fine arts
(B) contrast it informally with conducting
(C) help the reader get an image of the conductor's work
(D) illustrate the difficulties of the sculptor's task
(E) show how the study of sculpture can benefit the conductor

29. In line 44, "mold" most nearly means

(A) decaying surface
(B) fixed pattern
(C) decorative strip
(D) organic growth
(E) cooking utensil

30. Lines 51–55 indicate that the author believes that the ideal conductor's most important attributes are

(A) innate
(B) transient
(C) technical
(D) symbolic
(E) unclear

31. The author primarily regards the conductor's baton as

(A) a necessary evil
(B) a symbol of strength
(C) an electrical implement
(D) an improvement over hand gestures
(E) a tool for transmitting meaning

32. In dealing with musicians, the author believes conductors

(A) must do whatever it takes to motivate them to perform
(B) should never resort to pleading with their subordinates
(C) must maintain their composure under trying circumstances
(D) work best if they love the musicians with whom they work
(E) must assert dominance over the musicians autocratically

33. In lines 105–107, the author mentions "the last player in the second violin section" primarily to emphasize

(A) the number of musicians necessary in an orchestra
(B) the particular importance of violins in ensemble work
(C) how sensitive secondary musicians can be
(D) how the role of the conductor differs from that of the musician
(E) the distance across which the conductor must communicate

34. The author regards temperamental behavior during rehearsals on the part of conductors with

(A) disapprobation
(B) tolerance
(C) bemusement
(D) regret
(E) awe

35. To the author, the conductor's primary concern is to maintain

(A) rapport with the audience
(B) authority over the orchestra
(C) the respect of the musicians
(D) the tempo of the music
(E) the integrity of the musical piece

# STOP

**IF YOU FINISH BEFORE TIME IS CALLED, YOU MAY CHECK YOUR WORK ON THIS SECTION ONLY. DO NOT WORK ON ANY OTHER SECTION IN THE TEST.**

3  3  3  3  3  3  3  3  3  3  3

## Section 3

TIME—15 MINUTES
13 QUESTIONS

For each of the following questions, choose the best answer and fill in the appropriate circle on the answer sheet.

---

Directions: The two passages below are followed by questions based on their content and on the relationship between the two passages. Answer the questions on the basis of what is <u>stated</u> or <u>implied</u> in the passages and in any introductory material that may be provided.

---

**Questions 1–13 are based on the following passages.**

*The following passages, written in the 1960s, explore the roots of anti-Japanese and anti-Jewish feelings in America during the first half of the twentieth century.*

**Passage 1**

Prejudice, the sociologists tell us, is learned behavior. Twentieth-century Californians learned the lesson well. Although
Line racial prejudice, directed at various ethnic
(5) groups, flourished throughout the United States during the period under discussion, nowhere north of the Mason-Dixon line did any single group encounter the sustained nativist assault that was directed against
(10) California's Japanese. There seem to be four chief reasons for this. First, the Japanese were of a distinct racial group; no amount of acculturation could mask their foreignness. Second, unlike the Chinese, they rapidly began to chal-
(15) lenge whites in many businesses and professions—as a group, Japanese in the United States became very quickly imbued with what, in Europeans, would be called the Protestant ethic. Third, the growing unpopularity of their
(20) homeland . . . further served to make immigrants from Japan special objects of suspicion. These three conditions would have made any large group of Japanese a particularly despised minority anywhere in the United States.
(25) Finally, the fact that most of the Japanese were in California probably made things worse, for California probably had a lower boiling point

than did the country at large.

California, by virtue of its anti-Chinese
(30) tradition and frontier psychology, was already conditioned to anti-Orientalism before the Japanese arrived. Other special California characteristics abetted the success of the agitation. In the prewar years, the extraordinary
(35) power of organized labor in northern California gave the anti-Japanese movement a much stronger base than it would have enjoyed elsewhere; in the postwar years, open-shop southern California proved almost
(40) equally hospitable to an agitation pitched to middle-class white Protestants. In the two periods anti-Japanese sentiment flourished among completely disparate populations: the first- and second-generation immigrants who
(45) were the backbone of California's labor movement, and the Midwestern émigrés who came to dominate the southern California scene. For most of these Californians, opposition to the Japanese was based upon fears which were
(50) largely nonrational.

**Passage 2**

To say that anti-Semitism in America sprang chiefly from the difficulties of integrating large numbers of first- and second-generation immigrants is, inferentially, to stress its
(55) similarity to other kinds of anti-immigrant sentiment—to put it in the same class with

GO ON TO THE NEXT PAGE

3    3    3    3    3    3    3    3    3    3    3

dislike of the Irish, Italians, Japanese, Mexicans and other transplanted minorities, while making allowances for the differential
(60) characteristics of each group. Likewise, this approach minimizes distinctions often made between different kinds of anti-Semitism, in that it relates all of them to a common root. Yet we must also consider the role of irrational
(65) anti-Semitic fantasies that had no direct connection with real problems of ethnic integration. The ideological hatreds spread by the agitator and the fanatic have had a place in American history, too.
(70)      Unlike . . . more ordinary social prejudices . . . , ideological anti-Semitism condemns the Jews as incapable of assimilation and disloyal to the basic institutions of the country. In its more extreme forms, it portrays them as
(75) leagued together in a vast international conspiracy. The alleged plot usually centers on gaining control of the money supply and wrecking the financial system; sometimes it extends to polluting the nation's morals
(80) through control of communications and entertainment. The supposed eventual aim is to overthrow the government and establish a superstate. In America, anti-Semitism of this kind has not been so well organized or so pro-
(85) ductive of violence as other racial and religious phobias. But it has enjoyed an unusually rich and complex imagery.
      Religious motifs, by and large, have not figured prominently in American anti-Semitic
(90) thought. Except among certain preachers spawned by the Fundamentalist movement of the 1920s (notably Gerald Winrod and Gerald L. K. Smith), one looks in vain for a clearly religious animus. Though not entirely lacking
(95) in references to the treachery of Judas, ideological anti-Semitism has always dwelled mainly on the power of Shylock. Whether the Jew appears in his traditional role as exploiter or in his later incarnation as Bolshevik, his
(100) subversive influence supposedly flows from an unwillingness or inability to abide by the existing economic morality.

1. The author of Passage 1 makes the point that prejudice against the Japanese in the twentieth century
   (A) began in California
   (B) was comparable to racial prejudice in the South
   (C) was taught in the schools of California
   (D) often bred violence
   (E) was a shameful chapter in the history of California

2. Passage 1 implies that the Japanese would not have faced such intense prejudice if
   (A) their physical appearance had been different
   (B) they had arrived in California via New York
   (C) they had emigrated to California a century earlier
   (D) they had settled in southern California
   (E) Californians had themselves been recent immigrants

3. Passage 1 suggests that, after Japanese immigrants arrived in California, they
   (A) joined unions
   (B) often went on welfare until they got jobs
   (C) created Japanese ghettos in several cities
   (D) worked hard to be successful
   (E) contributed technical skills to the state's work force.

4. Based on information in Passage 1, World War II
   (A) provided California's Japanese population temporary relief from prejudice
   (B) caused prejudice against the Japanese to intensify
   (C) had little impact on prejudice against the Japanese
   (D) diverted the hatred from Japanese civilians to the Japanese military
   (E) shifted the center of anti-Japanese feeling in California

GO ON TO THE NEXT PAGE

5. One can infer from Passage 1 that hostility toward the Japanese flourished in California because

(A) California was closer to Pearl Harbor than any other state

(B) Californians are more intolerant than other Americans

(C) Japan-bashing was an official policy of the labor unions in the state

(D) Japanese were quickly buying up buildings, land, and other property throughout the state

(E) American workers felt threatened by Japanese workers

6. The author of Passage 2 believes that anti-Semitism in America differs from other forms of prejudice because

(A) it is based on a long tradition

(B) anti-Semites tend to be more hateful than other types of bigots

(C) most anti-Semites are fanatics

(D) it comes in many forms and guises

(E) each ethnic minority experiences prejudice in a different way

7. The term "ideological hatred" (line 67–69) refers to prejudice

(A) only against Jews

(B) that is openly declared in public

(C) that existed in an earlier era

(D) that is inspired by the victims' beliefs and values

(E) that has gone out of control

8. The author of Passage 2 implies that violence against Jews in the United States has been

(A) fed by social anti-Semitism rather than ideological anti-Semitism

(B) has been directed mostly at first-generation Jewish immigrants

(C) has helped other minorities to cope with violence against them

(D) has been more verbal and psychological than physical

(E) has been less severe than violence against other minorities

9. Passage 2 indicates that avid anti-Semites fear Jews for all of the following reasons EXCEPT that

(A) it is hard to tell a Jew from a non-Jew

(B) Jews crave power

(C) Jews are immoral

(D) the media are controlled by Jews

(E) Jews do not value democracy

10. Gerald Winrod and Gerald L. K. Smith (lines 92–93) are cited as anti-Semites

(A) who advocated the violent treatment of Jews

(B) whose hatred of Jews was based largely on religion

(C) who sought to convert Jews to Christianity

(D) who alleged that Jews were a danger to the United States

(E) who founded the Christian Fundamentalist movement in the United States

GO ON TO THE NEXT PAGE

3   3   3   3   3   3   3   3   3   3   3

11. Based on the two passages, it is fair to say that prejudice against the Jews in the United States compared to prejudice against the Japanese

(A) has been more violent
(B) has been more strenuously opposed by fair-minded people
(C) is more complex and diffuse
(D) has a longer history
(E) has increased at a greater rate since World War II

12. The authors of both passages appear to agree that

(A) prejudice in the United States is gradually diminishing
(B) prejudice in the United States is gradually increasing
(C) prejudice is based on irrational thinking
(D) physical appearance is a major cause of prejudice against both Jews and Japanese
(E) stereotypes are hard to break

13. In their explanations of the causes of prejudice, both authors

(A) stress economic reasons
(B) focus on the historical roots of prejudice in America
(C) are hopeful that justice will eventually prevail
(D) agree that the Japanese and the Jews have been scapegoats
(E) think that extreme nationalism may lie at the heart of bigotry

### STOP

**IF YOU FINISH BEFORE TIME IS CALLED, YOU MAY CHECK YOUR WORK ON THIS SECTION ONLY. DO NOT WORK ON ANY OTHER SECTION IN THE TEST.**

# ANSWER KEY

## Section 1

| | | | | | | | | | |
|---|---|---|---|---|---|---|---|---|---|
| 1. C | 4. C | 7. D | 10. A | 13. C | 16. D | 19. E | 22. E | 25. C | 28. C |
| 2. E | 5. A | 8. A | 11. A | 14. A | 17. D | 20. D | 23. C | 26. B | 29. B |
| 3. E | 6. C | 9. C | 12. D | 15. A | 18. B | 21. C | 24. C | 27. C | 30. E |

## Section 2

| | | | | | | | | | |
|---|---|---|---|---|---|---|---|---|---|
| 1. C | 5. D | 9. D | 13. E | 17. C | 21. D | 24. D | 27. D | 30. A | 33. E |
| 2. D | 6. B | 10. A | 14. D | 18. B | 22. C | 25. D | 28. C | 31. E | 34. B |
| 3. C | 7. C | 11. C | 15. C | 19. A | 23. B | 26. C | 29. B | 32. A | 35. E |
| 4. E | 8. B | 12. B | 16. A | 20. A | | | | | |

## Section 3

| | | | | | | |
|---|---|---|---|---|---|---|
| 1. B | 3. D | 5. E | 7. D | 9. A | 11. C | 13. A |
| 2. A | 4. E | 6. D | 8. A | 10. B | 12. C | |

## ANALYSIS OF TEST RESULTS

### I. Self-Rating Chart

| | | | | Total |
|---|---|---|---|---|
| **Sentence Completions**<br>Number Correct | Section 1<br>(Questions 1–9)<br>_____ | Section 2<br>(Questions 1–10)<br>_____ | | _____ |
| **Analogies**<br>Number Correct | Section 1<br>(Questions 10–15)<br>_____ | Section 2<br>(Questions 11–23)<br>_____ | | _____ |
| **Critical Reading**<br>Number Correct | Section 1<br>(Questions 16–30)<br>_____ | Section 2<br>(Questions 24–35)<br>_____ | Section 3<br>(Questions 1–13)<br>_____ | _____ |

Sentence Completions    Number Correct _____

Analogies    Number Correct _____

Critical Reasoning    Number Correct _____

Subtotal _____

*Guessing Penalty:* Subtract 1/4 point for each incorrect answer.    _____

(Do not take off points for questions you left blank.)

TOTAL SCORE _____

### II. Rate Your Performance

| | Sentence Completion/Analogy Score | Reading Score | Total |
|---|---|---|---|
| Excellent | 18–19 Correct | 37–40 | 73–78 |
| Very Good | 14–17 Correct | 27–36 | 55–72 |
| Good | 11–13 Correct | 19–26 | 41–54 |
| Fair | 9–10 Correct | 15–18 | 33–40 |
| Poor | 6–8  Correct | 10–14 | 20–32 |
| Very Poor | 0–5  Correct | 0–9 | 0–19 |

# ANSWER EXPLANATIONS

## SECTION 1

1. **C**   To complete the comparison, in the same way that the roads all led to the city of Rome, the heart of the Roman Empire, the blood vessels all lead to or *empty into* the heart.

2. **E**   Currently, the railroads can take on additional shipping only during the winter; at other times of the year, they can't absorb any more traffic. During the winter months the waterway could not take traffic away from the railroads (an icebound waterway is useless as a route for traffic). Thus, those in favor of the waterway argue that it will *supplement* or be a desirable addition to railroad facilities and not *threaten* or endanger the railroads at all.

3. **E**   To give the visual details of past events is to make *history* real to people.

4. **C**   George Burns had even greater celebrity or *renown* in the 1980s than he had known in the 1940s.

5. **A**   Given the potentially controversial nature of the discovery, a responsible scientist might well be *hesitant* or reluctant to *release* the information for fear that it could be interpreted in incorrect, stereotypical ways.

6. **C**   "Despite" signals the contrast between the mole rat's repulsive, disgusting habits and its *meticulous*, painstakingly careful cleaning of its burrow.

7. **D**   The president did not say much about farm subsidies: he was *noncommittal*, taking no clear position on this important issue. He also did not say much about the more important or *vital* issue of unemployment.
    (C) is incorrect. While it would be possible in this context to describe the president as *uncommunicative* about farm subsidies, it would be inaccurate to describe the critical issue of unemployment as merely *academic* (theoretical; of no practical significance).

8. **A**   It is a major *requisite* (requirement or necessity) of the genre that the biographer be able to *reconstruct* or mentally build up again his or her subject's inner life.

9. **C**   In navigating tricky legal waters, one hopes to be able to *avoid* judicial *quagmires* (marshes; swamps) in which one might bog down.

10. **A**   To step down from office, a *chairperson* must *resign*. To step down from office, a *king* must *abdicate*.

11. **A**   A *sled* slides over ice and snow on its *runners*. A *skateboard* glides over streets and sidewalks on its *wheels*.

12. **D**   To *dampen eagerness* (enthusiasm) is to lessen its intensity. To *muffle* or smother *sound* is to lessen its volume.

13. **C**   Someone merely *annoying* is less irritating than someone who is *insufferable* (unbearable). Someone merely *chatty* (inclined to talk in a friendly, informal fashion) is less talkative than someone who is *long-winded* (inclined to talk for tediously long periods of time).

14. **A**   In a book or speech, a *digression* is a departure or wandering away from the *topic*. In a journey, a *detour* is a departure or wandering away from the *itinerary* (journey plan).

15. **A**   A break or lull in *fighting* is a *truce*. A break or lull in *labor* is a *respite* or rest.

16. **D**   The shadowy, gloomy understory is dimly lit or *obscure*.

17. **D**   The plants that exist only within the compass of the canopy live within its *boundaries*.

18. **B**   The tree trunks provide the epiphytes only with a good location up in the canopy. Being nonparasitic, epiphytes *cannot draw moisture (or any nourishment whatsoever) from tree trunks*.

19. **E**   Having developed features that collect and retain rainwater, epiphytes clearly are particularly well suited to the *retention* (holding; storing up) *of liquid*.

20. **D**  Because epiphytes do not sink their roots into the earth, *they lack connections* to the earth and thus do not have direct access *to water in the ground*. They have direct access to water only when it rains.

21. **C**  Both desert cacti and arboreal cacti grow in environments in which access to moisture is difficult to achieve. The desert cacti lack access to moisture because the amount of rainfall in desert regions is minimal and little moisture exists in the soil. The arboreal cacti lack access to moisture because they grow high up in the canopy with no root connections to the soil. Thus, both kinds of cacti have had to develop *features to cut down or reduce their loss of moisture.*

22. **E**  The passengers were walking because pulling a fully loaded coach uphill through the mud had been too much for horses. Note that they had already come to a stop three times.

23. **C**  The author describes the immediate, rather unwholesome area. However, he never *contrasts it with more attractive areas.*

24. **C**  Given the inclement weather, the muddy footing, and the uphill struggle, the fact that *the horses* (brute animals) *strongly attempted to turn back to Blackheath* suggests that they were more reasonable creatures than the humans who forced them to struggle on.

25. **C**  The lead horse *shook his head and everything upon it, that is, his head and his harness*, which made a rattling noise.

26. **B**  It is not surprising that, at the sudden, emphatic noise the nervous passenger started or *jumped*.

27. **C**  All the descriptive terms in the paragraph—mist "like an evil spirit," "waves of an unwholesome sea," fog "dense enough to shut out everything from the light"—emphasize the *gloominess* and dark melancholy of the scene.

28. **C**  The sentence that immediately precedes the reference to the Captain maintains that anyone on the road might be in league with robbers, that is, might be a robber's accomplice or confederate. Thus, to be in the Captain's pay means to be a robber's paid accomplice, and the Captain is clearly a highway robber or *highwayman*.

29. **B**  Viewing one another with suspicion, the passengers maintain a *guarded* or wary stance.

30. **E**  By definition, *genial* means cordial or friendly. However, the situation shown here is grim and unfriendly rather than genial. Thus, the word is being used in an *ironic*, unexpected way.

# SECTION 2

1. **C**  Given the examples listed, the administration seems unusually considerate of or *attentive to* the well-being of its employees.

2. **D**  "Whereas" is a contrast signal. Its use indicates that, unlike China's economic growth curve, which is going up, Russia's economic growth curve is *descending*.

3. **C**  If trees have adapted to survive short, mild winters, then they're not likely to do well in harsh winters with extreme temperature changes. In fact, they will prove *vulnerable to* (defenseless against) cold snaps and sudden thaws.

4. **E**  Unlike a contemporary feminist, Abigail Adams *accepted* the then *traditional* view of the roles of women and men.
     The second clause of the sentence serves to explain in what way Abigail Adams was unlike feminists today.

5. **D**  The author is making highly negative comments, ones that go beyond being casually *dismissive* (indifferent or disapproving) to being bluntly *contemptuous* (scornful).

6. **B**  Though people assumed Doisneau's pictures were unposed, he *acknowledged* (admitted) he had staged some shots that were supposed to have been *candid* (informal, unposed).

7. **C**  The key word here is "ferocity" (fierceness). The writer contends that it is extremely hard for people today to comprehend or *grasp* how fiercely Russians in the early 1900s *assailed* (attacked) their country's materialism.

8. **B**  Someone insecure would be likely to *construe* (interpret) disagreement as *betrayal* (disloyalty).

9. **D**   The opposite of a purposeful, determined action is a *desultory*, aimless one.
   "Not" is a contrast signal. The missing word must be an antonym or near-antonym for "purposeful."

10. **A**   The dictionary defines *serendipity* as good luck, an aptitude for making valuable discoveries by accident. Newton's discovery of the law of gravity is a classic example of serendipity at work.

11. **C**   A *pen* is an enclosure for *sheep*. A *corral* is an enclosure for *horses*.

12. **B**   To *discharge* someone from the *army* is to dismiss or remove that soldier. To *expel* someone from *school* is to dismiss or remove that student.

13. **E**   By definition, a person who observes an *exhibition* is a *spectator*. Likewise, a person who observes a *crime* is a *witness*.

14. **D**   A *kit* is a young *fox*. A *cub* is a young *bear*.

15. **C**   One uses a *bow* to play on a *viola*. One uses a *pick* (small piece of plastic or metal for plucking strings) to play on a *ukulele*.

16. **A**   *Carriers* (people infected with a contagious disease) are *quarantined* (isolated) to separate them from others. *Prisoners* are *confined* (imprisoned) to separate them from others.

17. **C**   The purpose of *persuasion* is to *sway* or influence someone. The purpose of a *falsehood* is to *mislead* or deceive someone.

18. **B**   To be *careful* is less extreme than to be *meticulous* (painstakingly careful). To be *unreliable* (undependable, untrustworthy) is less extreme than to be *treacherous* (unfaithful, traitorous).

19. **A**   To *swamp* something is to flood or overwhelm it with *water*. To *overpower* something is to subdue or overwhelm it with *force*.

20. **A**   A *hutch* (chestlike piece of furniture) is a kind of *cabinet*. A *newspaper* is a kind of *periodical* (regularly issued journal or magazine).

21. **D**   To *dart* by definition is to move *swiftly*. To *lumber* by definition is to move *clumsily*.

22. **C**   A *countenance* (face; facial expression) that is *wooden* lacks animation and vitality. A *voice* that is *flat* lacks vitality and animation as well.

23. **B**   To *entertain* an *idea* is to hold it in one's mind, to consider it. To *harbor* a *suspicion* is to consider it as well.

24. **D**   The author tells or *narrates* what happens during the period of time just before the conductor gives the upbeat to signal the orchestra to begin.

25. **D**   The opening of the first paragraph states that "the qualities that distinguish *great* conductors," the qualities about which the author is going to speak, "lie far beyond and above *what we have spoken of*." Clearly, he has just been speaking of other qualities that conductors must possess. However, these are not the high, artistic skills that one needs to be a great conductor. They are merely *the technical skills needed to be a reasonably competent conductor*.

26. **C**   The magic moment for beginning a piece of music is the moment that "feels exactly right." The conductor's decision is based on instinct, on feelings, not on logic; it is *intuitive*.

27. **D**   The author does not mean we are literally trapped or captive; he is being *figurative* or metaphorical.

28. **C**   Throughout the passage, the author uses different approaches to give the reader an idea of the nature of just what a conductor does. Here, he compares a conductor's working with time to a sculptor's working with physical blocks of stone. He does this to *help the reader get an image of the conductor's work*.

29. **B**   "Mold" here is a *fixed pattern* or shape.

30. **A**   The author states that "no conductor can learn or acquire" the mysteries or most important attributes of conducting. The "natural faculty for deep perception" is inborn or *innate*.

31. **E**   The author looks on the baton as a tool he uses to help him communicate with the orchestra, in other words, as *a tool for transmitting meaning*.
   (A) is incorrect. The author does not consider the baton either necessary (he can gesture equally clearly with his hands) or evil.
   (B) is incorrect. The author is not talking about the baton as a symbol; he is talking about it as an instrument that gets used.

(C) is incorrect. In talking of the baton's being "charged with a kind of electricity," the author is being figurative, not literal. He does not literally look on the baton as an electrical appliance or tool.

(D) is incorrect. The author never states a preference for one means of communication over the other.

32. **A**   The author suggests a variety of things the conductor can do to get a performance out of the musicians—cajoling (coaxing), demanding, raging. Clearly he believes conductors *must do whatever it takes to motivate* the musicians to want to perform.

33. **E**   The author is talking about projecting his feelings, conveying his emotions so vividly and intensely that they reach each and every one of his hundred musicians, no matter where in the orchestra they are. Thus, in singling out the *last* player, the one farthest back, in the *second* violin section, the section behind the first violins, he is emphasizing *the distance across which the conductor must communicate*.

34. **B**   The author's concern is for the orchestra to learn to function as one. He views the temperamental behavior of conductors—ranting, cursing, insulting musicians—with *tolerance*, accepting these actions as either unimportant personal quirks on the part of the conductor or tactical moves in the conductor's grand design to stimulate the musicians to play at their best.

35. **E**   In dedicating himself to "the service of the composer's meaning" (lines 128–132), the conductor is laboring to maintain *the integrity of the musical piece* in accordance with the composer's design.

# SECTION 3

1. **B**   In the first paragraph the author, by likening the prejudice against the Japanese to the prejudice below the Mason-Dixon line, argues that anti-Japanese feeling *was comparable to racial prejudice in the South.*

2. **A**   The intensity of anti-Japanese feeling is explained in part by the fact that the Japanese "were of a distinct racial group; no amount of acculturation could mask their foreignness." Logically, then, had *their physical appearance been different*, they might not have experienced such intense hatred.

3. **D**   Among the causes of prejudice against the Japanese was the rapidity with which the Japanese immigrants adopted the so-called "Protestant ethic," which includes the notion that you must *work hard to be successful.*

4. **E**   Before the war, anti-Japanese feelings were most intense in northern California. Afterward, southern California became the locus of prejudice. World War II, then, *shifted the center of anti-Japanese feeling.*

5. **E**   The passage explains that labor unions provided the base of the anti-Japanese movement. Presumably, labor unions voiced their opposition because members felt that their jobs were being *threatened by Japanese workers.*

6. **D**   The author of Passage 2 cautions readers not to confuse anti-Semitism with other forms of anti-immigrant sentiment, but to be mindful of "different kinds of anti-Semitism." The passage then describes *many forms and guises* (appearances) of anti-Semitism.

7. **D**   The author refers to ideological anti-Semitism as that which has "no direct connection with . . . ethnic integration." In other words, it is hatred of others' assumed *beliefs and values*, such as the anti-Semitic notion cited in the passage that Jews want to take control of the United States.

8. **A**   According to the passage, ideological anti-Semitism has not been as "productive of violence as other racial and religious phobias." When violence has occurred, therefore, it has been inspired or *fed by social anti-Semitism.*

9. **A**   The second paragraph of the passage lists several explanations for hatred of Jews, but not that *it's hard to tell a Jew from a non-Jew.*

10. **B**  In the third paragraph Winrod and Smith are cited as examples of anti-Semites *whose hatred of the Jews was based largely on religion*. As the passage says, except for Winrod and Smith, "one looks in vain for a clearly religious animus" to explain anti-Semitic feelings.

11. **C**  The first passage pinpoints California as the center of anti-Japanese feeling and gives several precise explanations for its growth in that state. In contrast, Passage 2 portrays anti-Semitism as a *more complex and diffuse* (widespread) form of bigotry. It describes various reasons for anti-Semitism and fails to identify a place or region where it is concentrated.

12. **C**  Both authors cite *irrational thinking* as the cause of prejudice. The first says the "opposition to the Japanese was based upon fears which were largely nonrational" (lines 47–50), while the second refers to the role played by "irrational anti-Semitic fantasies" (lines 64–67).

13. **A**  *Economic reasons* dominate both authors' explanations of prejudice. The Japanese were hated for challenging whites in many businesses and professions, for working hard, and for competing with American workers for jobs. Jews were accused of plotting to take control of America's money supply, wrecking the financial system, and taking over the communications and entertainment industries.

# ANSWER SHEET FOR VERBAL REASONING TEST 3

| Section 1 | Section 2 | Section 3 |
|---|---|---|
| 1. Ⓐ Ⓑ Ⓒ Ⓓ Ⓔ | 1. Ⓐ Ⓑ Ⓒ Ⓓ Ⓔ | 1. Ⓐ Ⓑ Ⓒ Ⓓ Ⓔ |
| 2. Ⓐ Ⓑ Ⓒ Ⓓ Ⓔ | 2. Ⓐ Ⓑ Ⓒ Ⓓ Ⓔ | 2. Ⓐ Ⓑ Ⓒ Ⓓ Ⓔ |
| 3. Ⓐ Ⓑ Ⓒ Ⓓ Ⓔ | 3. Ⓐ Ⓑ Ⓒ Ⓓ Ⓔ | 3. Ⓐ Ⓑ Ⓒ Ⓓ Ⓔ |
| 4. Ⓐ Ⓑ Ⓒ Ⓓ Ⓔ | 4. Ⓐ Ⓑ Ⓒ Ⓓ Ⓔ | 4. Ⓐ Ⓑ Ⓒ Ⓓ Ⓔ |
| 5. Ⓐ Ⓑ Ⓒ Ⓓ Ⓔ | 5. Ⓐ Ⓑ Ⓒ Ⓓ Ⓔ | 5. Ⓐ Ⓑ Ⓒ Ⓓ Ⓔ |
| 6. Ⓐ Ⓑ Ⓒ Ⓓ Ⓔ | 6. Ⓐ Ⓑ Ⓒ Ⓓ Ⓔ | 6. Ⓐ Ⓑ Ⓒ Ⓓ Ⓔ |
| 7. Ⓐ Ⓑ Ⓒ Ⓓ Ⓔ | 7. Ⓐ Ⓑ Ⓒ Ⓓ Ⓔ | 7. Ⓐ Ⓑ Ⓒ Ⓓ Ⓔ |
| 8. Ⓐ Ⓑ Ⓒ Ⓓ Ⓔ | 8. Ⓐ Ⓑ Ⓒ Ⓓ Ⓔ | 8. Ⓐ Ⓑ Ⓒ Ⓓ Ⓔ |
| 9. Ⓐ Ⓑ Ⓒ Ⓓ Ⓔ | 9. Ⓐ Ⓑ Ⓒ Ⓓ Ⓔ | 9. Ⓐ Ⓑ Ⓒ Ⓓ Ⓔ |
| 10. Ⓐ Ⓑ Ⓒ Ⓓ Ⓔ | 10. Ⓐ Ⓑ Ⓒ Ⓓ Ⓔ | 10. Ⓐ Ⓑ Ⓒ Ⓓ Ⓔ |
| 11. Ⓐ Ⓑ Ⓒ Ⓓ Ⓔ | 11. Ⓐ Ⓑ Ⓒ Ⓓ Ⓔ | 11. Ⓐ Ⓑ Ⓒ Ⓓ Ⓔ |
| 12. Ⓐ Ⓑ Ⓒ Ⓓ Ⓔ | 12. Ⓐ Ⓑ Ⓒ Ⓓ Ⓔ | 12. Ⓐ Ⓑ Ⓒ Ⓓ Ⓔ |
| 13. Ⓐ Ⓑ Ⓒ Ⓓ Ⓔ | 13. Ⓐ Ⓑ Ⓒ Ⓓ Ⓔ | 13. Ⓐ Ⓑ Ⓒ Ⓓ Ⓔ |
| 14. Ⓐ Ⓑ Ⓒ Ⓓ Ⓔ | 14. Ⓐ Ⓑ Ⓒ Ⓓ Ⓔ | |
| 15. Ⓐ Ⓑ Ⓒ Ⓓ Ⓔ | 15. Ⓐ Ⓑ Ⓒ Ⓓ Ⓔ | |
| 16. Ⓐ Ⓑ Ⓒ Ⓓ Ⓔ | 16. Ⓐ Ⓑ Ⓒ Ⓓ Ⓔ | |
| 17. Ⓐ Ⓑ Ⓒ Ⓓ Ⓔ | 17. Ⓐ Ⓑ Ⓒ Ⓓ Ⓔ | |
| 18. Ⓐ Ⓑ Ⓒ Ⓓ Ⓔ | 18. Ⓐ Ⓑ Ⓒ Ⓓ Ⓔ | |
| 19. Ⓐ Ⓑ Ⓒ Ⓓ Ⓔ | 19. Ⓐ Ⓑ Ⓒ Ⓓ Ⓔ | |
| 20. Ⓐ Ⓑ Ⓒ Ⓓ Ⓔ | 20. Ⓐ Ⓑ Ⓒ Ⓓ Ⓔ | |
| 21. Ⓐ Ⓑ Ⓒ Ⓓ Ⓔ | 21. Ⓐ Ⓑ Ⓒ Ⓓ Ⓔ | |
| 22. Ⓐ Ⓑ Ⓒ Ⓓ Ⓔ | 22. Ⓐ Ⓑ Ⓒ Ⓓ Ⓔ | |
| 23. Ⓐ Ⓑ Ⓒ Ⓓ Ⓔ | 23. Ⓐ Ⓑ Ⓒ Ⓓ Ⓔ | |
| 24. Ⓐ Ⓑ Ⓒ Ⓓ Ⓔ | 24. Ⓐ Ⓑ Ⓒ Ⓓ Ⓔ | |
| 25. Ⓐ Ⓑ Ⓒ Ⓓ Ⓔ | 25. Ⓐ Ⓑ Ⓒ Ⓓ Ⓔ | |
| 26. Ⓐ Ⓑ Ⓒ Ⓓ Ⓔ | 26. Ⓐ Ⓑ Ⓒ Ⓓ Ⓔ | |
| 27. Ⓐ Ⓑ Ⓒ Ⓓ Ⓔ | 27. Ⓐ Ⓑ Ⓒ Ⓓ Ⓔ | |
| 28. Ⓐ Ⓑ Ⓒ Ⓓ Ⓔ | 28. Ⓐ Ⓑ Ⓒ Ⓓ Ⓔ | |
| 29. Ⓐ Ⓑ Ⓒ Ⓓ Ⓔ | 29. Ⓐ Ⓑ Ⓒ Ⓓ Ⓔ | |
| 30. Ⓐ Ⓑ Ⓒ Ⓓ Ⓔ | 30. Ⓐ Ⓑ Ⓒ Ⓓ Ⓔ | |
| | 31. Ⓐ Ⓑ Ⓒ Ⓓ Ⓔ | |
| | 32. Ⓐ Ⓑ Ⓒ Ⓓ Ⓔ | |
| | 33. Ⓐ Ⓑ Ⓒ Ⓓ Ⓔ | |
| | 34. Ⓐ Ⓑ Ⓒ Ⓓ Ⓔ | |
| | 35. Ⓐ Ⓑ Ⓒ Ⓓ Ⓔ | |

**1**  1  1  1  1  1  1  1  1  1  1  1  **1**

# VERBAL REASONING TEST 3
## Section 1

TIME—30 MINUTES
30 QUESTIONS

For each of the following questions, select the best answer from the choices provided and fill in the appropriate circle on the answer sheet.

---

Directions: Each sentence below has one or two blanks, each blank indicating that something has been omitted. Beneath the sentence are five words or sets of words labeled A through E. Choose the word or set of words that, when inserted in the sentence, best fits the meaning of the sentence as a whole.

Example:

Medieval kingdoms did not become constitutional republics overnight; on the contrary, the change was ____.

(A) unpopular
(B) unexpected
(C) advantageous
(D) sufficient
(E) gradual

Ⓐ Ⓑ Ⓒ Ⓓ ●

---

1. A subway modernization program intended to ____ a host of problems ranging from dangerous tracks to overcrowded stairwells has failed to meet its schedule for repairs.

    (A) augment
    (B) initiate
    (C) deplore
    (D) disclose
    (E) eliminate

2. Despite the current expansion of membership in America, the governing body of world fencing fears that fencing could be in danger of ____ if it does not become more ____ to spectators.

    (A) monotony…intelligible
    (B) overcrowding…resistant
    (C) extinction…accessible
    (D) corruption…cordial
    (E) remoteness…handy

3. To astronomers, the moon has long been an ____, its origin escaping simple solution.

    (A) interval
    (B) ultimatum
    (C) enigma
    (D) affront
    (E) opportunity

4. Precision of wording is necessary in good writing; by choosing words that exactly convey the desired meaning, one can avoid ____.

    (A) redundancy
    (B) complexity
    (C) duplicity
    (D) ambiguity
    (E) lucidity

GO ON TO THE NEXT PAGE

**1    1   1   1   1   1   1   1   1   1   1   1**

5. The amusements of modern urban people tend more and more to be ____ and to consist of the ____ of the skilled activities of others.

   (A) strenuous...contemplation
   (B) healthful...enjoyment
   (C) solitary...sharing
   (D) passive...observation
   (E) intellectual...repetition

6. Despite the ____ size of her undergraduate class, the professor made a point of getting to know as many as possible of the more than 700 students personally.

   (A) negligible
   (B) modest
   (C) infinitesimal
   (D) daunting
   (E) moderate

7. As matter condenses out of the thin disk of hot gas and dust revolving around a new sun, it ____ into larger particles, just as snowflakes stick together as they fall.

   (A) crashes
   (B) protrudes
   (C) coalesces
   (D) evaporates
   (E) dissolves

8. Biographer Janet Malcolm maintains that biography is a spurious art, for the orderly narrative it creates is ____; the "facts" aren't facts at all, but literary ____.

   (A) illusory...inventions
   (B) genuine...commonplaces
   (C) informative...allusions
   (D) brilliant...triumphs
   (E) sincere...criticisms

9. The term *mole rat* is a ____, for these small, furless rodents are neither moles nor rats.

   (A) pseudonym
   (B) digression
   (C) misnomer
   (D) nonentity
   (E) preference

GO ON TO THE NEXT PAGE ➡

1 1 1 1 1 1 1 1 1 1 1 1 1

Directions: Each question below consists of a related pair of words or phrases, followed by five pairs of words or phrases labeled A through E. Select the pair that best expresses a relationship similar to that expressed in the original pair.

Example:

CRUMB : BREAD ::

(A) ounce : unit
(B) splinter : wood
(C) water : bucket
(D) twine : rope
(E) cream : butter

Ⓐ ● Ⓒ Ⓓ Ⓔ

10. TAXI : FLEET ::

(A) soldier : squad
(B) truck : cargo
(C) waltz : dance
(D) ship : rudder
(E) train : caboose

11. UNEASINESS : PANIC ::

(A) revulsion : disgust
(B) uncertainty : doubt
(C) irritation : outrage
(D) illness : attack
(E) fortitude : weakness

12. ROUND : TOURNAMENT ::

(A) circle : friends
(B) conclusion : proceedings
(C) inning : game
(D) fulfillment : goal
(E) book : cover

13. BREATHTAKING : WONDER ::

(A) repugnant : revulsion
(B) devastating : defiance
(C) perplexing : lucidity
(D) inspiring : gratitude
(E) crude : refinement

14. QUIXOTIC : PRACTICALITY ::

(A) erratic : oddity
(B) apathetic : intelligence
(C) economical : thrift
(D) frivolous : gravity
(E) steadfast : loyalty

15. ACID : CORROSIVE ::

(A) lubricant : unhygienic
(B) vaccine : resistant
(C) antiseptic : astringent
(D) sedative : stimulating
(E) sap : viscous

GO ON TO THE NEXT PAGE

**1**   1   1   1   1   1   1   1   1   1   1   **1**

---

<u>Directions:</u> Each passage below is followed by questions based on its content. Answer the questions on the basis of what is <u>stated</u> or <u>implied</u> in that passage and in any introductory material that may be provided.

---

**Questions 16–21 are based on the following passage.**

*In this excerpt from* The Way to Rainy Mountain, *the writer N. Scott Momaday tells of his grandmother, a member of the Kiowa tribe, who was born at a key time in Kiowa history.*

I like to think of my grandmother as a
child. When she was born, the Kiowas were
living the last great moment of their history.
*Line* For more than a hundred years they had con-
(5) trolled the open range from the Smoky Hill
River to the Red, from the headwaters of the
Canadian to the fork of the Arkansas and
Cimarron. In alliance with the Comanches,
they had ruled the whole of the southern
(10) Plains. War was their sacred business, and
they were among the finest horsemen the
world has ever known. But warfare for the
Kiowas was preeminently a matter of disposition rather than of survival, and they never
(15) understood the grim, unrelenting advance of
the U.S. Cavalry. When at last, divided and ill-
provisioned, they were driven onto the Staked
Plains in the cold rains of autumn, they fell
into panic. In Palo Duro Canyon they aban-
(20) doned their crucial stores to pillage and had
nothing then but their lives. In order to save
themselves, they surrendered to the soldiers at
Fort Sill and were imprisoned in the old stone
corral that now stands as a military museum.
(25) My grandmother was spared the humiliation
of those high gray walls by eight or ten years,
but she must have known from birth the afflic-
tion of defeat, the dark brooding of old
warriors.
(30) Her name was Aho, and she belonged to
the last culture to evolve in North America.
Her forebears came down from the high country in western Montana nearly three centuries
ago. They were a mountain people, a mysteri-

(35) ous tribe of hunters whose language has never
been positively classified in any major group.
In the late seventeenth century they began a
long migration to the south and east. It was a
journey toward the dawn, and it led to a gold-
(40) en age. Along the way the Kiowas were
befriended by the Crows, who gave them the
culture and religion of the Plains. They
acquired horses, and their ancient nomadic
spirit was suddenly free of the ground. They
(45) acquired Tai-Me, the sacred Sun Dance doll,
from that moment the object and symbol of
their worship, and so shared in the divinity of
the sun. Not least, they acquired the sense of
destiny, therefore courage and pride. When
(50) they entered upon the southern Plains they had
been transformed. No longer were they slaves
to the simple necessity of survival; they were
a lordly and dangerous society of fighters and
thieves, hunters and priests of the sun.
(55) According to their origin myth, they entered
the world through a hollow log. From one
point of view, their migration was the fruit of
an old prophecy, for indeed they emerged
from a sunless world.

16. The author of this passage indicates in lines
12–16 that the Kiowas waged war predominantly because they

(A) feared the Comanches
(B) wanted more land
(C) were warlike in nature
(D) had been humiliated by the cavalry
(E) believed they would perish otherwise

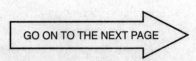

GO ON TO THE NEXT PAGE

1   1   1   1   1   1   1   1   1   1   1

17. Compared to the Kiowa warriors, the cavalry-
    men were

    (A) more idealistic about warfare
    (B) exceptionally fine horsemen
    (C) vulnerable to divisiveness
    (D) unswerving in determination
    (E) less given to brooding

18. The author's grandmother directly experienced

    (A) imprisonment at Fort Sill
    (B) the bleak attitude of the older Kiowa men
    (C) the defeat at Palo Duro Canyon
    (D) the loss of the tribe's provisions
    (E) surrender to the white soldiers

19. The author views the Kiowas of the late seven-
    teenth and eighteenth centuries with a sense of

    (A) urgency
    (B) ambivalence
    (C) remorse
    (D) admiration
    (E) irony

20. By "their ancient nomadic spirit was suddenly
    free of the ground" (lines 42–44), the author
    most nearly means

    (A) the wanderers were now free to worship
        the sun
    (B) the acquisition of horses liberated them to
        rove more freely
    (C) they did not have to pay the Crows for the
        gift of horses
    (D) the oldest of the migratory Kiowas lacked
        ties to the soil
    (E) they no longer believed in the earth spirits
        of their ancestors

21. An "origin myth" (line 55) as used by the
    author is

    (A) a theory of reproduction told to Native
        American children
    (B) a religion the Kiowas learned from the Crows
    (C) a type of tale known only to Kiowas
    (D) an explanation of how the Kiowas came
        into being
    (E) a natural tale about trees and the sun

**Questions 22–30 are based on the following
passage.**

*This passage is from a book written by a contempo-
rary American surgeon about the art of surgery.*

One holds the knife as one holds the bow
of a cello or a tulip—by the stem. Not palmed
nor gripped nor grasped, but lightly, with the
Line tips of the fingers. The knife is not for press-
(5) ing. It is for drawing across the field of skin.
Like a slender fish, it waits, at the ready, then,
go! It darts, followed by a fine wake of red.
The flesh parts, falling away to yellow glob-
ules of fat. Even now, after so many times, I
(10) still marvel at its power—cold, gleaming,
silent. More, I am still struck with dread that it
is I in whose hand the blade travels, that my
hand is its vehicle, that yet again this terrible
steel-bellied thing and I have conspired for a
(15) most unnatural purpose, the laying open of the
body of a human being.
      A stillness settles in my heart and is car-
ried to my hand. It is the quietude of resolve
layered over fear. And it is this resolve that
(20) lowers us, my knife and me, deeper and deeper into the person beneath. It is an entry into
the body that is nothing like a caress; still, it is
among the gentlest of acts. Then stroke and
stroke again, and we are joined by other
(25) instruments, hemostats and forceps, until the
wound blooms with strange flowers whose
looped handles fall to the sides in steely array.
There is a sound, the tight click of clamps fix-
ing teeth into severed blood vessels, the snuf-
(30) fle and gargle of the suction machine clearing
the field of blood for the next stroke, the litany
of monosyllables with which one prays his
way down and in: *clamp, sponge, suture, tie,
cut.* And there is color. The green of the cloth,
(35) the white of the sponges, the red and yellow of
the body. Beneath the fat lies the fascia, the

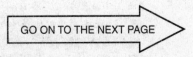

GO ON TO THE NEXT PAGE

**1   1   1   1   1   1   1   1   1   1   1   1**

tough fibrous sheet encasing the muscles. It must be sliced and the red beef of the muscles separated. Now there are retractors to hold
(40) apart the wound. Hands move together, part, weave. We are fully engaged, like children absorbed in a game or the craftsmen of some place like Damascus.

Deeper still. The peritoneum, pink and
(45) gleaming and membranous, bulges into the wound. It is grasped with forceps, and opened. For the first time we can see into the cavity of the abdomen. Such a primitive place. One expects to find drawings of buffalo on the
(50) walls. The sense of trespassing is keener now, heightened by the world's light illuminating the organs, their secret colors revealed—maroon and salmon and yellow. The vista is sweetly vulnerable at this moment, a kind of
(55) welcoming. An arc of the liver shines high and on the right, like a dark sun. It laps over the pink sweep of the stomach, from whose lower border the gauzy omentum is draped, and through which veil one sees, sinuous, slow as
(60) just-fed snakes, the indolent coils of the intestine.

You turn aside to wash your gloves. It is a ritual cleansing. One enters this temple doubly washed. Here is man as microcosm, represent-
(65) ing in all his parts the earth, perhaps the universe.

I must confess that the priestliness of my profession has ever been impressed on me. In the beginning there are vows, taken with all
(70) solemnity. Then there is the endless harsh novitiate of training, much fatigue, much sacrifice. At last one emerges as a celebrant, standing close to the truth lying curtained in the ark of the body. Not surplice and cassock
(75) but mask and gown are your regalia. You hold no chalice, but a knife. There is no wine, no wafer. There are only the facts of blood and flesh.

22. The passage is best described as
    (A) a definition of a concept
    (B) an example of a particular method
    (C) a discussion of an agenda
    (D) a description of a process
    (E) a lesson on a technique

23. The "wake of red" to which the author refers (line 7) is
    (A) a sign of embarrassment
    (B) an infectious rash
    (C) a line of blood
    (D) the blade of the knife
    (E) a trail of antiseptic

24. In line 8, "parts" most nearly means
    (A) leaves
    (B) splits
    (C) rushes
    (D) shares
    (E) quivers

25. The "strange flowers" with which the wound blooms (line 26) are
    (A) clots of blood
    (B) severed blood vessels
    (C) scattered sponges
    (D) gifts of love
    (E) surgical tools

26. In writing of the "strange flowers" with which the wound blooms (lines 23–27), the author is being
    (A) technical
    (B) derogatory
    (C) ambivalent
    (D) metaphorical
    (E) didactic

GO ON TO THE NEXT PAGE ➡

1   1   1   1   1   1   1   1   1   1   1

27. The word "engaged" in line 41 most nearly means

(A) compromised
(B) engrossed
(C) delighted
(D) determined
(E) betrothed

28. In lines 48–50, the comment "One expects to find drawings of buffalo on the walls" metaphorically compares the abdominal cavity to

(A) an art gallery
(B) a zoological display
(C) a natural history museum
(D) a prehistoric cave
(E) a Western film

29. In creating an impression of abdominal surgery for the reader, the author makes use of

(A) comparison with imaginary landscapes
(B) contrast to other types of surgery
(C) description of meteorological processes
(D) evocation of the patient's emotions
(E) reference to religious observances

30. One aspect of the passage that might make it difficult to appreciate is the author's apparent assumption throughout that readers will

(A) have qualms about reading descriptions of major surgery
(B) be already familiar with handling surgical tools
(C) be able to visualize the body organs that are named
(D) relate accounts of specific surgical acts to their own experience of undergoing surgery
(E) remember their own years of medical training

## STOP

**IF YOU FINISH BEFORE TIME IS CALLED, YOU MAY CHECK YOUR WORK ON THIS SECTION ONLY. DO NOT WORK ON ANY OTHER SECTION IN THE TEST.**

**2**   2   2   2   2   2   2   2   2   2   **2**

## Section 2

TIME—30 MINUTES
35 QUESTIONS
For each of the following questions, select the best answer from the choices provided and fill in the appropriate circle.

---

Directions: Each sentence below has one or two blanks, each blank indicating that something has been omitted. Beneath the sentence are five words or sets of words labeled A through E. Choose the word or set of words that, when inserted in the sentence, best fits the meaning of the sentence as a whole.

Example:

Medieval kingdoms did not become constitutional republics overnight; on the contrary, the change was ____.

(A) unpopular
(B) unexpected
(C) advantageous
(D) sufficient
(E) gradual

Ⓐ  Ⓑ  Ⓒ  Ⓓ  ●

---

1. Though financially successful, the theater season, once again, is more noted for its ____ than for its original productions.

   (A) musicals
   (B) revivals
   (C) failures
   (D) rehearsals
   (E) commercials

2. During the Ice Ages, muskoxen ranged as far south as Iowa, in North America, and Spain, in Europe, but in recent centuries the species has been ____ arctic tundra habitats, such as Greenland and the arctic islands of Canada.

   (A) barred from
   (B) confined to
   (C) dissatisfied with
   (D) enervated by
   (E) unknown in

3. Just as an orchestra cannot consist only of violins, a society cannot consist only of managers, for society is an ____ in which different parts have different ____.

   (A) anarchy...powers
   (B) edifice...complaints
   (C) organism...functions
   (D) institution...results
   (E) urbanity...ambitions

4. A ____ person is one who will ____ something on the slightest of evidence.

   (A) restive...forget
   (B) garrulous...criticize
   (C) maudlin...censure
   (D) phlegmatic...condemn
   (E) credulous...believe

GO ON TO THE NEXT PAGE ⟶

**2** 2 2 2 2 2 2 2 2 2 2 **2**

5. That the brain physically changes when stimulated, instead of remaining _____ from infancy to death, as previously thought, was Doctor Marian Diamond's first, and perhaps most far-reaching discovery.

 (A) mutable
 (B) static
 (C) sensory
 (D) vigorous
 (E) fluid

6. There were _____ in her nature that made her seem an _____ enigma: she was severe and gentle; she was modest and disdainful; she longed for affection and was cold.

 (A) aspirations…irreducible
 (B) contradictions…inexplicable
 (C) distortions…impetuous
 (D) disparities…interminable
 (E) incongruities…irrelevant

7. At a time when biographies that debunk their subjects are all the rage, it is refreshing to have one idol who not only lives up to her legend but _____ it.

 (A) complicates
 (B) surpasses
 (C) compromises
 (D) rejects
 (E) subverts

8. *Morphing* is a term _____ for the metamorphosis of one shape into another, such as the smooth formation of a live actor from a silvery puddle as seen in *Terminator 2*.

 (A) coined
 (B) denigrated
 (C) simulated
 (D) mistaken
 (E) repudiated

9. Einstein's humility was so _____ that it might have seemed a pose affected by a great man had it not been so obviously _____.

 (A) spurious…genuine
 (B) convincing…assumed
 (C) profound…sincere
 (D) heartfelt…hypocritical
 (E) modest…contrived

10. Something in Christopher responded to the older man's air of authority; he looked _____, used to _____.

 (A) magisterial…command
 (B) monumental…intimidate
 (C) diffident…domineer
 (D) masterful…obey
 (E) decisive…fret

GO ON TO THE NEXT PAGE

2   2   2   2   2   2   2   2   2   2   2

Directions: Each question below consists of a related pair of words or phrases, followed by five pairs of words or phrases labeled A through E. Select the pair that best expresses a relationship similar to that expressed in the original pair.

Example:

CRUMB : BREAD ::

(A) ounce : unit
(B) splinter : wood
(C) water : bucket
(D) twine : rope
(E) cream : butter

Ⓐ ● Ⓒ Ⓓ Ⓔ

11. COOP : CHICKENS ::

(A) school : fish
(B) flock : geese
(C) sty : pigs
(D) mutton : sheep
(E) forest : deer

12. MASON : STONE ::

(A) tailor : fabric
(B) dentist : drill
(C) sculptor : mallet
(D) actor : stage
(E) miser : gold

13. FLURRY : BLIZZARD ::

(A) hurricane : typhoon
(B) deluge : drought
(C) drizzle : downpour
(D) zephyr : breeze
(E) current : wave

14. CONSTELLATION : STAR ::

(A) delegation : representative
(B) meeting : acquaintance
(C) congregation : church
(D) courthouse : judge
(E) epidemic : disease

15. ANCHOR : NEWSROOM ::

(A) sailor : lighthouse
(B) novelist : plot
(C) artist : exhibit
(D) mourner : cemetery
(E) astronomer : observatory

16. BANAL : ORIGINALITY ::

(A) ribald : pleasure
(B) popular : novelty
(C) baleful : malevolence
(D) forbidden : progress
(E) clumsy : grace

17. BRIDGE : SHIP ::

(A) tunnel : automobile
(B) cockpit : plane
(C) closet : bedroom
(D) handlebars : bicycle
(E) annex : building

18. WASTEFUL : SQUANDER ::

(A) intrepid : fear
(B) cautious : procrastinate
(C) querulous : complain
(D) circumspect : fascinate
(E) gullible : question

GO ON TO THE NEXT PAGE

**2   2   2   2   2   2   2   2   2   2   2**

19. LISTEN : EAVESDROP ::

    (A) hear : recollect
    (B) witness : envision
    (C) ascertain : confess
    (D) wait : lurk
    (E) travel : meander

20. LOAFER : INDOLENT ::

    (A) laggard : restless
    (B) buffoon : clownish
    (C) clodhopper : energetic
    (D) miser : benevolent
    (E) sluggard : pugnacious

21. ADDENDUM : BOOK ::

    (A) extension : house
    (B) abridgement : novel
    (C) agenda : meeting
    (D) elevation : peak
    (E) acreage : land

22. EMBELLISHMENT : DECORATIVE ::

    (A) harvest : bountiful
    (B) circumlocution : indirect
    (C) landscape : pristine
    (D) accessory : essential
    (E) setting : elaborate

23. SELF-INDULGENT : ABSTAIN ::

    (A) self-effacing : defer
    (B) self-deprecating : boast
    (C) self-centered : alienate
    (D) self-willed : coerce
    (E) self-possessed : oblige

GO ON TO THE NEXT PAGE

2 2 2 2 2 2 2 2 2 2 2

---

---

**Questions 24–35 are based on the following passage.**

*The following passage is taken from an article by a contemporary poet about Clement Clarke Moore, the nineteenth-century writer best known as the author of "A Visit From Saint Nicholas."*

If he wasn't a myth maker himself, at least Clement Clarke Moore was a great myth refin-
er. He started with St. Nicholas, giver of pre-
Line sents, whom the Dutch settlers had brought
(5) over to New York. Moore's portrait of the good saint is as fleshy and real as some Frans Hals painting of a burgher:

> The stump of a pipe he held tight in his teeth,
(10) > And the smoke it encircled his head like a wreath.

But with American efficiency, Moore combines the figure of St. Nicholas with that of Kris Kringle, who (in Norwegian lore)
(15) helped the saint by driving a reindeer-drawn sleigh. Moore fires Kris, leaving St. Nick to do his own driving. The result is our own American Santa Claus. Moore removes St. Nick's bishop's miter, decks him out in fur,
(20) gives him a ruddy face and a pot belly, hands him a sack of toys and calls him an elf—sug-
gesting a pointed cap. Thomas Nast, our most authoritative Santa Claus delineator, stuck closely to Moore's description, and ever since,
(25) few artists have dared depart from it.

To see how good Moore's imagination is, you have only to compare his version of St. Nicholas with Washington Irving's of a few years earlier. In 1809, in "Knickerbocker's
(30) History of New York," Irving makes St. Nick a friendly Dutch-American deity "riding jollily among the tree-tops" in (of all things) a

wagon, not only on Christmas but also on any old holiday afternoon. What pulled that silly
(35) wagon Irving doesn't say, nor why it didn't snag itself on a branch and bust both axles.

But Moore in his genius provides St. Nick with reindeer power. And by laying marvelous names on those obedient steeds, he makes
(40) each one an individual. Though ruminants may be poorly designed for flight, Moore doesn't worry his head about aerodynamics; he just sidesteps the whole problem. Dasher, Dancer, Prancer, and the rest of the crew sim-
(45) ply whiz up to the rooftop by pure magic. It never occurs to us to question such a feat. We are one with Moore's protagonist, a man with "wondering eyes."

Delving into John Hollander's recent
(50) Library of America anthology "American Poetry: The Nineteenth Century," I was glad to find "A Visit From St. Nicholas" right there along with works by Whitman, Emily Dickinson and Jones Very. Professional decon-
(55) structionists may sneer, but popular demand has fixed the poem securely in our national heritage. If Mr. Hollander had left it out, it would have been missed. Statistics are scarce, but it seems likely that Moore's masterwork
(60) has been reprinted, recited and learned by heart more often than any other American poem—and that goes for "The Raven," "Casey at the Bat," and Sylvia Plath's "Daddy."

To be sure, mere popularity doesn't make
(65) a work of art great. If it did, then "September Morn," that delicate tribute to skinny-dipping once reproduced on calendars hung in barber-
shops and pool halls galore, would be a better

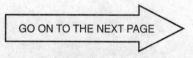
GO ON TO THE NEXT PAGE

2  2  2  2  2  2  2  2  2  2  2

painting than "Nude Descending a Staircase"
(70) any day. And yet a poem like Moore's that has
stuck around for 171 years has to have something going for it.

Well then, what? I submit that the poem's
immortality may be due not only to Moore's
(75) perfecting a great myth, but also to his skill in
music-making. It is a moribund reader who
doesn't feel the spell of its bounding anapests,
as hard to ignore as a herd of reindeer on your
roof. Poets today tend to shy away from such
(80) obvious rhythms. They shrink too from alliteration, which, applied badly, seems bric-a-brac.
But Moore lays it on thick, and makes it work
like a charm: the "fl" sounds in "Away to the
window I flew like a flash," the hard "c"
(85) sounds in "More rapid than eagles his coursers
they came." As for his rhymes, most clunk
along unsurprisingly (like "house" and
"mouse"), but a few sound Muse-inspired. If
any later versifier ever hits upon another pair
(90) of rhyming words as fresh and precise as
these, let him die smug:

*He sprang to his sleigh, to his team gave a
whistle,*
*And way they all flew like the down of a*
(95) *thistle.*

History doesn't tell us whether Moore's
daughters, who first received the poem as a
Christmas present in 1822, were disappointed
at not getting dolls instead. Anyhow, it is a
(100) safe bet that, a hundred years from now, many
a more serious and respectable poem will have
departed from human memory like the down
of a thistle, while Moore's vision of that won-
derful eight-deer sleigh will go thundering on.
(105) "A Visit From St. Nicholas" may be only a
sweet confection, yet how well it lasts. On a
cold winter night, it can warm you to the
quick: a homemade verbal cookie dipped in
Ovaltine.

24. The passage serves primarily to
    (A) inform the reader of a new anthology fea-
        turing "A Visit to St. Nicholas"
    (B) encourage contemporary poets to adopt the
        literary techniques used by Clement
        Clarke Moore
    (C) give an instance of a great work of art that
        has won universal renown
    (D) correct a misconception about the origins
        of Santa Claus
    (E) explain the enduring appeal of a classic
        example of light verse

25. By calling Clement Clarke Moore "a great
    myth refiner," the author intends to convey that
    Moore
    (A) was skillful at explaining myths
    (B) created brand new legends
    (C) studied the origins of myths
    (D) transformed old myths into something new
    (E) disdained the crudity of early mythology

26. Moore's sources for his Saint Nicholas can best
    be described as
    (A) eclectic
    (B) pagan
    (C) meager
    (D) illusory
    (E) authoritative

27. We can infer from lines 22–25 that Thomas
    Nast most likely was
    (A) an imitator of Moore's verse
    (B) a critic of Moore's changes to traditional
        figures
    (C) an illustrator of Moore's poem
    (D) an iconoclastic artist
    (E) a competitor of Moore's

GO ON TO THE NEXT PAGE

2  2  2  2  2  2  2  2  2  2  2  2

28. Which statement best summarizes the point made in lines 26–48?

(A) Moore's portrait of Saint Nicholas antedates Washington Irving's interpretation.
(B) Irving's version of Saint Nicholas surpasses the one created by Moore.
(C) Moore's interpretation of Saint Nicholas is less friendly than Irving's interpretation is.
(D) Moore preferred his version of Saint Nicholas to Irving's variant.
(E) Moore showed greater creativity than Irving in constructing his picture of Saint Nicholas.

29. The statement in lines 46–48 ("We are one . . . eyes'") is best interpreted as conveying the idea that

(A) we share the identity of the protagonist
(B) we too view the proceedings with astonishment and awe
(C) we do not understand the attraction of what takes place
(D) we question the events as they occur
(E) we also resemble Saint Nicholas in nature

30. The author's attitude toward "professional deconstructionists" (lines 54–57) can best be described as

(A) respectful
(B) dismissive
(C) adulatory
(D) timorous
(E) perplexed

31. In line 62, the phrase "goes for" most nearly means

(A) aims at
(B) passes for
(C) holds true for
(D) gives approval to
(E) attacks physically

32. The word "mere" in line 64 means

(A) insignificant
(B) involuntary
(C) momentary
(D) simple
(E) problematic

33. In line 76, the author uses the word "moribund" to emphasize the reader's

(A) immortality
(B) fear of dying
(C) ignorance of mythology
(D) reservations about magic
(E) insensitivity to verse

34. The author regards Moore's use of the rhyming words "whistle" and "thistle" with

(A) self-satisfaction and complacency
(B) amusement and condescension
(C) delight and admiration
(D) interest yet envy
(E) derision and disdain

35. One aspect of the passage that might make it difficult to appreciate is the author's apparent assumption that readers will

(A) prefer the realistic paintings of Hals to later artworks
(B) have read Hollander's anthology of American poetry
(C) be acquainted with statistics about the memorization of verse
(D) understand the author's childhood associations with Saint Nicholas
(E) already be familiar in great detail with Moore's poem

## STOP

**IF YOU FINISH BEFORE TIME IS CALLED, YOU MAY CHECK YOUR WORK ON THIS SECTION ONLY. DO NOT WORK ON ANY OTHER SECTION IN THE TEST.**

3  3  3  3  3  3  3  3  3  3  3  3

## Section 3

TIME—15 MINUTES
13 QUESTIONS

For each of the following questions, choose the best answer and fill in the appropriate circle on the answer sheet.

Directions: The two passages below are followed by questions based on their content and on the relationship between the two passages. Answer the questions on the basis of what is stated or implied in the passages and in any introductory material that may be provided.

### Questions 1–13 are based on the following passages.

*These passages are portraits of two fathers. The first appeared in a contemporary novel, the second in a memoir written in the 1990s by a person looking back on experiences in the San Francisco Bay area.*

### Passage 1

In 1948 my father was serving his second term as sheriff of Mercer County, Montana. We lived in Bentrock, the county seat and the
Line only town of any size in the region. In 1948
(5) its population was less than two thousand people. . . .

Many of the men in Mercer County had spent the preceding years in combat. (But not my father; he was 4-F. When he was sixteen a
(10) horse kicked him, breaking his leg so severely that he walked with a permanent limp, and eventually a cane, his right leg V-ed in, his right knee perpetually pointing to the left.) When these men came back from war they
(15) wanted nothing more than to work their farms and ranches and to live quietly with their families. The county even had fewer hunters after the war than before.

All of which made my father's job a rela-
(20) tively easy one. Oh, he arrested the usual weekly drunks, mediated an occasional dispute about fence lines or stray cattle, calmed a few domestic disturbances, and warned the town's teenagers about getting rowdy in
(25) Wood's Cafe, but by and large being sheriff of Mercer County did not require great strength or courage. The ability to drive the county's rural roads, often drifted over in the winter or washed out in the summer, was a much more
(30) necessary skill than being good with your fists or a gun. One of my father's regular duties was chaperoning Saturday night dances in the county, but the fact that he often took along my mother (and sometimes me) shows how
(35) quiet those affairs—and his job—usually were.

And that disappointed me at the time. As long as my father was going to be sheriff, a position with so much potential for excite-
(40) ment, danger, and bravery, why couldn't some of that promise be fulfilled? No matter how many wheat fields or cow pastures surrounded us, we were still Montanans, yet my father didn't even look like a western sheriff. He
(45) wore a shirt and tie, as many of the men in town did, but at least they wore boots and Stetsons; my father wore brogans and a fedora. He had a gun but he never carried it, on duty or off. I knew because I checked, time
(50) and time again. When he left the house I ran to his dresser and the top drawer on the right side. And there it was, there it always was. Just as well. As far as I was concerned it was the wrong kind of gun for a sheriff. He should
(55) have had a nickel-plated Western Colt .45, something with some history and heft. Instead, my father had a small .32 automatic,

GO ON TO THE NEXT PAGE

3 3 3 3 3 3 3 3 3 3 3

Italian-made and no bigger than your palm.
My father didn't buy such a sorry gun; he con-
(60) fiscated it from a drunken transient in one of
his first arrests. My father kept the gun but in
fair exchange bought the man a bus ticket to
Billings, where he had family.

## Passage 2

He was good-looking, in a Southern,
(65) romantic poet sort of way. He needed those
good looks, one of the aunts said; why else
would my otherwise sensible mother have
married a man like him, an actor-writer
hyphenate who lived on dreams and spent his
(70) free evenings carrying a spear at the Opera
House. But that was in later times, when he
had moved out of the rundown communal
house in the Berkeley Hills, leaving my mother and the ever-changing cast of nominal
(75) uncles and aunts to patch the ancient water
heater and pump out the basement when the
overpressured valve finally blew. He needed
separateness to write, he said, solitude, something we'd never given him, and he was tired,
(80) tired of being dragged from his study to tend
to the latest household eruption that bubbled
up "like gas from a Calistoga mud bath," he
said, with relentless regularity.

He looked tired by then, as tired of us as
(85) we were of him, of forgotten birthdays and
surprises that failed to surprise. When he did
bring us a present, I even wondered why, for it
was always somehow off: last season's hot toy
no one played with any more, or a complicated
(90) model no boy could assemble without a
father's help. Which we never got. He was an
actor, after all, not tech crew, an artist, not
someone who could fix a toy.

If he was an actor, we were props at best.
(95) Reluctant ones—had there been a Plantagenet
Pleasure Faire, he would have strutted his
hour as Wicked Dick III, while Geoffrey and I,
thrust into burlap sacks, were hauled off, two
little princes in shabby tights, to be disposed
(100) of elsewhere. That was his glory, kinging it.
Living History,[1] he called it, and in the early
days he followed the fairs up and down the

state, living the Renaissance first in Agoura,
then in Marin, finally winding up the acting
(105) season with Victoria's England in San
Francisco or even Oakland for one or two
slow years.

Not that anyone ever hired him to act the
king. No, he was a minor figure even on that
(110) rude stage, a charming but lesser nobleman in
Elizabeth's court, an attentive councilor in
Victoria's entourage. But he shared the perks
of royalty, such as they were, stood center
stage in black velvet pantaloons while the
(115) September sun burned overhead, or posed
handsomely (in a Prince Albert coat, no less)
as the royal party made its way through the
Christmas crowds at Dickens Fair. Why he
stuck to it, I never understood. Certainly not
(120) for the pay.

Between fairs he wrote, or thought of
writing, shut up in his study, into which we
children were not allowed, or did research for
his one-man-shows (in which he played a
(125) series of writers, one per show, so that one
year we saw his Edgar Allen Poe, another
year, his Ambrose Bierce). He was a writer, or
at least a writer once removed, writing down
other men's words and speaking them as if
(130) they were his own. At times it seemed he
thought they were his own, he paraphrased
them so freely, vamping upon the themes of
The Devil's Dictionary.[2] And he probably
thought we were his own as well, as little
(135) acquainted with us as he was. And so we were,
if only by example and heredity.

---

[1] Since the 1960s, California's Living History Centre has pro-
duced fairs and festivals in northern and southern California.
The Rennaissance Pleasure Faire is set in the time of Queen
Elizabeth I; the Dickens Christmas Fair and Pickwick Comic
Annual, in the time of Queen Victoria.
[2] A book of diabolical epigrams by Ambrose Bierce.

GO ON TO THE NEXT PAGE

**3    3    3    3    3    3    3    3    3    3    3**

1. In Passage 1 the narrator uses the parenthetical material (lines 8–13) to

   (A) suggest that his father became sheriff to compensate for his disability
   (B) highlight the difference between his father and other men in Mercer County
   (C) justify his father's peaceful nature
   (D) belittle his father
   (E) indicate that the voters felt sorry for his father when they elected him sheriff

2. Mentioning that Mercer County "had fewer hunters after the war than before" (lines 17–18) is the author's way of saying that

   (A) the men had had their fill of shooting and death
   (B) the men worked long hours and had no time for hunting
   (C) the narrator's father prevented the men from hunting
   (D) the men thought hunting was too dangerous
   (E) many of the hunters were killed in the war

3. By describing his father's work clothes (lines 44–48), the narrator is suggesting that his father

   (A) wanted to dress like other men
   (B) didn't take the sheriff's job seriously
   (C) was pretty dull
   (D) was a nonconformist
   (E) was concerned about his image

4. By wishing that his father had a gun with "some history and some heft" (lines 54–56), the narrator means

   (A) an antique gun
   (B) a more expensive gun
   (C) a gun used in the war
   (D) a gun that could be worn in a holster
   (E) a more impressive gun

5. In Passage 1 which of the following best describes the narrator's feelings about his father?

   (A) Regret
   (B) Hostility
   (C) Resentment
   (D) Affection
   (E) Indifference

6. The narrator of Passage 2 compares himself and his brother to "props" (line 94 because they

   (A) reinforced their father's image as a parent
   (B) were assets to theatrical productions
   (C) were physical objects handled onstage
   (D) supported their father's dramatic efforts
   (E) possessed essential attributes their father lacked

7. In line 110, "rude" most nearly means

   (A) roughly made
   (B) deliberately impolite
   (C) highly vigorous
   (D) inconsiderate
   (E) tempestuous

8. The narrator mentions his father's sharing the perks of royalty (lines 112–118) in order to emphasize that his father

   (A) had gone far in his chosen field
   (B) wanted to share these privileges with his children
   (C) had a particularly regal demeanor
   (D) demanded only the best for himself
   (E) received very little for his efforts

GO ON TO THE NEXT PAGE

3  3  3  3  3  3  3  3  3  3  3

9. Which of the following is NOT an accurate description of the narrator's father?

(A) He was not dependable to his children.
(B) He enjoyed being the center of attention.
(C) He had an appealing appearance.
(D) He was well-liked by those who shared his home.
(E) He was uncomfortable with his responsibilities.

10. The narrator's purpose in writing this portrait of his father was

(A) to show readers the effects of a bohemian lifestyle on one man
(B) to help himself understand his complex feelings toward his father
(C) to illustrate the importance of open communication among members of a family
(D) to tell about the difficulties of his boyhood
(E) to praise his father, a man he both loved and feared

11. In which respect is the portrait of the father in Passage 1 similar to the portrait in Passage 2?

(A) In both passages we see the father through the eyes of a young boy.
(B) Both passages portray the father as deficient in some important way.
(C) In both passages we get to know intimate details of the father's life.
(D) Both passages tell us as much about the narrator as about the father.
(E) Both passages imply that the narrators would like to emulate their fathers.

12. As presented in the two passages, the relationship between each narrator and his father is

(A) loving
(B) competitive
(C) cautious
(D) distant
(E) tense

13. The authors of both passages come across as

(A) loyal sons
(B) intolerant of their fathers
(C) respectful of their fathers
(D) rebellious sons
(E) puzzled by their fathers

## STOP

**IF YOU FINISH BEFORE TIME IS CALLED, YOU MAY CHECK YOUR WORK ON THIS SECTION ONLY. DO NOT WORK ON ANY OTHER SECTION IN THE TEST.**

# ANSWER KEY

## Section 1

| | | | | | | | | | |
|---|---|---|---|---|---|---|---|---|---|
| 1. E | 4. D | 7. C | 10. A | 13. A | 16. C | 19. D | 22. D | 25. E | 28. D |
| 2. C | 5. D | 8. A | 11. C | 14. D | 17. D | 20. B | 23. C | 26. D | 29. E |
| 3. C | 6. D | 9. C | 12. C | 15. E | 18. B | 21. D | 24. B | 27. B | 30. C |

## Section 2

| | | | | | | | | | |
|---|---|---|---|---|---|---|---|---|---|
| 1. B | 5. B | 9. C | 13. C | 17. B | 21. A | 24. E | 27. C | 30. B | 33. E |
| 2. B | 6. B | 10. A | 14. A | 18. C | 22. B | 25. D | 28. E | 31. C | 34. C |
| 3. C | 7. B | 11. C | 15. E | 19. D | 23. B | 26. A | 29. B | 32. D | 35. E |
| 4. E | 8. A | 12. A | 16. E | 20. B | | | | | |

## Section 3

| | | | | | | |
|---|---|---|---|---|---|---|
| 1. C | 3. C | 5. A | 7. A | 9. D | 11. B | 13. E |
| 2. A | 4. E | 6. C | 8. E | 10. B | 12. D | |

## ANALYSIS OF TEST RESULTS

### I. Self-Rating Chart

| | | | | Total |
|---|---|---|---|---|
| **Sentence Completions**<br><br>Number Correct | Section 1<br>(Questions 1–9)<br><br>_____ | Section 2<br>(Questions 1–10)<br><br>_____ | | _____ |
| **Analogies**<br><br>Number Correct | Section 1<br>(Questions 10–15)<br><br>_____ | Section 2<br>(Questions 11–23)<br><br>_____ | | _____ |
| **Critical Reading**<br><br>Number Correct | Section 1<br>(Questions 16–30)<br><br>_____ | Section 2<br>(Questions 24–35)<br><br>_____ | Section 3<br>(Questions 1–13)<br><br>_____ | _____ |

Sentence Completions    Number Correct _____

Analogies    Number Correct _____

Critical Reasoning    Number Correct _____

Subtotal _____

*Guessing Penalty:* Subtract 1/4 point for each incorrect answer. _____
(Do not take off points for questions you left blank.)

TOTAL SCORE _____

### II. Rate Your Performance

| | Sentence Completion/Analogy Score | Reading Score | Total |
|---|---|---|---|
| Excellent | 18–19 Correct | 37–40 | 73–78 |
| Very Good | 14–17 Correct | 27–36 | 55–72 |
| Good | 11–13 Correct | 19–26 | 41–54 |
| Fair | 9–10 Correct | 15–18 | 33–40 |
| Poor | 6–8  Correct | 10–14 | 20–32 |
| Very Poor | 0–5  Correct | 0–9 | 0–19 |

# ANSWER EXPLANATIONS

## SECTION 1

1. **E**   A repair program logically would attempt to *eliminate* or get rid of problems.

2. **C**   "Despite" signals a contrast. Right now, fencing in America is in a stage of growth; the fencing association's membership is expanding. However, the association fears it will not grow but die out (face *extinction*) if spectators cannot understand what's going on. Thus, fencing needs to become more *accessible* (comprehensible).

3. **C**   Something that cannot be solved with ease remains a mystery or *enigma*.

4. **D**   Precise wording reduces the chances of *ambiguity* (confusion about meaning).

5. **D**   If you simply watch or *observe* the skilled activities of others, you are *passive*, that is, inactive.

6. **D**   It would be a *daunting* (discouraging) task to get to know over 700 people in the course of one semester.

7. **C**   The key phrase here is "stick together." Small particles of matter join together to form larger ones. In other words, they *coalesce*.

8. **A**   *Spurious* means false or fake. Malcolm argues that biographers make up or *invent* the facts they narrate, so the orderly narrative you read and take as historically true is actually *illusory* (deceptive; unreal).

9. **C**   A *misnomer* (incorrect designation) by definition misnames something. The writer here is arguing that mole rats have been given the wrong name.

10. **A**   A *taxi* is part of a *fleet* (group of vehicles). A *soldier* is part of a *squad* (group of military personnel).

11. **C**   *Uneasiness* is a less extreme state of worry than *panic* (consternation); *irritation* is a less extreme state of displeasure than *outrage* (great anger).

12. **C**   A *round* is a division of play in a *tournament* or contest. An *inning* is a division of play in a *game*.

13. **A**   By definition, something *breathtaking* (awe-inspiring) fills one with *wonder*. By definition, something *repugnant* or disgusting fills one with *revulsion* (abhorrence; distaste).

14. **D**   By definition, someone or something *quixotic* (unrealistic; impractical) lacks *practicality*. By definition, someone or something *frivolous* (light-minded; superficial) lacks *gravity* (seriousness).

15. **E**   *Acid* is by nature *corrosive*, tending to eat away other substances. *Sap* (the fluid part of plants) is by nature *viscous*, tending to stick to other substances.

16. **C**   The author states that warfare for the Kiowas "was preeminently a matter of disposition rather than of survival." In other words, they were *warlike in their nature*.

17. **D**   The author comments that the Kiowas "never understood the grim, unrelenting advance of the U.S. Cavalry." They lacked the *unswerving determination* that kept the cavalrymen pursuing their foes long after a band of Kiowas would have changed its course.

18. **B**   Born too late to experience the actual fighting and famine, the author's grandmother did experience *the bleak, cheerless attitude* of the defeated warriors, "the dark brooding" *of the older Kiowa men*.

19. **D**   Describing the Kiowas as "a lordly and dangerous society of fighters and thieves, hunters and priests of the sun," members of a courageous and proud tribe, the author clearly regards them with *admiration*.

20. **B**   Before they acquired horses, the Kiowas were tied to the ground, forced to move slowly in the course of their journey toward the dawn. Once they had horses, however, they were *liberated to rove more freely*; their wandering spirit was no longer tied down.

21. **D** The Kiowas' origin myth describes how "they entered the world through a hollow log." Thus, it is *an explanation of how they came to be* on earth.

22. **D** Step by step, the author traces the course of a surgical procedure, from the initial grasping of the scalpel through the opening incision to the eventual sensory exploration of the internal organs. In doing so, he is *describing a process*.

23. **C** As the surgeon draws the knife across the skin, it leaves behind a thin *line of blood* in its wake (path or track passed over by a moving object).

24. **B** To part the flesh is to *split* or separate the skin.

25. **E** The "strange flowers" with their looped handles are the hemostats, forceps, and other *surgical tools* attached to the opening.

26. **D** To write of one object by using a term that normally indicates a different object, suggesting a likeness between them, is to make an implicit comparison, that is, to be *metaphorical*.

27. **B** The simile "like children absorbed in a game" indicates that in this context "engaged" means *engrossed* or deeply involved.

28. **D** Primitive drawings of buffalo and other wild beasts still exist in *caves* in which *prehistoric* humans dwelled.

29. **E** Writing of "ritual cleansing," entering the "temple" of the human body, the truth hidden in the "ark" or holy place, the author is referring to priestly or *religious observances* (rites).

30. **C** The author freely uses technical names for various *body organs*—"fascia," "peritoneum," "omentum"—tossing in occasional descriptive adjectives or phrases as if he assumes the reader is already *able to visualize* these organs in some detail. Readers without much background in anatomy might well feel the need for additional information about these organs (size, function, specific location) in order to appreciate the passage fully.

# Section 2

1. **B** The contrast here is between *revivals* (new productions of old plays) and original productions.

2. **B** "But" signals a contrast. In the Ice Ages, muskoxen ranged or roamed over much of the Northern Hemisphere. In recent times, however, they have been *confined* or limited to the far northernmost regions.

3. **C** The comparison suggests society is an *organism* made up of many parts serving different tasks or *functions*.

4. **E** By definition, someone *credulous* or gullible readily *believes* things without having much reason to do so.

5. **B** "Instead" signals a contrast. The missing word must be an antonym or near-antonym for "physically changes." Something *static* or unchanging by definition does not physically change.

6. **B** To be sometimes harsh and sometimes gentle is to act in *contradictory* ways. Such inconsistencies in behavior might well make someone seem an *inexplicable* enigma, a mystery that could not be explained.

7. **B** To debunk the subject of a biography is to expose the false claims about that person's virtues, to poke holes in the legend, so to speak. The subject of this biography, however, deserves the praise she has been awarded. She is even better than tales paint her, *surpassing* her legend.

8. **A** To come up with or invent a name for something new is to *coin* a term.

9. **C** Einstein's humility was not a pose that he put on for an audience. His *profound*, deep humility was clearly *sincere* (genuine; unfeigned).

10. **A** By definition, *magisterial* means authoritative or *commanding*.

11. **C** A *coop* is an enclosure for *chickens*. A *sty* is an enclosure for *pigs*.

12. **A** A *mason* (stoneworker) constructs things from *stone*. A *tailor* constructs things from *fabric*.

13. **C**    A *flurry* (sudden, brief snowfall) is less intense than a *blizzard* (severe and prolonged snowstorm). A *drizzle* (light rain) is less intense than a *downpour* (heavy rain).

14. **A**    A *star* is part of a *constellation* (grouping of stars). A *representative* is part of a *delegation* (body of delegates).

15. **E**    A *newsroom* is the place where an *anchor* (member of a newscasting team) works. An *observatory* is the place where an *astronomer* works.

16. **E**    By definition, something *banal* (trite) lacks *originality*. By definition, something *clumsy* (awkward) lacks *grace*.

17. **B**    The *bridge* is the part of the *ship* from which it is steered. The *cockpit* is the part of the *plane* from which it is steered.

18. **C**    By definition, someone *wasteful* (extravagant) *squanders* or wastes. By definition, someone *querulous* (peevish) grumbles or *complains*.

19. **D**    To *eavesdrop* is to *listen* in a secret, stealthy manner. To *lurk* is to *wait* in a secret, stealthy manner.

20. **B**    A *loafer* or idler is by definition *indolent* (lazy). A *buffoon* or jester is by definition *clownish* (like a fool).

21. **A**    An *addendum* (supplement) is an addition to a *book*. An *extension* is an addition to a *house*.

22. **B**    An *embellishment* (ornamentation) is by definition *decorative*. A *circumlocution* (roundabout way of stating something) is by definition *indirect*.

23. **B**    If you are *self-indulgent* (unrestrained about gratifying your own desires), you are unlikely to *abstain* or refrain from giving in to your appetites. If you are *self-deprecating* (inclined to undervalue or belittle yourself), you are unlikely to brag or *boast*.

24. **E**    Throughout the passage, the author praises Moore's "sweet confection," demonstrating its strengths and showing reasons for its popularity over the years. Thus, the passage chiefly serves to *explain the enduring appeal of this classic example of light verse.*

25. **D**    Moore did not invent any new myths. However, he *transformed the old myths* of Kris Kringle the sled driver and Saint Nicholas the bishop into our archetypal Santa Claus.

26. **A**    Moore uses sources from a variety of traditions—Norwegian, Dutch, possibly even American. To compose something out of elements drawn from such a variety of sources is by definition to be *eclectic*.

27. **C**    To delineate Santa Claus is to depict or portray him. The *illustrator* Thomas Nast closely based his illustrations of Santa Claus on Moore's own words.

28. **E**    One contrasts Moore's St. Nick with Irving's in order to see just how very good and imaginative a job Moore did compared to Irving. Moore goes beyond Irving in furnishing Santa with steeds, naming these steeds, and differentiating them from one another. In doing so, he shows considerable *creativity*.

29. **B**    We never think of questioning what the poem says, because, like the poem's protagonist, we are too awestruck by what we see to ask any questions. We view what occurs *with astonishment and awe.*

30. **B**    The author disregards or *dismisses* the sneers of the professional deconstructionists (literary critics, members of a literary school with little respect for light verse). He believes the lasting popularity of the piece should outweigh the deconstructionists' petty criticisms.

31. **C**    The phrase "that goes for 'The Raven'" means "that also *holds true for* 'The Raven.'" The author is asserting that he has not ignored the claims of popular favorites like "Casey at the Bat" and "The Raven" in saying Moore's poem is probably our most popular American poem.

32. **D**    "Mere popularity" here means *simple* popularity, considered apart from any other quality a work of art might possess.

33. **E**    A moribund reader is someone figuratively dead or *insensitive to the verse* he or she reads. (*Moribund* literally means approaching death; dormant.)

34. **C**    The author presents this pair of rhyming words as one of Moore's "Muse-inspired" better pairings. Clearly, he regards Moore's use of these words with both *delight* in the rhyme and *admiration* for the rhymester.

35. **E**    The author does not bother to summarize the story of "A Visit From Saint Nicholas" for the reader. He refers blithely to its anapests and alliteration, mentions its protagonist (whom someone unfamiliar with the poem, not knowing any better, might have confused with Saint Nick), and generally assumes that anyone reading his article will *already be familiar in great detail with Moore's poem.*

# SECTION 3

1. **C**    Throughout the passage, the narrator, a small boy, wishes that his father had been a tougher, more heroic sheriff. *To justify his father's peaceful nature* to himself as well as to his reader, he explains why his father had not gone to war like other men.

2. **A**    We are told that when the men returned from war, they "wanted nothing more than to work their farms and ranches and to live quietly with their families." In essence, the war veterans *had had their fill of shooting and death.*

3. **C**    The narrator disapproves of his father's clothes. At least the other men "wore boots and Stetsons." All told, the boy thinks that his father is *pretty dull,* especially for a sheriff in Montana.

4. **E**    The boy wishes that his father carried a "nickel-plated Western Colt .45," perhaps one that had been carried by a gunslinging sheriff in the old West. In short, it ought to have been a *more impressive* firearm.

5. **A**    The passage is tinged with the boy's *regret* that his father was not a tougher, more glamorous sheriff. In fact, he says that aspects of his father's job "disappointed" him.

6. **C**    Theatrical properties or props are usually movable items (not costumes or furniture) that actors use onstage during a performance. Note how the boys are hauled offstage as if they were inanimate *physical objects.*

7. **A**    The stage is rude in the same sense that "the rude bridge that arched the flood" is rude: it is a *roughly made,* somewhat primitive structure.

8. **E**    The narrator uses the phrase "such as they were" to dismiss the supposed perks or privileges of stage royalty. Considering that his father's reward was to stand under a hot sun wearing a heavy costume, it is clear that his father *received very little for his efforts.*

9. **D**    Given that he forgot their birthdays and never helped them fix their toys, the narrator's father clearly was "not dependable to his children." He "enjoyed being the center of attention": he gloried in acting like a king and starring in one-man shows. He "had an appealing appearance," evidenced by the good looks that attracted his wife. He "was uncomfortable with his responsibilities," tired of dealing with household problems. All he lacked was the liking of *those who shared his home,* who grew to be as tired of him as he asserted he was of them.

10. **B**    The narrator has told the story of his father to better *understand his complex feelings toward his father,* who abandoned his family responsibilities in pursuit of ambitions the narrator neither shares nor fully understands.

11. **B**    The authors of the two passages portray their fathers as *deficient in some important way.* The father in Passage 1 is not tough and courageous enough to suit his son, and the father in Passage 2 is flawed in many ways—from his inability to succeed in his career to his destructive self-centeredness.

12. **D**    Neither son seems to have a close relationship with his father. In essence, they are *distant.*

13. **E**    The author of Passage 1 seems to be asking how a man can be both a sheriff in Montana and a wimp at the same time? It's *puzzling* to the boy. The author of Passage 2 analyzes his father closely, but not with a sense of confidence in his findings. In many ways the father remains *puzzling.* As the passage says, the author never understood why the father endured his low-paid, uncelebrated career as an actor working for the fairs.

PART **VIII**

# SUGGESTED STUDY PROGRAM

Introduction
Your Personal Study
  Program

# INTRODUCTION

Over the past two years, teachers and students have written to Barron's to ask advice on how to work through the entire *Verbal Workbook* in a systematic, well-thought-out manner. Because today more and more students are applying to early acceptance programs, many young people are starting to prepare for their SATs as early as their sophomore year. These students need help in pacing themselves over the long months ahead so that they can build their SAT prep into their regular study schedules.

The program that follows is flexible enough to accommodate students with study time from two years to two months to prepare for the SAT. We hope it will also prove helpful to classroom teachers and tutors seeking guidelines as to how heavy a workload their students can handle.

# YOUR PERSONAL STUDY PROGRAM

Whether you have a year to prepare for SAT I or only a month or two, you will do best if you work regularly and follow a plan. Your preparation for the verbal reasoning sections of SAT I and PSAT should be as thorough as time permits. The assignments that follow have been designed to take you through this workbook step by step. Complete as many of the cycles listed below as you can in the time you have available. Each cycle you complete will improve your chances for a good score on the test.

Except for Assignment 1, the assignment for each day's work should take no more than an hour to complete. After completing the day's assignment, review any vocabulary words that gave you difficulty and study the answer explanations.

Space your assignments as you choose, or as time allows. If you have a full year to prepare, you can do one assignment a week and still have a full month free for vacation time. If you have only three months, you can do one assignment every other day. However you organize your study program, you know you're on your way to verbal expertise.

## CYCLE I

### Assignment 1

Take Verbal Self-Assessment Test (page 17).

### Assignment 2

Review answer explanations to Verbal Self-Assessment Test (page 37).

## CYCLE II

### Assignment 3

Read Tips on Sentence Completion questions, Analogies, and Critical Reading.
Take Verbal Reasoning Test 1, Section 1 (page 209).

### Assignment 4

Take Verbal Reasoning Test 1, Section ·2 (page 216).

**Assignment 5**

Take Verbal Reasoning Test 1, Section 3 (page 223).

Review answer explanations to Verbal Reasoning Test 1 (page 228).

## CYCLE III

Begin work on Sentence Completion questions, Analogies, Critical Reading, and Vocabulary.

**Assignment 6**

Do Sentence Completion Exercise 1, Level A (page 46).

Study Word Lists 1 (page 173) and 2 (page 173).

**Assignment 7**

Do Analogy Exercise 1, Level A (page 88).

Study Word Lists 3 (page 173) and 4 (page 174).

**Assignment 8**

Do Critical Reading Exercise 1, Questions 1–15, Level A (page 124).

Study Word Lists 5 (page 174) and 6 (page 175).

**Assignment 9**

Do Sentence Completion Exercise 2, Level A (page 49).

Study Word Lists 7 (page 175) and 8 (page 176).

**Assignment 10**

Do Analogy Exercise 2, Level A (page 90).

Study Word Lists 9 (page 176) and 10 (page 176).

**Assignment 11**

Do Critical Reading Exercise 1, Questions 16–40, Level A (page 127).

## CYCLE IV

**Assignment 12**

Do Sentence Completion Exercise 3, Level A (page 51).

Study Word Lists 11 (page 177) and 12 (page 177).

**Assignment 13**

Do Analogy Exercise 3, Level A (page 91).

Study Word Lists 13 (page 177) and 14 (page 178).

**Assignment 14**

Do Critical Reading Exercise 2, Questions 1–15, Level A (page 133).

Study Word Lists 15 (page 178) and 16 (page 179).

**Assignment 15**

Do Sentence Completion Exercise 4, Level A (page 53).

Study Word Lists 17 (page 179) and 18 (page 179).

**Assignment 16**

Do Analogy Exercise 4, Level A (page 93).

Study Word Lists 19 (page 180) and 20 (page 180).

**Assignment 17**

Do Critical Reading Exercise 2, Questions 16–40, Level A (page 136).

## CYCLE V

**Assignment 18**

Do Sentence Completion Exercise 1, Level B (page 55).

Study Word Lists 21 (page 181) and 22 (page 181).

**Assignment 19**

Do Analogy Exercise 1, Level B (page 94).

Study Word Lists 23 (page 181) and 24 (page 182).

**Assignment 20**

Do Critical Reading Exercise 1, Questions 1–15, Level B (page 141).

Study Word Lists 25 (page 182) and 26 (page 183).

**Assignment 21**

Do Sentence Completion Exercise 2, Level B (page 57).

Study Word Lists 27 (page 183) and 28 (page 183).

**Assignment 22**

Do Analogy Exercise 2, Level B (page 96).

Study Word Lists 29 (page 184) and 30 (page 184).

**Assignment 23**

Do Critical Reading Exercise 1, Questions 16–40, Level B (page 144).

# CYCLE VI

### Assignment 24

Do Sentence Completion Exercise 3, Level B (page 59).
Study Word Lists 31 (page 185) and 32 (page 185).

### Assignment 25

Do Analogy Exercise 3, Level B (page 97).
Study Word Lists 33 (page 185) and 34 (page 186).

### Assignment 26

Do Critical Reading Exercise 1, Questions 1–15, Level C (page 149).
Study Word Lists 35 (page 186) and 36 (page 187).

### Assignment 27

Do Sentence Completion Exercise 4, Level B (page 61).
Study Word Lists 37 (page 187) and 38 (page 187).

### Assignment 28

Do Analogy Exercise 4, Level B (page 99).
Study Word Lists 39 (page 188) and 40 (page 188).

### Assignment 29

Do Critical Reading Exercise 1, Questions 16–40, Level C (page 152).

# CYCLE VII

### Assignment 30

Do Sentence Completion Exercise 1, Level C (page 63).
Study Word Lists 41 (page 188) and 42 (page 189).

### Assignment 31

Do Analogy Exercise 1, Level C (page 101).
Study Word Lists 43 (page 189) and 44 (page 190).

### Assignment 32

Do Sentence Completion Exercise 2, Level C (page 65).
Study Word Lists 45 (page 190) and 46 (page 190).

### Assignment 33

Do Analogy Exercise 2, Level C (page 103).
Study Word Lists 47 (page 191) and 48 (page 191).

### Assignment 34

Do Sentence Completion Exercise 3, Level C (page 67).
Study Word Lists 49 (page 191) and 50 (page 192).

### Assignment 35

Do Analogy Exercise 3, Level C (page 104).
Study Word Lists 51 (page 191) and 52 (page 193).

# CYCLE VIII

### Assignment 36

Do Sentence Completion Exercise 4, Level C (page 69).
Study Word Lists 53 (page 193) and 54 (page 193).

### Assignment 37

Do Analogy Exercise 4, Level C (page 105).
Study Word Lists 55 (page 194) and 56 (page 194).

### Assignment 38

Take Verbal Reasoning Test 2, Section 1 (page 235).
Study Word List 57 (page 195).

### Assignment 39

Study Word Lists 58 (page 195), 59 (page 195), 60 (page 196), and 61 (page 196).

### Assignment 40

Take Verbal Reasoning Test 2, Section 2 (page 242).
Study Word List 62 (page 197).

### Assignment 41

Study Word Lists 63 (page 197), 64 (page 198), 65 (page 198), and 66 (page 198).

### Assignment 42

Take Verbal Reasoning Test 2, Section 3 (page 249).
Review answer explanations to Verbal Reasoning Test 2 (page 254).
Study Word Lists 67 (page 199) and 68 (page 199).

# CYCLE IX

### Assignment 43

Study Word Lists 69 (page 200), 70 (page 200), 71 (page 200), and 72 (page 201).

## Assignment 44

Study Word Lists 73 (page 201), 74 (page 201), 75 (page 202), and 76 (page 202).

## Assignment 45

Take Verbal Reasoning Test 3, Section 1 (page 261). Study Word List 77 (page 203).

## Assignment 46

Take Verbal Reasoning Test 3, Section 2 (page 268). Study Word List 78 (page 203).

## Assignment 47

Take Verbal Reasoning Test 3, Section 3 (page 275). Review answer explanations to Verbal Reasoning Test 3 (page 280).
Study Word Lists 79 (page 203) and 80 (page 204).

# College-bound students can rely on Barron's for the best in SAT II test preparation...

Every Barron's SAT II test preparation manual contains a diagnostic test and model SAT II tests with answers and explanations. Model tests are similar to the actual SAT II tests in length, format, and degree of difficulty. Manuals also present extensive subject review sections, study tips, and general information on the SAT II. Manuals for foreign language tests, priced slightly higher than the others, come with audiocassettes or CD's that present listening comprehension test sections and additional practice material. All books are paperback.

**SAT II: American History and Social Studies, 10th Ed.**
*David A. Midgley and Philip Lefton*
ISBN 0-7641-0460-8, $13.95, *Can$17.95*

**SAT II: Writing, 2nd Ed.**
*George Ehrenhaft*
ISBN 0-7641-0463-2, $13.95, *Can$18.95*

**SAT II: Biology, 12th Ed.**
*Maurice Bleifeld*
ISBN 0-7641-0461-6, $13.95, *Can$17.95*

**SAT II: Chemistry, 6th Ed.**
*Joseph A. Mascetta*
ISBN 0-7641-0331-8, $13.95, *Can$17.95*

**SAT II: French, 7th Ed.**
*Christopher Kendris, Ph.D.*
w/CD
ISBN 0-7641-7141-0, $18.95, *Can$25.50*

**SAT II: Japanese**
*Ikuku Torimoto, Ph.D.*
w/60-min. cassette
ISBN 0-8120-8276-1, $18.95, *Can$24.95*

**SAT II: Literature, 2nd Ed.**
*Christina Myers-Schaffer, M.Ed.*
ISBN 0-7641-0769-0, $13.95, *Can$19.50*

**SAT II: Mathematics IC, 8th Ed.**
*James Rizzuto*
ISBN 0-7641-0770-4, $13.95, *Can$19.50*

**SAT II: Mathematics IIC, 6th Ed.**
*Howard Dodge*
ISBN 0-7641-0462-4, $12.95, *Can$16.95*

**SAT II: Physics, 7th Ed.**
*Herman Gewirtz and Jonathan S. Wolf*
ISBN 0-7641-0482-9, $14.95, *Can$19.95*

**SAT II: World History**
*Marilynn Hitchens and Heidi Roupp*
ISBN 0-8120-9294-5, $13.95, *Can$17.95*

**SAT II: Spanish, 8th Ed.**
*Christopher Kendris, Ph.D.*
w/CD
ISBN 0-7641-7142-9, $18.95, *Can$25.50*

The publisher's list price in U.S. and Canadian dollars is subject to change without notice. Available at your local bookstore, or order direct, adding 18% for shipping and handling (minimum $5.95). N.Y. residents add sales tax.

**Barron's Educational Series, Inc.**
250 Wireless Blvd., Hauppauge, NY 11788
Order toll free: 1-800-645-3476
Order by fax: (516) 434-3217

In Canada: Georgetown Book Warehouse
34 Armstrong Ave., Georgetown, Ont. L7G 4R9
Order toll free: 1-800-247-7160
Order by fax Toll-free 1-800-887-1594

**BARRON'S**

**Visit us on our website at: www.barronseduc.com**

(#87) R10/99

ASPIRE HIGHER WITH THE POWER... OF WORDS!

**504 ABSOLUTELY ESSENTIAL WORDS, 4th Edition**
**$10.95, Can. $14.50 (0-8120-9530-8)**
Builds practical vocabulary skills through funny
stories and cartoons plus practice exercises.

**VOCABULARY SUCCESS, 3rd Edition**
**$11.95, Can. $15.95 (0-7641-0311-3)**
Covers all the methods of evaluating words to
improve communication skills.

**1001 PITFALLS IN ENGLISH GRAMMAR 3rd Edition**
**$10.95, Can. $14.50 (0-8120-3719-7)**
Examines the most common errors in the English
language.

**1100 WORDS YOU NEED TO KNOW, 3rd Edition**
**$10.95, Can. $14.50 (0-8120-1620-3)**
This book is the way to master more than 1100 useful
words and idioms taken from the mass media.

**WORDPLAY: 600 WORDS YOU NEED TO KNOW**
**Cassette Pkg. $19.95, Can. $25.95 (0-8120-8319-9)**
Based on *1100 Words You Need to Know;* included are four
90-minute audiocassettes presented in comedy-drama form
to add in the dimension of dialogue and the spoken word.

**A DICTIONARY OF AMERICAN IDIOMS, 3rd Edition**
**$13.95, Can. $19.50 (0-8120-1248-8)**
Over 8,000 idiomatic words, expressions, regionalisms,
and informal English expressions are defined and cross-
referenced for easy access.

**HANDBOOK OF COMMONLY USED AMERICAN IDIOMS,**
**3rd Edition $7.95, Can. $10.50 (0-8120-9239-2)**
With 1500 popular idioms, this book will benefit both
English-speaking people and those learning English as
a second language.

**BARRON'S EDUCATIONAL SERIES, INC.**
250 Wireless Boulevard
Hauppauge, New York 11788
Canada: Georgetown Book Warehouse
34 Armstrong Avenue
Georgetown, Ont. L7G 4R9
www.barronseduc.com

Prices subject to change without notice. Books may be
purchased at your bookstore, or by mail from Barron's.
Enclose check or money order for total amount plus
sales tax where applicable and 18% for postage and
handling (minimum charge $5.95). Books listed are
paperback editions.
$ = U.S. Dollars   Can. $ = Canadian Dollars
(#14) R11/99